Bridge to the Sky

Book III

God's Miracles
in
Lives of Regular People

TRILOGY

BOOK III

Bridge to the Sky

By Angelic Tarasio

iUniverse

GOD'S MIRACLES IN LIVES OF REGULAR PEOPLE

BRIDGE TO THE SKY

Graphic Design Credits: Johny Ivanov

iUniverse books may be ordered through booksellers or by contacting:

iUniverse
1663 Liberty Drive
Bloomington, IN 47403
www.iuniverse.com
1-800-Authors (1-800-288-4677)

ISBN: 978-1-5320-9439-2 (softcover)
ISBN: 978-1-5320-9441-5 (e-book)

Print information available on the last page.

iUniverse rev. date: 02/07/2020

I dedicate this book to my dear daughter Tatania,
a woman with a beautiful soul and infinite Faith.
She came into this world with vitally
important assignment –
to fight darkness that crashes the
human lives and happiness,
and to improve the quality of lives of paralyzed people
on different continents of the world.
I also dedicate this book to those,
who have been already very close to suicide
due to life hardships, but chose God's will
and live to serve the Lord with compassion to others.

Author Angelic Tarasio

Foreword

I consider that it is a great honor to write the forward to a literary work written by my own mother about the extraordinary life of my paternal grandmother Countess Maria Kotyk-Kurbatov.

Having the privilege of knowing my grandmother Maria, I can assure you that I was always amazed by her devotion to the Divinity, exuberance, caring about everyone and everything, generosity, creativity, deep wisdom and, at the same time, childlike playfulness.

From the depth of her wisdom, she shared with me that "if anything touches your body, then it must be the best, whether it is clothing, jewelry, bedding, paper, pen, etc.". Belonging to a conservative approach of upbringing the children, she introduced me to the concept that inappropriate behavior, actions and language were beneath human dignity, and there for must never be part of me. Her teachings have greatly influenced my preferences and choices in life.

Grandma Maria's creativity brough art into my life. She developed patience, taste, femininity and skills with crochet and knitting of one of a kind pieces of clothing with different intricate patterns and designs. Since the 1st grade, I began to win crochet competitions, and the trend continues, as in 2015, I won the 1st place in

State of Florida Arts and Crafts Competition of Greater Federation of Women's Clubs.

Grandma Maria's frequent visits made everyone happy. After putting us to beds, she spent time with my brother and I, and her playful nature came out. Like nobody else, Grandma Maria read out loud the fairy tales, with improvisation of voices and facial expressions of each character. It was a theater of one actor, of which my brother and I couldn't get enough, and she patiently indulged us for hours.

Many times, I was an eyewitness of immeasurable generosity of my grandmother Maria that manifested towards everyone. I have seen her compassionate giving for free to complete strangers her handmade remedies made of rare herbs and roots, that were costly in ingredients and time of preparation. Grandma Maria saw their suffering, and she wanted to ease their condition.

Here are additional examples of grandmother's generosity. From faraway trips, she brought to the neighbors whatever they were not able to find locally. Every Easter, she baked a lot of Easter breads, made hundreds of colorful eggs and took them to the church for blessing. Then she divided everything into baskets and delivered to the elderly people of the village, who were unable to do this for themselves.

Grandma Maria showered the family with her generosity, as she gave my Mom and I family jewels. She used to invite us for High Tea and, at the end of tea party, she packed the entire set of bone china for 8 to

12 persons to be our departing gift, simply because she saw how my mother and I loved it.

Grandmother Maria exhibited the ultimate act of selflessness, when she kept, as a secret from us, her suffering and death from cancer. In all the phone conversations and letters, she stated that no matter what happened, none of us could return to the Ukraine before our United States citizenship was granted. She didn't want us to repeat her mistake of home-coming to communist country and being trapped by KGB. We learned of her death only after her funeral. We fulfilled her last wish by publishing the trilogy about her life and God's miracles in lives of regular people.

May my grandmother Maria's legacy live on through the inspiration and faith in the Divinely that the readers obtain from reading her life-story!

Countess Tatania Kurbatov, B.S., M.A.

Founding President of International Wellness Foundation, Inc.

USA

2020

Preface

Importance Of life

The last book of the trilogy "God's Miracles in Lives of Regular People" is completed and ready to be published. My late mother-in-law Countess Kotyk-Kurbatov insisted in the specific name of the third part-"Bridge to the Sky". The circumstances of her life that I described in trilogy based on her journals were extremely dangerous for Countess Maria and her children. As she narrated, there were two choices left for her in 1961: to hide and wait until the representatives of the merciless demonic service KGB will find and kill her together with three kids, or to take a risk and fight for the last time. She chose the second and, with God's intercession, Maria won the liberation from unlawful persecution.

I asked Countess Maria, if she had ever considered suicide, as one of the ways of liberation from illegal discrimination, humiliation, harassment, physical torment, hunger, begging, homelessness, and slavery in soviet mines. She answered with her charming smile, "My dear, how could I betray my Father? I could not yield the demons and capitulate. It's my #1 assignment in this life." I asked what other assignment mother

Maria was given from Above. "To be compassionate with people in need and those who are lost in this life. I don't do much but pray in order the Lord could make them stronger at the time of their testing."

Countess Maria became my role model of selflessness. I stopped pitting myself. I admitted that everything I've been and am going through is my destiny and my mission. This attitude helped me to fight again for my daughter's life in 2016 after my daughter crash. Six hospitals rejected her case. Nobody wanted to take a risk and provide a complicated surgery with removal of the broken hardware that inflamed infection and 9 cm opened wound. The doctors expected sepsis any moment. We were suggested hospice with increased dosage of narcotics and "comfortable" painless death.

Staying for months in different hospitals with my Tatania and watching her suffering, I realized that my prayers were not enough to change the circumstances and save her life. I described her critical condition on Facebook. The collective compassionate prayers of hundreds of Facebook friends at churches, synagogues, and mosques were victories. The Creator sent right people to help. Everything was miraculously changed in 24 hours: the helicopter, right hospital, brilliant surgeon Dr. Hoh and an operation without a single complication. With God's blessing, Tatania continues the philanthropical projects of her life mission and defeat the darkness with helping people on all the continents of the world to improve their lives and succeed. She is a faithful and dedicated granddaughter of Countess Maria Kotyk-Kurbatov.

This article is my personal understanding of birth and life, suicide and survival, destiny and human choices, life mission and success, hopelessness and happiness. I want to accentuate your attention at our responsibility for every life that can be terminated by individual wish. I understand that your opinion can be different. Freedom to interpret these vitally important subjects gives everyone the opportunity to save the children, youth and adults, including our veterans from untimely death.

Besides my own rather long-life experience with life challenges, hardships and surviving, I underwent extended and time-consuming studies on the topic of suicide in 2008 at the period of severe economic downturn and in 2018. I learned the historical materials on the subject, horrifying Global and American statistics, conclusions of specialists, organizations, associations, foundations, as well as interpretations of different religions. Finally, I came to my conclusion: just studies of the repetitive information and illusory preventative measures took a lot of my time without the convincing findings, how our modern-day society can realistically help people with suicidal tendencies.

With God's blessing, a child comes into this world on the definite day, time and year. He/she comes with his/her own destiny and a personal assignment to fulfil. "For I know the plans, I have for you, declares the Lord. Plans to prosper you and not to harm you. Plans to give you hope and the future." (Jeremiah 29:11) Only then, upon the fulfilment of his/her purpose in human life, he/she returns home to the Creator on the definite day, time and year.

From the very first day of his or her human life, the child observes this world. The speed of the child's mental, physical and spiritual development depends on the surrounding. The closest people make the child's life joyful or sad, happy or stressful. It depends on the quality of accomplishment of our parental purpose in this life. The Creator trusts us, sending us His best gift – a child with the important life determination. It depends on us, how we prepare the child to succeed with God's assignment.

The health, happiness and success of a child begins its development nine months prior a child's physical appearance in this world. The parents play vitally important part in it. What feelings did you experience when you've discovered that your baby was on the way? Have you accepted it with gratitude and joy? Have you concluded that a child can be one of your greatest achievements in your life? Did you give a strong positive energetic charge to your son's or daughter's healthy development?

Maybe, you felt the opposite-admitted that a child was a big mistake that affected your finances, relationship and carrier? Have you become scared of unexpected expenses and difficulties? Have you decided to step out of the picture and never come back, leaving your neglected baby with unhappy single mother?

You should not be scared because you are not the only provider for your family. God provides you. Our Lord promised us, His children, "You will have plenty to eat… and you will praise the name of the Lord." (Joel 2:26) These words are for people who praise the name of the Creator for His bread that we receive daily. Do not destroy your baby, God's tiny perfect creation. Take good care of a child. The mutual faith and energetic supply of a man and a woman nourish the child's physical, spiritual and mental development, as well as his/her future success. You just honestly fulfil your parental assignment and believe that not you, but "He satisfies the thirsty and fills the hungry with good things." (Psalm 107:9)

Every child should be taught that he/she was born with the soul, as a spark of the Divinity. Every human soul is connected to the Creator, as our Source of Life. We are under the best supervision and support "Do not fear for I am with you. Do not be afraid, for I am your God. I will strengthen you; I will help you; I will uphold you with my victorious right hand." (Isaiah 41:10) With this knowledge, the child will live his/her life without initiating additional disturbances in complicated life situation. The child also needs to do his/her best and sincerely ask the Lord to assist in the resolution of the difficulties. He/she will always receive His help. It is up to the Lord in what way the situation is resolved. With correct spiritual development the child does not gain any predispositions for hyper-emotional sensitivity, caprices, anxieties, hysterical and depressive behavior.

By the age of 9-10, the child becomes a solid mindful individual. Nothing can push him/her from the way to success and happiness. It's already a grate credit of the parents. Their a simple but very clever saying: "The children of the responsible parents do not drown in street puddles." It is true.

In all the times, the childbirth required the blessing from Above. I did not repeat this in order to sound strange. Without God's blessing, we could not deliver a new life. The Creator gives us a child, as a tremendous test, maybe the most complicated among all those that we have taken and passed in our lives. I underline again: two parents are responsible for health, happiness and success of their child. The mutual faith and energetic supply of a man and a woman nourish the child's physical and spiritual development, as well as his/her future success. There is a funny proverb: "The children of responsible parents do not drown in street puddles". It is true.

In accordance with the God's plan, a human life is a long journey. We believe that we are not lost in our challenging world because every moment our souls receive Father's energy, guidance and support. In childhood, we need to learn to listen to our soul that has direct connection with the Divinity, and do not allow our mind to take a priority in our decisions. From my own life experience, I learned that God always shows us the exit from the most complex situations. There are no hardships that last forever. There is no pain that pushes to suicide. There are no ugly relationships that kill. The danger is from something different that I'll describe later. We pray to our Father, we talk to Him, we complain to him, we express gratitude to Him for every breath, new day, our survival in this day, success in overcoming the hardships, and certainly, for His fidelity.

The Global statistics alarms us: nearly 800,000 people die by suicide each year, which is roughly one death every 40 seconds. Suicide is the 2-nd leading cause of death for those aged 15-24 years.

The young people are not prepared for the realities of life. They need to recognize from childhood, what life means and how valuable and important it is. The parents are supposed to develop the right attitude of the children to life. Fr. Mark Brummel, CMF wrote, "To be alive, to be human means that we are blessed with the whole range of life experiences – including joy, sadness, health, illness, love, infidelity, happiness, disappointment, suffering and success. Throughout this acceptance of life, we know that we are connected to God." People need to accept that these experiences are part of the diversity of life's path. They make us stronger and wiser when we have the correct attitude towards them.

Then why the escalating statistics if suicide in the USA shocks us?

Suicide is the 10-th leading cause of death for all ages. Suicide takes the lives of over 44,965 Americans every year. An estimated quarter million people each year become suicide survivors.

It is 1 (one) death by suicide every 12 minutes. Every day, approximately 123 Americans die by suicide. (CDC)

Lesbian, gay and bisexual children are 3x more likely than straight kids to attempt suicide.

Suicide among males is 4x's higher than among females. Male deaths represent 79% of all US suicides. (CDC).

What is going on with our children and grandchildren?

Suicide is the 3-rd leading cause of death for 15-24-year-old Americans.

Suicide is the 2-nd leading cause of death for ages 10-24.

Suicide is the 2-nd leading cause of death for school and college-age youth and ages 12-18.

The specialized institutions that deal with suicidology created the list of emotional and physical traumas that could lead to suicide. They completely excluded the spiritual aspect of suicide.

Mental illness	Incurable disease / excruciating pains
Trauma of war	Domestic violence
Traumatic religious persecution	Financial loss
Difficulties of being refugees	Painful relationship
Family environment	Job troubles/loss

Substance (alcohol/ drugs) abuse

Culture conflicts

I added some more:

- Undeveloped spirituality, when the person does not believe in unlimited power of the Creator, guidance and protection from Divinity
- Absence of knowledge that the lost Divine guidance and protection opens the gate for dangerous choices in life
- Undeveloped sense of Gratitude to the Creator for all the talents, knowledge, skills and opportunities in everyday life
- Undeveloped responsibility for making the wrong life choices lead to interrupted connection with the Source of life and weakness of the soul. Weak soul can be easily possessed by dark forces
- Wrong annexation of suicidal thoughts to mental illness or stigma, and hiding them, as a secret
- Undeveloped sense of compassion toward the family and friends who are in the same or even worth physical, psycho-emotional or financial situation. Compassion is the key which can liberate from spirit of despair better and faster than any medical or psycho-therapeutic treatments
- Undeveloped ability to resolve life problems due to self-centrism, working out in isolation

without asking for God's guidance and support of the family and community

- Undeveloped sense of responsibility for lives of other people who could follow the terrible example of self-destruction
- Undeveloped appreciation for God-given chances to start a new meaningful life at any moment of the physical existence

The parents of God-given children are always responsible for the development of all the roots in their children. Everything is important: soul, mind and body. The parents of the children with suicidal behavior did not pay attention at the growth of the soul, and the most important root was not nurtured with spiritual sustenance. The world is shocked with the following fact:

More teenagers and young adults die from suicide, than from cancer, heart disease, aids, birth defects, stroke, pneumonia, influenza, and chronic lung disease COMBINED.

Father Dennis Palanco, SA said, "No mother should have to bury her child. Sadly, this is all too common in America today".

The children live in the society where nobody has time, patience or desire to explain the meaning and value of human life. School children are introduced to the topics of money and sex early enough. However, nearly nobody explains the kids anything about the most valuable subject – human life. Nobody helps kids to recognize the higher purpose of their coming into this world. Nobody reminds them the importance of every individual in successful accomplishment of the life mission for the progress of the country and global well-being. They need to know that they are not a one-day flower, which is beautiful, makes us pleased seeing it, but gone fast. God assigned people for longer undertaking on Earth. At the age of 12-13, they need to think consciously, define and recognize **their** calling (not anybody's else) in order to elaborate the strong foundation of knowledge and skills for future success in life.

Insufficient influences of the churches, synagogues, mosques, and especially schools on spiritual development of younger generations led our society to escalation of suicide and mass shootings of school and college students. Sorry to say, but the families, educational, political and religious institutions try to be "politically correct" and avoid the development of the spiritual root in children and youth. That's the way, how modern-day society destroys vitally important connection of young souls with the Creator. Do they prefer to sacrifice the lives of innocent children and young adults to being "politically correct"?

I can understand that public schools should not divide students into groups for religious education. Division and separation of people on religious basis had never brought positive results. On the contrary, we need to be united under one God, our Creator. We live in a wonderful multinational and multireligious country. It does not matter, how we call Him in our native languages. Schools can develop Faith in Higher Consciousness or Super Consciousness, as referred by Albert Einstein and sincere Gratitude to our Source of Life, Provider, and Supporter in everyday life for the opportunities to attend schools, obtain knowledge and meet friends.

Thank God that not all young people are succumbed to the idea of suicide. New Columbia university research suggested: "Teens, especially girls, whose parents are religious may be less likely to die by suicide, no matter how they feel about religion themselves." As one of the leading specialists of the American Association of Suicidology, Melinda Moor concluded in her article, "We know that spiritual beliefs and practices tend to help people feel a greater sense of connection, hope and meaning in their lives." Being also an assistant professor Kentucky university, Ms. Moor explains, "We know what places people at risk for suicide – it's a sense of not feeling connected to a community and feeling like you are burden, and your life does not matter… In addition, spiritual communities can help people who are in crisis by giving them hope, connection and meaning." Research found a lower risk for suicide among young people whose parents consider religion important. These parents proved that the spiritual development of children is equally necessary with physical and mental growth of their kids.

There are deterrent factors against suicide. Only some specialists out of hundreds suggested practical steps and established the rehabilitation centers and talk-lines for people with suicidal tendencies. A talented Muslim therapist Heather Laird founded the "Family and Youth Institute". Ms. Laird's research on suicide was focused on Southern California, where she saw a dramatic increase of suicides my Muslims with nearly 50 in 2017. Her institute issued a Toolkit, the 1-st of its kind in US, that charts a new way for Muslim communities to deal with suicide. I consider that our society is in big need of elaboration more toolkits that can be implemented in schools and colleges. Somebody has to save the young generation.

The Creator gives the parents and educational institutions freedom to make the correct conclusions regarding the youth suicide. God will not forcefully stop suicide, when the adult person makes his/her wrong choices and, losing the spirit of life, voluntarily interrupts the vitally important soul connection with the Divinity. When the natural connection with the Divinity is lost, there is no more guidance received from Above. Only naive people can believe that their intuition is so good that they avoid mistakes in this life. Nonsense. It's our spiritual guides and angels fulfil perfectly well God's assignments in leading and protecting us. People frequently push them away with dirty language and disgusting deeds and, in some time, they find themselves astray in immoral company or terrifying isolation.

The spirit of despair sneaks closer and closer to the confused person. Some disoriented people try drugs, alcohol, and experiments with different types of sex. Certainly, this 'treatment' does not restore the lost connection with the Divinity. Nothing satisfies and helps them and, being exhausted in the battles with shadows, they allow the evil spirit to possess them. They are on the second step to suicide after the wrong choices – suicidal ideation. They constantly think about ending of this life but still do not take active efforts to do so.

It's a short time, when the family, educational, religious and professional institutions, as well as our human surrounding can assist the person to reconnect the soul, as the spark of the Divinity, with its Creator. We should be a helpful and non-judgmental human force with a strong collective compassionate prayer that assists the weak soul to receive the charging, healing and complete restoration from Above.

Every case of suicide is deviant. Nevertheless, nearly all of them have the same 4 causes:

- ✓ absence of a strong Faith,
- ✓ absence of a strong connection with the Divinity
- ✓ absence of concept of the importance of life
- ✓ absence of compassion

When people take into consideration these causes that are common for 99% of suicidal cases, I believe in good results of prevention of suicide. These causes are missed in majority of scientific case studies. It looks like specialists are sidelined from including the root of the problem in preventative measures. Why? Are they afraid of backlash of the dark power that pulls misfortunate victims to the bridges, ropes, guns, knives and poison? Maybe, the specialists are not mindful enough of what people are going through before they kill themselves? The reports and articles of the specialists in suicidology are lacking in substance. They are reluctant to delve and find the true cause of somebody's miserable life, lost hope, guilt, hatred, anger, fear, isolation from society that pick up the victims and spiral them to the brink of terrible death.

I do not believe that doctors can successfully cure the condition of the patient with suicidal tendencies without recognition of the root of it the root of it – illness of his/her soul or psycho-spiritual disintegration. In most of the cases, the doctors treat the symptoms and can prolong the physical existence of the patient to some extent. Physical existence is not life with its productivity, joy, beauty, fulfilment and success. It's just hopeless and dangerous wandering in the darkness without seeing the exit.

People with suicidal tendencies are already under the influence of the evil spirit. They require another cure from another Healer. They need the assistance in restoration of their soul connection with the Creator through compassion in order their souls can channel again the healing power from Above. Only then "God will command his angels concerning you to guard you in all the ways." (Psalm 91:11) Absence of correct spiritual development and compassion to others led more teenagers and young adults to die from suicide.

The veterans increased this number by killing themselves as 20-24 individuals daily.

"The Road to Recovery Report" of Coalition to Salute America's Heroes, Volume 72, Summer 2019 brought the alarming facts. "America's veterans of the global war on Terror experienced horrors on the battlefield – and many returned home only to face a new nightmare. The multiple stories came from disabled heroes who served our country bravely… but struggled to face down the demons of post-traumatic stress and financial despair when they returned home." As General Lloyd J. Austin III said, "Suicide is the toughest enemy I have faced in my 37 years in the army." "Suicide epidemic takes heavy toll on active duty military, veterans, and family members. In 2018 the U.S. military experienced its highest number of suicides among active-duty troops in six years. 321 active-duty members took their lives during the year, including 57 Marines, 68 sailors, 58 airmen, and 138 soldiers. From 1999 to 2016 the suicide among active-duty troops doubled to 22 per 100,000 service members. Navy Captain Mike Colston, Department of Defense (DoD) mental health director, called it the DoD's "biggest public health problem." Suicide is an epidemic among the veterans' community, as well. Statistics show as many as 20 veterans commit suicide each day. Recent government reports show that 530 veterans in Texas died by suicide in 2016 alone – a suicidal likelihood double that of the general population. A recent troubling trend of "parking suicides" has seen veterans traveling to VA hospitals to commit suicide."

The veterans were courageous at war and helpless in transitional period of their lives. The heroes are home, but their battles are far from over. They and their families need help today. Victimizing of the warriors does not work. They are not victims. They are men and women who were courageous protecting us against Islamic extremists in the global War on Terror. Nearly 2 million troops have served in Afghanistan and Iraq, and now, over 50% are veterans, and nearly half of them severely injured. The odds are stacked against the young veterans when they leave the military service. Disabilities and marks of bravery make it difficult to find the right job and understanding of the same age people. Many young people complain, "I am sad when I wake up. I am sad when I go to sleep. I don't know what to do with my life. I do not belong here. Nobody needs me." We must help them escape real dangers and keep their body and souls together, as they are making not easy transition into civilian life. We must never forget the price veterans paid for our freedom in the Global War on Terror against Islamic extremists.

Now it's our turn to save their lives, assisting them in fight with mental, spiritual and physical wounds of combat and welcoming them back to life, so they can enjoy the country they defended. The veterans' legacy is the legacy of our country, and we should not take it for granted. This legacy should be passed to younger generations of Americans in schools, colleges and universities, making the spirit of the youth stronger and concept of life valuable. Let the students meet the veterans with their marks of bravery, let them learn from the veterans the value of life and grief for those who would never be back. Let the students stand for a minute of silence, saluting the memory of the young people who were brave to leave their homes and step in merciless fire of war in order to defend us and our peaceful lives.

Depression is considered the leading cause of suicide worldwide. Depression affects 20-25% of Americans ages 18+ per year. Depressed people lost interest in life, families, work and studies. They feel abandoned. And this is in one of the greatest nations on Earth, in the country of great opportunities.

What causes the depression in young and physically healthy people? What kind of the person can be diagnosed with depression? As the scientists have stated, there is no known unifying underlying pathophysiology for either suicide or depression. Low levels of brain-derived neurotrophic factor (BDNF) is associated with suicide and indirectly associated through its role in major depression, posttraumatic stress disorder, schizophrenia and obsessive-compulsive disorder. Serotonin, a brain neurotransmitter, is believed to be low in those who die from suicide. This deficiency could be balanced. Modern day holistic medicine, as well as nutrition and natural supplementation can provide the body with precursors that assist the human brain in secretion of serotonin in order to stabilized mood and the whole wellness.

From a spiritual point of view, depression is an illness of a soul. What makes a human soul sick? What separates the human soul from Creator? There are several reasons:

- Wrong understanding of value of life and life responsibilities
- Self-pity and entitlement
- Wrong choices in life
- Lack of accomplishment, caused by laziness and procrastination
- Envy of other people's accomplishments and possessions
- Dirty language, using the profanity
- Disgusting thoughts and deeds

All these reasons push away the celestial guides and guardians, interrupt the vitally important connection of the human soul with the source of life. The weak soul is easily possessed by the evil force. The demonic force torchers the soul, playing dirty tricks on its victim, making the person dispirited, distrustful, disappointed, dissatisfied, and discouraged. The darkness persuades him or her to live in disagreement with Faith and people. Most of the people with depressive and suicidal tendencies blame God in their hardships.

The evil force induces the victim to disbelief in goodness and disavow the family and even children.

Self-pity and isolation from the world which 'cannot understand the sufferings of the person', lead the victim to offence, anger, hatred and loneliness. The evil force eagers to obtain the victim's soul and pushes him or her to the brink of disaster. The evil thoughts to kill himself/herself in order to stop the emotional, physical, financial suffering possess the mind. The exhausted mind loses the power to think clearly and terminates life, giving the soul, as the most valuable God's creation, to satan to possess.

Why did most of the religions considered suicide, as a disgraceful act or stigma in the eyes of the Creator? Historically, the individuals that committed suicide were execrated and nobody had right for exoneration of the person who voluntarily destroyed his or her own life. The history of Judaism, Catholicism and Islam deny funeral rights to those who killed themselves. In Judaism, preserving human life is among the highest duties. In traditional Jewish understanding, the body belongs to God and untimed termination of life is not considered within a scope of human's authority.

Suicide is regarded as steeling from God and a rejection of God's sovereignty. "And surely your blood of your lives, I require." (Genesis 9:5) "Duty of preserving life, including one's own is considered paramount." (Jacobs 1995) "Suicide is regarded as a grave sin, worse than murder. Life is owned by God. It is not seeing as human possession. The individual does not have the right to wound his/her own body, and certainly not to take his/her own life." (Bailey and Stein 1995: Schwartz and Kalan 1992)

Prophet Muhammed warned, "Those who died by suicide will face hellfire and will experience their suicide again and again for perpetuity." In Hinduism, suicide is called 'atmahatya' or "soul murder", and it brings karmic reactions that prevent the soul liberation. To the opinion of Mr. Adnan Zulligar, an assistant law professor at Rutgers University and a specialist in Islamic law: "Suicide is particularly fraught, because in a way, it's the supreme denial of faith. You've lost faith in God's plan and are taking your own life."

Every single person is blessed with hope for healing of the soul and body. As Fr. Mark explains, "The ways we each need healing are personal and unique." One protocol will never work for every individual. "When the individual with depressive and suicidal behavior honestly recognizes the personal way of healing, it brings this individual closer to God, and it is one of the ways when the Holy spirit works within him/her for good". The sincere recognition of things and thoughts that need to be changed, released or improved navigates the individual closer to Divinity.

Every soul sick person can answer the non-judgmental simple questionnaire:

1. Have you ever thought about the importance of human life?
2. Have you ever recognized the importance of your personal life?

3. When did you get the idea of suicide?
4. Where did you get the idea of suicide from?
5. What makes you so disturbed that you prefer horrible death to life?
6. What do you contribute your suicidal thoughts to?
7. Do you contribute your suicidal thoughts to depression?
8. Do you contribute your suicidal thoughts to stigma?
9. Do you contribute your suicidal thoughts to family environment?
10. Did you try to fight with depressive thoughts?
11. In what way did you fight with self-destructive tendencies?
12. What help do you think you need in order to overcome the suicidal thoughts?
13. Who or what educational organization/church/synagogue/masque can help you in your fight?
14. What would you like to change in your life?
15. What would you like to change in the world?
16. What help do you need in order to live happily?
17. Do you think that murdering yourself is fair to your family?
18. Do you know that the suicide of a loved one is among the most challenging tragedies a person can face?
19. Do you think that they can live happily after with this loss?

20. Do you feel any compassion toward your mother/father/wife/husband/children?
21. What can you do to the needs of your family and friends?
22. Can you pray for them?
23. Do you know a Compassionate prayer? Read it, please.

"Heavenly God, Your compassion for me is unending. You hear me in my physical and emotional pain. You love me through my needs. Help me today and every day to hear others in their pain, to love them through their needs. Your Son sacrificed himself for me. Help me to find the right sacrifices to make for others, that they may know a glimpse of God's love through me. Amen."

When they write the answers honestly in the presence of the Lord, the miracle can happen: *"I am convinced that... neither things present, nor things to come..., nor anything else in all creation, will be able to separate us from the love of God."* (Romans 8:38-39)

Our compassionate prayer for people with suicidal tendencies plus the sincere compassionate prayer of the disoriented person for the needs of a suffering mother, father, wife, children and friends turns on the switch, and the weak soul can channel the healing power from Above. With God any miracle is possible. The religious, governmental institutions, and specialists can stop suicide of children, college students, veterans and elderly people. The words of the Lord comfort us: "Do not fear, for I have redeemed you; I have called you by name; you are mine… You are precious in my sight and honored, and I love you." (Isaiah 43:1b, 4a)

Thank God that not all young people are succumbed to the idea of suicide. New Columbia university research suggested: "Teens, especially girls, whose parents are religious may be less likely to die by suicide, no matter how they feel about religion themselves." As one of the leading specialists of the American Association of Suicidology, Melinda Moor concluded in her article, "We know that spiritual beliefs and practices tend to help people feel a greater sense of connection, hope and meaning in their lives." Being also an assistant professor Kentucky university, Ms. Moor explains, "We know what places people at risk for suicide – it's a sense of not feeling connected to a community and feeling like you are burden, and your life does not matter… In addition, spiritual communities can help people who are in crisis by giving them hope, connection and meaning." Research found a lower risk for suicide among young people whose parents consider religion important. These parents proved that the spiritual growth of children is equally necessary with physical and mental development of their kids.

In accordance with God's plan, a human life may be a short or long journey. We believe that we are not lost in our uneasy life because every moment, our soul receives Father's love, energy, guidance and support. We learn to listen to our soul and do not allow our mind to take the priority in our decisions. We pray to our

Father, we talk to Him, we complain to Him, we express gratitude to Him for every breath, new day, our success in overcoming the hardship, and His fidelity. Daily, we honestly accomplish our assignment, fulfilling the mission of this life. Our life way is not a wide and straight avenue, but a thorny path with dangerous situations when somebody plays dirty or traitorous tricks on us. It's life on Earth. We painfully fall many times and with God's blessing we arose again. It's life here and now. We are not in Haven. We must work hard to get there. We need to prove that our Father was not mistaken, giving us a chance in this life to achieve success and happiness in everything He blessed us for.

Author Angelic Tarasio

2020

Introduction

"Bridge to the Sky" is a final novel in the trilogy of ***"God's Miracles in Lives of Regular People"***.

I started my introductions to two previous books with the words that I consider myself a happy person. This time, my readers, I do consider myself that I am truly blessed. I am blessed for so many changes in my life. The most important blessing is that I learned to admit that whatever God changes in our lives, He does it for our good. Glory to the Lord for every day of my new life! God gave me another miracle to witness, participate in and survive. My next book is about it.

Countess Maria Kotyk-Kurbatov was a real person. She was my mother-in-law, who introduced me to Faith and revealed to me her life-story, so that I may share it with you, my readers, as an inspirational example of Faith and Love. She inspired me to believe that God's miracles often happen in lives of people, like you and me.

I used the chain of events from Countess Maria's journals, our verbal discussions with her interpretation of the recorded facts and depicted them in the book using my imagination.

The true story of my mother in-law became the keystone of the trilogy. The chain of the miraculous events happened, as described. However, most of the names, characters, titles, ranks and places I used fictitiously, and any resemblance to actual living or dead persons or places is entirely coincidental.

Author Angelic Tarasio
2020

Chapter 1

The shocking news about the horrific murder of Maria's husband Alexander Kurbatov, crucially distressed Maria. She lost consciousness, and the ambulance delivered her to the local hospital, where her husband and she were working after their discharge from GULAG labor camps.

It was the fourth day of struggle for Maria's life. Most of the time, the grief-stricken woman was in comatose state. Maria's colleagues considered her condition, as critical. There were two episodes when the doctors concluded that Maria approached the irreversible, dying state. Many times, her breath and heart rhythms were hardly obtainable, and one time, the diastolic blood pressure dropped to 29.

After staying for a short while in aberrant parameters, it looked as if somebody gave a new shot of life force energy to Maria's heart: it tried to catch its rhythm and compensate the pumping of the blood. Those changes in Maria's condition made the doctors confused. It gave the impression that somebody wanted to prove that she still had a chance to survive.

After the joined examination on the fourth morning, the doctors of the local hospital came to their mutual agreement to transfer Dr. Maria Kurbatov to Magadan regional hospital for more advanced evaluation, lab testing and treatment. The chief-of-staff Dr. Belikov concluded: "Let us observe Dr. Kurbatov for one more day at our hospital, and then we'll transport her to Magadan. I hope, the doctors of the regional hospital will be more successful in Dr. Kurbatov's case."

Sasha was the only visitor allowed in Maria's room; although there was nobody else in the whole world, who would come to see her. The neighbor Zina wanted to visit Maria, but Sasha asked her to stay longer with Tisha in order he himself could check on his mother after school. The boy became a man of the house on the very next day after the merciless event. He went to morgue to identify his father's body and did not faint there or become hysterical. The militiamen were amazed with the behavior of a twelve-year-old child. Sasha was not scared at all. He approached close to his father's body and touched his father's hand. Then he looked at the head twisted to the left and said in a low, but clear voice,

"Forgive me, father that I could not protect you. I would never pardon myself for staying at home instead of being with you on the train. Everything could be different, if two of us went together to Magadan. You were right, Dad: a single warrior could not win. You were the only warrior on the field among so many of them, and they won."

Then he turned to amazed militiamen and pronounced resolutely,

"I confirm that this body belongs to my late father, Alexander Kurbatov, Sr. What else do you expect from me?"

Both officers looked at each other and answered simultaneously:

"Nothing."

Sasha slowly moved to the door, stopped at the doorway for a minute and turned around,

"I have a question for you. When can I take my father's body for funeral?"

The militiamen looked at each other again and did not know what to say. Sasha noticed that they were not ready to answer his question. The senior officer tried to avoid the direct answer, saying

"We were not given the instructions regarding the body, except the recognition."

Sasha suggested:

"Let us go to the chief of the militia station. I need to talk to him about the arrangement of my father's burial."

Both men had nothing to do than to take the boy to the local militia station. When they arrived at the station, the senior officer wanted to enter the chief's office in front of the boy or with him. But Sasha stopped him at the door,

"You should not accompany me. I know well what I need to ask."

Both militiamen stood behind the boy in a small and stuffy waiting room, as Sasha knocked on the door. The unfriendly voice from the room asked,

"Who is there?"

"Alexander Kurbatov," the boy answered.

There was silence for a couple of minutes, and then everyone in the waiting room heard the heavy steps behind the door. The chief of local militia Major Gromov opened the door and asked angrily,

"Who is that wise ass that decided to play jokes with me?"

The younger militiaman moved forward and explained, pointing to the boy,

"He is also Alexander Kurbatov, only Junior."

Sasha made a step forward and introduced himself,

"Alexander Kurbatov. May I come in?"

The chief invited him to his office without any enthusiasm,

"Come in, if you are already here. What do you want, Kurbatov, Jr.? Let me guess. You want me to find who killed your Dad, am I right? You definitely want the killer to be caught, caged and executed, do you?"

"Not really. It's not my issue. I do not insist in wasting your time for any investigation, finding of anybody and punishment. I have two questions for you. First: I want to know, when I can take my father's body to bury. And second: where I can bury my father's body."

Sasha noticed that his questions or tone he asked them perplexed Major Gromov. The man was processing Sasha's questions for a while and then asked,

"Where is your mother? Is she still in the hospital?"

"Yes, she is."

"Do you know when the doctors plan to discharge her?" Gromov asked.

"No, I don't."

"How can you bury your father, if she did not see him and did not say "Good-byc"?

Sasha tried to talk without trembling in his voice, but it was very hard for a child,

"My mother is unconscious most of the time. This morning the doctors made the decision to transport her to Magadan regional hospital."

Gromov was not aware about the severity of Dr. Kurbatov's condition, and he sounded naturally surprised,

"Oh, really? Nobody reported to me about the seriousness of your mother's illness; I mean that it is so dangerous."

He thought for a minute and then continued,

"Listen, we still cannot give the dead body to a child. We need a signature of an adult person."

The boy asked,

"If my mother stays for a week in this condition, how can you keep him unburied?"

Gromov did not have an answer, but Sasha insisted in it,

"Tell me, Comrade Major, who, where and how will bury my father in case, if my mother stays in the hospital for another week or even longer? The doctors said that her condition is unpredictable …"

Gromov shrugged his shoulders and moved toward the window. The room turned dark the moment he stood in front of it. Major Gromov was a heavy built man with wide shoulders and huge fists. Staying in front of the window, he completely blocked the light coming to his office. Sasha was not frightened. However, the boy felt uncomfortable in the darkness of the room.

Gromov knew that he needed the further instructions from Magadan office. He thought: "What can I personally do in this situation? There is something unclear in the set of circumstances. I don't know why, but Magadan KGB is deeply involved in the case with Dr. Kurbatov. Captain Sidorenko called several times, asking different questions about the Kurbatovs. In general, he did not sound pleasant…"

Gromov lit a cigarette. "Wait a second: maybe, Dr. Kurbatov was not a victim of a criminal, as Captain Sidorenko described? Dr. Kurbatov visited Magadan on the day of his murder… Why did he go there? Most likely, this smart *junior* knows something about his father's visit. Let me ask him. The boy looks very clever for his age."

Gromov turned back and asked Sasha:

"Do you know, Alexander, why your father went to Magadan, and what he wanted to do there?"

Sasha answered honestly:

"Yes, I do. He went to Magadan KGB to make inquiries regarding the status of our case."

"What case do you mean, boy?" Gromov asked.

"My father wanted to find out their plans regarding us, I mean, regarding our family."

Gromov did not understand anything and asked again,

"What case do you have in mind, Alexander? What could KGB decide regarding your family?"

Sasha explained briefly the family situation,

"When my parents and I were discharged from the camps, the commandants of both camps received the instructions from Moscow regarding our case, and we were given surety to receive French passports in a short while, in order to be repatriated back to France."

This time Gromov did not hide his surprise,

"Damn it! What did you say? Where did they plan to repatriate you? France? Why did they promise to deport your family to France? Wait a minute, where were you originally from?"

Gromov was stunned, when the boy answered,

"My father was born in France and my mother was born in Poland. They had never been the citizens of the Soviet Union. My brother and I were born in Russia. I was born in Maltin labor camp that is not far from here. My mother was six months pregnant with me when my parents arrived to visit her family after WWII. At that time, the territory of my mother's estate was annexed from Poland. So, it belonged to the Soviet Union."

Gromov's face turned red, and he sat down in his armchair. The drops of sweat covered his forehead. He listened to the boy's story and saw how the pieces of the puzzle came together.

Gromov interrupted the boy:

"Well, you said that your parents came to visit the family. I mean your mother's family," "Did they have a chance to find your mother's family?"

"No, they didn't."

"What had happened to your parents? Why did they get into the force labor camps for political prisoners?" Gromov asked.

"My parents were arrested on the very first day of their arrival with false accusations in espionage and terrorism on the territory of the Soviet Union. NKVD paid zero attention at their French citizenship and legal entry documents issued by the soviet government. There was no court hearing. They were tortured and imprisoned for 12 years. In ten and a half years, we were discharged with admittance that "*the confinement transpired due to false accusations*."

"Where and when did you learn this story?" Major Gromov asked.

"This story I learned from my parents at the very beginning of our free life. They wanted me to know the truth," Sasha answered.

"How did your parents meet each other and get married, if they were born in different countries? You mentioned that your father was from France, and your mother was from Poland," Gromov inquired with the tone of suspicion in his voice.

It was difficult for a soviet citizen to imagine that people from other countries were free to travel to different places of the world. They studied there, met their new friends, or even beloved, got married or just lived somewhere else, beside their native land. The soviet citizens were not permitted to travel abroad in order to visit their relatives or friends there. They were not allowed to enjoy travelling, seeing the beauty of the world, and staying anywhere else than in the Soviet Union.

People abroad were considered enemies. They were capitalists, who exploited somebody's hands to become rich. The utopic theory of Karl Marx was planted and flourished among ignorant and illiterate population of the Soviet Union. Keeping the soviet people in a locked cage, made it possible for the soviet government to lie about the best quality of life in the USSR in comparison with other countries. They sang: "I do not know any other country where the man is so free to breath." Air was for free. It was true.

People worked hard nearly for free. The population in the towns and cities lived in communal apartments – five to ten families with one kitchen and a restroom. The communist government *fed* the citizens with slogans. Brain washing achieved the highest level, when the son wrote denunciation against his father. One accused other neighbors of the same apartment in "suspicious" activity or belief in God. The NKVD/KGB arrested and executed non-guilty people without court hearing. The mini committee of t*hree communists* made the decision of *life* or *death* for arrested citizens. Fear ruled the life of the country when everyone expected, if not that night than the next, the government officials would come, and the person disappeared forever.

Sasha saw that Gromov expected his explanation. The boy answered with a smile,

"They met each other in the medical school of Sorbonne University."

"Where is it?" Gromov was curious. He hadn't heard earlier about that famous university school.

Alexander answered,

"It's in France. It was founded in Paris and received its name in 1257 after Robert de Sorbon, French theologian. My parents graduated from the medical school there before WWII."

Gromov frowned and muttered,

"Oh, well…" He said and made a circle around his desk.

The picture was clarified for him to some extent. Not completely, but at least, something became evident. At the moment, Gromov was sure in one thing: he should not make any personal decision regarding Dr. Kurbatov's case. His mind suggested him, "It would be much better for you, Gromov, to make a couple of phone calls. Let somebody else makes a decision, sends you the order, and then you'll fulfill it in the best way."

He looked at the boy who stood in front of him, waiting for his answer, and felt ashamed, thinking, "The boy lost his father, and his mother is in critical condition. If not today then tomorrow, she can follow her husband. Well, the boy wants to bury his father's body. He has right to do it, doesn't he? Maybe, it's not a big deal, and we can assist him in arranging the burial. But who knows, what is in plans of Magadan KGB office?

Still, it's better to call and ask. I do believe that those Frenchmen got in fire for nothing and were destroyed. They arrived and were not given any chance to escape the trap. But why should I be hurt? It's much better for me to be cautious and avoid any complications."

Gromov felt sorry about the boy, and somebody mentioned that there was another child, a baby boy at home. However, the fear for his personal life, career and the lives of his family members cancelled any intent to help Sasha. His frightened mind sent him the repetitive thought, "Still, it's better for you, Gromov, to call to Magadan and find out what to do. It's always trouble-free just to follow somebody's commands. In future, it will not create you any headache."

Gromov came up to Sasha, put his heavy hands on the boy's shoulders and said,

"Alexander, I'll make some calls right now. If they do not need to work on your father's body, then I'll give you a call later today, and we'll arrange everything for tomorrow. Sounds good?"

Sasha clearly saw that Gromov did not come to any decision in the situation with burial and agreed to wait until the next day.

"Thank you. I'll visit my mother at the hospital, and then I'll be at home, waiting for your call. Our neighbor, Aunt Zina, had prepared my father's clothing for burial. If you want, I can bring it today."

Gromov answered,

"Bring it tomorrow. I think, tomorrow will be quite all right."

Sasha left. He felt confused after his visit to the militia station. His child's heart picked up something deceitful in Gromov's behavior. It added more pain. Sasha could not hold the unmerciful pain any longer. The child experienced one and the only desire to lament loudly, in order all the people of the village could hear his grief, sense his pain and understand his loss. Tears filled the boy's eyes, but he reminded himself: "I cannot cry. My father was strong, and I should be a young replica of my father. Since now on, I must live for two of us: my father and myself in order to help our Mama and Tisha to survive." The boy made his turn into the main street of the village, passed his school and the house where they lived, wending his way to the hospital.

On that morning, Maria did not regain consciousness even for a short time. Sasha sat down on the chair next to his mother and holding her by the hand, he silently begged, "Mama, please wake up. We miss you so much. We need you at home."

Sasha was sure that Maria could hear him, but in order to react and answer, she needed to gain some strength after the merciless shock. Sasha continued,

"Mama, I don't want to leave you here, but I have to. Tisha waits for me, and, by the way, Gromov promised to call regarding Dad's funeral. Do you remember Major Gromov? I am more than sure that you have met him before."

On that day, nobody from militia station gave Sasha a phone call. He did not hear any news on the next day either. The boy became nervous and could not stay in school. He ran to the militia station again, delivering a bag with father's clothing and a new pair of shoes. The child did not understand, why Aunt Zina put the shoes in the bag, but she explained that they had to be in his father's coffin.

A secretary had hardly looked at Sasha. She took the bag with cloths and put it under her desk. Still looking in the papers, the woman informed the boy,

"Go home, Alexander. There is no way to see Major Gromov today. He left for Magadan. They have meeting there. Do not wait for him, because he did not promise to come back to the militia station tonight."

"Did he leave any instructions regarding my father's body?" Sasha asked anxiously.

The secretary noticed that the boy was desperate, looking for her help. He tried to understand what was going on around his father's death and funeral. Then he asked,

"Why do they keep my father's body for five days and do not allow me to bury him."

The secretary answered with noticeable irritability,

"Come tomorrow. I cannot say anything. I don't know anything."

Sasha went to the exit door, thinking: "Why nobody wants to talk to me? The secretary did not even look at me. Why? She dissembles something."

He was already near the door, when the phone rang in Major Gromov's office. Somebody answered it. The boy clearly heard a deep baritone. There was no doubt, it was Gromov's voice. The secretary glanced at the child. Sasha realized: Gromov was in his office and that woman, his secretary, tried to persuade him to wait for another day. The boy looked at the secretary and whispered,

"Why did you lie to me? Why?"

Sasha wanted to get an answer and made a step toward her, but felt like somebody stopped him, sending a strange message to his mind: "Silly boy, can't you see that all of them avoid seeing you? Doesn't it look like these people refuse assisting you in any way? They don't want to be involved in your father's case. Run to the hospital. Your mother is helpless and under threat."

Sasha ran out of the militia station. The boy was really scared with the message, "I was not able to protect my father. Now, I must protect our Mama."

Sasha's biggest fear was to lose his mother. He did not want to believe that somebody decided to *dispatch* her, as the local criminals used to say. At the same time, the boy could not get rid of that "sick thought" that came to his mind at the militia station. He tried to push away the message, but everything looked so real. "Who could prevent another crime? Who will protect our Mama? The militia people don't want to talk to me or even look at me. All of them are liars. It looks like they would like to get rid of us. Why? What did we do?"

Sasha tried to calm down his thoughts and feelings while running along the street. He recollected his father's saying,

"Nobody can frighten anyone more that the person himself. If you do not panic, you can see clearly all the circumstances and find the possibility to escape. Sasha, the Lord conceders us capable to overcome any life-threatening situations, if you are not losing control of yourself. No panic, boy. Panic and fear cause the confusion, chaos and loss. We cannot allow ourselves loosing. We must resolve the situation and win."

Sasha was thinking, "Where is the escape? Father, why hadn't you found the escape? What should we do now? How can we hideaway from danger?"

Alexander opened the door of a new hospital building and ran fast to the second floor, directly to his mother's room. He was afraid of one thing: to find his mother dead. Sasha was about to enter the room, but the voices inside stopped him. The boy slightly opened the door and saw a stranger near his mother. The stranger talked to Dr. Belikov. Sasha stopped behind the door in order not to interrupt the conversation between the chief physician and the visitor.

His first thought was: "Probably, they invited a consulting physician from Magadan, instead of sending my mother there."

A stranger was asking the questions, and doctor Belikov answered them.

"So, you consider the condition of this woman as critical, don't you?"

"Yes, I do," Dr. Belikov answered briefly.

The man with unpleasantly high voice continued inquiring,

"Why do you consider the condition of citizen Kurbatov so serious?"

Dr. Belikov answered impatiently,

“All the symptoms, test results, vital signs, delirious state are abnormal, and they are so evident in the case with Dr. Kurbatov that nobody can find another classification of her condition. For the period of four days, she was conscious only for a couple of hours.”

“Dr. Belikov, how long can she stay in such a condition?” the visitor asked.

“If there is no improvement, she will not survive for another week.”

The unpleasant voice asked his next question,

“What do you think, does this woman need to survive and get well again?”

Dr. Belikov reported,

“Our doctors decided to transfer Dr. Kurbatov to Magadan regional hospital.”

“What’s the difference, where to die?” the visitor asked sarcastically.

Dr. Belikov was disturbed with the tone of the last question and answered with unhidden irritability,

“We anticipate that the specialists of Magadan regional hospital can obtain some additional test data, or they can prescribe new and more effective medications, which will help with heart arrhythmia and extremely low blood pressure. Something has to be done, otherwise we’ll lose her. She is a mother of two children. The kids lost their father, and somebody has to help their mother to survive.”

For a minute there was silence in the room and then the visitor pronounced the long and loud tirade,

"Do you know that she is from former Polish landowners? And her husband was Count from France. We consider them our social and idealistic enemies. We kept them in the camps for more than ten years. I cannot understand your personal concern about this woman."

Dr. Belikov answered in a cold manner,

"She served her term, if even she was guilty in anything. As for us, not only for me, personally, for all our medical personnel and patients, she was a knowledgeable, helpful and dedicated doctor. She was most likely from a noble family, but her professional attitude toward every patient, a child or adult, was an example for us."

"What a characteristic! It's nice, Dr. Belikov that you clarified to me your personal respect toward citizen Kurbatov. I believe that you spent enough time with this woman, observing her in different situations. But still, some people have another opinion regarding her case and the case of her husband."

The visitor burst into cynical laughing. He tried to continue but Dr. Belikov interrupted him, and Sasha noticed a metal sound in Dr. Belikov's voice,

"Her husband was murdered, and somebody ordered to bury him without making a post-mortem examination. Somebody from Magadan gave the special instructions regarding Dr. Kurbatov's funeral. He was buried outside the cemetery under the number instead of his name, as a killer, unknown homeless, criminal, drunkard, or a person who committed suicide. The militia arranged it *'secretly'* the day before yesterday, not giving us, his colleagues, and even his own son any opportunity to be there."

"Oh, Dr. Belikov, you'd better take good care of your live patients and personnel. Do not forget that you are the chief-of-staff, and there are so many unresolved problems in your hospital. The death of one more political enemy means nothing in comparison with your problems; I have in mind the tasks that had to be resolved weeks or months ago."

"It's interesting. Give me an example, please. What should I take care of?"

Dr. Belikov asked, sounding louder than usually. The visitor motioned to Maria.

"It's absolutely clear that you should not care of this dead case, Dr. Belikov. Don't you understand what I am talking about? Long time ago, we had finished with their aristocratic class. We won our political fight. Few of them left. Now it's their time to disappear. And you confirmed that her life is over, anyway. Just look at her: her husband was killed, and "poor" she could not deal with that news and fainted. What does this example illustrate to us? They are too weak to wrestle with us, with our proletarian strength and morality. They are boneless. They are made of soft flash."

The visitor came up to Maria, and Sasha's heart began pounding. The boy watched through a slightly opened door, how he picked up his mother's arm and said with disdainful smile,

"Cannot you see, Dr. Belikov that she is not our proletarian woman? The bad news about her "beloved blue blood husband" threw her "noble flash" into coma. She reacted, as if she was still a "sentimental young girl" that hadn't been prepared for the difficulties of real life. She was not brought up in our communist way. They do not have strong muscles and sharp teeth. Why should we take care of them? Think, Dr. Belikov! Think and make the right conclusion, I mean, politically correct conclusion."

The chief-of-staff was astonished to hear such a merciless opinion of KGB officer. It was impossible for humanitarian like Dr. Belikov to agree with it. He asked,

"Do you want me to call our doctors for a meeting and explain them your opinion, suggestion, or order regarding Dr. Kurbatov? What conclusion do you expect from me and other physicians? Do you want us to stop giving Dr. Kurbatov medications? Do you want us to kill the woman? I personally, cannot do it. I was taught to save patients' lives, not to murder them."

"Do not exaggerate, Dr. Belikov," the visitor screeched with hostility in his voice.

Then he continued,

"Nobody orders you to kill her. But think about your responsibilities, your civilian position in our democratic socialist society, and, at last, think about your own family. I'll be back to the hospital, and we'll continue the exchange of our interesting ideas."

Sasha heard the loud steps coming towards the door and stepped aside. The boy was trembling. The visitor passed by without paying any attention to the kid.

Lord, have mercy!

Chapter 2

The stranger rushed downstairs, and Sasha slipped into the room. It was difficult for him not to burst into tears. The boy tried hard to control his emotions. Dr. Belikov was near his mother, injecting the medication.

Sasha came up closer and begged,

"Dr. Belikov, please do not stop treatment. We need our Mama to live. More than anything else, I want her to get well. Tikhon cries all the time. He misses both of them, our Dad and Mama, and calls them constantly."

"Who told you, Sasha that I was going to interrupt the treatment?" Dr. Belikov asked, looking at the child with suspicion.

The boy could not stand any longer the severity of the situation and burst into tears. He cried helplessly, as if he was five. Then Sasha recollected again his father's teaching about being a strong man and handling any situation without weeping. The boy managed the restraining of his emotions. He came closer to Dr. Belikov and said,

"Excuse my tears, Dr. Belikov. Please, do not listen to that visitor and help our Mama. I want our Mama to be with us again."

"Sasha, trust me, we do our best for your mother, but the shock was too strong. Her body cannot endure it."

"She was twice in the same condition at the force labor camp, but the camp physician Dr. Leskov saved her there. Please, give him a call, and he'll arrive and help you with our Mama."

Sasha noticed that Dr. Belikov liked the idea. He wrote down Dr. Leskov's information in his small notebook. Then he asked,

"What do you think, Sasha, will Dr. Leskov remember your mother's medical history, if I call him now?"

Sasha confirmed,

"Certainly, he will. Doctor Leskov and his wife visited us several times. Once we visited them, as well. Now, he lives in village Eultin and works in their tiny local lazaret."

Dr. Belikov promised Sasha to contact him, as soon as possible. Sasha added with some guilt in his voice,

"Dr. Belikov, I'd like to stay longer with Mama, but I have to be with Tisha now. When I come home, Aunt Zina goes to her flat to have some rest. She is old, and she needs to 'stretch her legs' for an hour, as she says."

Dr. Belikov hugged the boy and said,

"Your father could be proud of you, Sasha. You look so much alike with your father, and even speak like him."

"Thank you," Sasha replied.

He stepped closer to his mother and asked the doctor,

"Dr. Belikov, do you know where they have buried my father?"

"I don't know exactly, Sasha, but we'll find it out. One thing I want you to remember forever-your father was an honorable man and a talented surgeon. I wish you become a surgeon, as well."

"Thank you, Dr. Belikov."

Sasha was about to leave, when both of them noticed that Maria moved the fingers of her hands. Then she opened her eyes and called with a weak voice,

"Sasha. Where are you, Sasha?"

Sasha and Dr. Belikov were near Maria in a blink of an eye. Dr. Belikov took her left hand and checked the pulse. He was pleased with his finding and smiled. Sasha kissed the other hand of his mother.

"Mama don't fall asleep, please. Mama, we love you. We need you, Mama. Don't die."

A new flow of tears rolled down his cheeks. Being a twelve-year-old child, he was incapable to stand two tragedies at the same time. He did not have enough strength to fight the dark shadows that had gathered around their family. He still needed his mother's protection.

"Mama, please get well soon and come home. Tisha and I miss you so much. You are the best Mama, and we need you badly. Mama, please understand me correctly. It's not because I am tired of chores at home or afraid to be there without you. It's because Tisha and I cannot live without you."

Dr. Belikov noticed that it was difficult for Maria to focus on what Sasha said. She was in her thoughts,

"What is going on? Why am I here, while both of my kids are at home alone?"

She distinctly remembered only one thing – the tragedy with her husband, who was murdered on the train. Maria touched the face of her son with a shaking hand, whipping his tears. She looked at the doctor and said quietly that they could hardly hear her,

"Dr. Belikov, I need to go home. I'll be fine. Please, discharge me now."

"Not today, Dr. Kurbatov."

It was obvious that Maria was too weak to be discharged. Then he looked at Sasha and suggested the boy to run home with good news.

Maria continued,

"Nevertheless, I need to go home, in order to arrange Alexander's funeral. He has been a faithful man, and I want to bury my husband in accordance with Christian tradition. I need to be discharged today, Dr. Belikov. I need to bring a priest to the cemetery, and he will serve Panikhida at Alex's grave."

Dr. Belikov interrupted Maria,

"Dr. Kurbatov, you were unconscious for five days, and the local militia had buried Alexander's body."

Maria was surprised to hear the news,

"Had they? But anyway, I want Panikhida to be served, and I must prepare the memorial dinner for our colleagues, if you and they do not mind coming to our place."

Dr. Belikov promised, "When you are stronger, you'll bring a priest, and he'll serve the Panikhida, as well as the memorial dinner will be prepared. We'll help you with the dinner. Don't worry, Maria."

Maria widely opened her eyes, and Dr. Belikov saw that she was close to collapse again.

He shouted,

"Dr. Kurbatov! Stay with me!"

Maria was passing out again. Dr. Belikov grabbed Maria's shoulders and shook her. He shouted in her face,

"Maria, think about your sons. Do you want them to be scared to death? Do you want them to be lost, separated and sent to different orphanages?"

He took a breath and whispered in Maria's ear,

"Do you want those monsters to come to your lonely kids at night and strangle them?"

Dr. Belikov did not know what other arguments to bring, in order to keep her conscious. Then he asked with the real anger in his voice,

"Do you want your sons to become criminals? Dr. Kurbatov, you cannot betray the memory of your husband, and leave the children on their own. Be a strong mother, Maria! Get well and go home. I don't think that you are weaker than your husband. You are a very strong person, too. Maria, can you hear me? Being a mother of two sons, you must take care of your kids."

Maria turned to Sasha and whispered,

"How's Tisha doing? How is his appetite? I took away his favorite 'dessert' and lost my breast milk due to stress. My poor baby..."

Maria wanted to add something, but Dr. Belikov interrupted her,

"Don't be just a *thoughtful* mother. Don't ask how your baby son is there. Don't pretend that you are concerned about his appetite. Maria, do not make the lives of your children more miserable and complicated after the death of their father."

Maria could not understand what was wrong with Dr. Belikov. Usually, he was so polite and friendly to the Kurbatovs. She asked with the annoyance,

"What do you want to say, Dr. Belikov? Why do you address so many unfair accusations toward me? Was it my fault that they killed my husband?"

Sasha watched, how Dr. Belikov tried to find the explanation of his unusual behavior. The man stood for a minute near his mother's bed, catching air with his opened mouth. Then he exhaled,

"Stop dying, Dr. Kurbatov, like you have nothing else to do."

Maria felt offended. She wanted him to know it,

"If Alexander is not here any longer and cannot defend me, I'll do it by myself."

Dr. Belikov was glad to hear such a reply. He answered with a happy smile,

"It sounds better, Maria. Don't you think, Sasha that your mother sounds much better now?"

The disturbed child did not understand, what made Dr. Belikov joyful, but he noticed that his mother did not pass out and, on the contrary, she talked louder.

Maria could not calm down. She sat in her bed and asked,

"Dr. Belikov, how dare you talk to me like this? I'll take care of my sons, and they would never be criminals. That's it, I want to go home. I do not want to comply with your regulations and stay another day at your hospital."

It looked like all her energy evaporated with the last words and dizziness returned.

Dr. Belikov understood that he went, probably, too far and said,

"Not today, Dr. Kurbatov. You'll be discharged tomorrow or the day after tomorrow. I'll give all the instructions to the personnel regarding your discharge."

Maria tried to get up but could not do it without assistance.

She asked,

"Dr. Belikov, will you help me? I need to walk. I stayed in bed for too long."

"As you wish, Maria. We can help you," Dr. Belikov said.

Maria stood up for a minute and asked,

"Sasha, will you help me to sit down?"

Dr. Belikov was the first near her. He said with his regular considerate intonation,

"You see, Maria, you are not ready to go home today. It would be better for you to stay for another day or two under our supervision. And, please forgive me, if I was rude. I did not mean to hurt you. I wanted you to understand one thing: you have no right to die for the sake of your children."

Maria smiled with her innocent smile and repeated his words,

"I have no right to die. I like it."

Then her smile disappeared, and tears filled her eyes. She whispered bitterly,

"Did Alex have right to die? How could it happen to him? He went to ask, only to ask them about the status of our case, about the French passports and repatriation... And look, what they did! Do they still have right to murder innocent people? Do they have right to arrest, torture, imprison and murder the foreigners without being punished for their deeds?"

In a second, usually calm and tolerant Maria turned into tornado that could not be kept under control. She was hysterical, and nobody was capable to stop the explosions of her deeply hidden emotions. Dr. Belikov pulled a chair closer to her bed and showed with the hand motion to Sasha not to interrupt his mother. The nurse heard Maria's squeal and opened the door to check, if Dr. Maria needed help. She closed it, seeing Dr. Belikov near Maria's bed.

Maria repeated the same questions,

"Why did they kill my husband? What could my husband ask them about that they decided to answer with brutal massacre? What could Alexander insist on, if the assassination was their answer? They are monsters. They are merciless demons."

Dr. Belikov could not understand Maria's saying and asked,

"Who do you blame, Maria? Who are '*they*'?"

Maria took a breath and continued,

"On that day, Alexander went to Magadan KGB to check the status of our case and find out anything about the French passports that were promised at the time of our discharge from the GULAG force labor camps. Alexander was absolutely right, when he said that they fooled us on the day of our liberation with making photos for our new passports."

Dr. Belikov was confused with the story about passports and wanted to clarify it,

"When you were discharged from the force labor camps, you were issued soviet passports, weren't you?"

"No, doctor Belikov, not at all! They did not issue any passports to us. We do not belong to the Soviet Union, even Sasha and Tisha who were born in this country are not soviet citizens. They skipped the line in their birth certificates with the name of the country where normally, baby's citizenship is filled in. My husband wanted us to return to France. He left his mother there and prayed every day to see her alive."

Dr. Belikov was surprised and asked the logical question,

"Why didn't you contact the French embassy in Moscow, if you wanted to leave for France?"

"It was absolutely impossible! How could we get in contact with the embassy, if in 1946 the KGB took away our French passports and after so called 'liberation' from the camps, nobody issued us Russian passports to travel to Moscow? You know that the law of the

USSR forbids travelling without passports, especially for former prisoners. We are slaves who belong to the evil, and that evil owns all the rights on our lives and the lives of our children."

Maria's eyes were constantly filled with tears. The misfortunate widow did not pay attention at the endless flow of tears that ran down her cheeks, dropped on her chest, hands and continued falling on her quilt. Dr. Belikov handed her a towel. She blessed herself and exclaimed in despair,

"*Help us, save us, have mercy on us, and keep us, O God, by Thy grace.*"

The nurse opened the door again, holding in her hands some sedative medication and a glass of water for Maria. Dr. Belikov stopped her with his gesture. He knew that after such a strong emotional outburst, Maria would feel physically drained and fall asleep without any calming medications. He did not want her to take any sedatives that would slow her heartbeat and decrease the blood pressure.

Maria kept on repeating the same question,

"Why did they kill Alexander?"

Nobody had an answer. Nobody was there. Nobody knew the details of Alexander's visit to Magadan KGB. Everyone knew the tragic end. Now, Dr. Belikov did not have any doubt that Alexander was just another victim of KGB. Otherwise, they would never *'care'* about the death of the former political prisoner, sending the obnoxious investigator to the hospital to find out the seriousness of his wife's condition.

Suddenly, Maria stopped crying and started to think about something really stressful. Even the thought about it terrified the misfortunate woman. Maria asked a question. It was very important for her to hear Dr. Belikov's answer,

"What do you think, Dr. Belikov, Alexander was the only victim from our family, or they will go after me and, God forbid, after our children?"

It was not in Dr. Belikov's plans to say anything about the spiteful officer from KGB. He found the neutral answer, hiding the fact of a ruthless visitor. He dealt, as a physician, who did not want to aggravate the emotional and physical condition of his patient.

"Maria, please get well soon and return home to your kids. I think that Alexander had paid the highest price for all of you."

Maria's eyes were filled with tears again. Dr. Belikov turned to Sasha, tapped him on the shoulder and suggested cheerfully,

"Alexander, go home and take care of your younger brother. Don't worry about your mother. I'll take care of her. Do not open the door to anybody except your babysitter. Did you understand me, young man? From now on, only Tisha's babysitter can be your everyday guest."

Sasha kissed his mother's hand, as his father used to do it, and left. The boy was running home with good news – his mother was alive and conscious. Tomorrow, or the day after tomorrow, she would be at home. Wasn't that wonderful?

Glory to Thee, O Lord! Glory to Thee!

Chapter 3

Dr. Belikov called the head-nurse and when she appeared in the room, he announced,

"As you understand, Dr. Kurbatov's condition is more or less stable now, and we do not transfer her to Magadan hospital."

Then he gave all the instructions regarding Maria's night medications. At the end, Dr. Belikov lowered his voice, in order Maria could not hear him, and instructed,

"I do not allow any visitors in her room. It doesn't matter, who they are, where they are from, and why they are in our hospital. The patient cannot be disturbed. If anyone insists in seeing her, give me a call right away. I'll be here and take care of everything."

The nurse answered briefly,

"I understood, Dr. Belikov. I will comply with all your instructions."

Everyone from the medical personnel of the hospital had a suspicion regarding the tragic death of Dr. Kurbatov. His secret burial without proper personalization was additional strange piece of the puzzle. The colleagues felt sorry about Alexander. They could not understand why a highly professional and nice man was brutally murdered. There was another detail that made the carnage doubtful. If the crime was committed by a former convict, as it was presented to them by a militia officer, how was it possible that he did not steal a heavy bag stuffed with good foods and the money from the pocket? On the contrary, the killer left his ax near the bag and disappeared. What other reasons could the bandit keep in his mind, if not the robbery?

Nobody could believe that Dr. Kurbatov argued with somebody, especially a mugger. What did they find reciprocal in order to start the conversation? Everyone considered the militia version regarding the arguing and fight, as a complete nonsense. The personnel of the hospital sincerely sympathized with Dr. Maria and her children.

Maria noticed that Dr. Belikov knew something else that she was not aware about, and she asked a direct question,

"You think they will come here, don't you?"

After some hesitation, Dr. Belikov decided to tell her the truth,

"They have been here, Maria. Today, I talked to one of the KGB officers. After his visit, I understood that it was nice that we had not transferred you to Magadan regional hospital."

Maria could not pronounce a word, so startled she was. Dr. Belikov continued with a biter smile,

"I must say that you have awakened right on time. As you understand, in Magadan hospital I cannot control the situation."

Dr. Belikov left. Maria whispered,

"Thank you, Lord. You were kind to me again with "awakening on time". Why did You allow the horrible murder of my husband?"

The tears rolled out of Maria's eyes. She thought, "The demons murdered my husband and destroyed the defense of our family. Why did the Lord allow the tragedy to take place?"

Maria sat down in her bed and started the prayer which she did not pray for a long time,

"*Lord, I cry to Thee, hear me. Hear the voice of my prayer, when I cry to Thee. I am a sinner because I am in despair. Incline not my heart to any evil thing or practice wicked deeds, just because at this moment, I experience hatred and anger. O Lord and Master of my life! Take away from me the spirit of despair, as well as the feelings of anger and hatred. Please, give rather to Thy servant Maria the spirit of patience, humanity and love. Amen.*"

Maria could not sit still: bitter emotions overwhelmed her. She got up slowly and walked to the opposite side of a tiny hospital room. At the beginning, she could hardly make several steps. It seemed to her that the floor rocked from side to side, as if she walked on the boat.

"Oh Lord, why have You allowed the murder of my husband, who loved me and who I loved so much? Why have You allowed leaving our children without the protection and support of their father? My Lord, I know that grumbling is sinful. We must accept everything, as it happens. But how can I be in agreement with the horrible loss of Alexander? You see that I have no strength to overcome the tragedy. Oh, my Lord! Please, do not turn Thy face away from me! Help me! Please, help our children!"

The nurse quietly opened the door and suggested Maria "just a few Valerian drops" and water.

"You know better than me, Dr. Maria that it will help you to calm down a little bit, and I hope that a tiny dosage will not slow down your heart rate."

The nurse pronounced it with heartfelt sympathy, and misfortunate woman took the relaxing remedy.

Maria returned to her bed, sat and bend down there, crying bitterly. It looked like there was no end to her tears. They were rolling and rolling on the cheeks, dropping on the floor. Suddenly, she imagined how unprotected Sasha and Tisha were at home. "They could be harmed easily," Maria thought.

She exclaimed with all her strength, "Dear Lord, please protect our sons. They are alone now. Help me to surmount my misfortune. Make me strong, in order I can be a good mother, and substitute their father, at least in some way."

Maria stood up again and moved to the window. That time she felt stronger for a couple of minutes, but the strength disappeared fast. She pressed her forehead to the cold glass of the window, stood there with her eyes closed and prayed in complete feebleness,

"Mother of God, you are support and benefit for everyone who is suffering. Lend a hand to our sons and make possible their survival in this Godforsaken land.

Make three of us strong. Make us tolerant in our deeds and pure in our thoughts. I do not want to plant a seed and grow hatred in the hearts of our children toward this country and its people. Impatience, anger and hatred made the tragedy possible. Alex's intolerance left our sons without father's love, protection and support. Help us, Mother of Savior, through your prayers to your Son in the name of the Father, and of the Son, and of the Holy Spirit. Amen."

Maria moved slowly to her bed and lay down. Her silent meditation was interrupted with loud voices in the corridor. Then somebody entered the room, without knocking on the door. The head-nurse tried to stop the visitor, asking him to wait until the chief physician came. But the man was bad-mannered. He pushed her out and closed the door. Without any greeting, a stranger addressed to Maria,

"Oh, citizen Kurbatov, I can see that now you feel much better in comparison with this morning. That's smart that you stopped pretending that you were dying."

Maria was surprised to see a man, who talked about her health condition in such a sarcastic manner. For a minute, there was silence in the room, and then Maria interrupted it with a question,

"I beg your pardon, who are you?"

"Captain Sidorenko, Magadan KGB."

Maria wondered, "Why is he here? Could he be a killer of my husband? I've heard that the killers are always attracted to the place of murder or family of the victim. Did he arrive to kill me? Is he a danger for our children?"

Maria sensed inner trembling in the area of her stomach. The terrified woman tried to take it under control, ordering to herself, "I must look calm. I shouldn't show to this KGB officer that I am scared." In reality, it was not easy at all.

Captain Sidorenko sat down on a stool near Maria's bed and distastefully observed her. She felt uncomfortable under his observation. Sidorenko reminded Maria the older demon, the torturer from her family manor in the Ukraine in 1946. "I have no doubt that he can do smutty things, as well. They even look alike, as if all of them are the children of one evil father."

The pause lasted too long, and Captain Sidorenko interrupted it with a question,

"Citizen Kurbatov, can you guess the reason of my visit?"

"Hardly, Captain Sidorenko," Maria replied in a calm manner.

Her short and quiet answer made Sidorenko nervous. The visitor jumped up and paced the room two times back and forth from her bed to the window.

"Do you want to say that you haven't expected our investigation?"

Maria shrugged her shoulders and did not answer. She noticed that the absence of the answer irritated him even more. He rushed to her and shook with his index finger in front of her face, saying angrily,

"I recommend you not to keep silence. I am not going to stay with you for hours. It's not a pleasure for me to watch you. Your answers must meet the requirements of the interrogation and protocol. I've planned to ask a couple of questions and leave. I must warn you from the very beginning: if your answers are considered by Magadan KGB, as incomplete, then we'll have to take you to Magadan office, and provide more detailed interrogation there. Is it clear enough, citizen Kurbatov?"

Maria turned her head to the wall, in order to avoid meeting with Sidorenko's furious eyes. The wave of anger arose inside of her. "Why should I watch him? I have zero desire to listen to him and answer the stupid questions of this obnoxious KGB officer," Maria thought.

Sidorenko seemed not to pay attention at her attitude and preceded with his questions.

"Why, do you think, your husband was killed?"

Maria thought, "Because you preferred him to be dead." But poor woman squeezed out loud another answer,

"I don't know."

"Do you have any idea?"

"What kind of idea do you mean?" Maria asked.

"Relating to the death of your husband, citizen Kurbatov," growled Sidorenko.

"No, not at all," Maria answered quietly.

Out of nowhere, Maria commented to him about the subject that she usually did not touch, and it was absolutely irrelevant to the questions she was asked,

"By the way, Captain Sidorenko, I am not *citizen* Kurbatov, because we are not and haven't ever been the citizens of Russia or the USSR. Nobody had "*granted*" us the citizenship of *your* country."

The statement with the emphasizing of two words was absolutely fearless. Sidorenko found it too impertinent. He definitely learned the fact of nonexistence of their soviet citizenship. Knowing that, he still was not ready to be reminded of the fact in such a forthright manner.

"How do you want me to address my questions to you?"

"Madam Kurbatov is quite all right."

He smirked,

"That's fine with me, too. Let's continue, Madam Kurbatov."

"Thank you."

Maria was stunned with herself, "Why did I do this? Where did it come from? My Lord, it can only aggravate the situation."

Captain Sidorenko repeated the same question:

"Why did they kill your husband, Madam Kurbatov? Did he have significant sum of money with him?"

Maria answered,

"Does it make any difference now? My husband was brutally murdered. This fact is the only one that matters for me and our children. Nobody can make any correction of the fact. The tragedy happened. I do not want to waste my strength by looking for any imperceptive reasons."

"You are wrong, Madam Kurbatov. We need to define all possible reasons of the crime. Only then we can find the killer or the person who was interested in death of your husband. Sometimes, it could be the closest friend or even a wife. Aren't you interested...?"

He interrupted his sentence, looking straight in Maria's face and pretending that he was checking for Maria's personal interest in death of her husband.

Maria asked unperturbedly, "Interested in what?"

Captain Sidorenko finished his question with unhidden irritability,

"In positive results of the investigation, Madam Kurbatov? Are you interested in it?"

Maria looked at him and thought, "I believe that you will take me to the office in the nearest time. It's absolutely obvious that Magadan KGB made the decision *to finalize* the Kurbatovs' case. These monsters can do it in a very easy way: to come to our place at night and to strangle our children and me. Since their revolution in 1917, they are trained very well to get rid of opposing people."

Maria looked at Sidorenko and another thought crossed her mind, "Wait a minute. If they have started *'the investigation'*, this means they have prepared already their *scenario* for us. I wonder, what is in their plans? Who plays the main role in their scenario-a wife-killer or wife's lover, as a killer?"

Maria felt completely exhausted. At the moment, the children were her biggest concern. After Alexander's murder, all the rest things became meaningless. Maria silently prayed to God's Mother,

"Holy Mother of God, I do not ask anything for me. I ask you to protect my sons in the name of the God's glory. Amen."

Captain Sidorenko repeated one more time his question regarding money. Maria was about to answer it, when Dr. Belikov rushed into the room. He was agitated.

"Excuse me, Captain Sidorenko. Five minutes ago, I made a call to your office and talked to lieutenant-colonel Zotov. I reported about seriousness of Dr. Kurbatov's condition. To my mind, your interrogation of an emotionally disturbed and physically weak patient was scheduled too early. Her present condition is far from being ready to concentrate and answer all your questions."

"Well, Doctor, I am here not for listening to your opinion regarding the matter. Just say, what was lieutenant-colonel Zotov's decision?" Sidorenko asked with impatience and hatred in his voice.

"He wanted you to stop the interrogation and return back to the office. We came to the mutual conclusion: when Dr. Kurbatov is strong enough, she'll give him a call and answer all the questions."

Maria saw that Captain Sidorenko was infuriated with doctor's interference. He did not even try to cover his rage. He jumped up to Dr. Belikov and hissed in his face,

"You went too far, Dr. Belikov. You cover this… this…"

He pointed at Maria, trying to find the right word to disgrace her.

"You took her side, the side of this Madam Kurbatov or Countess Kurbatov. We must investigate, why you hired her and her husband, as the physicians. They did not submit their passports and diplomas. What does it mean, Dr. Belikov? It means that you support spies and terrorists, the enemies of the soviet socialist democracy. You must be another black horse in this game. Your activities are very suspicious and require detailed investigation, as well."

Dr. Belikov was startled with a fact, how fast the obnoxious KGB officer had added him to the list of individuals who provided *suspicious activities.* He knew about the existence of two articles in the soviet legislation for the accusations that the KGB officer named: *sympathy* and *support* the enemies of the soviet democracy. Without further ado, they could promptly throw him into a prison for ten years, using any of these articles or both of them together. He replied in a low voice,

"How can I be a "black horse"? What nonsense do you say?! It's not fair. There is nothing suspicious in my actions. I am a physician and now, Dr. Kurbatov is a patient with severe emotional trauma."

Captain Sidorenko went to the door, paying zero attention to Dr. Belikov's explanations. Maria witnessed the expression of deep satisfaction on his hateful face. Sidorenko definitely felt himself, as a winner in the first round of fight.

Lord, have mercy!

⚜

Chapter 4

For the first time, Maria watched her chief-of-staff confused and scared. She felt sorry for this honest, highly professional and dedicated man. In some way, he reminded Maria her Alexander. He was a leader, who was capable to find the best solutions in the most complicated situations. Dr. Belikov was always properly organized, took good care of the patients, hospital and medical personnel. His personal example allowed him not to hide his dissatisfaction regarding anybody's work. But he did not hurt the colleagues, expressing his opinion in front of other doctors or nurses. Dr. Belikov's professional courtesy, human politeness, respect and fairness worked well for co-workers, and the medical specialists did not run away from the hospital.

The graduates of the Nursing and Medical schools in the Soviet Union were obligated to follow the federal law of "Distribution of the Graduates" among the hospitals, where there was shortage in specialists. They had to undergo residency or apprenticeship for two years. The diplomas were issued only upon two-year term of their practical work under the supervision of the highly skilled professionals.

The hospitals that experienced shortage in personnel usually located in faraway regions, in thousands of miles from the civilized part of the USSR. Nobody was enthusiastic to spend their young years working in wilderness, criminally dangerous areas, as well as in zones with extremely low temperatures and snow for nine months.

The young specialists, who were sent to Dr. Belikov's hospital, voluntarily stayed longer than it was required. They enjoy working side by side with experienced professionals in a friendly and helpful atmosphere. Even the lack of beauty of Magadan nature with its short, one-sided trees, nine-month winter, absence of any comfort, and high level of violence receded in comparison with their speedy professional development that the young specialists gained during several years of work at the hospital.

Maria felt guilty, watching Dr. Belikov who was mercilessly attacked and unfairly accused. For the first time in his life, a dedicated doctor got acquainted with the forceful, backbreaking accusations of KGB. He was unexpectedly dragged in the battle, where he was crashed during the first exchange of blows. The rival did not follow any rules. Maria saw with her own eyes, how an innocent person was knocked down and terrified. She felt sorry for him and said,

"Dr. Belikov, I realize that whatever I say now means nothing. Nevertheless, I want you to know that from the very first day of our work at the hospital, my husband and I did our best to avoid causing any trouble for you. We were always grateful for hiring us, for your human intuition and respect. Now, I need to leave and never return. Then you can be honest with them, saying that you fired me right away after this conversation. It could be considered, as your rehabilitation in the eyes of KGB authorities."

Doctor looked at Maria with admiration, identifying the fact that in that situation, she was much stronger than him. It was she, who found the solution of his perilous dilemma. His mind agreed immediately with her suggestion. He acknowledged, "This woman is ready for dramatic changes in her status after Alexander's death. She is a fighter."

Maria preferred never to see Dr. Belikov in his fearful weakness. She wanted to remember him, as a solid and strong person.

"May I ask you for the last favor, Dr. Belikov?" Maria asked.

Dr. Belikov answered with the sound of alertness in his voice,

"Yes, sure, Dr. Kurbatov, if… it's not beyond my power."

Maria tried to cheer him up with a smile, but the spasm in her throat did not let her do it. The tears poured again. The reality of the life hit her with double blow: five days ago, she lost her beloved husband, and a couple of minutes ago, she lost her most wanted job. Maria could not imagine how to live after these tragic consequences.

Dr. Belikov asked,

"What can I do for you, Dr. Kurbatov?"

Maria answered,

"I am not strong enough to walk home. Maybe, you can arrange an ambulance for me?"

Maria noticed the relief of inner tension on his face. Dr. Belikov was afraid that she would ask for something more significant. Her request made him contented.

"Of course, we'll arrange the transportation for you. Maria, if you need anything else, let me know. I wish you find the right way out of this horrible situation. When you feel stronger, come and work for the hospital again. In a month or two, they'll forget about Alexander and Maria Kurbatov, and we'll take you back. This is my opinion. However, in your situation, it would be better to leave the village forever for another place. Here, everything will remind you about the tragedy."

Dr. Belikov was going to continue, but Maria interrupted him.

"I am sorry, Dr. Belikov, I worry about my boys. I need to go home. Will you call for an ambulance, please?"

He looked straight at Maria and confessed,

"I am not as strong and courageous as you are, Dr. Kurbatov. For the first time in my life, I was in close contact with KGB. I must say, it was not a pleasant experience. Now, I understand how easy they can make any innocent person an *enemy* or *criminal*. Maria, I hope you do not blame me for early discharge and... loss of work."

Maria looked at Dr. Belikov with sympathy and reminded herself, *"Judge not, lest ye be judged..."*.

"I don't", she answered.

"I appreciate your understanding, Maria."

Dr. Belikov left to make a phone call to the emergency department regarding the transportation for Maria. Maria stared at the door where the chief physician left, and a new wave of grief, deep resentment, physical weakness and sharp heart pain gave Maria a nasty blow that she could not move. A disturbed woman meditated,

"O Lord, who upholds all things in the purest hollow of Your hand. Remember Your compassion and Your mercy toward us who repent to You regarding our weakness and wickedness. Look upon us with Your goodness; grant unto us by Your grace. Through the reminder of the present day, avoid the diverse subtle snares of the evil, and keep our lives protected through the grace of Your Holy Spirit. Amen."

The nurse entered the room and announced,

"Dr. Kurbatov, the ambulance waits for you at the entrance. I'll help you to go downstairs."

"Thank you," Maria whispered.

She collected all her strength to get up from the chair and stood for a minute, catching the balance. Then she slowly moved towards the door. The nurse helped Maria to get downstairs and sit into the ambulance. The thought that she would never come back to the hospital, as a physician, hit her hard. Maria looked up at the hospital building and noticed Dr. Belikov in one of the windows, watching her leave.

Maria thought,

"I should not blame him for his fearfulness. Probably, his personality is not super strong. He would not step into the line of fire, as my Alex did, and maybe, he is right. I wish him all the best."

The ambulance stopped at the door of Maria's apartment house. She could hardly get out of it and climb five steps to the entrance door. She was shaking, ready to faint any second. The driver saw Maria's feebleness and rushed to help her. He knocked on the door, but nobody opened it. Maria called, "Sasha." The immense weakness did not allow her to shout. Instead of yell, she barely whispered the name of her son. Maria was losing the last strength when somebody opened the door. Zina picked Maria up and brought her in with the words,

"Dr. Maria, why are you here? Why did they allow you to come home?"

Zina put Maria in bed and Sasha ran into his mother's bedroom. The boy was happy to see his mother at home,

"Hurray! Our Mama arrived home!"

Then he looked attentively at his mother and asked,

"Mom, are you all right? Did Dr. Belikov allow you to go home today?"

Seeing mother's frailty, Sasha doubted,

"Is Dr. Belikov aware that you have left?"

"Quiet, Sasha. Please, quiet," Zina interrupted the boy.

She saw that Maria was unwell, and the smart woman understood, "Something serious had to take place at the hospital. Otherwise, Dr. Maria would never take a risk to arrive home in such a poor condition. She could barely breathe. Lord, have mercy!"

Tisha screamed in Sasha's room. He was left there with the door closed while Zina and Sasha ran to meet Maria. Nobody released the baby-boy after his mother's arrival, and he reminded with a loud yell about his presence. Maria missed Tisha very much and felt guilty that she had lost her milk due to shock. She could not keep waiting to see her baby and whispered impatiently,

"Sasha, let him in."

Zina looked at Maria with deep sympathy. The appearance of a young woman had changed so much for five days. She looked, as if she was in her late sixties. Zina thought, "Oh Lord, Maria must be dreadfully stressed out and completely drained. For several days, she lost not only her weight, but all her strength and beauty. She must be hungry. I need to feed her."

Tisha appeared in the room, crawling fast toward his Mama. He got up near Maria's bed and tried to climb it. Her first thought was, "Alexander would never see his first steps. He had never entirely enjoyed his fatherhood. He missed all the precious moments with Sasha. And now with Tisha…"

Severe throat spasm caused suffocating cough. Zina brought Maria some warm chamomile tea, but poor woman was choking with it. Sasha looked at his mother with dismay. Only Tisha was glad to see his Mama with or without cough. Maria put her hand on the throat, and it seemed like the spasm was partially released. Tisha climbed up to Maria with Sasha's assistance. The baby-son hugged his mother, then looked at her face, and hugged her again. Then he spread his tiny hands and pronounced one of his first sentences,

"No Daddy."

He pronounced those two words so clearly that all three heard the real meaning of his complaint. Maria sat down in bed, hugged her baby, and burst into tears. Sasha embraced both of them, crying quietly. Zina joined the company of lamenting people, repeating,

"Cry, children, cry. It's better for all of you to cry out your pain and let the grief go. Do not hold it long in your hearts. Memory is one thing, but disparaging pain is another. It destroys our hearts."

Tisha separated himself from Maria and watched his mother. He was too small to understand why all of them were sorrowful. He was not able to comprehend what an irreversible calamity occurred with their family. He was unable to realize that he lost his father forever, and there was no more a man in the whole world who would love him, as his Papa did. Somehow, Tisha sensed the irregularity of the moment with his babyish heart. Recollecting something important, the baby stopped them with his loud request,

"Mama, am-am."

Maria helplessly looked at the clock and then at Zina. It was seven o'clock in the evening-time for supper.

She whispered,

"My baby is hungry. Zina, Tisha is hungry. What shall I give him? I have lost my milk."

Tisha wrestled with Maria, trying to lie down in the position for nursing. Maria was panicky and asked,

"Zina, do we have anything for supper? What will Tisha eat?"

Zina answered with a smile,

"Please, don't worry, Dr. Maria. I'll feed all of you. During last four days, Tisha ate everything that I cooked. I pureed the food for him with the fork, diluted with milk or broth, and he enjoyed it. Thank the Creator, the baby has wonderful appetite."

Maria got up from her bed, holding Tisha in her arms. She made a couple of steps and Zina picked up the baby: his mother was too weak to carry him. Their supper was ready. On that very day, Zina prepared more food, as if she knew that Maria would come home.

The incomplete family sat down around the table, and Zina put a plate with food in front of each. In the middle of the table, she put a basket with sliced bread that she baked two days ago. Maria took a slice and chewed it slowly. Zina noticed that Maria's thoughts were far away from the supper. Home-coming was difficult for the widow. At home, the absence of her husband was intolerably painful. Right at this moment, Maria realized that Alexander was unreservedly gone. The grief-stricken thoughts climbed in her head,

"My husband has gone forever. We are here around the table, but my husband is not in the room with kids or on duty in the hospital. He will never open the door to the flat with his key and enter the kitchen with the words, "Smells wonderful. I am hungry, my dear. Please, feed me." He will never hug and kiss us. He will never be with me. His sons will never see him again. Oh, my Lord! How can I resign myself to the tragedy? They seized my Alex from me. They made me a widow and a miserable single mother with two kids. It's terrible! Who can survive such a tragedy? Where shall I find strength to live, work, raise our children, do my chores and be happy without my husband? I hate my life without Alex. Forgive me, my Lord, but I don't want to live without him. I wish I could die in the hospital in order to be in the same grave with Alex and never again come back to this life."

Maria bit her bread and found it wet and salty. She put it on the table. Tisha broke off a piece of mother's bread, chew it for a second, and spit it out. Zina and Sasha smiled. Maria noticed it and could not apprehend the reason for their smiling. She looked at Tisha. The baby made a funny face, pushed the slice of bread with mother's tears further away and pulled Sasha's bread closer. He pinched a small piece of it, chewed well with his front teeth and liked it. Then he pulled the whole Sasha's slice, but Zina gave him a smaller one instead, and returned the bigger slice to his elder brother.

"Look, Dr. Maria, you dropped your tears on the bread, and Tisha did not like it. Who would like the bread with mother's tears? Tears are salty, right Tisha? Baby, now you know, even the tears of your sweetest mother are not sweet. Sorry, kid, you learned it too early."

Maria dived in her thoughts again,

"My grandfather was right, saying that I would be blessed with children but lose early my woman's happiness. According to Grandpa's prophesy, my kids destined to grow up without their father. I remember clearly that grandfather mentioned three kids. One thing is unknown, where the third child came to his mind from? There is Grandpa's slip or maybe, I've lost my husband extremely early, so I've missed the opportunity to bring the third child into this world."

It seemed that Tisha read his mother's sad thoughts. He opened his plump hands again and pronounced with heartfelt bitterness in his tone,

"Daddy. No daddy."

Sasha stroked Tisha's short hair, saying,

"Eat, Tisha. Continue eating. Don't make Mama cry."

Maria's tears were rolling constantly on her cheeks. She did not even try to wipe them up. She was dying for her husband. She did not imagine living her life without him. She did not know how to exist for another day without her Alexander. Maria wanted to scream:

"Why didn't I die at the very first moment I've learned about the murder? I was close to passing away. Why did I recover? Did I need to survive? Oh, Lord! Why didn't You take me to my Alex? I long for being together with him. If we cannot be together here, take me there."

Abruptly, Maria stopped crying and sat quiet for a while. It looked like she listened to her Angel who explained something really important, and he made her feel ashamed. He guiled her with the reason of being back into this world. The distressed widow answered him in her thoughts,

"Forgive me, my Guardian. I am sorry for my weakness and lack of consideration for my children. Now, I know why I was destined to survive. You are right: my sons are in danger, and they need me. Certainly, they need me. There is no way for them to survive in this country, being orphans from a noble family."

Maria said out loud,

"*Dear Lord, cleanse me a sinner. Have mercy on me and save me. Keep all of us, O Lord in Thy grace. Amen.*"

Zina came up to Maria and hugged her, but Maria hardly noticed Zina's touch. Only when Zina mentioned,

"Dr. Maria, we need to talk about something important after I put Tisha to sleep."

Maria *woke up* for a second from drowning in sorrow and the conversation with her Guardian Angel. Zina took Tisha to the bathroom to give him a bath, while Sasha did the dishes. When the boy had finished with his chores, he came up to his mother and stood still in front of her. Maria did not lift her head up, and Sasha saw that his mother did not notice him.

Sasha had to call her, in order to draw her attention,

"Mama, I want to tell you something. Please, get well. I promise to fulfill Dad's and my chores every day. Please, be with us. We need you, Mama. I don't know how we can live without Dad and you."

Maria hugged the child and answered in tears,

"I'll be all right, son. Thank you, Sasha for your understanding. You are Dad's son, for sure. You inherited everything from him."

"Like what?" the boy inquired.

Sasha wanted Maria to name all the identical features. The boy was not ready to lose the connection with his father. On the contrary, Sasha wanted to develop the best of father's characteristics. Who has the best knowledge of them, if not his mother?

"You are honest, brave, strong, smart, hardworking, helpful and devoted. You are real Count Kurbatov, and from now on, not Jr.," Maria explained.

"Mama, I wish I could be always Alexander, Jr. I miss my Dad so much. People from militia visited us two times. They checked on us, if we were not alone. Every time, they spoke with Aunt Zina. They saw that she took good care of us. Mama, Zina cried every day, but she didn't want us to see it. By the way, Dad bought in Magadan my favorite sausages besides the bread flour. He also brought Aunt Zina's most wanted candies and cookies."

Sasha looked at Maria and asked her, using the French version of the word "father",

"Why did they kill Papa? I wish he would never go there! Do you know, I cannot imagine our life without Papa. I miss him so much!"

"Me too, Sasha," Maria whispered.

Maria and Sasha sat together, cuddling each other until Zina came into the kitchen.

"Tisha sleeps and sees sweet dreams. It's late, Sasha. Go to bed, please. I need to talk to your mother."

Sasha gave Maria a hug and asked her,

"Please, Mama, don't cry. I cannot see you crying. We are incapable to return our Dad, even if we cry all the time. I love you, Mama so much. I am afraid to lose you."

Sasha had been already at the door, then turned around and came up to Maria again. He took her hand and kissed it, as Alexander used to do. Maria smiled through tears.

"Good night, Alexander. Sleep well!"

Lord, have mercy!

Chapter 5

Zina sat down next to Maria and embraced her. She felt sorry for this fragile and helpless woman, unmercifully bitten with callous life circumstances. Two nights ago, Zina saw Maria in her nightmare. Maria was there as a dove-mother. The black kites pounced and killed her loving guard and destroyed safety of the family. Then they started to trace her and both chicks. The black kites were pitiless, and their intent was to condemn their victims to failure without food, water and warmth. The black kites did not allow the dove widow and chicks to take wings and fly away. They did not give them chance to hide, attacking the misfortunate birds all the time. It was horrible to see how they got pleasure, watching the demise of their innocent victims.

Zina awoke in tears around three in the morning and was not able to fall asleep again. Her nightmare was so apparent: they murdered Dr. Alexander and planned to kill Dr. Maria with her children. Zina had figured out already their horrifying plans, when one of the militia men forewarned Zina of danger in Zina's stay with the Kurbatovs' kids, particularly at night. Zina tried to find any possible way for Dr. Maria's and kids' rescue, but she realized that nobody could protect them. Sasha heard, how Zina prayed, asking the Lord to save the helpless family. She talked to the Savior in her simple words,

"Dear Lord, please hear my request. This time, I do not ask You to help me, a sinner. I beg You to help Dr. Maria and her sons. You know that there is nobody in the whole world, but You, who can be their support. In a week, they have no bread and they have no money to pay for their flat. Please, provide their safety, daily bread and don't make them homeless."

Another moment Zina was meditating about something that Sasha could not understand:

"My Lord, I ask You about one thing-do not allow the kites to destroy completely this wonderful family. Help them in the way that is possible only for You. Amen."

Zina was sure that there was no probability for Maria and kids to survive without God's intervention, especially, after Maria had lost her doctor's position at the hospital. Another thing was obvious: Maria's stay at home did not protect her and children's lives. Zina remembered the words of her acquaintance from militia station, "It's dangerous even for you, a baby-sitter, to stay together with the Kurbatovs." Honestly, the devoted woman hardly experienced any fear. Zina believed that it was her destiny to stay with the Kurbatovs at the most difficult time. For nearly two years in neighborhood with the Kurbatovs, she felt herself as a happy member of their loving family. After the brutal murder of Dr. Alexander and a word of warning about her personal peril, she chose to be with the family to the very end. Zina made her evident decision and declared it to Maria,

"Regardless of what is in Magadan KGB plans about you and children, I have decided to stay here and to be sure that everything dangerous is over, and there is no more threat to your family. It will be better, if I sleep at night on the couch in Sasha's bedroom."

Maria leaned to Zina. She was grateful to God for sending their family such a brave and helpful woman.

"Thank you, Zina. I am so happy to have you in my life, especially now. Alexander used to enjoy our nine o'clock tea. Let us continue this family tradition. I believe he'll join us, … only in spirit."

Maria sighed deeply and asked,

"Tell me, how they buried Alexander. Tomorrow, I want to go to the cemetery. Will you join me?"

"Maria, I was not there. Nobody knew when and where they buried Dr. Alexander's body. But one man from the militia station told me that they buried him not on the cemetery. You'll find his grave beside the cemetery wall. That man gave me this piece of paper with the number that was scratched on an aluminum plate."

Zina handed the paper to Maria with the warning, "Keep it hidden."

Maria was surprised to hear such strange news. She could not understand, why the local militia buried her husband under the number, instead of his own name. Moreover, it was strange that they buried Alexander's body beside the cemetery."

"Where did they fix the plate with the number?" Maria asked.

"I don't know," Zina replied.

Maria looked at the paper. She found one letter and four figures there: *K 5916*.

Maria read them out loud and could not find the meaning of any figure: they did not match any number in Alexander's personal data. She asked Zina about the details of a strange funeral. Zina did not know additional details, except what she heard from her acquaintance:

"He said that they followed the instructions of Magadan KGB. I sent Sasha with Dr. Alexander's cloths, but they had buried Dr. Alexander a day before. I guess, you can go and bring back your husband's cloths and shoes, but I beg you, never mention there the informer's and my names."

"Earlier, I did not even think, Zina that they are closely interconnected: I mean the local militia and Magadan KGB."

"Yes, they are. With Dr. Alexander's case, the local militia had followed all the instructions of the KGB. By the way, it was the same militiaman, who suggested me to find somebody who could stay with you for a while. He did not explain why and what we should expect from them, but he called my attention to it several times. We don't need anybody, Maria. I will be here days and nights."

Zina lied. She was advised the opposite: not to stay with the Kurbatovs. The elderly woman made her personal choice: to take a risk but stay with Maria and kids for days and nights. The woman supported herself with a repetitive affirmation, *"Lord is merciful."* Zina's belief in God's mercy alleviated her nervousness and fear.

Maria recollected her conversations in the hospital with the chief physician and Captain Sidorenko. She started retelling them to Zina and burst into crying again.

"Zina, now it is a problem to find another place, where I can be hired, as a physician. The KGB insisted in my dismissal from the hospital. They accused Dr. Belikov in admitting Alexander and me, as the professionals in medicine without passports and diplomas. Where can I earn money to feed my children and pay the bills?"

Zina was supportive, saying,

"Stop crying, Dr. Maria. Everything could be changed in a week or two. They will close Dr. Kurbatov's case, and you'll go back to the hospital. You know, it's difficult to find another specialist, like you."

Maria answered,

"I doubt, Zina. In spite of the fact that our hospital has always shortage in physicians, I don't think that Dr. Belikov would take a risk and responsibility for my employment. The KGB officer frightened him with terrible accusations. Now, Dr. Belikov is afraid of consequences."

Zina was deeply disappointed with everything that was going on at the hospital, and Maria's words made Zina more upset. She asked Maria,

"Do you think Dr. Belikov was really so frightened? What's wrong with your co-workers? I thought that after the tragedy with Dr. Alexander, your colleagues would support you. I cannot understand their indifference. By the way, I had better opinion about Dr. Belikov."

"Don't judge him, Zina. He protects himself, his family and professional credibility. I won't be surprised, if the rest of the people are also scared to be in touch with the Kurbatov family. Alexander was murdered, and I can be the next one. That's why I want you, Zina, to leave us in order to avoid the complications in your life. They made us like "leprous" for the local people, and people understand that leprosy is highly dangerous. It scared our colleagues. Who wants to get in trouble? So, leave us, Zina. It's dangerous for you, too. Now, I don't have money to pay you. I appreciate everything you've done for us."

Zina did not respond at once and continued making tea. The woman put the tea kettle on the table and looked at Maria with disappointment.

"Why do you want me to leave?" Zina asked. "Tell me, dear, how long people can live? Do you think that I need to live forever? I am not afraid to die or lose my 'administrative position' which I had never had. Cannot you see that in some situations, it's better to be old, and not to belong to the political rulers, party leaders, commanders, local authorities, or any government?"

Zina tried to cheer up Maria,

"Years ago, I was in your position of outsider, and with God's blessing, I survived with my four children.

God is always merciful. He blesses us with children and teaches how to live on."

Zina poured the tea in two cups and said,

As for your payment to me for this month, I'll take home some candies and cookies that Dr. Alexander brought from Magadan."

Both women smiled.

Maria monotonously sipped her hot tea, when an interesting idea arose in her mind.

"Zina, I have a plan. First of all, I need to arrange everything here with Alex's church funeral service and memorial dinner. Then, I'd like to take kids and go away for a while."

"It's a good idea. Where would you like to go?" Zina asked.

"We'll go to Eultin. We'll stay there for some time with Dr. Leskov and Sofia. They were always friendly with us. Maybe, Dr. Leskov can help me with my health condition and find some work in his lazaret."

"Good idea, Maria. Let's pray and go to sleep. You are hardly sitting."

"I agree, Zina. Tomorrow, I'd like Sasha to go to school, in order to catch with the material that he, probably, failed to take for several days. As for me, I'll go to the militia station. I need to find out the place where they have buried Alexander. Don't worry, Zina, I promise you not to mention there you or anyone else who brought to me the important information."

Zina was against Maria's plans for tomorrow,

"Maria, I insist in your staying at home for a day or two. First, you need to gain some strength. Your visit there won't be easy and painless. Second, one more day of home staying will not make big difference for anybody. Let us go and pray. Today was not an easy day, but thank God, you are alive and at home."

They prayed together "The Agreement Prayer",

"Dear Lord, You told us with Your pure lips, if two or three people on the Earth make a mutual agreement to pray together for something in Your name, they'll receive it from Your Father Almighty. Where two or three people pray together then You are among them. Your words are unalterable. Your mercy is incomparable. Your love of mankind is everlasting. Praying in our mutual agreement, the God's servants Maria and Zina dare to ask You: dear Lord Jesus Christ, accept our prayer and save, help and keep by Your grace the children Alexander and Tikhon, as well as us, Maria and Zina. Do it not as we wish, but in Your way. Amen."

Both women went to sleep. Maria was surprised, how fast she slumbered in her roomy bed without Alexander.

"I must be dead beat."

This thought was the last one that she remembered, and the physical and emotional exhaustion knocked disturbed Maria down.

Next morning, Maria was not able to get up. She tried to move out of bed but felt enormous weariness that interfered even with keeping her eyes opened. Extreme exhaustion put her back to sleep. Zina sent

Sasha to school, as Maria wanted. The moment nanny locked the door after Sasha, Tisha woke up. It looked like he opened his eyes and mouth simultaneously, greeting his mother with happy sounds. Zina stepped quietly into the room, took the baby out of his bed and left Maria to rest.

"Quiet, Tikhon. Your Mama is very weak and needs some breather. She'll gain her strength faster while sleeping," Zina whispered. The boy answered his nanny loudly, in a funny babyish language.

Maria listened to their "conversation" and could not help smiling. Then she sighed.

"Yesterday, Zina was completely realistic regarding my weakness," she thought.

The tragedy appallingly drained Maria's strength. She agreed, "Dear Lord, today is definitely not my day to go anywhere." Maria closed her eyes listening to Zina's voice in the kitchen. Zina was patiently explaining something to Tisha.

The disturbed mother sounded weak, "Thank you, Lord that you sent me a woman who is a grate help for us, especially during this horrible time."

Maria dozed again. She had a dream. It was absolutely unreal and scary dream. She vividly saw both kids and her, taking a train. It was an endless train, consisting of innumerous green and dark blue carriages. Maria found herself and kids somewhere in the middle of the train. The carriage, they walked in, was stuffed with passengers, and they could not find a single seat there.

Then she saw how three of them were moving from one carriage to another. Even in her dream Maria realized that they were not looking for seats, but … begging. Yes, they asked for food. Her children were hungry, and Maria did not have anything to give them. She clearly saw how Tisha stretched his small hand, and somebody gave him a slice of bread and a sugar cube…

Then Maria saw herself talking to a nice couple – a well-dressed woman in a beautiful hat and a military officer. They were kind and gave Maria some money. The couple was in their late forties and, as they mentioned to Maria, they did not have children. They suggested "easing" the life of a single mother with adoption of Tikhon. Maria remembered clearly that she declined.

Maria could not recollect one thing-what exactly diverted her attention for a short while from her boys. It looked like at one of the train stops, she ran out of the carriage to a railway station canteen to buy some foods for kids. She nearly missed the train, and when the train had moved, she jumped into the carriage. What Maria observed out of the window shocked her. A poor mother perceived that a *nice* couple took Tisha away without her permission. She clearly saw, how they walked her son along the platform of unknown railway station. The train was catching speed and a shocked mother lost Tisha out of her sight. Maria screamed and woke up.

She said to herself, "What a nightmare! Actually, it's daymare. Get up, Maria and move on. Staying in bed does not work for you."

Maria stood in front of the iconostas with the icons beautifully arranged on the wall and began her morning prayers. In a short while, she felt dizzy and sat down on a chair. Zina quietly opened the door and saw Maria sitting and praying. She entered the bedroom and opened the thick curtains on the windows. The rays of the spring sun filled the cozy bedroom with pleasant light. Maria finished her morning prayers with praising the Lord for keeping her and children alive.

"Maria, you need something to eat," Zina suggested. Then she continued, "I cooked oatmeal with dried apples for breakfast. Eat and lay down again."

"Thank you, Zina. I agree that I need to eat, but I don't feel that I am hungry. To begin with, I must take shower, and in half an hour, I'll be ready for my breakfast," Maria replied. "Do we have a bucket of warm water for my shower?"

"Yes, we do," Zina answered.

"Very well, Zina …" Maria wanted to say something else, but the thought slipped away.

Zina shook her head, watching Maria's feebleness. She interrupted her with the words,

"Stay here, please, and wait for me, Maria. Before you go to take shower, I'll give you something."

In two minutes, Zina handed Maria a small plate with a sandwich made of a slice of rye bread and some sunflower oil on it.

"Eat this sandwich first and then go and take shower. You know, bread and oil will give you some strength."

"Thank you, Zina. I forgot the feeling of those mornings, when somebody took care of me. I appreciate your care very much."

"Don't mention, Maria," Zina answered. She stopped adding "Dr" with Maria's name due to two reasons: first, she avoided recollecting Maria about her unemployment, and second, after all the tragic events, Zina felt closer to Maria and boys. She came up and began to undo and loosen Maria's long braids.

Maria burst into crying, recollecting her nightmare. It was important for misfortunate woman to have somebody, who could understand her misery, nerve-racking fears, terrible feelings and horrifying worries. Zina was sincerely sorry. She knew how to listen and ease Maria's fears.

"Zina, I saw a weirdest dream. It terrified me," Maria said between sobbing.

Zina did not know what dream Maria was talking about but tried to calm Maria down.

"Don't worry, Maria. It's due to all shocking events that took place during last week. When I am panicky, my dreams are always scary. Pull yourself together and ask Archangel Gabriel to supply you with strength. Focus on your boys. Pray and you'll see how merciful our Lord is."

Zina saw that Maria did not listen to her, so much she was frightened with the vision. Zina asked,

"Well, what was your dream about? Was it really so scary?"

"Zina, my dream was not only scary for me; it was more alarming. I saw an unusually long train with old dark green and blue carriages. My children and I could not find unoccupied seats and moved slowly from one carriage to another. Do you know what wc did on a train?"

Maria looked in the mirror to see Zina. Zina shook her head.

"Zina, we were begging there. Can you imagine? However, our begging was not the most thrilling thing. My boys were hungry, and I had nothing to give them. That's why we became beggars on a train. I saw clearly, how we went from one carriage to another, begging."

Zina interrupted Maria with a strange question,

"Was your begging answered?"

Maria looked at Zina with surprise and asked,

"Why did you ask about it?"

"It's important to get something, when you beg. So, was your request answered?"

"Yes, it was. The passengers gave alms, slices of bread and some sugar cubes," Maria answered, crying distraughtly.

Zina watched her with sympathy. However, it was difficult to find the right words that could calm Maria down. Zina stroke Maria's hair, saying repeatedly,

"Calm down, darling. It was not a scary dream. It was a dream of a distressed woman."

Maria continued,

"Then one couple took my Tisha away. I saw them out of the train window. Zina, they talked to me politely.

They were nice people and gave me some money, and then they kidnapped my child and walked him away."

At that very moment, Tisha appeared in the doorway, as if he wanted to prove his disturbed mother that nothing bad happened to him, and nobody took him away. He moved toward his mother with his unsteady waddle gait. When he reached Maria's bed, she picked him up and covered with kisses. She exclaimed with mother's joy,

"Look, Zina! Tisha walks!"

Then she turned to the iconostas and prayed emotionally,

"Holy Mother of God, please, ask your Son to cast out any danger from my children, and cover them with the Divine protection and mercy. Dear Lord, hide us from the predatory view of the beasty demons. Help us, save us, have mercy on us, and keep us, O God by Thy grace."

Zina embraced Maria and Tisha, saying:

"That's right, Maria. For now, praying is the best thing you can do. Do not tear your heart. God is merciful. You know it very well. Gain strength, and we'll go to Eultin. You must see your friends. I have my strong feeling that Dr. Leskov is the one who will find the way to help you."

Lord, have mercy!

Chapter 6

The first day after the hospitalization started not in the way Maria planned it in the previous evening. Weakness interfered with everything.

Zina asked Maria,

"Please, get well, Maria. You need strength for so many things. All of them cannot be postponed."

"I agree, but now, I need to find strength to take a shower and wash my long hair," Maria replied.

Zina suggested,

"Wait for me, Maria. I'll put baby in bed and help you."

Maria looked at her boy and smiled. It was his time for a day nap, and the child leaned toward his mother, falling asleep. Suddenly, she recollected her vision, and mother's instinct worked-she hugged him tightly. Tisha whimpered. Zina took him and put in his crib.

Maria felt better after shower. She put on her new flannel lilac nightgown and a light pink robe with small lilac flowers. Maria always paid attention to the details of her wardrobe, even sleep wear. The doctor's salaries did not allow her to have many cloths, but whatever she sawed was always nice and feminine. Zina assisted Maria with calming her long and beautiful hair. Poor woman looked in the mirror and bitterly smiled to her thought, "Alex always liked my hair. He could not wait until it grew after the force labor camp. Do I need to keep it long?"

There was no answer to her question. The person, who could answer without any hesitation, '*Yes, certainly, sure, Mon Chere'* left this world.

She went to the kitchen and sat down at the table. To her great surprise, Maria experienced strong hunger.

"Everything is strange," Maria thought. "I am hungry and eat my oatmeal with big appetite, like nothing happened. How could I be hungry after everything that occurred? Does the law "survival of the fittest" work this way? I believe that God wills to save me. He wants me to rejuvenate, gain strength and protect my kids. *Glory to Thee, O Lord! Glory to Thee*!"

Maria looked up at Zina. The woman had finished cooking soup for lunch and wrapped it in the kitchen towels to keep it warm. After several days of starvation, it smelled delicious for Maria.

"What time is it now?" Maria asked.

"A quarter to two. Sasha will be home in half an hour. The fresh soup waits for the boy."

Eating made Maria dozy. She returned to her bedroom, laid down in bed and closed her eyes. Though she felt drained, a new wave of grief did not let her take a nap. She had to deal with an obstinate loneliness and irreparable loss. Maria suppressed sobbing. She did not want to awake Tisha and hided her face in the pillow. The woman was inconsolable. Her tears poured, making her pillow wet. Then she pulled Alexander's pillow, hugged it with both hands and continued crying. She repetitively called his name, "Alex, my dear Alex…"

Maria did not know how to deal with tragic situation. Again and again, her mind raised the same question, "Where can I find emotional, physical and financial strength to run away from the evil or struggle with it and win?"

Maria's heart was in complete disagreement with another question, "How can I live without Alex, his devoted and passionate love, his care and protection?" All her nature refused to accept the fact that she had to learn living without Alexander, who left her forever. She still needed to hear his straight answers to the questions she asked. She always relied on his opinions and decisions. Maria trusted her husband because Alexander was right in all their life situations.

"Alex, what should I do now? Darling, I don't know how to stay in this intimidating world without you. I am lost. I was fired yesterday, so we do not have money for living. Alex, why did you decide to go and talk to monsters? What did you ask them about or what did you insist on, if the brutal murder was their answer?"

Maria held her breath but did not hear any answer. Nevertheless, she anxiously continued talking to her beloved.

"Mon Cher, I understood that you were sick and tired of *existence*. I understood that you were seriously concerned about the future of our sons. I could easily understand that you were unhappy in this Godforsaken land. You felt guilty and responsible for your old and lonely mother, who could be still in this world, waiting for you. However, you should be more patient and avoid the merciless demonic fire. Being a single warrior, why have you declared the war against the army of demons?"

Maria caught some air and continued, as if she saw her husband in front of her,

"I know darling, it was your battle for better life. Where is life, Alex? What did we get instead? You found terrible death. Mon Cher, you have left us forever. What destiny is prepared for our sons and me? Since your visit to KGB, the demons followed us. They blamed Dr. Belikov in the sins, he had never committed. How can all of us live in trepidation?"

Maria took a deep breath again and ended in a low voice,

"Mon Cher, please forgive me. I know that I must live for our kids. I must protect and support them in this life. The grief and fear make me shattered. The grief and fear do not let me gain my strength; they also tried to paralyze my mind and will …"

Maria heard that somebody knocked on the door. Her first thought was: "Sasha is back home after school." She did not want her son to see her in despair. The woman got up and moved to meet her boy. Maria was ready to open the door of her bedroom, when she heard a voice of a visitor. The blood of a terrified woman nearly curdled in her veins. She recognized the voice of Captain Sidorenko, who talked to Zina in his usual obnoxious barky manner.

Maria's mind screamed, "My Lord, the demon appeared in our place. Alex, they would never leave us alone…"

Maria felt lightheaded and was close to pass out. The frightened woman lay down on her bed, closed her eyes and began to pray repetitively the Jesus prayer,

"O Lord Jesus Christ, Son of God, have mercy on me, a sinner. Amen."

Zina opened the door of Maria's bedroom and asked,

"Doctor Maria, Captain Sidorenko is here. What should I tell him? Can you talk to him now?"

"Let him in, Zina."

Captain Sidorenko stood behind Zina trying to catch Maria's response. He entered the bedroom, and Maria immediately noticed how her room became dark and stuffy. Zina brought Sidorenko a chair. He sat down, opened his briefcase and started questioning without any greeting.

Maria assumed, "Politeness does not exist for this person. Probably, he was not introduced to such a subject, as politeness in his *proletarian* childhood. Actually, for his job he does not need such a tool."

"I can see, Madam Kurbatov that you are at home that means, you feel better. Am I right? Why did you decide to leave the hospital so hurriedly?" Sidorenko sounded sarcastic.

"I prefer to be at home."

Maria noticed that Sidorenko did not even register her answer. He continued in monotonous manner,

"Madam Kurbatov, I warned you last time, if our committee found your answers, as incomplete, we had to ask the same questions again and again. Well, let us begin. When did you learn that your husband decided to take a trip to Magadan?"

"In the evening of his departure," Maria replied.

Sidorenko asked,

"When exactly did he say about his plan to visit Magadan …?"

Maria noticed that Sidorenko wanted to say "Magadan KGB", but interrupted himself.

"When he came home after work, he announced to us about his decision to go to Magadan with the late evening train," Maria answered.

"You mean, he announced about his trip to Magadan in the evening of the previous day?"

Maria sensed how all her nature arose against answering his questions. She hated him and preferred to ignore that goose-like man. Maria cogitated, "Why should I answer all his preposterous questions? Why should I play the part, he wants me to play? I know for sure how all these interrogations will end. Why should I act? I hate pretending. If it is the end, so it's the end. I am more than sure that my husband did not pretend or amuse them there. He died, as an honorable man. Died … Is this what I want for myself? Maybe. But what about our children?"

For a while, Sidorenko was recording something in his notebook, giving Maria the opportunity to think about taking real or fictitious parts in life. Then Maria pushed away the depressing thought about the *end* and answered,

"My husband told us about his trip on the day of his departure. To be more precise, Alexander informed us in the evening, when he returned home from the hospital."

"What was the reason of keeping his trip in secret to the very last minute?" Sidorenko asked.

Maria shrugged her shoulders. Sidorenko insisted in answer,

"Why didn't he say anything earlier or at least one or two days before his trip? Probably he mentioned to you a week ago that he planned to go to Magadan?"

"No, he didn't."

"Did he talk to your son about his plans?" Sidorenko continued.

"Ask Sasha. I hadn't heard such a conversation."

"I will. Did your husband have enemies in the village?"

Maria tried to be calm, but it was not easy for her.

"No, he didn't."

Sidorenko continued inquiring,

"Your husband was a surgeon. Maybe, there were patients or patient's relatives, who did not like the results of your husband's work?"

"I haven't heard anything like this."

Sidorenko degradingly looked at Maria and concluded with anger for himself,

"There were no delinquencies made by your *saint* husband. He deliberated every step, except the last one.

The Count made a mistake. He made a huge mistake, Madam Kurbatov."

Sidorenko hated Maria for everything: for her brief and honest answers, the necessity to arrive to this dirty village several days in a raw, and for senselessness of his interrogation. Without Maria's answers, Sidorenko irrefutably knew everything about the case of murder better than "Madam" Kurbatov could imagine.

He concluded for himself,

"I am here for the third time in one week. Damn them and, particularly, this bitch! She does not want to look at me, hardly answering my questions. She is smart enough to guess that the death of her husband has not been an accident. A couple of things I know for sure: she will never try to investigate it, and she will never prove that her husband had been purged, just because his name was on the list of people under the secret code for eradication."

Sidorenko repeated the question,

"So, Madam Kurbatov, you are absolutely sure that your husband did not have enemies."

"Yes, I am."

"Who do you think kill your husband? Could it be your admirer?" Sidorenko asked with a smirk that made Maria furious.

His obnoxious supposition aroused a new wave of hatred. Hardly controlling her feelings, Maria asked with a trembling voice,

"I hadn't been introduced to that person. Had you?"

Sidorenko liked her answer, "This bitch has sense of humor. Maybe, I need to introduce her to Sergeant Frolov. We'll wait until Madam looks better. Maybe, she is good enough in bed for her 39. I must admit that she has beautiful hair. I wish Frolov and I meet her under different circumstances, where she does not have any way out …"

He shook his head and continued with questioning,

"Did your husband plan to buy anything valuable in Magadan?"

"I don't think so," Maria answered.

"Did you want him to bring home anything particular?"

"Yes, I did."

"What did you want?"

"Some foods and flour," Maria answered emotionlessly.

"What happened to it?"

Maria did not understand the question and asked,

"What happened to *what*?"

"What happened to the foods he bought in Magadan?"

"Nothing. The militiamen delivered it to us in the evening, when Alexander was found murdered on the train."

Sidorenko was bored and decided to finish the pointless interrogation.

"Why did you decide to leave the hospital, if you do not feel well?"

Maria replied,

"You must know the Russian proverb: 'Even the walls help us at home.'"

Sidorenko smirked, "Ha, this bitch learned something in Russian prison."

Then he asked the next question,

"Did your chief physician discharge you yesterday, or you left without his permission?"

"He did it," Maria could not understand what he meant.

"When do you go back to the hospital?"

"You mean the next visit for my treatment? I prefer not to go," Maria replied.

"When do you plan to return for work?" The KGB officer became mad again at Maria. "Never," Maria answered with irritability.

Sidorenko was surprised with her straight answer and jumped off the chair, leaned over Maria and asked,

"Why is it so, Madam Kurbatov?"

"Dr. Belikov fired me. He said that I cannot work there any longer."

Maria watched how Sidorenko's facial expression had been shifted for demonic satisfaction. The monster enjoyed his victory.

Maria was tired and asked,

"When is the end of your interrogation? I feel nauseous."

"I have finished it. This time, you were more cooperative, Madam Kurbatov."

Sidorenko put an accentuation on the word *Madam*. For a couple of minutes, he stared Maria with disgrace, as if he wanted to tell her something dirty, dishonorable or scary. Then he left without saying "Good-bye".

Maria heard how Sidorenko questioned Sasha and Zina, repeating the same questions several times. She felt disturbed again. "How dare he interrogate twelve-year-old boy for such a long time? What an abominable person Sidorenko is!"

Tisha woke up, saw his mother in bed and stretched his arms, calling,

"Mama."

Maria pretended that she was asleep, and the boy called louder,

"Mama."

Maria recollected how every new word of their baby son awoke Alexander's joy. However, at that moment, Maria experienced emotional pain of a single mother, knowing that from now on, she was the only parent who delighted with her boy. Tisha called for the third time. Maria got up and asked Tisha with a smile,

"Who called his Mama so nicely?"

Tisha burst into laughing.

Maria made a serious facial expression and looked at Tikhon. The boy stopped smiling. Maria asked,

"Who interrupted mother's sleep? Who woke up his mom?"

Tisha looked at her attentively, sensing the difference in mother's voice.

Maria smiled again, and the boy smiled in answer. She took him in her bed, and Tisha gave her a hug. The child put his head on Maria's chest and closed his eyes with his tiny hands. He played hide-and-seek with her, as Sasha played with him.

Maria pretended that she looked around for her son. Then she called,

"Tisha, where are you? Where is Mama's boy?"

The boy was happy to play with his Mama, watching her through the fingers of his tiny hands. He loudly laughed every time, when she called for him again, "Tisha! Tisha! Where are you?"

This child was destined to lessen his mother's grief, because there was no better medicine for a mother than her children.

Lord, have mercy!

Chapter 7

Zina closed the door after Captain Sidorenko and rushed into Maria's bedroom. Sasha followed Zina and embraced his Mom and Tisha.

Zina asked Maria,

"Why did that *serpent* arrive to us? I worried, Maria. He questioned you for so long! What did he want to know? I was nervous because you are weak. He didn't have any mercy for you."

"He asked nearly the same questions that he asked at the hospital," Maria answered.

"Mama, why did he arrive for the third time?" Sasha asked anxiously.

Maria did not want to frighten her son and answered in a calm manner,

"Who knows, son? I think they just follow their protocol. They demonstrate us, how thoroughly they provide the investigation of "Dr. Kurbatov's case". We know well that they are deeply involved in your father's murder. With killing your father, they got rid of one of the '*annoying*' cases. They performed everything in their usual brutal way. They sent Sidorenko to check, if anybody in the family has a suspicion about dirty part of Magadan KGB in your father's death."

Zina was frightened with Maria's conclusion. She whispered,

"Maria, I hope that you haven't shown him that we know who has ordered and carried out Dr. Kurbatov's murder."

"Definitely not, Zina. Why should I take a risk? I must protect my chicks from those monsters. Sasha, what did Sidorenko ask you about?"

"He wanted to know, if Dad talked to me about his visit to Magadan, and when and where that conversation took place. Sidorenko asked what my father planned to do there. Do you know, Mama, I mentioned on purpose that we were out of bread flour, and Dad went to Magadan to purchase flour and my favorite sausages. I simplified everything, as a child, and avoided bearing out my understanding of what had happened to Papa in reality."

Sasha's voice sounded unusually low. He breathed out the next two sentences,

"I did not want to speak out that it was they – the people of KGB, who had killed my Papa. One day, I'll tell them how I hate all of them. I hate them, Mama."

Sasha was hysterical for the first time after the tragedy occurred. He ran out of the room. Zina wanted to follow him, but Maria stopped her. She sensed the necessity to talk to Sasha. He had to learn from her something vitally important. The explanation could not be postponed. It had to be done at that very moment, otherwise Sasha was in danger.

Maria found Sasha in his room. He sat at his desk, crying bitterly. Sasha met Maria with the words,

"Mama, I hate them all! I hate them!"

The child could hardly take a breath between sobbing. Then he continued,

"First, they have killed my Papa. Then, they sent an officer, who did not even pretend that he was sorry for you, Tisha and me. He wanted Dr. Belikov to interrupt your treatment and make you die. They fooled me with Dad's burial. Now, they continue fooling us with their farcical interrogations and promises to find the man who had killed our Papa. Can we trust them, Mama? Never! They are liars. All of them are pretenders and liars. They are murderers."

At that very moment, Maria realized how much her son undertook during five days of her stay at the hospital. She sat down next to him and embraced his shoulders. Maria did not want to interrupt his heartbreaking narration. Sasha stopped sobbing and continued,

"When I was at the militia station after the recognition of my father's body, Major Gromov promised to call me the same day with the instructions from Magadan regional office regarding father's burial. Mama, that man is the biggest liar. He had never kept his promises. For two days, I was waiting for his call and then brought Dad's cloths and shoes to the militia station. His secretary took Dad's things without looking at me. She did not allow me to talk to Gromov. Mama, she is also a liar. She said that Gromov had left for meeting and was not going to be back to his office on that day."

Maria tried to explain the behavior of the secretary,

"Sasha, that woman is just a secretary. She follows the orders and instructions, she receives."

"But I have heard his voice in the office," Sasha screamed.

"It was he who answered the phone call. He was not on his business trip. Mama, all of them are terrible people. They hate us and I hate them all."

Maria embraced Sasha's shoulders again, leaned to his head, trying to calm her child down. She wanted Sasha to release his pain which her boy accumulated after Alexander's death. Maria patiently listened to his distressing story. Sasha went on,

"On the next day, I went there again, and the secretary informed me that they had buried my father's body *somewhere*, but she did know where exactly. Mama, I ran to the cemetery. I searched everywhere, but I did not find any fresh grave there. I ran back to the militia station, and one older militiaman stopped me at the entrance door.

Sasha looked at his mother and asked,

"Do you know what he suggested?"

Maria asked,

"What did he say?"

"He said, 'Well, I would not suggest you, boy, to come here again. You are a good son, but it's better for you not to be involved in the case of your father. You cannot make him alive, but you can aggravate your family's situation. You have a small brother at home. Go and take care of him, until your mother gets well."

Mama, I went home, like a coward. I did not say straight to the militia people, what I thought about all of them."

"Thank God! Lord was merciful to you," Maria exclaimed.

Then she asked,

"Have you seen that older man anywhere after?"

"Yes, I did. When you were at the hospital, he came several times here and talked to Aunt Zina and me."

Sasha sighed and asked Maria,

"Mama, what did the old militiaman mean, when he wanted me to stay away from anything that was related to my father, his death and burial? How dare they advise you or me not to be involved in Dad's case?"

After the painful emotional explosion, the boy felt exhausted and put his head on mother's shoulder. For some time, they were sitting in silence.

Maria felt sorry for Sasha, but she wanted her son to realize the danger of a trap the Magadan KGB prepared for their family. She hesitated for a minute, watching her son. She wanted to be sure that at his age, he was able to comprehend everything that she was ready to reveal. Maria thought, "Sasha has to be aware of our precarious state. Otherwise, any noticeable disobedience that Sasha's hatred initiates will provoke a new wave of violence against him and the entire family, including Zina. The hostility easily brings to an appalling end. So, I must introduce Sasha to the demonic nature and plans of our enemies."

Maria interrupted Sasha's distressing thoughts with the words,

"Let's go to the kitchen and have some tea. I need to talk to you, son."

She poured two cups of hot tea and put some cookies on a plate. They sat down at the dining table, facing each other.

"Oh, Lord, I want to be sure that it's the right time to share with Sasha my embittered knowledge and warning experiences," Maria thought.

"Sasha, I have to talk to you on the subject that you are not familiar with. I believe that you are old and strong enough to comprehend my conceptions. What I reveal now, you would never hear again. Those people, you have dealt with for the last week, are not the regular people."

Maria noticed that her introduction surprised Sasha a bit. She continued,

"Trust me, my son, I know what I am talking about. Once, your father and I were '*introduced*' to the cruel nature of those people, people without hearts and with the brain of the predators. They were marauders and sadistic species in military uniforms of NKVD. Now it is KGB. We learned hard way about the existence of demons in the world. They mutilated your Dad in 1946 but did not murder him on that time. They dishonored me and threw into prison where you were born. They did not change their nature for twelve years. This time, they have finished their evil mission with Count Alexander Kurbatov, Sr. Trust me, son, they have their vicious plans regarding us, as well. We must be cautious, Sasha."

Maria's voice was quiet, but firm. Sasha could not understand the depth of mother's statement and asked,

"Who are not people? I mean, who are not the *regular* people?"

Maria reached Sasha's head and stroked his wavy hair. She would prefer her child not to learn anything about co-existence of two worlds. The dangerous situation forced her to precede with more detailed explanation. Otherwise, misunderstanding of the situation and lack of knowledge could burn her boy to ashes.

"Alexander, what I am going to tell you is not a fairy tale, nightmare or a product of my sick imagination after the severe shock. You learn it once and, since now on, you'll see our world from different prospective. The human world is alienated into two subdivisions: the constituent of light and the constituent of darkness. God runs the enlightening part, and Satan is a ruler of the dark demonic forces. Satan always competes with God and tries to seize more people, breaking down their nature, and forcefully keeping them on his dark side."

"Oh yes, Mama, I remember how Dad explained it to me on our very first day together. But how does it affect the present situation? I can believe that the demonic person murdered our Dad just because Dad was good. Then it means that in Dad's case the demonic darkness has won. Why did our God allow it to happen? Maybe, He forgot about us?"

Maria continued,

"Be careful, my son with your conclusions. When a normal person's life is distorted by hardships, he or she feels lost, disappointed, impatient and hopeless. The impatience and hopelessness make the person angry, envious and weak. The weakness and hatred allow the *spirit of despair* to possess his or her soul and run the mind. The person becomes depressed."

"What does it mean to become depressed," Sasha interrupted.

"Depressed people do not see anything good in their life. Nothing looks beautiful or interesting for them. The darkness separates them from the main light – our Creator, Savior and Holy spirit. People stop praying to the Lord, *'Create in me a pure heart, O God, and renew a right spirit within me. Cast me not from Thy presence and take not Thy Holy Spirit from me. Restore unto me the joy of Thy salvation, and with Thy governing Spirit establish me... A sacrifice unto God is a broken spirit; a heart that is broken and humbled God will not despise...'* Nuisance, impatience, anger and hatred work like *firewood* and *flames*. The more firewood and flame you collect and store inside, the easier you can be destroyed."

Maria looked at her son and saw how deeply he had been already damaged. She had her hope for God's mercy.

Her voice was calm when she continued,

"Demons grow and become stronger on human hatred. Anger and hatred are fertilizing material for demons. Your father's hatred and impatience let them get closer and murder him. Now, the same executers try to confound you and me, contaminating us with anger, fear, hatred and hopelessness. At this moment, they do not abolish us physically. They work at our moral and spiritual destruction. Remember, *spiritual and moral destruction is worse than physical death.*"

Sasha looked at Maria with surprise and asked,

"What can be worth than death? If I knew that I could survive, I was ready to kill all of them at the militia station. They were not sympathetic for us after everything that happened with Papa and you. When I asked for their help with father's funeral, they ignored me, lied and did not even look at me. They did not have any pity. I hate them, Mama. How can I forgive them?"

Maria smiled bitterly and answered without any distressing intonations in her voice,

"You are wrong, darling. Physical death happens once. Moral suffering is endless. Sorry to say, Sasha but for less than a week after your father's death, evil successfully seeded anger, hatred, fear and doubt in your mind and heart. He was not successful with the soul, not yet. Preserve it, my boy. I beg you, son, do not let harmful, devilish seed to grow! They want to turn your pure grief into moral eradication in order to celebrate their victory with trapping one more ingenuous man into demonic darkness."

Alexander did not answer, trying to understand the depth of his mother's words. Her explanation impressed him. From the very beginning, his hatred surprised and scared the boy. He remembered the exact day and occasion, when he noticed how a strong hot wave of hatred hit and covered him. The clash was so strong that the boy lost the balance, drowning in that heat. It took place in the office of Major Gromov, when the boy brought his father's clothing for funeral. Entirely ignoring the boy's tragedy, Gromov refused to see him, and his secretary deviously lied.

Maria noticed how strenuous it was for her son to absorb the new knowledge. He was sitting across the table, but it looked like the invisible force took the boy away from her to the place where they seeded hatred in his young mind.

Sasha looked at his mother and described another painful situation that affected him a lot and did not let the hatred go,

"Mama, they are liars, and they hate us. They killed our father and buried him naked. I saw him on the table in a basement. They did not even clean the blood from his neck, right side of his face and shoulder."

Maria did not know that Sasha was taken for post-mortal recognition. It was another shock for poor mother. She turned pale and was close to collapse again. Sasha rushed to her, supplicating,

"No, Mama. Please, do not faint. I love you, Mama. If you want me to cleanse my hatred, I'll do it for you. You explained the origin of my new feeling that suffocated me for all these days and nights. I promise not to grow it. It's a word of a man. Still, Mama, I cannot understand why it happened to all of us."

Maria recognized Alex's firmness in Sasha's words and persistent attempt to fully comprehend the reason of the family tragedy. She thought, "My poor boy went through a lot of stress and disappointment. He learned unforgettable loss, grief and hatred. He turned older. The unmerciful events of the last week had completely changed his childish appearance. The tragedy left its merciless imprint not only on the face of my son, but in his mind, heart and soul. *Oh Lord, restore a right spirit within my son. Amen.*"

Maria saw that Sasha was thinking about something important and did not interrupt him until he broke the silence,

"Mama, how shall we live without Dad, especially when you have lost your job? We have nobody who will help us. Where can we get money for living? Aunt Zina said that God is merciful and would take care of us. She promised to help us. Do you know, Mama her pension is enough for having only bread for four of us, but Tisha needs milk and ..."

It was the second proof of Sasha's grown-up. The upsetting thoughts flashed in Maria's mind, "It's a pity, but my son is not a child any longer. It's my fault that he is not destined to have his normal childhood. My desire to see my family and to take them to Europe with me made our life extremely painful."

"I want to be honest with you, Sasha. I do not know how we'll live without your father and my work, but I agree with Aunt Zina that our Lord is the best provider. We'll pray, live with the faith and keep hope only on

Him. He'll have mercy for us. It's not the first hard-hitting situation in our life, is it? You remember the camp life. I remember my home-coming. We must praise the Lord in the best way for waking us up every morning, for seeing each other and our devoted friend aunt Zina. We must be grateful that we can watch Tisha's growth… With the support of our Holy Father, we'll survive. You and I have to pass our life test in faith in order to overcome the hardships."

Maria's voice trembled, but she pulled herself together and continued,

"We'll survive, Sasha. Remember, son: *With God all things are possible*."

"Mama, is there any way to fight the darkness and win?"

Maria smiled,

"I expected this question from you. You are a son of your father, Sasha. I want you to learn the most important rule in the fight with darkness: anger and hatred are forbidden. These two strong feelings unarmed thousands of good people in their struggle against demonic force. The evil won when you are armed with anger and hatred instead of light of the Divinity that comes from a strong soul. Learn to believe in Divine intervention and resolution of any life hardship. Don't start futile fire and don't be mindless to jump in it, pulling all of us there. Be always patient and keep faith. Enlighten your life path with praising the Lord. Then with God's help, the dark forces will retreat."

Sasha listened to Maria with admiration. She continued,

"Every day, please pray for your father's soul, and merciful God forgives him all his sins. Pray for yourself, in order the Savior cleans and protects you. Ask Him with the words, *'Dear Lord, restore unto me the joy of Thy salvation, and with Thy governing Spirit establish me. Amen.'*

Maria smiled, watching how genuinely Sasha absorbed her last direction, repeating the prayer several times,

"Pray for your enemies, son."

"Why should I?" Sasha was surprised with the mother's request.

"In order the Lord converts them into people of the light. Promise our Creator, *'I shall teach transgressors Thy ways, and the ungodly shall return unto Thee'*. Always keep your promises in front of God. What victory may be more desirable than to return lost and possessed souls to the light, and they'll serve the righteousness? Remember: the greatest gift is to share the enlightenment."

Sasha came up to his mother, put his hands on her shoulders and asked,

"Mama, are you an angel? You know so much about righteousness and wickedness, about enlightening, love and hatred… You must be an angel."

Maria sighed and brought her argument:

"If I am an angel, I would never let your father to leave us. Being an angel, I would be able to stop him. I miss him so much ..."

Sasha shook his head and pleaded,

"Mama, please live forever! Teach Tikhon and me, how to stay on the right side, serving the Divinity and overcoming the hardships of life with true faith."

Glory to You, o Lord! Glory to You!

Chapter 8

Maria felt ashamed, recollecting her hysterical condition in the morning.

"Sometimes, Sasha, it's rather difficult for people in distress to hear the word of the Lord's guidance. Most of the time, it comes through your Guardian angel. Learn to sense your angel. You think that it's your own *intuition* gives you an idea or hint how to attain it in life." Maria smiled, repeating again and again with a bit of sarcasm, "Yes, our intuition. Certainly, our intuition…"

She continued, "Your angel receives the messages from Above and teaches you what is right or wrong. God was so kind to me, giving multiple opportunities to learn the difference. Once in my life, I was not patient enough to listen carefully. I made the wrong decision and arrived home in 1946..."

Maria sighed and continued: "Remember, son: the satan is strong. He always pushes stubborn or angry people in the wrong directions."

"How can we escape his influence?" Sasha asked with the fear in his voice.

Maria advised:

"Stop yourself right at that very moment when you sense that something is going wicked. Listen to your Guardian or 'intuition', if you want."

"Did you have that feeling?" Sasha asked. "I mean the feeling that your trip was the wrong thing to do?"

"Yes, I did," Maria answered honestly. "The unusually strong force pushed me to go home, and I did not postpone the trip. Even my pregnancy did not change the plans of home-coming."

"And what about our father?" Sasha asked.

"Your father couldn't stop me and jumped in the same fire," Maria said with deep regret.

"And you think, Mama that God punished us for your mistake?" Sasha asked and continued with passion: "You wanted the best for your family, Mama. How He could punish you for it?"

"Sasha, I was punished for my disobedience, my stubbornness and refusal to listen to my guardian Angel and the advice of so many nice people. I needed to wait until you were born. I felt that something was not right. My "intuition" screamed…"

"Mama, what did you feel regarding Dad's trip to Magadan?" Sasha asked.

"I was against it. The same feeling of danger. My angel tried to cancel the tragedy."

"Why didn't Papa's angel stop him?" Sasha asked.

Maria explained: "It was the situation when father's anger and impatience pushed the angel away."

Sasha was surprised to hear that the angels could be pushed away and asked,

"How could it be possible that people can push the guardian angels away? What can push my guardian away?"

"There are so many things that turn the guardian away," Maria answered.

"Things, like what..?" Sasha tried to get the full answer.

Maria saw that the boy needed her explanation. She named the human weaknesses:

"Lost faith and gratitude to the Divinity, daily disobedience in the eyes of the Lord, stubbornness, bad deeds, anger, cruelty, bad words, hatred, unforgiveness..."

"You mean bad words, like profanity?" Sasha asked.

"Exactly, my boy."

"Most of the people around use them all the time. Even my classmates make the sentences out of bad words," Sasha said. "Major Gromov also uses profanity."

Maria smiled bitterly and said,

"Look, Sasha at the people around, who know how to build the sentences out of dirty words. Are they happy? Are they able to sustain their lives and the lives of their families? Do they have enough money to feed and dress their children? Look at the children in your school. The muttered words *slap* the angels and turn them away. From their parents, they inherited profanity, poverty and misery without God's guidance and protection."

Zina entered the kitchen, holding Tisha in her arms. She brought the apology.

"We are sorry, but we have to interrupt your conversation. Please, don't think that we came here to listen to your secrets. Right, Tisha? A little boy is hungry."

The baby was happy to see his Mama and brother. He 'talked' to them fast in his language with frequent repeating 'Mama' and 'Sasa', mixing those words with some cheerful exclamations that always exist only in babyish language.

Sasha began testing the baby's memory, asking,

"Tisha, where is our Mama?"

Tisha turned toward Maria and screamed joyfully. Sasha continued,

"Tisha, where is Aunt Zina?"

Tisha turned and looked at Zina. Then he stretched his arm, opened his tiny hand and asked in a childish way with his hand motion,

"Give me, give me!"

He made the funniest 'unhappy' face, as if he wanted to show that he was neglected and not fed, at least, for several days.

All of them laughed. Maria concluded,

"Zina, now Tisha associates you with his meals," They laughed again. Only children made the atmosphere at home alive.

Then Maria joined the game, asking,

"Tisha, where is Sasha?"

A little boy turned toward Sasha and repeated several times,

"Sasa, Sasa."

He moved toward his elder brother with piercing lament, as a brave leader of American Indians. Sasha picked up his baby brother and gave him a hug. The baby turned to his mother, opened both hands and said quietly,

"Daddy… No Daddy."

Maria's eyes were immediately filled with tears. She took Tisha in her arms and repeated his words,

"No Daddy, Tisha. Sorry, but you are right, baby. Your Daddy left us forever."

Zina brought a soup-tureen, put it in the middle of the table and opened the lid. The smell of home-made pea soup evaporated and spread all over the kitchen. Sitting high on his mother's lap, Tisha tried to reach the tureen.

Zina warned,

"It's hot, baby. Don't touch."

Maria interrupted,

"Zina, do we need to buy some food tomorrow?"

"Tomorrow, I'll go to the market and buy only milk. Let us pray."

Maria began,

"Dear Lord, please bless our food with Your Holy Spirit and us, who are grateful to You for whatever you provided today. Amen."

Everyone was silent at the table. Maria was feeding Tikhon. The hungry baby enjoyed soup, and he finished his meal without a single sound. Sasha cleaned the table, washed dishes, and went to do his school homework. Maria let Tisha walk, and he was circling around the kitchen furniture, trying to touch, open and pull everything that he could reach. Maria was quiet for a while, watching her baby and then asked,

"Zina, do we have any money left?"

"Yes, we do. Most likely, it's enough for a whole week."

Maria noticed for herself, "Zina is always positive. Even now, she underlined that we have money for the *whole* week. She avoided telling me, "We have money just for a week."

Then Maria asked the question that disturbed her all the time:

"What should we do after?"

The distressed woman sat down on her low stool in the corner of the kitchen. She cried quietly. Zina put her wrinkled hand on Maria's shoulder and suggested with consideration,

"Maria, stop crying, please. In your situation, even constant crying will not help. We'll ask for Lord's assistance, and He'll provide. But for now, it's better to ask the Lord to help you with your escape."

Maria did not understand Zina's words and asked,

"What should I ask the Lord about? What help do I need from Him?"

Zina re-phrased her suggestion, "I think that you need to leave this place. Sorry, Maria, but it would be better for you and kids to runaway forever. We'll try to arrange it, as fast as possible and nobody should know the place of your destination."

Maria was shocked to hear it. At that time, she saw zero possibility for runaway.

"Zina, how do you see it? Since next week, we do not have money for food. Do you think it is doable to escape with two children without money?"

"Next week, we'll go to Eultin to see doctor Leskov. Maria, I am more than sure, he'll help you. It's too dangerous for you and kids to stay here after everything that they have done to Dr. Alexander. Nobody can stop them. Nobody."

"Why? I will not insist in investigation of Alexander's murder. I don't want them to search for the killer. I will not insist in my position, as a physician. I need money to feed my boys and, due to this only reason, I can do anything: wash the floors in the hospital, do the laundry of their linen, or wash and feed the patients."

Maria burst into tears. She stated between sobs,

"Zina, I had never been issued my passport. I have no money for a long journey. There is one more obstacle and, to my mind, it is very important-I have no place to go."

Tisha started crying, as well. He opened his small plump hands and pronounced with bitterness in baby's voice,

"No Daddy."

"Zina, how can I leave Alexander's grave here? Who will take care of it? Why did you start this topic?"

"Maria, can you hear me? I want you to recognize the fact that your kids and you are in danger. God forbid, but different things can happen."

"How do you know? Who has told you that we are in jeopardy? Zina, why do you decide to scare me? Don't I have enough?"

Maria stopped crying and observed Zina with suspicion. She realized that their nanny knew something that Maria was not aware of. "It's obvious, otherwise Zina would never aggravate the difficultness of our situation. She knows something precarious but avoids terrifying me with scary details."

Maria was right. The only thing Zina cared about was the safety of Maria and her kids, otherwise the kind and caring woman would never insist in Maria's runaway.

"Zina, I can see that somebody has provided you some alarming information. Am I right? It must be truly unsafe for us to stay here, isn't it?"

"Yes, it is. I am sorry, Maria, but it's really dangerous," Zina answered in a low voice.

"Well, how urgently we have to run off?" Maria asked.

Zina answered without hesitation,

"To tell you the truth: the faster is the better…"

"Zina, I need to earn some money, first. How can I make money quickly?"

Maria looked around with the eyes of a stranger and asked,

"If we must disappear, I need to sell everything, including our furniture. Zina, how much can we make?"

"Let me see," Zina got up and went around the flat.

She counted everything that could be sold. Maria waited for her in the kitchen, thinking about the possibility to hide somewhere in Ukraine. When Zina returned to the kitchen with the approximate number, Maria realized that it was not enough to get to Ukraine.

Maria concluded for herself,

"With this financing we can hardly reach the area of the Ural Mountains – the beginning of European part of Russia. It's not the resolution of our problem."

Zina interrupted Maria's cheerless thoughts,

"The worst thing is that selling of the furniture requires time, and it will definitely attract *somebody's* attention. I wish, Maria, you can get your strength fast. Then, we'll visit the cemetery and leave for Eultin. You can suggest the furniture money to your friends in Eultin in exchange for tickets on the train and leave in the nearest time to … I don't know, where you can go, darling."

Maria's head became cloudy. She could not process in her mind all Zina's suggestions. Maria tried to focus her thoughts at vitally important things, but Tisha did not allow his mother to do it. Zina picked the boy up and left to give him a bath giving Maria an opportunity to think over their hastened journey.

In five minutes, Maria came to her strategic decision, "Nothing can be more important than safety of my children. Where should we go? Maybe, Sister Olga will help me. I have nobody else to go. I prefer staying away from Blue Creeks. People can recognize Pannochka Maria. Well, then Sister Olga's Ostrig is better again. Nobody knows me there. It's the only place where we can hide us for some time."

Maria got up and went to the entry hall to look at herself in the mirror. In accordance with the religious traditions, all mirrors in the apartment had been covered after Alexander's death. Maria opened the right side of the mirror and looked at herself. She could hardly recognize herself. Significant changes transpired in her appearance and posture. An elderly, skinny woman looked at Maria. That woman in the mirror with deadly pale face and hardly opened puffy eyes had nothing in common with Dr. Kurbatov who was here a week ago and, definitely she could not remind anybody Mademoiselle Maria Kotyk or Madam Kurbatov, who arrived at her home estate in 1946.

Maria whispered,

"My Lord! Who will recognize their Pannochka in this ugly woman?"

She covered the mirror and returned to the kitchen, planning their escape,

"All right, let Sister Olga be our *quiet harbor* for some time."

Sister Olga was discharged from the camp seven months earlier than Maria. At her discharge, she invited Maria with family to visit her in Ostrig. "I have enough space, and you can stay with me, as long as you need it." She left a note with her home address, which Maria hided with Alexander's secret letters from his camp in a blue envelope at Dr. Leskov's office until they were discharged.

"It's good that nobody knows me there," Maria concluded. Later, I'll visit Ganja in Blue Creeks. I miss our nanny so much. If she is alive, she'll tell me the complete story about my family…"

For a couple of minutes, Maria flew away in her thoughts to Blue Creeks. She did not have a chance during the last week for memories. Since 1946, there was no more nostalgia regarding the estate. She did not recollect it, as her home. It was a place of demonic tortures. She could hardly call to mind the sweet memories about her pre-WWII life.

"I did not find and save my father and siblings, but ruined the life of my own family," Maria concluded one more time. Even the term longer than twelve years did not clear up or reduce the bitterness of her home-coming. After Alexander's murder, Maria's guilt arose again. She blamed herself with new strength for the death of her husband.

In a while, Maria returned to the reality,

"Well, I have to find the way for runaway. Let's consider that the destination point is found."

Maria hit the bigger problem than finding the destination point.

"How can we get there without documents and money? I certainly need to visit Dr. Leskov. Maybe, he'll find any solution. *Dear Lord, help me to save my boys. Find the safe place for us,*" Maria meditated.

She got up from the chair, but strapping dizziness forced her to sit down again. New stress quickly exhausted Maria. "I must get well," Maria thought. "I must become stronger, otherwise, there is no way out. We'll be trapped."

Any new attack of a strong dizziness frightened Maria, arising an annoying thought in her mind, "It could be the symptom of passing out for unpredictably long term. I don't have time for it. I cannot leave my children alone. I must be functional."

It was easy to say, but weakness did not evaporate with the correct affirmations. Maria repeated desperately, as a child,

"*Dear Lord, have mercy on me and save me. Make me strong, my Lord. Amen.*"

She tried not to cry, but the tears were running uncontrollably. "I've lost my husband and now, I am the only one who is responsible for the lives of our children. We are trapped here. *Dear Lord, please show us the way out. Mother of God, please hide my children, covering them with your mother's love and patronage. Almighty Savior, for the sake of the prayers of all the saints, have mercy on us and save us. Amen.*"

Maria waited until dizziness and nausea alleviated and started meditating louder,

"Dear Lord, You are watching my illness. You know how weak and sinful I am. Help me overcome my weakness and sinfulness. Please, make my illness for cleansing of my multiple sins. I am in Your hands, my Lord. Have mercy on me and heal me. I accept everything in accordance with my deeds, and I am always grateful for Your Divine mercy. Amen."

Meditation always balanced Maria. She got up easier and put the kettle on a primus-stove in order to make the traditional evening tea. An odd and dreary thought struck her mind, "How can I stay here and prepare tea? My husband is not with me any longer, but I continue making our traditional tea, like nothing has happened. How can it be?"

Suddenly, Maria clearly heard the message from her Angel, "Never allow the demon of despair approach to you. Even the biggest tragedy with one person is unable to stop the flow of life of the entire family. You are destined to live, love, give birth to children and take care of them. Maria, you must continue serving the purpose of your life. Stay blessed!"

Maria closed her eyes and whispered,

Glory to Thee, O Lord! Glory to Thee!

Chapter 9

The morning of the next day was unexpectedly pleasing, if anything could be considered *pleasing* due to happenings that took place in the life of Maria's family. The chief-physician Belikov arrived for home visit of his patient. Zina opened the door. Tikhon could not see Dr. Belikov from the kitchen but heard the male voice in the corridor. He screamed loudly:

"Daddy! Daddy!"

Dr. Belikov rushed to the kitchen to show the boy that there was just a stranger, not the person who the baby called for with such an excitement. He came up to Tisha, stroked baby's blond curly hair, and a spasm in the throat did not allow doctor to talk for a minute. Then he whispered with sincere sadness in his voice,

"Tikhon, I also miss your father. Believe me, boy, all of us in the hospital are still in shock. Everything happened so … unexpectedly. Nobody could imagine that such a tragedy was possible with your Dad."

Maria looked at Belikov and concluded, "In general, Dr. Belikov is still a good man." It was hard for Maria to see how the vicious force has instantly succeeded in terrifying this man. She concluded for herself,

"It was his first face-to-face fight with the demons. The honorable man tried to follow the rules. On the contrary, the demon played without rules. Sidorenko was well-trained in unpredictable nudging of the honest people with his terrible accusations."

Maria could not forget Sidorenko's evil enjoyment, when Dr. Belikov lost the balance from an unexpected punch. She was sincerely sorry for their chief. Who won't be scared to death in his place? It is always a shock for an innocent person to be accused with serious crime he had never committed.

Zina invited Dr. Belikov for a cup of tea. He took Alexander's seat and Maria felt how all her nature was against it. She could hardly stop herself from saying,

"Oh, no ... It's my husband's. I do not want anybody to take his seat."

Maria found how to resolve her concern, asking: "Dr. Belikov, will you sit across the table in order I can see you better?"

"Certainly, Dr. Maria ..."

It appeared that Dr. Belikov understood the true reason of Maria's request, and he glanced at ill-fated woman with sympathy. He was sipping hot tea, attentively listening to Maria's health report. Then he opened his doctor's case, took out some medications and put them on the table in front of Maria. On the top of three boxes with pills Dr. Belikov put something else, wrapped in a sheet of school paper.

"Maria, I will not leave any written instructions, because you know well how to take these medications," Dr. Belikov said.

"Yes, I do. What is in there?" Maria asked, pointing to the wrapped package.

"The book-keeper prepared Dr. Kurbatov's and your salaries. We understand that you need it now."

Maria opened the pack and counted money. It was two times more than it was expected.

She mentioned it out loud. Dr. Belikov answered,

"Your husband had many hours of overtime. It's his bonus. Sorry, that he did not receive it by himself."

"Thank you, Dr. Belikov," Maria whispered.

The visitor got up and stopped in the doorway of the kitchen. Maria and Zina noticed that he wanted to tell Maria something else, something very important. Zina picked up Tisha and left for Sasha's room in order not to intervene in the conversation.

Dr. Belikov asked,

"Maria, wouldn't it be better for you and your boys to leave for another place?"

Maria was not sure that it was his personal question. The woman was suspicious regarding the topic. She thought,

"Where did this question come from? Who wants to know my plans regarding our escape?"

Maria answered with a chain of questions,

"Where can we go without assets? Who waits for us? Where can a single mother with two children find a new job and home to stay?"

One thing Maria did not mention for purpose – the documents. She believed, if *somebody,* like people from KGB, wanted to learn her opinion about leaving the village, then *that somebody* knew everything about the absence of Russian citizenship in the children's and her documents.

Dr. Belikov went on in a low voice,

"I've been to militia station this morning. The hospital personnel wanted to arrange some kind of farewell meeting at Alexander's grave. Do you know what Major Gromov suggested?"

Maria was silent, and Dr. Belikov continued,

"He advised us, not to organize anything. Magadan KGB is deeply involved in this case, and they would never allow it to happen. Gromov mentioned two more things: your son impressed them very much. They were astonished with his behavior in such an extraordinary situation. And another thing he mentioned... It was Gromov's advice, recommendation, suggestion... Whatever."

Maria noticed that Dr. Belikov was not sure, whether he needed to deliver Major Gromov's advice to Maria due to a new wave of fear that hit him. He thought, "If I do not reveal Gromov's advice, Maria will stay here. One day or night, the KGB people will come and destroy poor woman and kids. Gromov is sure that Magadan KGB has planned this operation. Gromov does not know the details, how and when the order will be fulfilled."

Maria watched Dr. Belikov's struggle between his fearful emotions and caring intentions. His frightened mind concluded that he told already too much,

"What can happen to me and my family, if she decides to tell them, that I am that person who has warned her about their plans?! I have my life, my family and my work. I should not take a risk, should I?"

Maria decided to help him, asking,

"What did Gromov want me to do?"

"Not to come back to the hospital for some time," answered Dr. Belikov.

Maria recorded, "He did not find strength to tell me the truth."

"Did he mean it, as a patient or as a physician?"

Dr. Belikov did not look at Maria when he answered her question,

"To my understanding, it's as a physician. It is better to wait, until the case of your husband is closed. Nobody can stop your visiting the hospital, as a patient."

Maria knew that Belikov lied. She decided to let him go, saying with a smile,

"Thank you, Dr. Belikov. Tell the hospital personnel that I am grateful for their sympathy. In one or two days, I'll go to Alexander. I'll tell him 'Farewell' from all of you."

Maria's words had scared Belikov to death,

"What is she talking about? What does she mean that she goes to Alexander in a day or two? Has Maria learned already that they plan to murder her? How can she talk so calm and easy about it?"

He glanced at her again and concluded,

"Then, it's up to her. I cannot share with her the information that I know. She is a strong decision maker. It's good that I did not *deliver* Gromov's warning to Maria."

Dr. Belikov moved to the door, saying,

"I wish you, Dr. Kurbatov, all the best. I hope everything will be all right with you and kids."

"God is merciful," Maria answered.

Belikov looked back and smiled. Maria did not want to see that scared man any longer.

"Thank you for medications and money, Dr. Belikov. It's an unexpected support. Sorry, I don't feel well and need to lie down."

Belikov opened the entrance door with the words,

"You are welcome, Dr. Kurbatov. Obviously, you need to gain strength after such a blow. I can understand it …"

Staying outside, Dr. Belikov looked around and rushed back in Maria's flat. He locked the door and whispered in her ear,

"Run away, Maria. Grab your kids and disappear today. Forgive me my cowardice. I've learned that I am a weak person. Please, forgive my weakness. I don't worry about myself. I have a family, and I do care about my family, as Alexander cared about his. I do not want anything unpredictable and inhuman happen to them."

He hugged Maria, as he could do it to his sister or mother, and whispered again in the ear,

"Maria, leave today, please. Do not wait till tomorrow. The militia received the order not to answer your phone calls today and tomorrow."

"Thank you. I'll do my best," Maria promised.

"Maria, let me talk to Sasha. Where is he?" Belikov asked.

"He is at school."

"What? Why did you send him there? Why did you separate him from you? They could kidnap the boy."

The phone rang and Maria startled from a sudden sound. She answered the phone,

"Hello. Dr. Kurbatov is here. Who is there, and how can I help you?"

There was no answer. Maria put down the phone, looked at Dr. Belikov and asked,

"Who could it be? They began calling us every hour since early morning."

Dr. Belikov answered quietly,

"Get ready, Maria. Pack and wait for me. I'll bring Sasha home." He rushed away.

Zina appeared in the hall with a backpack, stuffed with something. Maria recognized it: it was Alexander's bag, the one he took to Magadan. Zina washed it and attached two wide straps to the bag.

Maria understood,

"She "remodeled" it, as a backpack, in order to free my arms for carrying Tisha. Zina also wants me to leave."

Maria silently took the backpack and recorded in her mind, "It's too heavy. What has she packed there?"

The distressed woman went to her bedroom to dress for unexpected trip. She had to sit down. Her mind was "boiling". She could not stand that state of mind, where several thoughts appeared simultaneously, causing dizziness.

One serious question disturbed Maria mostly,

"My Lord, where can I find strength to run away with kids? How can we disappear without being watched?"

Every stressful situation immediately deteriorated Maria's condition, adding headache to her dizziness. The woman was realistic about the life-threatening situation.

"My Lord, You can see that I have no strength to carry Tisha from the kitchen to my bedroom. What should I do? Should I stay and wait until they murder my children and me? *Help us, save us, have mercy on us, and keep us, o God, by Thy grace.*"

Then several absolutely irrelevant thoughts appeared in her mind simultaneously:

"We have to leave the moment Sasha comes home. With God's blessing, we'll leave for Eultin… Children need to eat and drink at least two times per day… The money that Dr. Belikov brought is not enough to get to Moscow…"

Maria went to the kitchen, as if there she can find easier resolution of a dangerous situation. Her dream was to reach the French Embassy in Moscow and finish once and forever with their horrible life in this country. Maria's mind worked intensively, processing several thoughts at the same time: "I don't have a passport, and we don't have enough money to get to the Embassy... Still, I need to take a risk and buy the tickets to any town in central Russia, in order to hide for a while…"

Maria looked out of the window waiting for Sasha. The mind continued jamming one thought on the top of another: "We can take a night train and, with God's protection, nobody of the local people could see children and me, running away. Is it possible in reality? I doubt… It goes without saying that it's much better to take a train not at the local train stop but depart from the next one. The question is: how can we reach the next train stop? And again, my passport…"

Maria felt dizzy and her heart was pounding, causing pain in the middle of the chest. She tried to calm down, went back to her bedroom and meditated there to her Guardian Angel:

"Out of the love of my heart I cry to thee, O guardian of my soul, my all-holy Angel! Protect and guard me and my children from the hunting of the evil. Guide us to the heavenly life with Your teaching, enlightening and strengthening. Ask the Lord to have mercy on us. Amen."

Somebody knocked on the door. Maria heard Zina's voice in the corridor and rushed there. Dr. Belikov brought Sasha home. Doctor looked at Maria and concluded with satisfaction, "She is ready to go." He talked quickly, as he usually did when he gave the instructions to the personnel,

"Dress the kids and pack everything necessary for a trip. You have ten minutes to get ready, and I'll take you to your friends in Eultin. By 5:00 p.m., I must be back to the meeting at the hospital. You understand, Maria, nobody should find me absent for the whole day. The personnel and patients saw me at work in the morning, then I stopped there again fifteen minutes ago. I just *flew* through all the departments. At 5:00

p.m., I have scheduled a meeting with the heads of all the departments regarding a couple of vacancies, including your children's department.

Everyone should know that you are not working at the hospital any longer, and now, the hospital is in the process of hiring a new specialist. Maria, hurry up! Six minutes left. We'll wait for you in the ambulance in Market Street. I've shown Sasha the place of pick up. Maria, hurry up!"

Zina helped Maria to dress the kids and took Tisha outside "for a walk". It was nice that Zina had left with the baby alone without Maria. If even the KGB assigned anybody from the neighbors to watch Maria, nothing looked suspicious. The neighbors, who met Zina near the entrance door of the building, were not surprised to see her with the baby. They knew that the nanny with the boy were walking outside every time when the cold weather allowed. Zina talked to the neighbors for a minute, and slowly went on along the street. Sasha was the next. He took a sack with cloths and bread, went in the opposite direction, making a turn to the rare side of the building and got into the ambulance. Maria was the last one. Somebody called again. She did not want to pick up the phone, but at the same time, she found it smarter to answer and let them know that she was unwell and stayed at home. She picked up the phone and said with her weak voice,

"Hello. Maria Kurbatov is here. May I ask who is calling?"

Nobody wanted to talk to her. Maria requested,

"Will you, please stop calling. I do not feel well."

They did not put the phone down and Maria added,

"Thank you."

Maria switched on the light in the kitchen and Sasha's room, in order *they* could see that the family is at home. In a minute, she left. She saw an ambulance coming toward her. It stopped in some distance, and two people in white medical coats went to somebody's house. Maria was nervous,

"It's not the right one," she thought.

She slowly passed by the ambulance, answered "Good-afternoon" to a driver, and turned to the next street. Maria noticed that another ambulance was slowly moving in her direction. In some distance, Dr. Belikov stopped the ambulance, and Maria gathered all her strength, in order to reach it faster. Sasha and Zina helped her to get inside. The moment Maria got in, she fainted. They put her on a stretcher. Maria opened her eyes, saying,

"I am sorry. It was not easy to catch your *trolleybus*." All the passengers laughed. Zina praised the Lord, "Thank You God, for making Maria conscious quickly. You are so merciful. Glory to You."

Dr. Belikov drove fast. It was hard for him to observe two undefended kids and a woman that was falling apart. Both boys watched their mother and expressed their nervousness in different ways: Tisha was cranky, and Sasha sat near Maria on the stretcher, trying to keep her attention chained to something vitally important. He did not want her to collapse again and be in unsafe condition for days. The boy realized that they had limited time for escape.

Sasha talked to Maria,

"Mama, I feel sorry for you. You did not have time for recovery after the hospital. We must run away. Please, get well. We know that you are out of strength, but if we do not leave today, they'll find us at night or the latest-tomorrow... Tell me, Mama, where do you want us to go after Eultin?"

Maria whispered,

"I don't know, Sasha. I need to discuss it with Sofia and Dr. Leskov. It depends on their advice and … financial support."

"But still, where would *you* like us to go?"

Sasha inquired with emphasizing "you". The boy wanted to know his mother's choice. Sasha saw how difficult it was for Maria to focus on his questions. They rode in silence for some time until she answered,

"I wish I can take you home." Maria signed. "It's sad, Sasha, but there is no more home for us in the whole world."

Sasha did not understand Maria and asked,

"You mean that you want us to go to France, don't you?"

"No, Sasha. Probably, it sounds deviant, but I mean to take you to Ukraine. At this point, I cannot find any other place to go."

Lord, have mercy!

Chapter 10

Maria looked at Sasha and noticed that her boy was surprised with his mother's choice.

"I am not delirious, my son. I remember well that the horror started there, but I do not know any other place to go. I have no passport to get to the Embassy of France in Moscow. I do not know anybody in Russia, who can help us."

"Is there anybody in Ukraine who can help us?" Sasha asked.

"I hope that my sister and brothers had returned to Blue Creeks. Certainly, they did not reside in our mansion, but they could be in the area. I don't think that they were blamed and punished, as "*the enemies of the USSR and the communist government*". They were children when WWII began. They did not live in capitalist France or Nazi Germany before or during the war."

Maria sighed deeply.

"When we reach Ukraine, my siblings will be happy to give us a place to stay, at least for an initial couple of months. I have one more devoted person there-our nanny Ganja. She considerably helped your father and me in September of 1946. She took a risk, visiting us daily in hell. I doubt that we could survive without her prayers and physical assistance."

Sasha asked,

"What did Ganja do for you and Papa?"

"Ganja brought us daily food, delivered healing herbs for your father, brought a woman who fixed his fractured bones. She was our angel."

After Maria's explanation, why she would like to return to Creeks, Sasha still was astonished with his mother's wish. He remembered that there, in Creeks, his parents were arrested, callously tortured and his father became a mutilated and crippled person to the end of his life. The boy did not like to hear anything about Blue Creeks. Here and now his mother expressed her desire to return to that demonic place. It sounded more than strange.

"Mama, why do you want to return there? You lost everything in Creeks. All our post-war misfortune started from Creeks. You told me shocking stories that took place in your mansion in Creeks and finally, you decided to return there again. Why? You know better than anybody else that you have no home in Creeks. It was taken away from your family long time ago. As a result, your siblings did not have place to return. Think about it, Maman! I don't want us to escape this fire in order to be destroyed there. I need to protect you and Tisha from being wiped out."

The boy sounded, as a mature man. Maria calmed him down,

"All right, Sasha. It is and always will be my dream to return to Blue Creeks. However, we'll go to Sister Olga. Do you remember her?"

Alexander kissed Maria's hand and replied joyfully,

"Certainly, I remember her. It sounds much better, Mama. It's an absolutely different decision. Nobody knows us there. I believe that Sister Olga will be happy to see us at her place. Thank you, Mama."

Maria felt exhausted. She did not have strength to breathe and could not think clearly again. The disturbed woman kept silence to the end of the ride, and Sasha did not know, whether she dosed or was unconscious again.

At last, the ambulance made the final stop at the point of their destination. Sofia Leskov was outside, when Maria got out of the ambulance. Maria slowly went in the direction of the Leskov's house. Zina carried a sleepy baby-boy, and Sasha talked to Dr. Belikov on their way to the Leskov's place. Sofia rushed to meet the guests. Doctor Belikov introduced himself and after greeting, he asked Sofia,

"Where is your husband now?"

"He is still at work. Usually, he is at lazaret until 6 p.m. Do you want to see him? It's not far, only five minutes of walk from here."

Sofia looked at Maria and asked Dr. Belikov,

"What's wrong with Maria? She is not well, is she?"

Dr. Belikov led Sofia away from the visitors and explained the situation in the shortest way.

"She is very weak after the tragedy that happened. Dr. Kurbatov was brutally murdered a week ago. The KGB is involved in it. Now they went after Maria and children. Please, help them to hide for a day or two.

They must disappear from here, as soon as possible. Maria needs to decide where they can go."

Sofia was shocked with the news. The self-protection worked prier than all other senses.

"Why did you bring them here? How can we help them? Dr. Belikov, what shall we do, if the KGB finds them at our place? Take them somewhere else, please. We cannot hide them. Please, take them somewhere else."

Dr. Belikov did not like Sofia's reaction. He thought, "Poor woman, she is worse than me. The fear completely paralyzed all her other senses."

Then he said,

"There is not any other place for them to go. By the way, Maria and Alexander considered you and Dr. Leskov their true friends."

Dr. Belikov emphasized on the word *friends.* The responce of the frightened woman reminded him his initial reaction, and he tried to calm her with the words,

"They are here for one-two days, because they must leave in the nearest time."

"But still they cannot stay with us. Take them back or somewhere else..."

Sofia looked around and noticed three neighbors across the street, watching her and her visitors in a distance. Then she looked at Dr. Belikov again and noticed his disappointment. He felt sincerely sorry for Maria and kids.

Sofia came to human senses and apologized,

"I am sorry, Dr. Belikov. What am I talking about? We'll take care of them. Do you need to go back tonight?"

"Yes, I am in a hurry."

He motioned with his head in the direction of three visitors and added to Sofia,

"I also don't want anybody to see our hospital ambulance and me at your place. They can easily prove that it was me, who has helped the misfortunes to hideaway. It's a pity that I haven't met Dr. Leskov. My best regards to your husband. We'll be in touch."

He came up to fugitives and said,

"Maria, you considered these people your friends, you were right. They'll do everything they can and put you on a train tomorrow or the day after tomorrow. I must leave. My best wishes to you. Have a good trip. Good luck."

Belikov hugged both kids and Maria. Tisha opened his hands and complained to him,

"No Daddy."

Doctor jumped into the ambulance, waved with his hand and left. Maria did not have strength and sat down on the steps, covered with ice and snow. Mourning black shawl covered nearly all her face. She was crying quietly, and Sofia felt guilty for her first selfish desire to send back the despondent woman and her children.

Sofia had already recovered from the initial shock and invited the runaways into the house.

"Please, come in. Maria, accept my condolences. It is a shock for us. I feel sorry for Dr. Alexander. I feel sorry for all of you."

Maria did not answer out loud, just nodded. Sasha helped his mother to stand up and enter the house.

"You must be hungry," Sofia said. "I'll feed you with whatever we have."

Sofia rushed to close the curtains on the window, in order nobody could see her guests. Then she covered the table with clean tablecloth, put a basket with homemade cookies near the big hot samovar and went to the kitchen to cook something for supper. The unexpected visitors sat quietly around the table and drank hot tea with cookies. Somebody opened the front door. Maria stood up with her eyes widely opened.

Sofia calmed her down,

"Don't worry, Maria. It's our doctor came home."

Sofia was right. When Dr. Leskov opened the door to the room, he was surprised to see the visitors at their place, and Maria's mourning black shawl stopped him in the doorway. He asked several questions at once,

"What's wrong, Maria? What happened? Where is Alexander?"

Maria did not answer a single question. She looked at him with her puffy eyes, filled with tears. The hot flow of tears poured on her cheeks, shawl and hands. The choking spasm in the throat did not allow Maria to pronounce a word. She was unable to explain the reason of Alexander's absence. Zina described with the least of details the tragedy that occurred with Dr. Alexander a week ago and the horrible plans of the Magadan KGB, regarding the other members of Dr. Alexander's family.

Zina concluded with a trembling voice,

"They need to runaway, as soon as possible. Dr. Belikov delivered them here and, in the nearest time, Maria and kids must leave for some other place, in order to hide from the followers."

Dr. Leskov brought one more chair to the table and sat down between Maria and Sasha. He embraced their shoulders and promised,

"We'll help you, Maria. I'll purchase the tickets on a train to Moscow, and in a day, you'll be far away from Magadan."

Lord, have mercy!

Chapter 11

Dr. Leskov attentively observed Maria and noticed that she was very pale and could hardly comprehend his words.

"Maria, you do not feel well enough to travel, do you? What's wrong with you, dear?"

Sasha answered the question on his mother's behalf,

"Doctor, our mother is sick. I doubt, that she is able to take a journey anywhere in the nearest time."

"Do not forget, Sasha, your mother is a special woman who has a very strong personality. In a way, she was stronger than your father and me. I believe, she'll be all right on a train."

Zina stepped out of the room and called Dr. Leskov outside for a conversation. The woman avoided disturbing Maria and children with additional hurdles. Standing on the porch, Zina inquired,

"Doctor, what do you think about Maria's hideaway? When can Maria and kids go? Tell me, is there any chance for them to fade away from KGB followers?"

"I think there is the chance for them to get to the Ukraine," Dr. Leskov replied.

Zina asked, "Why the Ukraine?"

"First of all, it's pretty far from Magadan. The second, Maria needs somebody she trusts to stay with, at least, for a short while," Dr. Leskov patiently explained it to Zina and continued,

"Then, she'll do her best in order to contact the Embassy of France in Moscow. But she must disappear from here, as soon as possible, until they find her and arrest. Eultin is too tiny to be hidden in and very close to Magadan."

"I agree that it is dangerous to stay here. But, doctor, Maria does not feel strong for such a long journey. Ukraine is far away..."

"If we put Maria and kids on a train, she should not do a lot there. Maria's journey to the Ukraine will take longer than 2 weeks. During this term, she'll pull herself together emotionally and physically."

"What do you think, doctor, when does Maria need to leave?"

"Not later than tomorrow morning. The train Magadan-Moscow leaves at 11:20 a.m. We'll be there much earlier, and I'll go and buy tickets."

"Do they ask for a passport?" Zina asked with fear.

"Yes, usually, they do, but not always."

"When you go to buy the tickets, we'll pray with Maria an Agreement prayer, and I hope, they will not ask for Maria's passport," Zina promised.

Dr. Leskov smiled. He had wonderful experience with that prayer. Sofia and he prayed it and their daughters were found.

"You'll wait for me in the square or even inside of the railway station. The only thing is important-we should not stay all together. At the railway station, you will take a seat with Tisha in some distance from Maria. Sasha will go with me. Maria will stay with Sofia."

Zina explained the financial side of the plan,

"Maria has some money, but it is not enough to get to Moscow or the Ukraine. She left their furniture, personal things and kitchen goods. If it is possible, borrow her some money. I'll sell everything that is good for sale and cover Maria's debt. Whatever I gain is yours, Dr. Leskov."

"It's all right, Zina. Tomorrow, we must put Maria on a train. The KGB is looking for them. Fast runaway will give Maria and her kids a chance to survive. There is no way for postponing their departure. One extra day could be fatal."

Zina liked doctor's plan for the next day. His clear vision of the situation slightly quieted down her fear.

"Thank you, Dr. Leskov. I knew that you'll find the right way out," Zina said.

When they returned to the house, Dr. Leskov invited Maria to another room for examination. The blood pressure was severely low, and the heartbeat was weak and arhythmical. Dr. Leskov knew better that anybody else that Maria was not ready for a long journey. However, threats did not leave her any opportunity to have some rest and rejuvenate after tragic event.

During the evening, Sofia tried to feed Maria and insisted in drinking several cups of tea with honey cookies. The women and children went to sleep earlier, and Dr. Leskov ran to his assistant to discuss the work schedule for the next day. He wanted to do it without explaining a lot of details and before the assistant went to sleep. The doctor would not get to work earlier than around 2 p.m.

"What happened, doctor?" His assistant was surprised to see Dr. Leskov again.

"I need to take Sofia to Magadan to the dentist. Can you substitute me during tomorrow morning?"

"Sure, I can. Don't worry, doctor. I'll be at the lazaret at seven in the morning. Everything will be all right. I wish Sofia good luck."

When Dr. Leskov returned home, everyone was asleep. He lay down on the sofa and closed his eyes. He could not doze after the shocking news. Dr. Leskov considered Alexander Kurbatov the person of honor, knowledge and respect. Besides, they were best friends. He witnessed how difficult Alexander survived ten years of his imprisonment. Doctor was amazed observing what a high-skilled surgeon Alexander was, even with the complicated fracture of the right wrist.

He recollected how Alexander mentioned the last time when the Leskovs visited them, "If not Marie and my son, I would never survive torchers, more than ten years of imprisonment, and life in this uncivilized wilderness. I am ready to die for them and their happiness."

Dr. Leskov sighed deeply. He recalled different episodes from the Kurbatovs' family life and thought,

"Alexander kept his word: he paid with his life for the happiness of his wife and sons. I cannot imagine Maria's life without him. It was amazing relationship from the beginning to the very last day. I did not see another relationship like theirs."

Dr. Leskov's memories brought new episodes from Alexander's and Maria's life. He concluded, "To my mind, their family dynamics was not earthly."

One day, when they were on their visit to the Kurbatovs, Alexander described their relationship, as *spiritually enlightened romance*.

Dr. Leskov remembered, how desirous he felt, when he saw such love. Their relationship was not based on passion only. It combined many components, and Dr. Leskov didn't know what was stronger in their relationship – mutual understanding, friendship, love, respect or passion. Maria and Alexander were blessed from Above with building a solid union, which at the same time, was gentle, flexible, patient and beautiful.

Strong memories overwhelmed Dr. Leskov, and he sat down on the sofa. He recollected how Maria said one day, "Every marriage is blessed from Above, and our marriage is a true creation of God. Otherwise, Alexander would never find me in Germany in the fire of the dreadful war. Literarily speaking, he found me "in the fire of war".

Dr. Leskov realized that with killing of Alexander, monsters destroyed one of the most stunning God's creations.

His thoughts were interrupted by loud knocking on the door. Dr. Leskov jumped up and looked at the clock. It was half past three. They knocked impatiently again. The doctor came to the door and asked,

"Who is there?"

He wanted to believe that it was an emergency, and somebody needed doctor's help. The answer was different,

"KGB. Open the door."

Dr. Leskov understood: the search was very intensive, and they found Maria and children faster than he expected. His first intent was not to open the door. Then he realized the ridiculousness of his intent. He made a step forward, unlocked the entrance door and stepped aside. He turned around and saw Maria standing in the doorway of the room.

She pronounced in a low voice,

"Let them in, doctor. I don't want them to wake up my children."

He opened the door widely, and three KGB officers rushed into the house, leaving two soldiers on the porch. Maria went into the kitchen, and the officers followed her. One of them introduced Maria with a demonic sarcasm in his voice,

"Comrades, let me introduce Madam Kurbatov. She preferred to be called this way. Do not forget it. The last wish should be satisfied."

"Last wish…" Maria registered it in her mind.

She was surprised sensing no fear at all. She sat down on the sofa and watched their preparation. One of the lieutenants took a seat at the table and opened the portfolio with protocol papers. Another young officer sat down across the kitchen table, pulled a sheet of paper from his portfolio and wrote the date on it.

Captain Sidorenko was the senior officer of the group, and Maria saw that he was the one, who demonstrated to the younger officers, how to conduct the interrogation of an enemy.

"Let's begin. Madam Kurbatov, what do you do here?"

Doctor Leskov was the first, who answered,

"She came here due to her health reason. I used to be Maria's doctor at the camp and knew how to deal with her health condition."

Captain Sidorenko pretended that doctor's intrusion with an explanation made him furious. He jumped up and shouted into the doctor's face,

"Did I ask you to answer? Did I *invite* you here? Get out of here!"

The theatrically loud shouting of the demon awoke and frightened Tisha, and the baby burst into crying. Dr. Leskov went into the bedroom to calm him down.

Maria asked in a very calm voice,

"Captain Sidorenko, will you, please ask all your questions in a civilized, urbane manner without theatrical jumping and disturbances of the house residents? As for me, I got used to your voice during this week and can hear you perfectly well."

Maria noticed how both Captain's assistants smiled to her request. It was good that Sidorenko did not notice their reactions. He jumped up to Maria and hissed in her face,

"I do not talk to enemies in an urbane manner. Can you hear me, Madam?"

Maria did not answer. Everyone in the room noticed that he had lost the heat of questioning from the very beginning.

Captain Sidorenko looked out of the window, as if he could see something or somebody in the darkness, then asked in lower voice,

“Why did you come here? I need the truth. What did you plan to do?”

“I was looking for a medical assistance. I cannot gain strength after my husband’s murder.”

“Madam Kurbatov, you were hospitalized into your local hospital. Why did you decide to leave it, if you did not feel well?”

“Dr. Belikov concluded that they were unable to help me. They wanted to transfer me to Magadan central hospital.”

“Does this doctor know better how to help you?”

“He helped me several times in labor camp, and I hope that he’ll succeed with this episode, as well.”

“What are you going to do, if he cannot help you?”

“I don’t know,” Maria answered.

“Who knows, Madam Kurbatov?”

“Only God knows, Captain Sidorenko. Everything is in His hands, and I pray for His mercy. Regarding Dr. Leskov, I believe in his knowledge and experience… With Lord’s blessing, everything will work right.”

Sidorenko shook his head, “Not this time, Madam. Not this time.”

He laughed loudly and suggested,

"You'd better pray for my or our mercy, Madam Kurbatov. These officers know my mercy…"

Sidorenko saw that Maria got tired and could hardly breathe. He pondered about taking Maria to Magadan KGB "for real work". However, there was something that stopped him,

"If I take this bitch with us, how can it affect the whole situation? If she dies in the car, then everyone confirms that it was me, who has arrested an *innocent widow* in a 'distressed' health condition. I wish her to die, but I don't want to be accused in her … death."

Sidorenko paced the kitchen several times, brooding over the idea of arresting *Madam* and bringing her to the committee's basement.

"Everything has been changed since her husband was murdered. In the committee, some people suspect me in his termination, knowing that I've been the only one who saw him and listened to his stupid and obnoxious request regarding their repatriation to France. It's good that I did not leave the office on that day."

Sidorenko looked out of the window again. It seemed to him that he saw a shadow there, a limping shadow of Madam's husband. He sensed how goose bumps covered him from head to toes. He tried to continue the interrogation, but different notions, sounds and strange visions behind the window did not allow Sidorenko to focus on the subject.

"What a nonsense! There is nobody there. I thought that it would be better, if Kurbatov disappeared once and forever: *no person, no case*. But Major Gromov discussed it with our chief Zotov. What did they agree on? They concluded that the "angelic" couple was initially accused *by mistake* in 1946 and *punished for nothing* with ten and a half years of imprisonment. What was the worst for me in their mutual agreement-they decided to find the killer."

Captain Sidorenko paced the kitchen again, looking at Maria with hatred and thinking, "I definitely need to introduce Madam to Sergeant Frolov. He professionally chopped off her husband's head, and he can easily dispatch this bitchy Madam."

Maria noticed how his hatred brewed up and made his thinking unclear. He stopped in front of her and said,

"You go with us. Get ready. We'll escort you to Magadan."

Maria noticed that Sidorenko's assistants were surprised with his decision. She understood that her arrest was not in the assignment of their visit. Maria asked,

"Why should I go with you? I wish you show me the order for arrest."

Sidorenko did not know what to answer. Her calm manner made him mad. He hated that *madam*. He felt how the black wave of outrage covered him, and he lost his temper. He was eager to smack her with all his strength that she stopped breathing forever. Then he would like to get into the bedroom and strangle both boys of this obnoxious madam. Instead, he screamed with all his strength,

"Get up, bitch! You go with us. If I order you to go, you go! I'll show you the order for arrest! Wait until we get to Magadan. I'll teach you a lesson there! It will be the last one that you learn."

He looked at his assistants and ordered them,

"Take her to the car before I kill her here."

Both officers stood still and did not make a motion. Sidorenko pulled Maria from the sofa and pushed her to the door. Maria reeled, losing the balance. Sasha rushed out to help her,

"Mama, I'll go with you."

"No, Sasha. Stay here. God forbid you to go there, my boy."

Sasha looked at Sidorenko and said with his father's firmness in his voice,

"I will go with my mother. You had enough having my father alone."

"What? Go away, son of a bitch!"

He blew Sasha in the face with all the demonic strength, the blood poured over the boy's face and on the wall. Sasha fell on the floor, as a young tree that was easily chopped down. Maria screamed,

"Sasha!"

She kneeled beside her son's body, but furious demon did not allow Maria to touch her son. He pulled her outside with all his evil strength and packed her on the rear seat of the car. Then he jumped on the front passenger seat and ordered, "Go!" The rest of the KGB people rushed to another vehicle and followed the first one.

Zina and Sofia ran out of the house, but nobody could stop the demonic tyranny. They helplessly watched the car that was taking Maria away. The women returned into the house. The doctor was working with Sasha's dead faint. Tisha was sitting on the floor near his brother, loudly crying and calling for his mother.

"O my God! What did they do? What that beast did to a boy?" Zina lamented, as they entered the house. She kneeled near the kid and called him,

"Sasha! Sasha, wake up! Open your eyes, my boy!"

The boy parted his lips and the blood leaked out from his mouth. Then he pronounced soundless,

"Mama, where are you?" He fainted again.

"Doctor, I can help you to remove the boy from the floor to the sofa," Zina suggested,

Sofia covered the pillow with towels, and three of they brought Sasha there. Sasha opened his eyes. He looked around and whispered,

"Where is Mama?"

Zina told him the truth,

"They took her with them."

The tears rolled down from Sasha's eyes. Tisha climbed up near the sofa and looked at Sasha, hardly recognizing his brother's face. Dr. Leskov asked Zina to take the baby away and sent Sofia to bring warm water and towels. Zina picked up Tikhon and left, while Sofia fulfilled the job of the doctor's assistant.

Dr. Leskov cleaned Sasha's face from blood and asked him to stay still, avoiding any motion of the head. He had a suspicion that besides the nose fracture, there was severe concussion. In two hours, there was no doubt that extremely strong double blow caused the concussion with all the symptoms. One contusion was from Sidorenko's feast in the face and the second-from the wall that Sasha hit with the back of his head.

The boy experienced excruciating headache. He felt nauseated and dizzy all the time. The boy complained that the sofa was 'floating' under him.

By the night, the fever rose up, and persistent pressure headache increased. The icy water compresses did not lower the temperature but helped a bit with the headache. The night was extremely difficult: Zina, Sofia and doctor Leskov were near Sasha. Every 20 minutes they replaced the towel on his forehead and nose. Twice during the night, the boy lost consciousness, talked deliriously, called for his mother and father.

In the morning of the next day, Dr. Leskov examined Sasha and found the condition of the child very perilous. Sasha's forehead became purple and both eyes looked swelled and bloody. The swelling of the face did not allow the doctor to define the severity of the nose fracture that could be the main cause of constant nose bleeding. He gave all the instructions for both women and left for lazaret. Sasha fell asleep.

Lord, have mercy!

Chapter 12

Maria sat quiet on the rear seat of the KGB vehicle. The driver watched her in the mirror, as she whispered her prayers. Sidorenko felt tired and dozed on the front passenger seat. They were in twenty minutes of drive to Magadan office, when Sidorenko woke up and looked back at Maria, asking,

"What are you doing there, madam Kurbatov?"

The driver answered,

"She was praying all the time. I cannot understand, how they can learn all those stupid and endless prayers. Is she a nun?"

"I wish we can stop and check her on this subject, but I have to be in the office by seven thirty in the morning."

Sidorenko looked at the watch and realized that fifteen minutes left to the beginning of the meeting. He commanded to the driver,

"Don't sleep! Move faster! I cannot be late. I must transfer Madam Kurbatov to Sergeant Frolov. He'll check her in to our basement *hotel*. Nobody should see this bitch."

Both men neighed. Maria shivered, "So many years passed since 1946, but I still remember this neighing. Even their neighing proves that they are not humans."

Sidorenko turned to Maria and said,

"I hope you understand clearly that for you, madam, there is no way back. This is your end, bitch, and don't even try to find the way out."

Maria asked,

"What do you mean?"

Sidorenko neighed and answered, pronouncing every word with sarcastic enjoyment,

"The possibility for surviving does not exist for you any longer, as it was not possible for your f… noble husband. He worried a lot about his family and his mother in France. We helped him with all his concerns. We can help everyone to forget all qualms and worries. Tomorrow or probably even tonight, we'll help you with your trepidation for your life and lives of your f… kids. From this moment, you should not be focused, madam, at the earthy things. You are unable to change them. Do not waste your strength. Wait for me and I'll be there. I'll be the last man in your life."

They neighed again. Maria listened to Sidorenko and realized that nothing could stop that demon from brutality. He looked vicious and even sounded in the same way, as the Major of NKVD/KGB in her estate house in Blue Creeks. The Creator burned that demon, but a younger version was seeded and grew in another part of the country to murder her husband and torture her to death.

She continued praying,

"O my Lord! Defend my children from the wickedness of demons! Holy Mother of God, please watch over my sons and protect them from harm! Holy

Spirit, I leave my children under Your Holy protection. Help them, save them, have mercy on them and keep them, o Lord, by Thy grace. I do not ask mercy on me, a sinner, who exposed my family to danger with home-coming. I am ready to follow my husband. Amen."

Two cars stopped at the gate of KGB regional office. Sidorenko looked back and muttered. He said to the driver, without paying attention at Maria,

"If we arrived five minutes earlier, nobody could see this bitch. We could easily hide her in the basement cell and do with her whatever we want. The officers come to the meeting, but they should not see her in the car. Stop near the front entrance and I'll jump out there. You'll take her to the rare entrance. Wait for Frolov to take her in."

The guard at the gate checked the documents and opened the gate. Both cars entered the territory of Magadan KGB.

When they parked near the front entrance to the building, Sidorenko ordered,

"Sit quiet, madam, if you want to live for another hour."

Then he instructed the driver again,

"Watch her until I send Frolov to take *Madam* to her cell."

At that very moment, the car of the head of Magadan KGB stopped from the left side of Maria's vehicle. The head of the local committee opened his front passenger door, when his driver ran to open the rare door for another Colonel, the inspector from Moscow.

Sidorenko jumped out of the car, stood straight and saluted the senior officers. At that very moment, the invisible force pushed Maria out. She saw Sidorenko startled, seeing her out of the car. Maria asked both Colonels,

"I am Dr. Maria Kurbatov. Please, protect my children and me from this man. I beg you, officers, do not allow this person to murder my kids, as he murdered my husband last week. He wanted to *introduce* me to Sergeant Frolov, who, as Captain Sidorenko described, brutally *chopped off* the head of my husband. In Sidorenko's plans is to dishonor and torture me tonight in the cell of the basement before they murder me. You have your own wives, sisters and children. For the sake of your beloved, please help me."

Sidorenko wanted to say something, but the angry look of Colonel Zotov did not leave him a chance for explanation. Maria acknowledged that it was definitely not the head of the committee who ordered Sidorenko to search for her, arrest and bring here. Zotov was not aware of Sidorenko's plan to torture her to death. It was Sidorenko's sick demonic desire that initiated this lawbreaking. Another Colonel came up and asked,

"What is your name?"

"Dr. Kurbatov, a widow of Alexander Kurbatov, a citizen of France."

The inspector from Moscow found out her answer so surprising and undeniable, that he expressed his wish to talk to Maria and personally learn her case. The head of the local KGB was mad with Sidorenko's offensive actions.

The inspector assumed,

"The woman appeared out of the blue, and she could be one more proof to the numerous signals that confirmed the impenetrable activity of the Magadan committee."

The head of the local committee Colonel Zotov tried to save the situation. He came up to the inspector and whispered,

"Can't you see that she is a kind of insane?"

The inspector did not notice any insanity in the request of a woman. He did not like that the local committee tried to hide something even in his presence. He thought, "That's why I was sent here. They practice the illegal things."

The inspector answered,

"As for me, I did not notice any insanity in the words of this woman. I want to check everything by myself. Please, invite Dr. Kurbatov to the office and bring her husband's and her files."

The head of the local committee made one more attempt to save the reputation of the regional office,

"Comrade Colonel, maybe we can postpone the investigation of her case for later. She can wait. I know that the officers are already gathered in the conference room, waiting for us to start our meeting. They need to return to their work today."

The inspector glanced at him and did not reply to his request. Then he looked at Maria. Her eyes were filled with tears. She realized that that was her last chance and promised,

"It would not take long, citizen Colonel. I know that a week ago, Captain Sidorenko murdered my husband or ordered Sergeant Frolov to murder him. This night, he arrived with several officers and attempted to kill my twelve-year-old son. I don't know, if my child survives the blow and severe bleeding. The coming night, Sidorenko plans together with Sergeant Frolov to dishonor and kill me. I beg you to protect us. Why does he follow us?"

Maria felt dizzy. She knew that any sign of physical weakness could be considered as her insanity. She caught her breath and continued,

"Captain Sidorenko arrived at the hospital, where my husband and I worked since the time of our discharge from the camps. He scared the chief-physician to the point that he immediately fired me and discharged, as a patient."

Maria's Angel gave her the right tactic to follow. If she blamed the KGB in general, they will be on Sidorenko's side. If she made him and only him guilty, she had a chance. The inspector took Maria inside, and she overheard how the head of Magadan KGB hissed to Sidorenko,

"Who ordered you to bring her here?"

The inspector from Moscow got in a very unclear situation. He decided to check up the facts before his meeting with the KGB officers. Maria was surprised with a strong desire of the inspector from Moscow to listen to the whole story. She introduced him to her tragic events of home-coming in 1946, her and Alexander's imprisonment and incomplete release. She blamed only several people, and the inspector was on her side.

The meeting was re-scheduled for 10 a.m. The Colonel from Moscow needed time to make the right conclusions regarding the Kurbatovs' case. Maria observed, how he demonstrated for the local committee the fast way of taking actions. For complete liberation and permission to leave the Magadan region, they took Maria's signatures on the document with *four* NOs and *four* YESs:

- not to release any information about the Kurbatovs' case to the media or any foreign embassy,
- not to try contacting the Embassy of France with the request about the repatriation to France,
- not to restore the title of nobility and true personal data,
- not to reside in big cities with the population over a million inhabitants.

They insisted in changing:

- the last name Kurbatov for Gnatiuk, that was taken from nowhere,
- all three dates of birth for Maria and children,

- first name Tikhon for Ivan,
- for initial five years, they allow to reside only in villages or small towns of Russia or Ukraine that are far away from highly populated political or industrial centers.

Maria was not given a chance for disputing or disagreeing. Misfortunate woman concluded that life and security of her children might cost all those concessions. She also realized that with signing of all their requirements, she received their permission to leave the Magadan zone legally and forever.

The inspector ordered the secretary to issue on that very day Maria's passport, birth certificates for children, and Alexander's death certificate. He gave two hours to prepare all the documents and left for meeting. Maria was invited to stay in the waiting room of Colonel Zotov and could hardly believe that a new God's miracle happened. She praised the Lord while they worked on her new documents.

In two hours, the secretary brought in brand new documents. She also handed Sasha's school documents with his new last name and the extracts from the medical charts of both boys.

Maria registered in her mind, "What a system! They keep everything under their control. O Lord! My Alexander paid with his life for our liberation."

Maria checked all the data in the new documents. She looked at the picture on her passport and thought,

"I will be forty in July, but I look like I am sixty."

Maria shook her head and concluded,

"That's all right, Maria."

The meeting was over. The group of officers was out of the conference room. The inspector came up to Maria,

"Did you receive everything you need for moving from Magadan?"

"Yes, I did. I appreciate everything you've done for me and my sons. I will pray for you."

The Colonel smiled,

"Dr. Kurbatov, you have to understand, that every system makes mistakes. Do you need anything else? Where did they bring you from?"

"From Eultin. I am sorry, but I don't have money to get back to Eultin."

"They will take you back."

"Thank you."

Maria wrapped all the documents in a newspaper. The local Colonel ordered to take her back to Eultin. Maria thought,

"My Lord! I wish they do not assign the same driver."

The recollection about her trip with Sidorenko and his driver was petrifying. Maria walked along the endless corridor and thought about choices in human life, "Both men have chosen to serve Satan. Satan gave them demonic power. Nevertheless, that there were so many different human choices in their lives, they preferred horrifying darkness…"

The guard opened the heavy door and Maria stepped outside. "Am I free?" She could hardly believe in everything that happened to her. She felt like the Savior relocated her in another world that positioned in safe distance from her dangerous reality. The same vehicle that brought her here in the morning was parked near the entrance of the Magadan committee. The driver was a young soldier, and he stood near the rare passenger door. He noticed Maria approaching the car and opened the door. His speedy motion frightened the woman. The thoughts like lightening emerged in Maria's mind,

"It's a trap. Where do they want to take me? I have a suspicion that they have ordered him to transport me to another KGB place, where there is no inspector from Moscow. Quite possible! That's why the driver is in a hurry to let me in. *Lord have mercy.*"

Maria slowed down her pace and looked back at the building with metal rods on every window. She noticed how a tall silhouette retreated from one of the windows and assumed,

"Sidorenko watches me. I can imagine what a pleasure he failed to take, strangling me with his own hands. It was his sick dream to finish once and forever with the Kurbatovs. It is a miracle that they let me go."

Maria stopped for a second and concluded,

"There are no winners in the situation, because the Kurbatovs do not exist any longer in this world. As long, as I accepted and signed the resignation document in exchange for three lives, they will leave my children and me alive."

Maria was near the car when she questioned herself,

"Was there another choice for my children and me? Not at all. I had to be submissive with enemies due to absence of other choices. Everything is about human preferences. Alexander preferred resistance and death. He was a strong man and did not allow to surmount him. I am a mother. My sons' lives are the most important for me."

Maria experienced dizziness again. The night and day were extremely stressful. She got into the car and closed her eyes, trying to stay focused and not to fall in a faint. It was not easy. She was blessed with strength and clear thinking at the committee. After everything Maria went through in their office, she lost her strength. She started her meditation, knowing how well it usually worked,

"*Dear Lord, support me, please. Travel together with me. O Master, deliver me from all agitation and slander raised against me. According to Your will, return me home in peace and strength. Amen.*"

At the gate, the driver handed two papers to the guard. After careful check of the documents, the gates were opened, and they drove out to the road. Maria continued her praying,

"O Lord, Heavenly Father, in Whom we all have our beginning and end: we come to You with humble hearts and contrite spirits, entreating mercy, salvation and help in our time of need. By Your infinite power move to compassion and mercy the hearts of those who hold in cruel captivity me and other innocent people.

Restrain the captors from bringing harm to us. Cause them to relent and to release us. Restore us, the captives, to our families and friends, whole and unharmed, that together with them we'll lift our voices in prayers of thanksgiving and praise to You, O Heavenly Father, our merciful Benefactor..."

The young driver interrupted Maria's quiet prayer with naming the destination point,

"I was ordered to take you to village Eultin. We'll be there in forty minutes."

Maria's tension was released, and she added,

"With God's blessing..."

She finished the meditation and dozed. Maria was again in her picturesque dream: endless field, high grass of emerald color, a single birch tree and the clear blue sky. She was wandering there looking for the path out. The flashes of the bright light in Maria's dream awoke her, but every time, the pleasant waves of warmth penetrated her body and put her back to sleep.

In her dream, Maria waited for the voice of an Angel, who used to help her with his advice; however, that time she could not hear him. What was new in the dream: her boys were lost together with her. They annoyed, asking for food all the time. There was a moment when she blamed her sons for making her unable to pick up the voice of the Angel. Maria did not remember the end of her dream. Hunger was the only thing she distinctly registered in mind.

The car stopped and Maria awoke immediately. The driver opened her door. Maria praised, "Thank You, Lord for returning me alive to my children."

Lord, Have Mercy!

Chapter 13

Zina and Sofia heard the sound of a car that stopped near the gate of the house. Zina looked out of the window and exclaimed,

"Maria is back!"

Both women rushed to Maria. They noticed a thick newspaper in Maria's hands that she held tightly to her chest. They did not know that it was the newspaper in which Maria wrapped all the new family documents.

Sofia asked,

"How are you, Maria? What did they do to you?"

"Thank God, I am back. They did a lot," Maria answered. She looked at the stunned women and smiled.

"How is Sasha?" Maria asked.

None of them answered her question. Both women were rendered speechless with Maria's unexpected return and could not hide their astonishment. Maria thanked the driver for the fast ride and entered the house.

She rushed to her son. Sasha was asleep. Maria looked at his face, and the terrible picture reminded her the face of Alexander after the torments in Blue Creeks. Maria kneeled near the sofa, touched Sasha's hand and burst into tears. Sasha made an attempt to open his eyes, but severe swelling prevented it. Then he asked anxiously,

"Mama, are you here? Are you released? They let you go, didn't they? Are they also here?"

The severe headache interrupted the boy.

"I am here, Sasha. They released me. They brought me back."

Maria kissed her son's hand and listened to his complains.

"I have a terrible headache, Mama. Dr. Leskov wanted me to stay in bed for two-three days. He thinks that I have concussion."

Maria pulled herself together and said,

"Calm down, Sasha. I am with you, my boy. Nobody will hurt us anymore. I want you to gain some strength, and we'll leave. They permitted us to leave the Magadan zone."

Somebody knocked on the door. Zina opened it. It was the young driver who brought Maria in Eultin. He held an envelope in his hand. Zina was ready to take it, however the soldier asked,

"This is for citizen Gnatiuk. May I hand it to her personally?"

"Who is it for?" Zina asked.

"Maria Gnatiuk. It's the Death certificate of her husband Alexander Gnatiuk," the driver explained. "She left it on the car seat,"

The soldier pointed at Maria. The young man stepped in and handed Maria the envelope. Maria said,

"Thank you."

Zina and Sofia inspected Maria with the suspicious looks.

"I'll give you the explanation a little bit later," Maria said.

She turned to Sasha again and noticed that her boy fell asleep, holding her by the hand. Maria gently released the hand and turned back to both women.

"Where is Tisha?" She asked.

"He has a nap in the bedroom," Zina answered.

Maria asked again,

"What did doctor say about Sasha's condition?"

Sofia answered,

"It's concussion. The night was difficult. The boy needs some time for healing. Oh, Maria, you must be hungry."

She left to prepare Maria's meal. Zina sat down near Maria, embraced her and asked,

"How are you, Maria? How was it possible for you to escape Dr. Alexander's destiny?"

Maria looked at Zina and asked,

"Did you pray for me when the monster Sidorenko took me away?"

Zina exclaimed,

"All morning we prayed for you and Sasha. Nobody could sleep after they arrested you. Sasha was in poor condition. Dr. Leskov is sure that the monster broke Sasha's nose. But how was everything with you?"

Maria smiled,

"Zina, the Lord is so merciful. He heard our prayers and responded immediately. It is difficult to comprehend, what has happened there this morning. When I tell you what had happened, you can hardly believe me. Thank God, I have numerous proves of God's miracle in multiple documents. I'll show you now."

Sofia brought Maria's plate with her food. Both women took the seats across the table and poured tea from the samovar. They could not wait to hear Maria's story. Maria was hungry and ate with good appetite for the first time during the last week. Her exhausted body required nourishment and rejuvenation.

Somebody opened the storm door. The women were afraid of any visitors. It was Dr. Leskov. He entered the room and smiled.

"Maria, it's wonderful that you are back! How did the monsters let you go? By the way, how could you get back so fast? Did you fly, as an angel?"

Maria nodded. Doctor came up to Sasha and checked his temperature.

"The boy still has high fever. However, his heartbeat is slower now. He sleeps quietly. You know, Maria that sleep is the best medicine for him."

Sofia put a cup of tea in front of her husband.

"Is this all?" Dr. Leskov asked. Zina brought some slices of bread and a bowl of bean soup. Dr. Leskov smiled and repeated his question, "Is this all?"

Sofia went to the cupboard and brought two small jars with apple preserves and honey. She put apple preserves on doctor's side of the table and honey on the opposite side.

Doctor made a joke:

"Thank you, darling. You are so kind. Something has to make our life sweet. Let it be apple preserves, if not the honey."

Zina apologized: "The honey is only for Sasha and Maria. It will speed up their healing."

Dr. Leskov asked, "Well, Maria, tell us what happened in Magadan?"

Sofia interrupted her husband:

"Please wait. Let Maria finish with her meal. She is hungry. She did not eat for a week."

Maria said,

"I am done. Still, I do not know what to start with."

Doctor Leskov suggested with a smile,

"Start from the very beginning, Maria. Start from the moment the demon pulled you to the car."

Sasha moved on the sofa. Maria rushed to him.

"Mama, give me something to drink, please."

Maria made him some tea with a teaspoon of honey, while the doctor checked his temperature. Maria watched the doctor. He brought some medications and gave two of them to Sasha. Then he made an injection. Maria read the name of the medication and asked quietly,

"Is he so bad, doctor, or you decided to prevent the development of inflammatory reaction in the brain?"

Doctor Leskov explained,

"Maria, it is better to prevent. With these medications, we can easier keep the inflammation under control, avoiding the complications."

He looked at Maria and asked theatrically,

"Do you agree with my strategy, Dr. Kurbatov?"

"Absolutely. I always agree with everything you do, doctor. How could it be different? I remember very well, how you saved me several times in the camp. By the way, Alexander had always considered you, as a very knowledgeable physician. He trusted you and that's why Alexander invited you last year to work together with him in the Emergency and Intensive Care department." He assured me, "With God's blessing, two of us can make miracles. I'll do the surgical work, and Dr. Leskov will take care of the therapeutic treatment."

Zina entered the room with Tisha in her arms. The boy was happy to see his mother. He stretched his hands and pointer at Sasha,

"Mama, Sasa a-a-a." He wanted to show his mother that he knew about Sasha's sleep. Then he climbed on Maria's laps and hugged his mother. The last, what he did, made Maria cry. The baby opened his arms and called with all his strength,

"Daddy! Daddy!"

Then he made unhappy face and pronounced bitterly,

"No Daddy."

Everyone witnessed, how the loss of the father disturbed Tisha. His father has been already in another world, but his absence created an upsetting emptiness around the baby boy. Tisha continued waiting for his Daddy, calling him every day. He walked around the flat and looked for him everywhere.

Maria hugged her baby. She held him cozily, waggling from side to side and cried. Today, she has paid for the kid's lives and freedom with renunciation of their last name, title of nobility, and family history. This fact upset Maria very much. She thought: "My husband would never sign any agreement with the monsters. He preferred death to renunciation. Forgive me, Alex, but I am not so strong. I am just a mother. As for me, the lives of my children mean everything."

Zina came up to Maria and lifted Tisha from Maria's knees.

"Maria, please stop crying," Zina asked and continued: "Look, you made the baby's shirt wet. Drink your tea, it is cold already."

Sofia interfered,

"Don't forget, please, we want to hear, how you have managed to return to us save and sound after your arrest. What miracle had happened there?"

Zina added,

"You are right, Sofia. Something really miraculous must have happened in order the demons escort home the former political prisoner. Maria, please tell us your story!"

Glory to Thee, O Lord! Glory to Thee!

Chapter 14

Maria returned to the dining table and told her friends with details the miraculous story with the inspector from Moscow and his personal investigation of the Kurbatovs' case. Then she made an announcement that shocked everybody in the room.

"I am a traitor, my friends. I betrayed the memory of my family and the family of my beloved husband. Probably, my children will never forgive me, when I tell them this story."

Everyone was silent, and Dr. Leskov was the first, who broke the silence with a question,

"What do you mean, Maria? How could you betray your family and late Alexander?"

There was heavy stillness in the room. Everyone was guessing in what way the devoted woman could betray the beloved. Maria was sitting silently. She could not find strength to explain the price of her miraculous liberation. Maria unwrapped the documents and put them on the table in front of the doctor. He attentively read all of them. He understood what they did to poor Maria. Dr. Leskov tried to help her,

"Hai Maria, you are still anxious after everything that has happened this night and in the morning. You exaggerate with your concept of betrayal. The person like you cannot be a traitor or unfaithful. You accepted their requirements just due to defenselessness and incapability to change anything. Did you have a chance to be released and returned to your children without accepting their prerequisites?"

Maria shook her head and explained,

"I realized from the very beginning of the inspector's personal interrogation that they wanted me to forget about the histories of Alexander's and my family. Why? In order to cover up their dirty crime regarding the innocent couple that did not belong to this country. Who can prove the existence of real data now? Where are our genuine passports? They destroyed them now or probably even then in 1946."

Maria stopped for a moment and put an end to her sad story,

"The Kurbatovs disappeared forever in this godforsaken land…"

"Maria, trust me, it was smart to except their terms," Dr. Leskov approved. "Otherwise, you would never be back. Think about the children."

Maria looked very disturbed. She continued,

"They did not feel guilty of what they did to us. Not at all! Today, just today, they wanted to look nice, in order the inspector from Moscow Central office recorded in the protocol of his inspection that they are "loyal" to innocent people and ready to "correct" the mistakes. It doesn't matter that only a week ago those "loyal authorities" have brutally murdered my husband and destroyed the whole family."

Maria could not control her feelings. When she was in the office, it seemed to her that those people turned off her senses and froze her soul and heart. She complied with everything and did not experience any pain. Presently, she was in harsh pain. Even the complete understanding of her weakness in comparison with their gigantic demonic power, her inability to fight their evil structure did not help Maria to forgive her guilt.

She looked at her friends and told them,

"It is true that I did not fight there, because I knew that I could not win the fight. My husband tried it. And what? What did he gain? I was not so brave. I was terrified, as a tiny kitten in the paws of a huge and unmerciful monster. They illegally separated me from kids, pushed in the car with one purpose that Sidorenko explained to me on our way to the office. He wanted to lock me in the cage, where they planned to *show* how dreadful they were. He promised to introduce me to Sergeant Frolov, who murdered my husband. He also promised to be the last man in my life because I did not have a chance to be found alive tomorrow. I was sure, they would do with my kids whatever their sick psyche hungered for."

Both women cried listening to Maria's dreadful story. Sofia put a glass of cold water in front of a disturbed woman. Maria sipped some and continued,

"Now you know, why they did not murder me, and why I was "escorted" home so quickly. Alexander refused to renounce who he was. He repudiated any changes of his and our personal data. He disagreed with their "*thoughtful*" insinuation to disown his title of nobility. He insisted in repatriation to France. He wanted us to go home."

Only now, her friends entirely recognized how the Kurbatovs were exhausted of being enslaved from the very first day of their arrival to the Ukraine. The woman paid high price for the liberation. She considered that she betrayed her husband, father and grandfather, all her ancestors and the future generations. Was she given another option, another choice or another possibility to save the lives of her sons and herself? No.

Maria completed her narration, "On my way home, I praised the Lord for a miracle that he created for me."

Dr. Leskov came up to Maria and asked a reasonable question,

"Listen, Maria. What do you think is wiser for a mother – to die and let them kill the children or denunciate the title and accept a simulated last name?"

"I understand that lives of my boys have exclusive value for me," Maria answered.

Everyone kept silence for a while, trying to process Maria's information. It was nerve-racking situation for an honorable person. They knew a nice and strong family, and now they witnessed how the whole family was ruined. The KGB destroyed the vivaciousness of the family with brutal murder of Alexander and death-defying warning for Maria and children.

Zina broke the heavy silence,

"Maria, look at the other side of this medal. You signed an agreement that gives your children and you the possibility to start a new life. Believe me, Maria that your new life will be, as honorable, as you are. For us, it's difficult to feel what you feel in this situation."

"Where and how can we start our new 'honorable' life?" Maria asked anxiously.

Sofia supposed,

"Being Gnatiuk, it will be much easier to start your work in the Ukraine. We understand that they will not admit you, as a physician. However, you have different talents Maria.

"Like what?"

"You can teach children music at school," Sofia suggested.

"Maria, you can teach schoolgirls sawing, knitting and cooking," Zina added.

Sofia asked,

"Where were you born, Maria?"

"Let me see. I have to learn the data of my passport," Maria answered, placing all the documents in front of her. She smiled bitterly.

"Oh, great! I am Gnatiuk Maria, who was born in 1918 in Proskurov and did not have a father. My mother's name was Anna Gnatiuk."

Dr. Leskov took Sasha's birth certificate and read out loud,

"Alexander Alexander Gnatiuk. Father: Alexander Gnatiuk. Mother: Maria Gnatiuk. Date of birth: January 03, 1947. Place of birth: Magadan."

Doctor noticed,

"With Sasha, everything has been changed, except Sasha's name. That means, he is eleven now. That's all right, Maria. One year doesn't mean a lot."

Maria was reading Tisha's birth certificate,

"Name: Ivan. Last name: Gnatiuk. Father and mother are the same, as Sasha's. Thank God, they are brothers according to their birth certificates."

The last document was Alexander's Death certificate. Dr. Leskov read it out loud,

"Alexander Gnatiuk. His real date of birth is here. Place of birth: Kiev region, village Bobry. Date of death: five months from today. So, Maria, you became a widow long time ago and, probably, you were one of us, who hadn't been aware of it for five months."

Maria smiled bitterly and explained,

"It's hard to imagine, but it took only two hours for them to prepare all these fake documents, including Sasha's school reports and medical records for both children."

Dr. Leskov replied,

"We know well that it's a very powerful system, Maria. Alexander was unable to change anything. They keep everything and everyone under their control. Alexander was a smart man. How could it happen that he lost cautiousness?"

Maria wanted to explain those nice people that Alexander was tired of *existence*. Her husband wanted to live and enjoy every moment of his life, work, love and fatherhood. He dreamed for his boys to attend the same school which he attended in childhood. He wanted Maria to become again a beautiful, elegant and highly professional lady. He wanted to take care of his lonely mother. Those people in KGB were unable to comprehend his desires. That's why he was unmercifully grinded and burned to ashes by their demonic system which forbad people to dream about a delightful life in well-developed countries.

However, at the very last moment, Maria brought it to a standstill, considering that she should not reveal the thoughts and feelings of her late husband. Maria concluded for herself, "Alexander is not with us any longer, and these kindhearted people can hardly understand Alexander's dreams and desires. They did experience any other lives to compare with. They can hardly understand the difference between life and existence."

She looked at her friends and felt sorry for them. "They did not know the huge difference in quality of life. Their rulers did everything possible and impossible in order to destroy faith, wealth, and comprehension of a rewarding life. They proclaimed their false *equality* of all the citizens in social, moral and financial spheres of life. The laws made the educated, talented and hardworking people equal to illiterate, drunkards, immoral crooks and lazy unemployed elements of the soviet socialist society."

Maria's friends were right, saying that Alexander was not destined to change anything, even for his family. He aspired but did not ask God to support him.

He considered that his wish was insignificant and too personal in order to attract the attention of Divinity. He expected that one day, justice and democracy would win. Wrong! The whole system was not built on justice and democracy. They did not make a secret, proclaiming the *dictatorship* of workers. Any dictatorship would never represent Justice and Democracy.

The system was against anybody's desire to have a beautiful life. The system wanted everyone to exist equally in a herd. Maria imagined how outraged they were watching that Alexander refused to exist, like all the rest, just making ends meet. He managed to survive the camp and was not scared to dream about better life. The demons hated him, "How could he have the courage to wish a beautiful life?" They did not forgive him such courage. The destructive system pushed him in the grinder of injustice and unmercifully triturated.

Maria was right with not explaining the real cause of Alexander's death to her friends. Being born in another life conditions, he was tired of dragging a wretched life. Maria believed, "These people are honest, kind and helpful, but they would hardly understand my husband. They have not been introduced to human life of another quality."

Maria sat quiet. She questioned herself,

"Who knows, what is easier-to have a miserable life, when previously, you have experienced luxury and interesting one, or to keep going without being introduced to it? If people hadn't known anything better, they would not fight for uptraining anything better."

Maria sensed again the flow of warmth inside of her. She deemed with a smile, "It was my Angel, who stopped me from explanation. Thank you, Angel."

Dr. Leskov began to work at the plan of actions. The first thing that Maria needed to do was finding the grave of Alexander and arranging the Panikhida. There was a priest in Leskovs' neighborhood, and the doctor asked Sofia to visit him right away.

Zina advised,

"Maria, put Alexander's new name on the cross. I am sure that they will allow you to do this. Then you can be confident that in ten or twenty years, when you or your children decide to come and visit his grave, the name will be there."

The doctor asked,

"Maria, where do you decide to go?"

Maria handed a piece of paper with Sister Olga's address.

"Do you mind, if I keep it?" Dr. Leskov asked.

"It's my only notice with Sister Olga's handwriting of the address. I am sorry, I need it," Maria answered.

Doctor copied the address in his notebook without sister Olga's civilian name. He was thinking about Maria's long trip to the Ukraine.

"Maria, you need a substantial sum of money in order to get to the Ukraine. Maybe, you can ask people at the hospital to help you."

Maria looked at Dr. Leskov and replied,

"I need to sell our furniture and everything that can be sold from our flat. I hope it would be enough for three tickets."

Zina added,

"It could be enough for tickets, but you need assets for a month, at least, to live somewhere and feed your kids. You know that Sister Olga is unable to support anybody financially."

Dr. Leskov suggested, "There is another issue, Maria: I would like you not to stay here for a long time. People from KGB are so unpredictable in their decisions. Sale might take long time. You have to leave, as soon as Sasha is able to take a train," doctor suggested.

Zina agreed with the doctor,

"You cannot trust them, Maria. Are you sure with the complete closing of the Kurbatovs' case? You know who we are dealing with…"

Maria shook her head. Zina added,

"Doctor is right, it would be safer for you to go away, as fast as possible."

Maria was thinking about money. They lived with Alexander without any savings, as most of the soviet people. Who could save at that time? And what could be saved? The salaries were so tiny that two physicians with two kids had hardly enough money to meet the ends.

Doctor advised Maria to go to the hospital and find people who were interested in purchasing her belongings. Then he thought for a while and made up his mind,

"I need to call Dr. Belikov and give him the idea of crediting. I know you, Maria. You would never go and ask for yourself."

Zina assured the poor widow,

"People know your family very well, Maria. Everyone in the village was in shock with the tragedy that happened to Dr. Alexander. I am certain that they will help you."

Maria was upset. She knew that it was necessary to go and ask people to help her through buying her furniture, kitchenware and clothing. She contemplated,

"Everything looks exactly, as I have seen in my nightmare, when I was begging with kids on a train. Well, I am a beggar. The nightmare has come true time before our voyage."

Lord, have mercy!

Chapter 15

On the next day, Sasha felt a little bit better, and Maria left him in Eultin with the Leskovs. Zina and Maria decided not to waste a single day. They went home. They had a lot of work to do there. First, they made their stop at the militia station. Major Gromov was in the office and did not reject his meeting with Maria Kurbatov. He promised her that on the very next morning, his people would show Alexander's grave, and on her demand, they put the stone plate with the name Alexander Gnatiuk there.

Zina did not accompany Maria to Major Gromov; she was walking outside with Tisha. The secretary saw Zina through the window and returned Alexander's cloths that Sasha brought in. On their way home, Maria and Zina were talking about the Panikhida and the traditional Christian commemorative dinner after the service on the cemetery.

They stayed at home just for a few minutes, when the telephone rang. Maria stood frozen for a minute and then picked up the phone. She recognized the voice of Dr. Belikov. He pronounced just one sentence,

"I'll be there."

Zina was cooking dinner, when he arrived. Maria opened the door. He asked Maria,

"What happened? Why did you come back?"

Zina invited him for a cup of tea, and Maria told him briefly her story. She did not want to mention the details, because she still felt dishonored and ashamed that she had accepted their prerequisites. She mentioned only that they allowed Maria and children to leave Magadan zone forever when Sasha got well.

"When do you want to leave?" Dr. Belikov asked.

Maria answered,

"There are two reasons that did not permit me to leave right away, and both of them are serious enough."

"What are they, if it is not a secret?"

"I mean Sasha's concussion and finances. I have to stay here, selling the furniture and the rest belongings in order to make money for the train tickets and, at least, for the initial week in the Ukraine. I'll do my best to find any job there. However, it cannot happen on the next day upon the arrival. A week is necessary to find something."

Dr. Belikov focused on counting something in his notebook and then concluded,

"In the morning, I received a call from Dr. Leskov. We understand that the tickets and your journey require a lot of money. There are two kids on a train with you, and the trip lasts nearly a month, Maria. You need to eat every day. All right, I must talk to our doctors. We'll find out how to help you, at least with purchasing the tickets."

He left and Zina commented,

"When Dr. Alexander was alive, none of us knew what a helpful person Dr. Belikov could be. O Lord, bless him with everything he dreams about for his help for Maria and children."

Maria called Dr. Leskov and found out that in the morning, Sasha was sitting for some time in bed, and his dizziness was not as bad, as it was yesterday. Sofia added that Sasha had some chicken soup for lunch. Maria thanked them for taking good care of Sasha and for their morning phone call to Dr. Belikov. Dr. Leskov confirmed bringing priest Vladimir with him on the next day to serve the Panikhida for Alexander.

All the time, Maria returned in her mind to one thought that Alexander was not buried in a proper way. She blamed herself for being unwell, for her hospitalization and inability to arrange the funeral for her beloved husband. The unremitting guilt for everything that had happened to Alex, children and their family life converted into heavy, pressing weight, and Maria wanted to confess and repent in front of God and priest Vladimir with hope of decreasing her permanent chest pain and heaviness. She was good in medicine and could easily define the difference between a physical problem and suffering of her soul.

In the evening, the women arranged Tisha's bath earlier than usual. Three of them were exhausted and went to sleep around eight. There was one more reason for it: both women did not expect the next day to be hassle-free. Zina wished Maria,

"Have a good night. After all unmerciful, shocked and alarmed events, you positively need good rest. Sleep well, Maria and don't worry about the baby. Tisha and I will sleep in Sasha's room."

Maria closed the door of her bedroom and took off the robe. She was ready to pray her night prayers and thank the Lord for His miraculous intrusion in her fight against the demons. Maria felt that her strength has evaporated, and an icy pierce stabbed misfortunate woman in her chest, causing unbearable chest pain. She did not want to disturb Zina and her baby in another room, but she was not able to stand that pain without weeping and groaning.

Maria tried to catch breath between sobbing, and when she had chance to breathe in, she whispered,

"Alex, please forgive me for everything I did wrong. I do not know how to live without you, my love. I have no idea how to survive without you."

Maria pulled Alexander's pillow and hugged it with both arms. He slept only two nights on that pillow after she had changed the linen, but it seemed to her that the nice smell of Alex's cologne was still there. Maria kissed the pillow and hugged it tightly. She tried to remember this smell before it evaporated forever. She kneeled and whispered,

"O Lord, help me, please! Show me the right path, and this time, I promise to You to follow it. Even during the war, it was easier in a way. I was alone in Germany and kept hope that one day my Alexander would come and save me. Now, everything is different: two children suffer together with me. Tisha's grief does not allow the baby to gain his usual joy. Alex, he is not our happy child any longer…"

Maria complained to her husband, as if he could come and resolve all the complications in their lives. Suddenly, she noticed that her chest pain became lighter. She assumed, "Maybe, my endless and hot tears thawed out that sharp chest pain?" Maria lied down on their bed, put her head on Alexander's pillow, and in a short while, she dozed.

During that night, she saw different dreams, but closer to the morning, Maria saw a nightmare in which her kids and she were homeless beggars in the streets of a big city. Maria awoke and sat down in bed. She was praying passionately to Holy Theotokos,

"O Theotokos and Virgin Mary, rejoice, full of grace, the Lord is with thee; blessed art thou among women, and blessed is the Fruit of thy womb, for thou hast borne the Savior of our souls. O most holy Theotokos, save us. Amen."

The repetitive nightmare in which they wandered and begged along the streets of unknown city alarmed Maria. She did not want to fall asleep again in order to avoid the continuation of that horrible nightmare. She stayed in bed with opened eyes, pleading the God, "*Lord, have mercy!*" Maria promised to endure everything He prepared for her. She did not notice the moment when she fell asleep again.

In the morning, an early phone call awoke Maria and Zina. Dr. Belikov promised to be at their place in half an hour. The women jumped out of beds and moved fast. Maria was combing her hair when he arrived. He was in a hurry and announced from the entrance door,

"Please, don't prepare tea for me. I don't have time for a cup of tea."

Then doctor added,

"Maria, I found people who are interested in purchasing your furniture and whatever you leave here."

Zina asked straight question,

"Who are they? How fast they can pay money?"

"They will move in your flat right after you leave. Let them take a look at everything that is for sale and arrange the deal. You asked who they are. They are our new doctors. They will be here in fifteen minutes. I prefer to leave. So, Maria everything will be all right, trust me."

He looked at Maria and recognized once more the value of her loss, "Nothing is "all-right" for this grief-stricken woman with her long beautiful unbraided hair. The person who made her happy and joyful left forever, and nobody can substitute him, at least in the nearest time."

"Thank you, Dr. Belikov," Maria answered emotionlessly and noted for herself that it was the polite intonation, required at the German hospital from the inmates during the war. The chief-of-staff left in a hurry, and Zina locked the door after him. Then she rushed to the kitchen to cook breakfast. Maria finished with her braids when somebody knocked on the door. The widow opened it and saw a young couple.

"Come in, please," Maria invited.

The couple looked young. They were expecting a child to come. The man introduced his wife and himself,

"We are the Petruks, Oleg and Natasha. We are new physicians at the hospital. Last year, we graduated from the medical school in Kharkov and were sent to Magadan. The Magadan health department directed us here."

Natasha interrupted her husband,

"Dr. Kurbatov, please accept our condolences. The medical personnel at the hospital told us your story. To tell you the truth, I was so frightened that I was ready to go back immediately. The criminals are everywhere. I am scared."

Maria watched them and could not find the arguments for their stay in Magadan region. Then she recollected Alexander's and her work at the hospital and said,

"You should not run away because something had happened to us. The hospital personnel is wonderful. It is a very strong professional team. You will learn a lot from them. I know that you came here to take a look at our place. I leave everything, as is, taking only some of our personal cloths."

Maria made a tour for the young couple. They were surprised to see well-matched furniture, rugs, tablecloths, bedspreads, curtains and lampshades. Everyone, who visited the Kurbatovs, was amazed with the interior design of their apartment and admired it. All the guests kept asking, where the Kurbatovs found so many special pieces of home beauty that matched each other so well.

The guests could easily notice that the hostess was a woman with good taste. She used to go for shopping to the same place, as all the rest residents of the village. One thing made Maria different from the other consumers: Maria did not purchase anything that was not beautiful or special enough for their home. It did not matter, that it took longer time finding an enchanting fabric for making tablecloths or bedspreads. Once she had found what she liked, she added her personal fantasy, design and touch to it, and finished with the handmade fringes, tassels and lace. When it was done with elegance and love, it made their home cozy and beautiful.

The Petruks did not hide that they were impressed to see such a well-designed European home in non-civilized part of the country. They liked everything very much.

"We are impressed. We like everything in your rooms and kitchen," Natasha said.

"Excuse us, Dr. Kurbatov. We need to talk to the chief-physician regarding the financing of our project," Oleg added.

"Dr. Kurbatov, if the chief-of-staff agrees to give us a loan with monthly payments, we will be at your place in the afternoon with our final decision," Natasha promised.

The young doctors went back to the hospital. Zina heard the conversation and was happy for Maria, "At least something started to move in the right direction. Thank You, Lord!"

Maria noticed,

"Zina, if this couple moves into our flat, you'll have another baby in a short while to baby-sit and to make additional income to your tiny pension."

Zina answered,

"This is good, but there are so many 'ifs', Maria. Now, Tisha and I are ready for breakfast. Will you join us?"

Zina did not pay attention that she pronounced Alexander's phrase, because the woman got used to it. The Kurbatovs always invited Zina for their evening tea and discussing their plans for the following day.

"Will you join us?" Maria whispered.

Maria's eyes were filled with tears and, in a second, they ran out on her cheeks. She thought,

"No more evening "tea parties", no more polite invitations, no more Alex's calm and beautiful voice in the house, no more love and no more … life."

Maria burst into sobbing and could not pull herself together. She tried to sip some tea in order to calm down, but everyone in the kitchen, including Tisha, could hear how her teeth were tapping on the edge of the cup, and she was not able to swallow. Tisha made a funny face, watching his Mommy with curiosity and pity. Maria noticed it and smiled.

Zina tried to subtract Maria's attention from the grief. She said,

"Maria, in a couple of hours, Dr. Leskov and the priest will be here. I need to go to the grocery market, and buy some meat, potatoes, cabbages and milk. We should feed people after the Panikhida."

The necessity to do something brought Maria back to stern reality of her life. She counted money and asked Zina to buy some more meat and vegetables for dinner than they planned before. Probably, it was her angel who prompted Maria that they could have unexpected guests.

Maria added,

"You know better, Zina what we need for today. Please, take care of it. Cook more foods, maybe somebody else will stop by. I do not expect anybody from the hospital to come, but who knows?"

Zina asked with unusual for her irritation,

"Why do you think that none of your colleagues will come? What's wrong to come and express their condolences to a widow?"

Maria answered,

"People could be afraid, Zina. The case is obviously questionable. And there is another obstacle for many of them – I invited a priest for Panikhida. I must go this way because Alexander was a person of faith. You are right, Zina. Maybe, we will have some guests from Alexander's department…"

Lord, have mercy!

Chapter 16

Maria picked up her baby son and went to call Dr. Leskov's lazaret for confirmation that the doctor and Father Vladimir were on their way to Maria's place. Doctor's assistant said that Dr. Leskov left an hour ago. Maria dressed Tisha and they went outside.

She talked to Tisha,

"So, Tisha let us go for a walk now, while we are waiting for our guests from Eultin. Later, nobody will have time to take my baby for a walk."

The boy was quiet and did not express any resistance to putting on his winter fur coat, valenki and hats, as he usually did. "Maybe, he gets used to it and enjoys digging in snow or climbing in it?" Maria thought.

It was still difficult for a tiny child to move outside, but he did his best, trying to climb the snow hills around the building. Maria supported the baby's balance, holding him by the scarf that she tightened around him under his arms. Even with Mama's support, Tisha fell frequently in the snow, but never cried.

Maria concluded that morning,

"Tisha, you are your Daddy's son. You are a very strong and persistent baby boy."

Tisha smiled to his mother, as if he understood what she said. The child enjoyed staying with his mother, and the frosty weather could not spoil their walk outside. Maria continued her conversation with him,

"Tisha, later today, you will stay at home with Zina, while she cooks dinner for our guests. Your Mama will go to … to the cemetery."

Maria wanted to say, "to your Dad", and her angel stopped her. She saw her son's eyes. It seemed to her that he waited for that magic word to be pronounced. Maria continued,

"Actually, it will be your nap time, and you will not disturb Zina with cooking. Right, Tisha?"

Maria noticed that she became stronger. She was grateful to the Divinity that supported her and did not let her follow her husband, making the existence of their children totally destroyed. Maria praised God,

"*Oh Almighty God, who casts down and lifts up again and by whose wounds we have received healing; Who strikes and bandages us: We thank You that You have not given me death, but have shown Your compassion upon me and have preserved, corrected, and helped me in my affliction. Amen.*"

Tisha got tired "to dive" in deep snow. He raised his arms, asking Maria to carry him. Maria was too weak to walk, carrying her baby-boy in her arms. At the same time, she did not want to go home. She sat down on the edge of the steps, picked him up and put on her lap. Tisha was "telling" his mother his "long story" in his own babyish language, looked in Mama's eyes and laughed. It was fun, listening to his babbling through the shawl, as well as watching his serious or comical facial expressions. Sometimes, he stopped for a second, gave her a hug and continued the "monologue". His mother was with him, and the boy was happy.

Maria noticed for herself, "During the whole morning, Tisha did not call his Daddy."

The moment when that thought appeared in Maria's mind, Tisha opened his hands in the warm and beautiful mittens that she knitted for him and said in a low voice,

"No Daddy."

Maria noticed that the intonation was different. He stated the fact but did not complain any more. Maria gave him a hug and whispered, *"Have mercy on us, O God, according to Thy great goodness, we pray Thee, hear us and have mercy. Amen."*

Zina was on her way home from the grocery market when Tisha noticed her in a distance. He greeted his baby-sitter with piercing and excitement. Zina delivered the heavy bags with foods. She put the bags on the steps and sighed deeply. Zina did not pronounce anything out loud, but Maria guessed that the reason of their dinner made this kindhearted woman sad. In a minute, Zina caught her breath and praised Maria,

"That's nice that you decided to have some fresh air. You also need it, Maria. You are so pale. One thing is not good: it's too cold to sit on the steps. How long did you stay outside?"

"I think, a little bit longer than half an hour," Maria replied.

"It's enough for such a cool weather. Are you ready to go home? I'd like to have your advice regarding the dishes you want me to cook."

Maria got up from the steps, and they entered the flat. Every time, when Maria opened the door of her home, she was expecting Alexander to be there. It was purposeless, but she could not get rid of that obsessive feeling. It looked like Tisha read mother's mind and called loudly,

"Daddy! Daddy!"

Then looked at Maria and complained,

"No Daddy."

Her tears were ready to pour. Zina took the boy to undress and said firmly,

"Be quiet, boy! Please, be quiet! You are right, Tisha, Daddy is not here. He is far away from us. Your Daddy was a wonderful man, and now, he is with the Lord. Daddy watches you, baby, and asks God for everything good for you. Please, Tisha, do not tear your Mama's heart."

Maria could not stand this conversation, rushed into her bedroom and fell on the bed. She talked to Alexander,

"We will always miss you, darling. Why did you make the incautious decision? We have no strength to overcome your disappearance from our lives. Even your baby-son calls and looks for you everywhere. He complains at your absence, and his unhappy voice kills me. Now you see, darling what they did to Sasha. The misfortune and danger followed us after your death. Who can help us?"

Maria's tears were endless. Zina opened the door and, staying in the doorway, asked,

"Maria, please stop crying. You have to help me with the dinner."

Maria followed Zina to the kitchen. Zina cuddled her, as she used to do to children and asked,

"Do you think crying works for you, Maria? Do you feel better with crying?"

Maria shook her head. Zina continued,

"If not, Maria, please try to control yourself. We have a lot of work to do. Start packing the kids' and your cloths that you need to take with you to the Ukraine. If you remember, you have nice cotton fabric in your wardrobe. Make a new summer dress. With the speed you saw, it won't take long. Usually, it is warm there in May, isn't it?"

Maria nodded, as a child. Zina continued,

"And you can saw new white shirts with long and short sleeves for your boys. Maria, do you remember, you prepared the white fabric for Dr. Alexander's shirts and professional coats? Now, you can use it for the kids and yourself. Keep yourself busy, Maria. Prayers and work always help. You cannot be focused only on your grief. You have a lot of work to do."

Maria interrupted her,

"Zina, please do not remind me anything, I need to do. I don't want to saw or knit. I do not know how to live without Alex. I am dying for him. I am a sinner, but I do not want to live without him…"

Maria burst into tears again, and Tisha began to cry. Zina hugged Maria and stroked her hair, trying to calm her down,

"Maria, I went through the same experience in my life. I understand you well. You'll be their mother and father that I was unable to combine. You'll do your best for your sons. I did not have the strength, education, and intelligence that you have. You will make them decent in the eyes of God and people. Trust me, Maria they will be proud, having such a mother, like you. Be patient, please. Be patient. The Lord is merciful. He will heal your wounds with the help of your kids. Children are the best medicine for widows."

There was something boiling on the stove and Zina rushed there. Maria was sitting on the edge of her chair, as a small bird, waggling slowly from side to side. She did not notice when Tisha fell asleep in her arms. When Maria looked at him through tears, she recollected Zina's words and smiled, "You are my best medicine, darling. I agree with Zina."

She got up and took the baby to his crib. Maria blessed the baby and silently, asked the Lord to help her children and her to overcome the bereavement.

When Dr. Leskov and Father Vladimir arrived, Maria and Zina worked intensively, taking care of the dinner. Maria invited them to have some hot tea, but both visitors wanted to get to the cemetery first.

Dr. Leskov explained,

"You know my wife: she prepared good snacks for us. We had finished them on a train less than an hour ago. Let us start with Panikhida. In an hour, it will be dark outside."

Maria stopped at the militia station, and Major Gromov sent a militia man to show the grave of her husband Alexander Kurbatov. When they came to the cemetery, the militia man brought them to the grave that was outside the cemetery wall. Maria thought, "Poor Sasha. How could my boy find his father's grave?" On the metal plate there was only a number, written with black paint. The number was the one that Zina gave Maria several days ago. Maria learned it by heart. The militia man brought the stone plate from the truck. Somebody engraved there: "Alexander Gnatiuk" and the real dates of birth and death. Maria kneeled at the grave, crying quietly. She did not lament, talked or complained to her husband. She was bitterly weeping. The militia man fixed the stone with a new name and left.

Father Vladimir started the Panikhida. Staying on her knees with closed eyes, Maria could not see when they came-Alexander's and her co-workers. She remembered only the deep baritone of the priest, singing solo, "Memory eternal…" Maria believed that the spirit of her husband was somewhere near her, listening to the sounds of the farewell prayer.

When the service was over, somebody helped Maria to get up. She looked around and found more than twenty people, standing behind her. They sincerely cried, feeling sorry for their brutally murdered colleague Dr. Alexander Kurbatov and for Maria with her heartbreaking grief.

Maria could hardly walk. The co-workers asked her about her boys. Dr. Leskov told them a story about boy's concussion after his accidental fall, skipping the most significant detail-why the boy fell. All of them went to Maria's place for memorial dinner. The first thought that brought Maria to the reality was,

"Oh, my God! Where can I find food? What will we put on the table for so many people? I thought that only Dr. Leskov and the priest will participate in our farewell dinner."

Lord, Have Mercy!

Chapter 17

Maria opened the door of her apartment and froze in the doorway. The co-workers from the hospital first stopped at her place and did the necessary preparations before they went to the cemetery. They put two tables together in the living room, covered them with white compress paper and put their dishes on the tables. They cooked food at their homes. Maria looked around, observing the faces of her female co-workers in black shawls and pronounced,

"I appreciate everything you've done for Alexander and me. May the Lord bless you with all the best!"

Maria turned to the priest Vladimir and asked,

"Father, bless!"

The priest blessed foods, and Maria tried not to cry, but it was impossible. She loved those Russian people, she liked her work, and she liked her home. She presumed that she got used already to Magadan climate and poverty, if it was possible for anybody to get used to it. With the loss of her husband, Maria clearly apprehended that her life in Russia was over. In her forty, she had to leave the grave of her beloved, move somewhere else, and start from a new page another part of her life, a life of a widow with two children.

Maria silently asked the Lord,

"Is it possible for me to survive in this cruel world?"

Another essential thought struck her,

"Wait a minute. Why did I ask that question? I've been already several times in life threatening situations. The tornado of WWII grabbed me out of my home and threw to German slavery. I survived. After home-coming, the merciless events captured Alex and me, separated us and threw to Magadan force labor camps for longer than a decade. We survived. I know that it was easier to survive at that time, because our love supported us. Now it's different… I am with one wing without Alexander. Who can fly with one wing?"

Maria vividly saw the patterns of her life, "This time, the tornado pulled the whole family out of the ground, destroyed the roots and mercilessly crashed the main tree. Now, the furious evil wind bends and twists us; it drags us somewhere, and I have poor belief that it let us stop, rejuvenate, re-grow and flourish in another place. Lord, have mercy!"

It was the moment of her deepest anguish. Sitting with the guests at her husband's memorial dinner, Maria picked up the voice of her Angel,

"Do you remember, Maria that only God's miracles saved you. Pray to the Lord for a new miracle, call upon it, and you'll obtain it. You should not allow any hesitations." Maria smiled bitterly, thinking, "No hesitations are allowed."

The co-workers recollected many interesting stories about her husband. They described various successful cases from Alexander's professional life. She thought, "Why didn't he mention them at home? Probably, he did not consider those cases in an emergency/critical care unit, as something extraordinary. As for him, they were just the emergency cases that required prompt professional response."

Maria knew Alexander's nature better than anybody else. Her husband was always ready to save somebody's life, and the emergency/critical care unit was perfect place for him. Upon the receiving the emergency call in 1944 from nazi Germany, it was so natural for Alex to break through the fire of the war without any hesitation, cross three borders in order to save his Maria. It was he, who did not hesitate and stepped into the ruined German house in Meiningen, in order to save the lives of a young woman and three kids that could be buried alive under the ruins of their house. It was his purpose in life to think prier about somebody's life, health and happiness, making the most dangerous and challenging decisions for himself.

Dr. Belikov recalled their initial interview when they came to see him after the discharge from the camp, and Maria wore a dress of a prisoner. It was smart that he did not mention in front of people that both of them applied for doctors' positions without diplomas and passports. Nevertheless, God's miracle happened, they were hired and successfully worked for several years. Maria noted for herself, "Undoubtedly, it was God's miracle."

One thought did not give Maria a chance to calm down and participate in the conversation, "How is it possible for the Russian society to be distinctly subdivided into two opposite campsites? They are clearly either good or mean, either light or dark, either kind or nasty, either God's or Satan's. It is a very interesting phenomenon. Thank God that the most of our colleagues are decent, highly professional, helpful and trustworthy people. To my mind, weak and self-centered person would never work in this zone for prolong time. They are looking for warmer and more civilized conditions of life. Thank God, the nasty people run away from the hospital with the speed of the wind."

Dr. Leskov and priest Vladimir were the first who decided to leave. They needed to find the transportation to get to Eultin. Usually the public transportation did not work after 8 p.m. People were leaving one by one. Maria knew, it was her last gathering with Alexander's and her co-workers, and the feeling of new loss greatly distressed Maria. She was sincere when expressed them her appreciation for coming and support.

Maria did not know that besides food, the colleagues brought a blue envelope with some money, collected for kids. They did not want Zina to inform Maria about its existence until they left. Why? Normally, the Russians were introverted, especially when they expressed their generosity. When the guests left, Zina showed Maria the envelope and commented,

"In addition to this money, Dr. Belikov confirmed that he found the possibility for the Petruks to buy your furniture. Don't despair, Maria. God is merciful, and you know this better than anybody else. Tomorrow, we need to pack and go to Eultin. You'll stay there, until

Sasha is well. I will miss you, Maria. I got used to be part of your family. I have been changed a lot for the time with you. Your family warmed up my soul."

Zina did not let Maria to interrupt her and continued,

"Your grief is my grief, Maria. I love you and, more than anything else, I wish you and kids to find safe home, a real home where nobody will disturb you. You are young and forty is not the age to be alone. Think about it."

"Please, Zina I do not want to hear this. My love, passion and happiness passed away together with my husband. I have two sons to live for," Maria answered firmly.

The elderly woman had another vision,

"Maria, do not repeat my mistake. I did not know what they did to my beloved husband and waited for him. Decades passed, and I found that with getting older, it was more difficult to be alone. When I was younger, I did not allow myself to find a true fried or companion. I had my children, but you know them. They cannot support their old mother, because they cannot support themselves and their families. Poor drunkards! I am absolutely lonely. I am afraid that one day, I can die, and nobody will notice it."

Maria promised,

"If everything is all right with me and children in Ukraine, I'll let you know, Zina, and send some money for a ticket. I want you to live with us. Can you imagine the happiness of my boys, when you arrive?"

Zina smiled, envisioning, how nice it could be,

"Oh, yes. In the Ukraine, they do not have winter up to nine months, and every summer, they eat fresh fruits, berries and vegetables."

Then she embraced Maria's thin shoulders and said with hesitation in her voice,

"No, Maria, I will not go anywhere. I think that it's not right to make such changes at the end of the life. I am old, and I don't want you to take care of me. You have enough in your life."

Marie guessed,

"Zina, only God knows when is the last day of our life."

Zina and Maria heard strange sounds from the living room. They rushed there and saw how Tisha pushed a heavy chair closer to the table. They left the boy there for a short while without their attention, and he tried to climb the chair in order to reach some food on the table. Maria picked him up and asked,

"You must be hungry, baby, aren't you?"

She kissed him and sat down to feed. Zina was cleaning the table and named to Maria who of the guests brought the foods. They did not bring the same dishes, and Maria had her strong suspicion that Dr. Belikov "assigned" her co-workers to cook something specific in order to help Maria with memorial dinner. He was so kind to her family.

Maria wished him from the bottom of her heart,

"May God bless him and his family with good health and real happiness. Zina, if not him, it would be more complicated for me to deal with my loss."

Then she complemented to Zina,

"Zina, your meat stew, potatoes and stuffed cabbages were delicious."

"How do you know, Maria, if you did not try anything?" Zina asked.

"I saw how fast it disappeared from the bowls."

Zina brought Tisha's kasha and put it in front of Maria and Tisha. The boy screamed joyfully and opened his mouth before his Mama found a small spoon.

Maria asked with her pleasant smile which Zina saw for the first time after the tragedy took place,

"Do you have anything left for me, Zina?"

"Certainly, Maria. You are also hungry."

Maria looked at her child, who ate with enjoyment and asked,

"Tisha, who will cook for us these tasty dishes in the Ukraine? Who will take care of you, chick, when your Mama goes to work?"

Maria sighted deeply. Zina tried not to allow sadness to capture Maria. She answered,

"It will be you, Maria. Who has taught me all the tasty recipes? I do not think that you forgot how to make them. You are great in cooking and baking."

Maria froze up for a while, concentrating at one thought, "We talk, eat, feed Tisha, do chores, like nothing happened in our life. When Maman left for Canada, I could not eat and sleep for a long time."

Tisha opened his mouth and waited for the next spoon of food. His mother's memories took her far away. When he was not given anything, the "neglected" child put a piece of potato from Maria's plate into his mouth. Maria noticed his motion and said,

"Zina, look at Tikhon. He helped himself. Now, he does not want to wait for me; he eats my potatoes."

Maria's mind pulled her again in another direction, "How can I notice these tiny things? How can they make me joyful after everything that had happened?"

Zina watched Maria and praised the Lord,

"Thank you, Lord for keeping Maria and her kids alive. I am so grateful for Your protection and guidance. What can we do without You?"

Glory to Thee, oh Lord! Glory to Thee!"

Chapter 18

Another long and stressful day came to the end. Zina had finished with chores, while Maria put Tisha to sleep. Everyone felt exhausted, even the baby fell asleep immediately, while Maria was praying her Evening prayers. Zina prepared tea for Maria and herself, as it used to be. Sitting at their traditional "tea party", both women felt the hurtful emptiness – Alexander was not with them.

"I wish Sasha is with us," Zina said. "He was big help in the house. I used up all water in the buckets. Now, we need to go and bring water from the well."

"I'll do it by myself," Maria promised. "You had a lot for today, Zina. I appreciate your help with today's dinner. Everything that you cooked was delicious. Thank you, dear. Now, go and sleep and don't worry about water."

Maria missed Sasha, as well. She sighed and concluded in her thoughts,

"My brave defender, I'll pack tomorrow and go to you. I miss you very much, my boy. Probably, sonny, one more week is required before you'll be able to take a long trip on a train."

Maria put on her coat and stepped in her bedroom to get a warm wool shawl. The nights were very cold. Tisha woke up and sat down in his crib, trying to explain something to his mother in his babyish language. Then he showed at her bed and said, “A-a-a, Mama.” Maria smiled: he invited her to sleep.

Maria kissed Tisha and promised to do it a little bit later. She put him back to sleep, saying,

“Do not stand up, my boy. I’ll bring two buckets of water and come to sleep. In the morning, all of us need water. Good night. Have sweet dreams!”

When she went to the kitchen to take the buckets, she heard how Tisha called,

“Daddy! A-a-a, Daddy!”

Maria knew that for ten days, baby Tikhon experienced unusual emptiness around him. All the children pick up easier than adults the disappearance of something imperative, protective, warm, established and cozy that surrounded them from the very first moment of being born. For eleven months, the child naturally got used to all those important components of the family. He was blessed to have both loving parents. Presently, Tikhon’s baby soul was exposed to cold danger, and felt itself unprotected. The kid sat down in his bed again and called,

“Mama!”

He waited for a minute, but his mother did not appear in the room. The boy called,

“Daddy!”

He started to cry. Then he stopped crying abruptly and called impatiently for his brother,

“Sasa! Sasa!”

Maria grabbed two buckets from the bench and ran out of the flat. It was dark and nobody could see her hysterically crying on the way to the well and back. She experienced one desire – to run away in nowhere and never come back in her appalling life. She blamed herself again and again in everything that happened to them, especially Alexander. She shouted to the Lord,

"Home-coming was my biggest mistake. I am guilty. I am a sinner that should be punished. Why should my husband pay for it? Why did you allow them to kill Alex?"

At that very moment Maria slipped on the icy path, lost the balance, kneeled on the ground and spilled out all the water from both buckets. Maria stopped crying for a second, watching how the water from her buckets drained into the snow.

She exclaimed,

"I am scared, my Lord! With all my feelings I can slide to the wrong path, like my husband did. Please, help me! Right at this moment, you've reminded me your words: we shall eat the fruit of the labor of our hands, and we shall be happy, and it shall be well with us. My husband hated the fruit of his labor that kept us in slavery and poverty. He had lost patience, happiness, gratitude and joy. Poor Alexander forgot Your teaching, my Lord. *O God, cleanse me, a sinner, have mercy on me and save me! Amen."*

Maria sensed warmth inside. She got up, picked up the empty buckets and ran back to the well. On her way home, Maria promised herself, "I should not blame my husband in the eyes of the Lord for leaving me alone with our sons, for making my life thornier and more dangerous. I must stand the hardships. Dear Lord, forgive my husband! Forgive his sins! Forgive his impatience! That was his level of tolerance. Accept his physical and emotional suffering, as a credit for the remission of his sins. Enlighten my mind and strengthen my faith. Establish me in hope and perfect me in love. I do not want to grow hatred in my heart and in the hearts of my children. Hatred kills."

Maria put the full buckets on the steps of her house. At that time, nobody was outside, and Maria prayed out loud, *"Dear Lord, pardon the weakness of my husband and all his voluntary and involuntary transgressions. Grant him Your forgiveness, place him in Your eternal kingdom of goodness and light."*

The pleasant warmth covered Maria and filled her with its healing, cleansing and strengthening power.

"Thank you, Lord. Thank you, my Guardian Angel," Maria replied.

When Maria opened the door of her flat, it was quiet inside. Zina and Tisha were asleep. Maria went to the kitchen and put the buckets with water on the bench. She was tired, but her physical energy arose after the sincere meditation, and she did not want to stay sleepless in bed, thinking again and again about her derisory situation. She sat down on her low stool and pulled the basket with knitting. Maria didn't like to be pitiful to herself. Self-pity did not help her in any of her perilous life situations. She remembered the night of self-pity in the barn in 1941, where the Nazis locked her and Rosa together with hundreds of Jews. The self-pity did not help her a bit, but nearly destroyed her spirit.

Maria looked at the work that she started to knit some time ago. It was Zina's wool vest. It looked beautiful. Maria did not mention to Zina what a nice and useful birthday gift she was preparing for that kind woman. The knitting-needles moved fast in Maria's hands, and she thought, "I can complete this work tonight. It wouldn't take longer than an hour. I'll present it tomorrow because we are not here on Zina's birthday."

Maria used to knit every evening after "tea party" when they sat together with Alexander during *their hour* before going to bed. Maria remembered how they discussed all the important topics and made the mutual decisions. Everything was over. Her life, which she considered the life of a happy and loved woman, was irreversibly destroyed ten days ago. The tears filled Maria's eyes, and she could not see her work. Maria stopped knitting, listening to a distinct voice of her angel,

"Marie, live your life. You are not given any other choices."

It seemed that Maria felt light touch to her right shoulder. She wanted to look back and see her Alexander, safe and sound. Alex had always been a gentle man. For a minute, Maria was in anguish again. Then she whispered,

"My Guardian Angel! Thank you for being with me during all the sorrowful days. You protected me from demon of despair. Please, always stay on my side."

Maria began to meditate,

"Remit, pardon, forgive, O God, my offences, both voluntary and involuntary, in word, thought and deed, in knowledge and ignorance, by day and by night; for You are good and the Lover of mankind. Amen."

Maria sensed that there was no more painful tension in her chest. She pronounced with restored firmness in her voice, *"Glory to Thee, o Lord! Glory to Thee!"*

Maria was able to continue knitting. To her surprise, it took less than an hour and the work with Zina's vest was over. Maria pressed it, took it to Zina's room and left it on the chair near the sofa where Zina slept soundly. She thought with appreciation,

"Tomorrow, Zina will wake up and find a nice gift. I am grateful to You, my Lord, that You sent Zina into my life."

Maria was already in bed when the warmth penetrated her chest, causing some light pain for a minute. It seemed that the Holy Spirit squeezed out the remaining fear and worries.

Around 3 a.m., Maria saw a repetitive nightmare, where both kids and she were beggars. That time, it did not look so stressful. The kids smiled, sitting on the upper berth of a train, dividing alms between two of them. Then they decided to give everything to their Mama. The dream awoke Maria. Maria pronounced in a low voice,

"Glory to Thee, O Lord. Glory to Thee!"

Chapter 19

The telephone in the entrance hall rang loudly when Maria was still asleep. She jumped out of bed and rushed there. It was a quarter after seven. Dr. Leskov came to the lazaret and decided to call Maria with a good report on Sasha. He was glad to reveal,

"Maria, the boy walks outside. You see, God is merciful to him. He can walk without Sofia's support. She is there just because she wants to be certain that his dizziness is not so bad and does not interfere with his walking. How do you feel yourself? What are your plans for today?"

"I am quite all right, doctor. We plan to pack. I need to move out and let the young family move into our apartment. Yesterday, I did not have chance to talk to you. Dr. Belikov found a young couple of physicians who will move into our place and purchase everything, except our personal clothing."

"I know, Maria. I talked to Dr. Belikov about the credit for young specialists," Dr. Leskov replied with satisfaction in his voice.

Then he added,

"Everything goes in the right way. Take another day for your rest, Maria."

Maria explained,

"There is no time for rest. With God's help, we'll be in Eultin tomorrow by the end of the day. Best regards to Sofia and my boy. Say that I love him. I love you all. Thank you, doctor for everything."

Maria looked into Sasha's room and did not find Zina and Tisha there. She went to the kitchen. Nobody was there, as well. Maria's thoughts jammed in her mind, creating apprehensive ideas. Poor woman forgot what she promised in her daily meditation, "*The Lord is my miraculous Defender, and I will not be afraid; I will not fear evil, for my Lord is with me.*"

Out of the blue, one thought climbed on top of another,

"Maybe, they were kidnapped by Sidorenko? What should I do? Where can I find them?"

Maria looked in the mirror and found out that she was going to run somewhere in her nightgown. She rushed into the bathroom, washed and dressed herself, combed her hair and "flew" into the entrance hall to put on the coat. She looked at the clock-it was a quarter to eight. Maria heard a sound of somebody's steps behind the entrance door. That *somebody* tried to unlock the flat but was not successful in it. Maria stepped forward, waiting for the door to be opened. Then she recognized Zina's advice-giving intonation. The considerate baby-sitter talked to Tisha, as if the baby could understand her,

"Tisha, be quiet, baby. We should not awake your Mama. She is very weak. First, we'll cook breakfast, and then you'll go and wake her up."

Maria opened the door for them. Zina looked at Maria with surprise and asked,

"Where are you going so early? You are so pale, Maria! Are you all right, dear?"

Maria wanted to help Zina with carrying Tisha, but a smart woman preferred to carry Tikhon by herself and suggested Maria to help her with the shopping bag.

It was obvious: Maria was panic-stricken. Seeing the milk container with milk, she still asked the question,

"Where have you been, Zina? Why did you leave so early?"

Zina embraced Maria's shaking shoulders and answered,

"Maria, calm down, please. We went to buy milk. When you were in the hospital, I used to go every other morning together with Tisha, in order to buy two litters of milk for two days. Right, Tisha? As you know, they give just one liter of milk per person. If we go after 8 a.m., there is no milk left at the village store. But where were you going, Maria?"

"Zina, look at me, please. I am a paranoiac patient. To my mind, I am quite ready to be in a psychiatric unit," Maria replied, while taking off her coat.

Poor woman entered the kitchen, sat down at the table and put her baby-son on her lap. Zina was observing Maria. She did not find anything abnormal in Maria's appearance and asked,

"Why psychiatric unit? What's wrong with you? I see that you are still in shock, but you acknowledged that nobody can return Dr. Alexander. I am sorry, he left for a better world..."

Maria interrupted,

"Zina, I thought that Sidorenko or somebody else from KGB took revenge and kidnapped Tisha and you."

Zina burst into laughing, as she used to do, when everything was all right in before-tragedy life. Then she stopped laughing and replied,

"I am sorry, Maria. Certainly, Sidorenko came to kidnap me, personally me, Maria. Tisha was just an addition to a "desirable" me. Only due to "unpredictable circumstances" that this kid *accompanied* me to the village market, Sidorenko had to kidnap both of us. Oh, Maria, you can create funny stories in minutes."

"You are right, Zina. For one minute, I imagined your kidnapping so vividly, as if it has happened in reality."

"You need Valerian drops, Maria. Take them at least twice a day," Zina suggested with a compassion in her voice.

Maria went to Sasha's room and brought a new vest. She asked Zina to try it on. It looked gorgeously. Maria hugged Zina, saying,

"I have made it for your birthday, but on that day, we'll be far away from here."

Maria genuinely loved this kindhearted and helpful woman. She could not imagine her life without Zina during the last year. Zina was pleased,

"Thank you, Maria. You are so nice to me. May God bless you for your kindness with everything you need! Nobody gave me anything for my birthdays."

She smiled and added with bitterness in her voice,

"Nobody gave me any gift at all. To my mind, my children do not even know my day of birth or my Saint's day."

Tisha interrupted women's conversation, asking loudly for breakfast. Zina took off her new vest and rushed to the kitchen stove. She boiled eggs, made sandwiches with zucchini pate and poured fresh milk in the cups. Maria was sitting at the table, thinking about something that was meaningless and absolutely irrelevant to the events of the last eleven days. She did not even hear Tisha's voice, asking for the next portion of food. The child touched her hand and Maria "awoke" with apology,

"I am sorry, my boy. Today, there is something wrong with your Mama."

"It's all right, Maria. It will be treated with time," Zina promised.

Maria was surprised that she had a good appetite after everything she went through. The hunger forced her to ask Zina to give her more milk and bread. She continued feeding Tisha and enjoyed watching how her boy "worked" on his breakfast. Being a thoughtful and loving mother, Maria was pleased with him. The child did not give her any problem during this difficult time.

Then Maria recollected Dr. Leskov's call and told Zina,

"I forgot to tell you that Dr. Leskov called us at 7:15 in the morning and updated us with good news about Sasha. My boy walked outside with Sofia. Thank God, doctor prevented the complications. By the way, his phone call awaked me, and I rushed to share the good news with you, Zina. When I did not find you in Sasha's room and Tisha in his crib, I became paranoiac."

"Lord is merciful, Maria," Zina said. "Pray and you'll be healed."

After breakfast Maria and Zina went to Maria's bedroom.

"Now, Zina, we'll take out everything from the wardrobe and dresser and put on the sofa and table in the living room. I need to sort it out. What do you think about Alexander's clothing? Where should I take his shirts, jackets, boots, shoes and coats?"

"If you do not mind, Maria, I will take some older pieces for my sons. They will be happy to have Dr. Alexander's things. They did not have anything alike for the whole live. You sawed everything wonderfully. His pants, shirts and coats were always elegant. The rest that is newer, I'll sell for you today. I've talked to some people earlier, and they were interested in buying it. You know, they will never find anything like yours in the village or even Magadan store. Everything that you sawed for your husband, yourself and kids, you made stylish and with love."

Maria experienced spasm in her throat. The spasm caught her breath every time when she was disturbed or deeply upset. She turned to the window and whispered,

"Help us, save us, have mercy on us, and keep us, O God, by Thy grace. Amen."

Then she asked again for Zina's advice,

"Zina, do I need to take my uniform to the Ukraine? I do not think so."

"Your doctor's coats are so crispy, that you can sell them for somebody in the hospital, who is of your size and complexion. Do you remember anybody, like you?"

"Yes, I do, Zina. There were two or even three women, like me. You will go to the hospital and suggest them, won't you? I don't feel like going there and selling by myself …"

Zina understood Maria's reluctance and agreed to sell the things by herself right after sorting everything out. It could release the difficultness of situation and, at the same time, make some extra money for Maria's trip.

Zina continued to sort out and said,

"I am sure that they will be happy to have the doctor coats, like yours. You sawed them in a *feminine* way, Maria, not like our regular doctor's coats. We can sell Dr. Alexander's coats, too. Let people have a pleasant memory about both of you. Your colleagues respected you and Dr. Alexander. They knew that you were different, but very knowledgeable, intelligent, and helpful doctors."

Zina pointed to the sky and added with a smile,

"You were people from *another planet*. Everyone realized it from the initial days of your work at the hospital."

"Oh, really?" Maria was surprised to hear such an interpretation. "I thought that they were cautiously watching us for several months just because we were labeled as "people's enemies" and served long term in the force labor camps."

Zina laughed,

"No, Maria, not at all. Imprisonment cannot scare anybody in our region. You are different. I am an illiterate woman, but I can see that you belong to another type of people. Everyone noticed the difference in the way you speak, walk and react toward everything around. You behave in an uncommon way."

Maria confessed,

"Well, probably that *difference* made us outcasts for some time. We noticed that everyone was watching us. Alex and I could not find another explanation, except suspicion and distrust."

"No, Maria. You were wrong. They simply haven't seen such a couple before. Even so, that your unlikeness did not interfere with your hard work and your attitude toward co-workers, both of you looked different, the manner how you talk to people was different, and your relationship in the family was an example of real love, care and respect. Nobody was suspicious. On the contrary, I knew from my own experience that daily work next to both of you, made positive influences on many people. I am old, and still have changed a lot. You brought life to all of us. Not the regular, rough one, but beautiful life…"

Maria smiled to her thought,

"Zina knew better than us about everything that was going on at the hospital. A village is a village. Everyone is exposed. People could not hide their manners, images, ideas, especially at work."

The thought about selling the doctor's coats to her co-workers was still uncomfortable for Maria. Nevertheless, she packed six of them and wrote a note for Zina with the names of the people and units where they worked.

Maria looked at Zina and said,

"I wish I can give these coats, as gifts…"

"Not at the moment," Zina answered reasonably and left for the hospital.

Maria pulled down a big suitcase from the top of the wardrobe. Some time ago, Alexander purchased it in Magadan not for travelling, but for keeping the quilts and linen. They used it for a year, before they could afford their wardrobe with three doors and a mirror in the middle. Later, they used the suitcase for quilts, linen and cloths of a new baby. Maria took everything out of the suitcase and put in piles on the sofa. Then she removed everything from the shelves of the wardrobe and put it on the table of the living room. After that she started sorting out the belongings.

Some of the linens, towels, quilts and baby-cloths were in a pretty nice condition, and Maria put them back on the shelves of the wardrobe, in order the young family could use them for their baby. She separated a big pile for Zina and her children.

Maria made separate piles of cloths for her sons and herself. She thought, "It is heavy to carry while traveling, but wonderful to have it at hand, when it is needed. After moving to a new place, I could hardly find moncy and timc for buying anything ncw. I hopc that I can find job in a short while, otherwise …"

Maria tried to be optimistic and not to concentrate herself on "otherwise". She talked to God in her thoughts, "I believe, O Lord that you are my best Provider. I know that everything will be given on time and in the way, it is supposed to be. I cannot change anything. Dear Lord, help us to survive our long trip. Please, support my boys while travelling. It's my fate to be a single mother, but it does not mean that my kids should experience deprivation, hunger and poverty. I keep my hope on You, my Savior. With Your help, we'll reach the Ukraine. I'll do my best in finding job position, as quickly as possible. My sons will go to school and nursery there. With Your blessing, everything will be all right…"

Maria packed her suitcase fast. When Zina returned from the hospital, the widow had finished with sorting out of all the things and preparation of several packages.

Zina was satisfied with her visit to the hospital.

"What did I tell you, Maria? The doctors were happy to buy the Kurbatovs' lab coats. I decided not to nominate any prices. I've just explained to them what the money is needed for, and the doctors paid with the higher prices than I could expect."

Zina went to the kitchen and prepared small snacks and tea for Maria and herself, and a real lunch for Tisha. She said with noticeable sadness in her voice,

"Sorry, Maria, but I want to feed the boy by myself and put him to sleep. I feel sad, when I think that today is the last day of my baby-sitting. You are my family. You are the family from my dreams…"

Maria passed the boy to Zina. When the boy fell asleep, Zina said,

"Now, I'll go and sell some more things for you, Maria. Before I go, let me take a look at what you have packed for me and my children."

Zina re-sorted all the things that Maria had separated for her family. She made two piles of them. One pile she took to her flat, and another pile she packed with the rest of the cloths in a big bag and left. When she returned home, she handed Maria some more money with the words,

"I sold some cloths to our neighbors. For my sons, I have left only those things that I cannot sell fast. You are very kind, Maria, you gave us a lot. I do not want to take advantage of you and your situation. God knows, I am here to help you."

Maria came up to Zina, took her hands and said,

"You are my angel, Zina. I cannot imagine what I can do without you. Let's go together to the Ukraine. Maybe, today, we can make money for one more ticket?"

Zina smiled, but did not answer anything to Maria. She packed another bag of Dr. Alexander's belongings and left. It was about 3 p.m. When she returned home,

Maria opened the door and realized, Zina's mission was successfully fulfilled, because she handed Maria an empty bag.

"You go with us, don't you?" Maria asked with excitement.

Zina replied,

"No, my girl, I don't. Not now. At the present time, this is not the topic for discussion. I am happy that I have found how to help you. The Lord was merciful, and I sold everything. Here is your money, Maria."

Maria counted money and looked at Zina with admiration. That woman made her trip possible.

"Thank You, God! Thank you, Zina." Maria was pleasantly surprised.

"I knew where to go," Zina explained with the tone of conspiracy in her voice and added, "Where could they find so elegant dresses and suits, like yours, as well as so beautiful shirts and trousers, like Dr. Alexander's? Nobody could buy it in our village. I must say the truth: nobody has learned your art of sawing, embroidering, knitting and lacing."

Maria interrupted Zina,

"Zina, will you stop praising me? I know that you are tired, but we need to continue our work. I did everything with our and Sasha's rooms. Let me see, what I need to take from the kitchen."

By the end of the day, everything has been done, and Maria called Dr. Belikov, as she promised. This time, he was not afraid to arrange the transportation to Eultin.

Zina suggested,

"We need to eat our dinner. There are some leftovers from yesterday."

"I agree," Maria replied. "It's better to go to sleep earlier tonight. Tomorrow is our departure to Eultin."

Maria felt tired after packing and was contented to get the last chance to sit down at her table in the kitchen, having the last supper.

Glory to Thee, O Lord! Glory to Thee!

Chapter 20

Dr. Belikov appeared in their flat when they had finished with after breakfast chores, putting the clean dishes on their places in the cupboard. Maria covered the table with a new white tablecloth. It was beautifully embroidered with small pink flowers in the middle and bigger in the corners. She prepared it for Easter. "Let the young couple enjoy it," Maria thought.

"Ladies, your transport is at the door," Dr. Belikov announced theatrically, entering the kitchen. Maria did not find strength to smile and replied quietly,

"Thank you."

He handed Maria the envelope with the money for her furniture. Maria repeated again,

"Thank you."

Zina made some tea and a sandwich for Dr. Belikov. Three of them were sitting silently together. Maria had a heavy feeling. She realized, "With the loss of my husband, the whole world became colorless. We are together for the last time… The horrible tragedy ruined everything: love, friendship, happiness and joy."

Her mind concluded that after Alexander's murder, many vitally important human connections were destroyed forever. At that very moment, she painfully sensed how two more were splitting up. Maria did not identify the taste of her favorite tea. Bitterness of thoughts and feelings disallowed enjoying it.

Zina got up with exclamation,

"Oh my God, I forgot to pack your dry bread and sugar."

She took a new sack that Maria sawed and embroidered before a new year and packed two brown paper bags with dry bread for Maria's train journey. Then she pushed in a small bag with sugar cubes that was also made and embroidered by Maria.

"Thank God, I recollected about dry bread and sugar. In the evening, I sliced all our bread and dried it in the oven. Maria, the sugar is chipped off, so you do not need to chip it on the train from a big piece. On the train, you'll drink sweet tea with dry bread. It always helps when people are hungry."

Maria whispered,

"Thank you, Zina."

She recorded in her mind, "Again long journey, again dry bread to reduce hunger, and again Alexander is not with me. But this time, there is one heartbreaking divergence-he will never be with me…"

All this time, Maria was looking out of the window. Her soul was still waiting… She tried not to cry, but tears dropped out of her eyes.

Dr. Belikov interrupted Maria's despondent thoughts with a brief question,

"Ready to go?"

All three of them got up and Zina prayed,

"O our Father, the True and Living Way, Who travelled with His servants Joseph and Maria. Please, travel together with Your servants Maria, Tikhon, Dr. Belikov and Zina. Please, deliver us from all agitation and slander, and keep us in peace and strength. For Yours are the Kingdom, and the Power, and the Glory. Amen."

Maria looked at Dr. Belikov and noticed that he smiled during Zina's praying. He explained when Zina stopped,

"At least, Zina included me in her prayer. Since my grandmother and mother died, I have not heard anybody praying. My wife and I are atheists. She baptized our daughter secretly, more as a tradition. We do not practice religion at home. However, it was nice to be included in Zina's meditation."

"It's not only your fault that you are atheists, Dr. Belikov. Those, who govern this country, prefer people to believe in them, instead of God, in their power instead of the Divinity's," Maria replied emotionless.

Zina dressed the child and was waiting for Maria on the porch. She opened the door and asked,

"Maria, please let's go. It's better to arrive there before the dusk. And it's long way for Dr. Belikov to get home tonight."

Maria walked around the rooms for the last time. She left everything in a neat way, in order the young couple could move in without more ado, and from the very first day, enjoy their living in their new home. Dr. Belikov took Maria's suitcase to the ambulance.

"How will Maria manage this suitcase alone? It's heavy."

Zina replied with pettiness in her voice,

"Poor Maria… I don't know, how she can manage her life with two boys without Dr. Alexander. She is tiny and fragile. Dr. Alexander helped her a lot. They liked to be together, and he didn't refuse to help her with cooking, cleaning the flat, doing laundry or ironing. I did not hear arguing regarding kitchen choirs, as well. They were perfect for each other. I doubt that she can easily survive without him. She definitely needs some pillar… Dear Lord, send Maria support."

Dr. Belikov agreed with Zina,

"Particularly now, Maria is very weak. Nobody gave her time to recuperate after tragedy. She wasn't given any chance to build up her strength. Sasha is also sick; he is not her help at this point, because he needs some time for his recovery. Both of them require not less than a month to get better. We let them go, just because it's more secure for their lives to be further from this village. Any day, the KGB could reverse everything. They are unpredictable in their decisions."

"Only God will support Maria and kids. He is merciful and will not leave them unaided," Zina concluded.

Dr. Belikov thought, "They trust God more than anybody or anything else. I wish God prevent the tragedy with Alexander and avert making the life of this chaste woman and a talented doctor so tragically destroyed."

Maria picked up Tikhon, and Zina locked the door of the flat. She returned the key to Maria. Maria, in her turn, gave the key to Dr. Belikov with the words,

"*God bless the young couple for a happy life in their new home. Amen.*"

Usually, Zina was calm, but this time, she was nervous. She knew that KGB had their "*eyes*" everywhere, and it was better to avoid their new reports. She thought,

"Maria leaves forever, but Dr. Belikov has to stay and work here. O Lord, protect him from all the complications. He is a decent man."

The road was difficult. It was with post-winter big deep holes that the ambulance could hardly move around. They arrived to Eultin when it was completely dark. Dr. Leskov was outside, waiting for his visitors. Dr. Belikov refused to enter the house.

"Sorry, but I need to go back, as fast as possible. My family is waiting for me," he said to Dr. Leskov.

Both men quickly unloaded Maria's suitcase and two bags. Dr. Leskov acknowledged well that helping the Kurbatovs was dangerous for both physicians. Who could guarantee that KGB did not prepare the revenge?

Maria came up to Dr. Belikov and said,

"I am grateful to Lord for sending us to your hospital. I appreciate your trust and support of Alex and me from the very first day of our work under your supervision. Most of all, I was impressed with your courageousness after Alexander's death, when you did not leave my kids and myself single-handed and continued your thoughtful patronage, especially, after the fear-provoking visitors from KGB."

Maria did not cry, but she felt sad that a very important part of her life was over, and she would never see that respectable person again. She made another step toward Dr. Belikov and hugged him. Doctor whispered to Maria,

"Maria, I wish you good health and happiness. Take care not only of your sons, but yourself, as well."

Sasha walked outside and came up to his mother and Dr. Belikov. After greeting both of them, the boy said,

"Doctor Belikov, thank you for your assistance. I will always remember you, as an honorable person and reliable friend of our family."

Doctor Belikov heard the intonations of Alexander Sr. in every word, pronounced by the boy.

They embraced each other, and the doctor asked him to take care of his mother and Tisha,

"You have to remember, Sasha that the tragedy with your father arose you from childhood to a man of a family. You are not Alexander, Jr. any longer."

Then he jumped into the ambulance and started the engine. Maria came up to his window, blessed him and promised,

"From today, I will keep you in my daily prayers together with my children and Zina. I am so much obliged to you... Stay always blessed!"

Dr. Belikov's ambulance receded in darkness, and the frost below 30 hastened the guests inside of the house. It was pleasantly warm indoors, and the smell of freshly baked bread and something else woke their hunger up.

Sofia took supper out of the oven and invited all of them to the dining room. During supper, the Leskovs suggested Maria to leave on the very next day.

Maria and Zina were surprised. Maria expected to stay for at least three days, giving Sasha more time for healing. The nose that was fractured was still significantly swelled up. The sides of the face looked different due to general distention of the left side, and it was clearly visible that the health condition of the boy was far from being normal.

Doctor explained,

"Maria, Sasha is quite all right to be on a train. Sometimes, he experiences dizziness and headaches, but you know well that complete recovery after such a trauma with concussion takes always rather prolong time. I am sure that his present condition will not interfere with a long train journey."

Sofia added, "Everyone perceives that an elongated stay is truly unsafe for your family. Who could be certain that Captain Sidorenko let you easily go? You put him down. Usually, demonic people, like him, could not forget it."

Maria decided not to argue. Those people did everything possible for her children and her. She did not feel that just the fear for their own lives ruled out this unexpected suggestion. They were sincerely concerned regarding the revenge. Sensing their desire to assist her, Maria asked,

"How can we arrange everything for tomorrow? The train to Moscow is in the morning."

Dr. Leskov answered,

"I've made the arrangement with one of my former patients."

"Camp patient?" Maria asked.

"Yes. He'll give you a ride, but nobody should see him with you at the railway station. You have to manage everything by yourself."

Zina asked with fear in her voice,

"Who is that man? Do you know him well?"

Dr. Leskov explained,

"After the discharge from the camp, this man works as a driver of a small bus at one of the local mines. He rides to the railway station every other morning and picks up there the team of mechanics and two engineers from 7 o'clock train. He transports them to the mine. Tomorrow is his day to pick them up."

Sofia added,

"He promised to be here at six in the morning to pick you up with the kids and bring you to the railway station by 7 a.m."

"I'd like to go with Maria, can I?" Zina asked.

Dr. Leskov replied with joy,

"Of course, you can. Then you'll help Maria at the railway station with getting the tickets and taking the train. Maria, I prepared the health notice for Sasha to the railway station cashier, in order you can purchase two lower berths. Otherwise, they can give you only one lower berth. Sofia and I worried about your departure. Zina changed the whole situation. However, you are the woman who understands us. I am honest with you. We are chained by the government officials to stay and work here, and it's better not to aggravate our situation, as well."

"Certainly, doctor. I feel bad that my tragedy made your life more complicated," Maria responded to his straight explanation.

"Zina resolved our worries to some extent. I mean, how you'll manage staying in line for more than an hour for the tickets, and then loading heavy things into the train with Tikhon in your arms. Sorry to say but Sasha is not a big help for now."

Sofia added,

"Maria, the train stops for five minutes. Be careful. Watch…"

Zina decided to go to the railway station due to two reasons that she did not want to mention at the table. Maria interrupted her thoughts with a smile,

"Zina, you'd better tell us the truth-you want to be certain that nothing unexpected will happen to us, and we'll take the "*right*" train, in the "*right*" direction, and without *"special assistants* from KGB."

"You are right, Maria. But there is another important point: it is easier for me to return home from railway station with the evening train for the workers."

Glory to You, O Lord. Glory to you!

Chapter 21

Next morning everything went in accordance with Dr. Leskov's plan. Zina helped Maria with purchasing of the tickets and bringing the suitcase to the compartment. Two minutes left to the departure of Maria's train Magadan-Moscow. Maria's suitcase and both bags with dry bread and some other foods were packed inside of the box under Maria's lower berth. Zina warned Maria regarding the criminals,

"Maria watch, they can steal everything, if you do not keep an eye on your belongings." Maria could hardly focus at the warnings of a caring woman. She hugged Zina and thanked sincerely for being a great support to everyone in Kurbatovs' family.

"Zina, I wish I can take you now with me! For the whole my life, I missed a devoted and considerate mother. I was happy when I found such a wonderful person, like you. However, the tragedy separates us. Zina, the moment I am saved and settled with kids, I want you to arrive and stay with us. We love you, Zina. You are our family."

"Maria, I also love all of you, but I am too old to change anything in my life. Be happy, take care of yourself and kids, and please, do not forget my words – you are too young to be alone. You need a strong shoulder and a good heart to help you with upbringing your boys.

Another thing you need to keep in your mind-your sons will grow and leave. With God's blessing, they will have their own families. It's very difficult to be alone for the rest of your life."

They announced the departure of the train, and Zina kissed the kids and Maria. The woman moved quickly to the exit door, and in a minute, Maria saw her outside near their window. Zina burst in tears, as if it was the departure of her own daughter and grandsons. The train moved slowly. Zina walked, looking at them and waving with her hand. She cried bitterly. Both boys waved her, too. The train moved faster, and Maria saw how the elderly woman tried to catch the speed, in order to see longer their faces. She stopped only at the edge of the platform, and they could not see her anymore. Maria could not stop crying.

The conductor was collecting the tickets of the passengers and asked Maria,

"Who was that nice woman?"

"A mother, a real mother," Maria answered.

"She is very kind, isn't she?" the conductor asked.

"She is the best," Maria replied. "I was blessed to find the kindest mother."

Maria's answer made the conductor smile,

"All mothers are good. You must be a good mother, too. Look at you boys. They are sad, because they miss their grandma. You are a good daughter. When you love your mother, your kids will also love their grandma. One love creates another love from generation to generation."

Maria did not argue with the conductor, but had her own opinion, "It's not always so simple that one love creates mutual love. My father, brothers and I loved Maman, and she loved, but not us-another man. The affection for another man was more important for her than all of us with our love."

Maria hugged her boys and thought, "They were born from our never-ending love with Alex. Then Zina added her heartfelt love. Now, they have only me. For less than a month, my boys lost two loving people. Who will substitute the incomplete love for my sons? Up till now, I experience the absence of Maman's love."

Maria kept in her mind that she did not have chance to talk to Sasha about the changed personal data. She looked around. All the passengers were busy with making their berths and preparing small train tables for lunch. The scenery outside was dull: snow, hills and one-sided short trees.

Maria looked around and thought, "Most of these people would accompany us for several-week journey, until we arrive to Moscow – our destination point. I have to be careful, but I must talk to Sasha without delay. It was nice that Dr. Leskov gave me a notice that Sasha is after severe concussion. In case I need it, I can explain to the authorities that my boy does not remember one or two data due to his recent trauma. Poor Sasha, it was not easy for him to learn from the Leskovs that he was not Kurbatov any longer. Dr. Leskov told Maria that the boy was disappointed with the news and for some time, he did not want to discuss it. Later, he came to the conclusion,

"I know why our mother retreated. She settled on our lives; I mean, Tisha's and mine. Our Mama learned that they would never release her alive and leave us alone. There was no any other way to protect us from life-threatening menace."

Tisha watched passengers in their compartment. Their neighbors were ready to have lunch. When the boy saw food on their table, he looked at his mother and asked silently with his stretched hands his usual "Give me". Maria opened the bag, prepared by Zina and Sofia in the evening, and fed her boy.

The monotonous sound of the train made Tisha relaxed, and he fell asleep after his lunch. Maria decided to use the time while the baby slept, and asked Sasha to sit next to her on her berth. She opened him the secret of their true liberation. She was pleasantly surprised to learn, that Dr. Leskov had prepared the boy, and Sasha knew his new-fangled last name, date and place of birth.

Maria inquired with some fear,

"Sasha, what is your opinion regarding all the changes in our personal data? Was I right signing their requirements in exchange for our leaving from Magadan zone?"

It was so important for Maria to hear her son's verdict regarding her renunciation from the family history. New guilt stuck in her mind, as the old one that she carried from home-coming in 1946. The double guilt did not want to move away. Maria felt, as she had betrayed everything that bonded them in their mutual life. The guilt restated again and again that she dishonored the memory of her beloved husband, as well as his and her ancestors. Maria felt close to passing out, while waiting for Sasha's delayed response.

In one thing she was certain, "I would never do it, if I was by myself. The lives of our sons were in danger. Being a mother, I had no right to allow the kites tear my sons up. Otherwise, I am not a mother. I hope, my sons will understand my deed and will not blame me in future."

As long as Sasha did not answer right away, Maria figured out, "My son is against my decision. He considers my deed, as a treachery. Since now on, I am a traitor for him."

Maria touched Sasha's shoulder. He turned and looked at her. His eyes were filled with tears. He whispered,

"Mama, I can understand that there was no any other way for us to stay alive. For seeing you again, for touching your hands, for Tisha's smile, I would do the same. I prayed a lot and asked God to explain to our late father that you chose our lives. You are brave and smart. Thank God, we have you, Mama, and three of us are released."

Maria hugged her son and burst into tears. She felt like a heavy weight fell off her chest. It was not easy to receive her son's approval, because he was a younger version of his father, and any negotiations with an enemies, yielding or compromising was not acceptable by their honorable nature.

Sasha felt sorry for his mother. He whispered several times, using French word *Maman*,

"It's all right, Maman. Everything will be all right. Tisha and I love you very much. Thank God, that the monsters released you, and you are with us. Now, Maman we travel together to our new life. Isn't it great? It's a pity that Dad could not make it..."

Sasha wanted to add something else, but he was interrupted by loud announcement of the carriage conductor, distributing freshly made tea to all the compartments.

"Hot tea. Freshly made hot tea. Who would like to have some tea?"

The conductor delivered hot teas to each compartment on a big tray. A strong, freshly made teas were poured in glasses with beautiful metal glass holders. It reminded Maria silver glass holders in Kurbatovs' and her houses. Maria ordered three teas. When the conductor put teas on their table, she glanced at Maria with sympathy and said,

"Don't worry. Your mother is still strong. I saw how she ran along the platform. When she is older, you'll take her from here."

Maria smiled and did not answer.

In a couple of hours, Maria got acquainted with three more people in their compartment. One of the top berths in their compartment was occupied by an engineer from Moscow. It was his business trip to

Magadan. The side berths were occupied by an elderly couple from Magadan. Maria could easily see in both of them the former camp personnel. They examined everyone with suspicion, including Maria and children. Then a woman asked,

"Where are you from?"

Maria named the place, and it developed even bigger suspicion.

"What did you do there?" asked a man.

"My husband and I worked there at the local hospital."

"What are you and your husband?" the neighbor woman continued her investigation.

"We are doctors," Maria answered.

"Ah, they sent you there after school, didn't they? And you stayed for longer term than you planned. Am I right? The kids were born there, weren't they?" It was clear that the woman was satisfied with the results of her observation. Then she continued,

"It happens pretty often. The specialists come for their residency and stay for several years, making bigger money in Magadan region than in central and western part of the country."

Maria thought with a skeptical smile, "If these salaries are bigger, then what do they pay doctors in the central regions of the country? Poor Alex! He did not even learn how *rich* we were in comparison with the physicians in European part of Russia."

Maria did not want to release any personal information. She agreed with the woman, saying,

"Yes, you are right. Many young specialists arrived for two years and worked longer for our hospital."

The woman was ready to continue the conversation. She noticed Maria's black shawl and asked again,

"Somebody died in your family. I saw your mother, so it must be your father?"

For the first time, Maria declared it to a complete stranger:

"No, my husband passed away."

The man asked,

"When did it happen?"

"In March," Maria answered.

"Oh, really? How did it happen?" the annoying woman asked.

"I am sorry, but I am not ready to talk about it. It is still very painful for me," Maria replied with some irritation in her voice.

"He probably drank a lot, as most of the doctors. You know, they receive alcohol and drink it instead of using for the treatments," the woman concluded out loud to her husband.

"Now all of them are drunkards," her husband replied.

Maria did not argue with the rude couple. "Nevertheless, that she looks different, but she reminds me nurse Slender from the lazaret in GULAG (force labor camp for political prisoners). Nothing can change these offensive, disrespectful and bad-mannered women."

Maria unpacked her food bag and covered their table with beautifully embroidered placemats. Then she found Tisha's small plate and put two slices of a cabbage pie on it for Sasha and herself. They drank tea with pie and watched Tisha, who was happily smiling, while sleeping.

Sasha suggested,

"Mama, let us teach Tisha his new name during this trip. He needs to get used to it for a month. I am grateful to God that they did not insist in changing of my name."

Maria agreed,

"Sasha, you are absolutely right. We'll teach your brother a new name while traveling. We should not waste time. He is small and for a month, he'll learn his new name."

Sasha thought for a minute and said,

"I'll call him Va-nju-sha. It's closer to Tisha. How are you going to call him?"

"I don't know. Maybe, Ivanko," Maria answered. It was the Ukrainian version from Ivan. She recollected her childhood and their coachman Ivanko, who continued working for her Papa, when other servants had left them. He was always respectable to Count Kotyk and nice to his children. Ivanko used to take them for a ride around the estate.

Tisha interrupted their quiet snack time with a loud scream. Maria turned to her baby, calming him down,

"Be quiet, my boy. Be quiet, Ivanko. Your Mama is with you."

She pronounced for the first time a new name of her baby.

"Why does he cry?" Sasha asked.

Maria explained,

"Ivanko opened his eyes and saw everything new around him. Poor boy, he was scared."

Sasha called his brother,

"Vaniusha, are you hungry? Look what I have-it's a pie. It's a very tasty cabbage pie. Aunt Sofia baked it for us yesterday."

Tisha sat down on the berth and bit from his brother's pie. Maria cut a boiled egg for him, and food changed Tisha's mood: the baby-boy became happy and began to talk to Sasha in *his* language. From time to time, Tisha made funny faces. He looked a bit disturbed, probably, due to Sasha's insufficient comprehension and poor knowledge of Tisha's language. It looked funny, and even the rude couple of former camp watchers laughed.

Maria's mind redirected her from boys, "It's a very long journey, but I have food only for four-five days. What shall I do then? Today or tomorrow, I must talk to the conductor. I am not the only one who travels with kids. The conductor looks like a compassionate person. She knows the big railway stations on the route of our train. Normally, they have buffets there, where I can run and buy some food, at least for children. Tea with dry bread is good for me."

Maria prayed silently, "*Help us, save us, have mercy on us, and keep us, O God, by Thy grace.*" Then she prayed for Alexander's soul and asked the Lord to forgive her late husband all his sins. Maria wanted to believe that it was Alexander, who helped them in spirit to leave the Magadan zone alive.

Lord, have mercy!

Chapter 22

It was the end of the second week of Maria's and children's journey. Dr. Leskov was right: it did not interfere in any negative way with Maria's and Sasha's physical conditions. On the contrary, they felt better and gained strength during their trip. One morning, Maria woke up at 4:25 a.m. and sat down by the window. It was too dark to observe the scenery along the train track. Maria was thinking about her dramatic life changes during the last month. She lost the most devoted and loving person. No matter how difficult it was, but Maria had to admit that the tragedy brought liberation to her children and her. "With the price of his human life, Alexander opened the door of the cage and let us go." Maria whispered, "Thank you, darling."

Maria did not want to think about their future life in the Ukraine. She still had more than two-week voyage to Lviv. She was grateful to God, their journey from Magadan could not be compared with her banishment to GULAG in 1946. At the big railway stations, Maria learned to run and buy from the women on the platform some bread, salty fish, or potato-cabbage pies, hard boiled eggs, boiled or baked potatoes, beets, onions or fresh dairy products, such as milk and cottage cheese, so her children were not hungry.

Maria dreamed, "I wish, I meet my sister Jennie in the Ukraine upon our arrival. She will help my kids and me. She is thirty now. I am sure that she has her own family. She will be happy to see us – survivals. She does not remember me, but as our Papa used to say, blood is thicker than water. It means that she will not allow us to be homeless beggars, just because we are sisters. She was the one who I wanted to rescue the most, when I decided to come home in 1946."

The recollection of those events was very disturbing, and Maria started to pray. It was nice to pray when her fellow travelers were still asleep. She did not like somebody's watching and interruption of her meditation. Maria learned to connect herself to the stream of pure Divine energy while praying. Her strength, emotions and thoughts became balanced, and Maria sensed herself more aligned. She felt more energized after each meditation and could continue easier with her daily routine. Maria always ended her morning prayers with the words, *"Having asked that the whole day may be perfect, holy, peaceful, and sinless, let me commit myself and all my life unto our God. Amen."*

Maria smiled, watching her boys sleeping peacefully. She thought, "Thank You, my Lord, for my wonderful boys. I love them more than anything in my life. I am eternally grateful to You for miraculous chance given to me on the parking lot of Magadan KGB office. It made this trip possible for my children. Glory to You, oh Lord! Glory to You!"

The monotonous noise of the train and sincere worshiping made Maria relaxed, and she dozed, sitting by the window. She saw a short dream, as she used to see them in the early mornings. Maria saw herself with three children in a magnificent cathedral, where nuns directed them out. They were not angry with Maria, but they wanted her to move forward, not to hide there, waiting for some kind of resolution. Then she found herself in a palace, screaming loudly for help. She attracted somebody's attention and that "somebody" invited her and three children into his office. Maria was awakened with Tisha's voice, calling her,

"Mama, Mama."

The woman experienced a pleasant sensation after her unusual dream. She did not see its final part but being there and fighting for something vitally important made Maria blissful. The disturbed woman hadn't seen her victory, but somehow, she sensed it.

Maria hugged her boy and exclaimed,

"What a dream your Mama had! Why did you interrupt it, Ivanko?"

Sasha asked from the upper berth,

"What are you talking about, Mama?"

"I saw a dream, Sasha. At first, we were in the cathedral and then in a beautiful palace. The architecture and design of the palace were magnificent. By the way, there was a tiny girl with us. The people in the palace were polite to me. However, I was yelling at them, blaming them in our misery. Somehow, it was more like acting, in view of the fact that I felt happy inside."

“Mama, why did we go there?” Sasha inquired.

“I don’t know, Sasha. I only remember my unusual behavior. It’s hard to imagine that I have been in disagreement with those nice people and screamed at them and called them names. Not nice names.”

“What names did you call them?” Sasha asked with laugh.

“I called them demonic leaders, traitors, criminals, executioners, and some other names…” Maris explained.

“How did they react?” Sasha asked.

“They were not angry. I didn’t pick up their hatred,” Maria answered and concluded, “They were concerned about us and our situation.”

“Then tell me whose baby did you see in your dream? Where did you get the baby girl from?” Sasha was teasing Maria.

“Oh, it was another strange part of my dream. It looked like it was our girl there, your younger sister. Isn’t it funny?” Maria smiled.

“How old was she?”

“She was like Ivanko now… or a little bit younger,” Maria said.

She thought for a while and concluded,

“Nevertheless, it was just a strange dream.”

“It’s an odd dream, Mama,” Sasha replied with Alex’s intonation in his voice.

“Maybe, you are right, sonny. It’s a very strange dream, but it did not leave a heavy feeling inside. It was a dream that brought a feeling of hope and uplifting.”

Sasha sat down on his mother's berth. He embraced the shoulders of his tiny mother, saying,

"You are special, Mama. I wish you always remain like this, our romantic Maman, who still enjoys fairytales. I like your smile and want you to be happy."

On April 10, 1958 at 7:45 a.m. the train Magadan-Moscow arrived to one of the Moscow Railway stations. In order to continue their journey to the Ukraine, Maria and children had to change the train station and take a train "Moscow-Lviv" that would take them to Lviv. Maria carried Alexander's bag and was grateful to Zina for attachment of wide padded shoulder strips to it. Zina made it convenient to wear it, as a backpack, and Maria had free arms to carry Ivanko. Sasha carried their suitcase. He gained his strength during their trip and became again a good assistant for his mother. They did not have a single bag with food. On the morning of their arrival to Moscow, all of them were hungry.

They took a taxi and moved to Kiev railway station. There, they found the train schedule on the wall and defined that a direct train Moscow-Lviv departed an hour and ten minutes ago. They had to stay at the station until 7:05 next morning. Maria was not against staying for several hours out of the train on non-shaking ground. She was not sure about Ivanko. It could be difficult for a boy to wait for 24 hours in the railway station.

During the trip, the boy got used to his new name, and Sasha joked that his younger brother liked his new name better than Tisha. Maria was not sure about it, but nobody could express another option: the boy was still too small to say anything against it. They took their luggage to the cloakroom and went to have a hot breakfast at the nearest café. Everyone missed freshly made hot soup and kasha. Even small Ivanko ate it with pleasure. For a month, they were tired of cold foods and hard-boiled eggs.

They were about finishing their breakfast at the café, when a man from a Tourist office appeared at the door and invited new guests of Moscow on a daytrip around the city. Maria asked for the ticket prices and, when she found out that she had to pay for one adult and half of the price for Sasha's ticket, she agreed to participate in a trip to the places of interest of a famous historical city.

Maria thought, "Seeing the sights of Moscow would be beneficial for Alex. For 12 years in this country, we were not given a chance to be anywhere and see anything. Those Russians who lived in Magadan region had no idea how Moscow or Leningrad looked like. Few of them had knowledge about those big historical cities, just because time ago, they resided in those cities and were arrested and thrown into GULAG. After the discharge from the labor camps, none of them was allowed to return back home."

Maria recollected that the Kurbatovs used to have their winter house somewhere in Moscow and mentioned that fact to Sasha. Maria remembered Alexander's dream to visit Moscow after the release from the camps. He would like to find their family house, if it was not destroyed during the revolution and World War II.

Then Maria added with her beautiful smile,

"Your grandmother, Madam Kurbatov, recollected several times the magnificent beauty of their house and spectacular balls that her parents liked to arrange during winter season."

Sasha listened with great attention, absorbing each word from the history of his family.

"Sasha, your great-grandparents and grandparents lived really amazing life in this country, serving God and tsar. To their huge regret, they had to immigrate to France after the revolution of 1917 and underwent the hardships of a very difficult transitional phase. They lost everything in Russia."

"Mama, how did they survive in France?" Sasha asked.

"The parents of your grandfather Count Kurbatov owned several houses in southern part of France. In 1915, your great-grandparents purchased a huge Parisian house in a very prestige and picturesque area. It was a wedding gift to their son and his wife – your grandparents. The hardships forced your grandparents to sell it. You father took me there one day, and I saw the castle from a distance. It was a real castle, Sasha. It was two times bigger than your grandmother's castle in western Ukraine."

"Where did they live after selling it?"

"They purchased a small house in Paris. On that time, they could hardly afford an assistance of a single servant. When they moved into a small house, your grandmother expected your father Alexander to be born. Your grandfather invested the rest of their money from selling of the castle in purchasing shares of one of the leading steel companies. He was a successful businessman. They sustained well their life in France but had never achieved the same level of life that they had in Russia."

The tour bus was half empty, for the reason that it was too early for people to go on three-hour ride. Ivanko fell asleep after warm and tasty breakfast, and Maria comfortably positioned him on a seat. Sasha and Maria had a great opportunity to see all the monuments, historical and modern buildings, theaters, libraries, cathedral and university without baby's interruption.

They made a ten-minute stop at Novo-Devichy Monastery. Sasha stayed in the bus with Ivanko, and Maria entered the monastery church. When she was lighting a candle for the soul of her murdered husband, she noticed a heavy look of one of the women from their group. Maria did not have any doubt about that person who belonged to KGB and was assigned to escort the groups of tourists. She did not want to think that the representative of the KGB pursued her personally. "I do not think that they are still interested in my kids and myself. I am a widow Maria Gnatiuk and have nothing in common with Countess Maria Kurbatov."

The excursion was interesting, and Maria was pleased with her correct decision to take a tour and see a real beauty of the historical city. In a way, the trip connected Sasha to the history of his family.

When they were back to the Kiev railway station there was plenty of time for discussion. Usually, Maria was preoccupied with some work at home. At the moment, there was no work, as well as there was no home, and she was there for her kids only.

Sasha was disappointed with one thing,

"They did not show the Kremlin for tourists. It's the most interesting place to see."

Maria replied,

"The soviet government sits there, running the political, financial and economic life of a gigantic communist country, as well as its security. They make the decisions to humiliate and imprison millions of their citizens or "*humanely*" release their ideological *enemies*, sanctioning them to live far away from here without the right to be settled in their own houses and with their families. They can do anything, even to murder *accidently*, like in the case with your father."

Maria smiled bitterly, recollecting the words of the camp commandant:

"Sasha, the commandant of our camp used to say, 'No person, no case.' There was no punishment for their evil deeds, on the contrary, the government rewarded them for *uncovering* so-called, *suspicious elements*, who were not supportive enough of the decisions and orders of the communist party and the *dictatorship of the workers*."

Maria thought for a while and then added,

"I feel sorry for them, since they are destined to witness how their innocent children and grandchildren will pay for their mortal sins. In all the times, it was the most painful punishment to those who initiated the cruelty. They watched the misery of their children and grandchildren. Poor following generations! They will not understand why their lives are so complicated and misfortunate. Their grandparents and parents will always deny that their vicious actions are the main source of despondency of twelve following generations."

Sasha asked anxiously,

"Mama, what was done in our family that my Dad was killed, and you suffered a lot?"

"I don't know a lot about the ancestors of your father. My mother caused an issue. She left us when I was ten, as the oldest out of four children. She chose personal happiness and made Papa and us unhappy. That's the only wrong personal deed in the family that I acknowledged," Maria answered.

"One sinful deed, and all of us suffer. If the person repents with time, will it work?" Sasha inquired.

Maria thought and explained,

"We talk about mortal sins, son. In some way, probably, it will."

Maria re-directed the subject,

"Let us talk about the case with your father. How can the killers be remorseful to your father? Who can they ask for forgiveness? How could they be in harmony with the person they brutally murdered?"

Sasha tried to find the way out for the children of the sinners and asked,

"If they pray to the Lord, asking for forgiveness, will it improve the life of their children?"

"It doesn't matter that later, some of them would blame their blind belief in communism and curse the dictatorship of workers. They allowed themselves to forget the God's laws. They gave permission for evil to mislead them in order to obtain the power over other people. It was their choice to jump out of the God's boundaries, become crazy, and dance under evil's accords."

Sasha concluded, "Well, they are people without faith. They became atheists. They live without God. They do not believe in God's punishment."

"You are right. They live under their crazy slogans:

"Religion is the opium for people. Faith controls human instincts. Destroy timidity! Freedom to instincts! And so on, and so forth…"

Then the boy asked,

"Can anybody escape the punishment?"

Maria answered,

"Not from Above. However, it depends what punishment they are *sentenced* for. Sometimes, nothing dreadful can happened to them, but I feel sorry for the following generations."

"Do you think they know, why everything goes wrong with their children or grandchildren?" Sasha asked.

Maria said with firmness in her voice,

"When people become older, most of them comprehend the weirdness of their mindset in younger years. God shows them signs of His disapproval through observing an arrogant thinking and eccentric behavior of their children, they recognize themselves."

"How do they know that it's their punishment?" Sasha inquired.

"One day, the Creator forces them to admit it," Maria replied and continued,

"They live in fear that pulls many of them to suicide. They live in fear due to suicidal tendencies of their children. The fear and anger make them addicted to alcohol. They witness how their children are involved in vandalism, homosexuality, inhuman sex addiction with sexually transmitted diseases and abortions, as a sinful murdering of the next generation."

Sasha listened to his mother, holding his breath. She stopped her explanation, and he immediately asked,

"Mama, you mentioned the strongest signs or *sentence* from Above, but what are secondary or less painful warning signs of the Lord? I think that different people were involved differently in crazy life, so the punishment may be less."

"You see, Sasha, for a parent, even the secondary signs are painful. What could be worse to know that you instigated physical and emotional suffering of your children, grandchildren, great-grandchildren to the twelfth generation? Consciously, the sinners may deny that they know the reason why their children aren't blessed with good health, success, true love, and real happiness. However, their subconscious mind knows the truth and they never find serenity."

"Mama, what can be done for breaking this pattern?" Sasha asked emotionally, looking for an exit from a vicious circle.

"People have to learn human responsibilities for every thought, word, step and decision in their lives, otherwise consequences can destroy not only the irresponsible person, but also the innocent one."

Glory to Thee, O Lord! Glory to Thee!

Chapter 23

Four hours left to arrival of the train "Moscow-Lviv" to Lviv. Maria was happy to hear the soft melody of her native Ukrainian and Polish languages in the carriage. She realized how much she missed her beautiful languages for over twelve years. She remembered everything that had happened to her and her husband in the Ukraine in 1946, but her unconditional love for her homeland was not diminished at all. She knew who destroyed their peace and had never mixed in her mind two structures together – her Motherland and harsh dictatorship of the *red octopus*.

Sasha interrupted Maria's thoughts with a question,

"Mama, where should we go from Lviv?"

"We'll go to Ostrig, Sasha. We'll go to Sister Olga's place. We need to find out how to get to Ostrig from Lviv. If we have some free time before the departure of our bus or train, I would like to show you one more historical city. Who knows what to expect in future? I wish you can understand why I brought two of you to this land."

"What city you would like to show me? Ostrig?"

"No, Sasha. I do not know a lot about Ostrig. I meant Lviv. It is not because I lived here, attended school, visited theaters, library, exhibitions or cathedrals with your grandfather. I want you to learn more about the land, where your mother was born, and see the real beauty of Lviv architecture."

Maria thought for a while and then continued,

"I haven't been to Lviv since World War II. To my mind, it was not ruined completely. Usually God protects such places."

"Mama, do you remember anything from its history?" asked Sasha.

"Certainly, Sasha. We must learn and remember the history of our land, city, town or village. We have to be grateful to God for His creations and for His blessing to live there happily, enjoying important moments of our lives."

Sasha smiled, looking at his mother. His mother returned to life. It was she who could discover the beauty and significance in every moment of their life. For the last half a year, his father stopped noticing the importance of the moments. Most of the time, he was probably in his mind-numbing thoughts that faded the colors of the life, making the whole picture uninspiring and lifeless.

"Mama, how old is Lviv?"

"If I remember it clearly, the first mention of Lviv in historical chronicles was in the middle of the 13th century."

"Do you know, who was the founder of Lviv?" Sasha asked.

"Certainly, Sasha. The city was founded by Prince Danylo Halitsky of Galicia, and he named it after his son, Lev. Prince Danylo built his High Castle on the edge of the picturesque Roztochia Upland and the old walled city Lviv was built at the foothills of the High Castle on the banks of the river Poltva. It belonged to Kievan Rus. Lviv quickly became the center of trade and commerce for the region. The city's favorable location on the crossroads of trade routes and the river Poltva that was used for transporting goods led to its rapid economic development. When King Danylo died, his son made Lviv the capital of Halych-Volynia."

"Historically it belonged to Kievan Rus, didn't it?" inquired Sasha.

"Not always, Sasha. The Galicia with its capital Lviv was taken by Poland in the 14th century. The part of nobility eventually adopted the Polish language and religion – Roman Catholicism. But vast majority remained Greek Orthodox. With time, a new subdivision or Orthodox Church took place, and Greek Catholic Church was founded which acknowledged the Pope's spiritual supremacy but followed the Greek Orthodox forms of worship and holiday calendar. Lviv became an important city in Polish-Lithuanian Alliance. During the Polish historical period, many churches were built in Lviv, such as Dominican, Carmelite, Jesuit, Benedictine, and Bernadine."

"So, Lviv belonged to Poland until the soviets annexed it, right Mama?"

Maria saw that she started the fire of interest in her son. She answered also with excitement,

"Wrong, Sasha. You are wrong. There was another period in Lviv's history. The 17th century brought to

Lviv's gates invading armies of Swedes, Hungarians from Transylvania, Russians and Cossacks. However, Lviv was the only major city of Poland that was not captured by those invaders."

"So, Mama, it looks like Lviv was unbeatable," Sasha concluded.

"Not always. The first time Lviv was captured in 1704," Maria answered.

"Who succeeded then?"

"As far as I remember, it was Swedish king Charles XII."

Maria looked seriously at her son and recommended,

"Sasha, learn history! Read historical books. It is very interesting to know about the historical development of different countries and cities."

"Mama, your history is various from my school history," Sasha complained. "I wish, I can learn your history at school."

Maria disagreed with Sasha,

"History is history. How different could it be? Usually, the historical facts are described in different sources, by different people, who lived at that time. What do you mean, saying that my history is different? You do not believe in accuracy?"

Maria smiled again and Sasha concluded, "How wonderful to see Mama smiling. After Dad's murder, I was so much afraid that she would never become my Mama. Thank You, Lord."

Maria tried to find out what was different between her and Sasha's history.

She agreed,

"Sasha, I can lose some details, because they slipped away from my memory. Other than that, history was one of my favorite subjects at school. Without knowing the history of your family, land and country where you have been born, you are not able to understand the present-day life. You acknowledge everything in comparison."

"Mama, it is obvious, but you have to read my school history book. The history of the whole world went somewhere in parallel with our history. The history of this country, the USSR, is the only one that is important, and the only one that we must know well. I learned from you and Dad that it is not true, and they are fictitious in description of many historical events. You are right, Mama, I have to learn the world history."

Maria hugged Sasha and said,

"It's awful, that you lost your father. He knew the history of his family perfectly well. They became noble since the time of Peter the Great. I cannot help you much with the Kurbatovs' side. The Kurbatovs were supporters of Tsar Peter's reforms. They assisted Peter the Great in his development of diplomatic, political, educational and economic connections with European countries. The Kurbatov brothers participated in construction of navy and merchant fleet that realized one of the Tsar's dreams and '*opened the window to Europe*'."

"Mama, you can be a teacher of history. I am eager to learn with you," Sasha was excited. "It's so interesting to learn the family history."

Maria replied,

"We'll start with the history of my family, the history of the land where my ancestors were born, lived and died. Then we'll study the history of the countries, which our ancestors visited or lived in. They were studying, working with diplomatic missions, doing business, or became camp inmates during or after WWII. We'll learn where your Mama became the happiest woman in the whole world, when my brave savior Count Alexander Kurbatov found me in the fire of the war."

Sasha listened to Maria with amazement. Then he asked again,

"When shall we start learning?"

"We have already started, haven't we? Ask and I'll answer," Maria replied.

"What happened to Lviv later, after 1704?" Sasha asked.

Maria paid Sasha's attention to the fact that the human world has been always undergoing different developmental changes, stages or cycles.

"The history of mankind is alive, Sasha. It exists since the Creator brought into being our land and the first people. The history is as interesting, as the life itself. Both phenomena are always in their progressive evolution. The dramatic or even tragic historical events cannot be explained by people, as negative or positive, correct or wrong. The fact that takes place in human life should be described by historians without judgment or personal interpretations. We need to learn the true historical facts."

"Why do you say this?" Sasha asked.

"Don't waste your strength in fighting with shadows. You see, Sasha, many people, including your father, cannot understand my non-fighting position. He wanted to correct the history when he blamed Captain Sidorenko for everything that had happened to him and his family. Well Sasha, answer my question, is there anybody who can change the tragic historical facts that took place with your parents in 1946?"

"I don't think so," the boy answered.

Maria continued,

"The situation has been aggravated by Dad's accusations of the demons. The demonic force always gets rid of the fighters with the past. People cannot change anything that occurred a second ago. If we did something wrong, it is better to analyze the situation and, facing the reality, find the reason why we did wrong. Analysis keeps us from repetition of our mistakes."

"You said that we cannot change anything that took place a second ago. What analyzing does? How can it improve the situation?" Sasha asked.

"We have to understand why we acted in the wrong way. When we find out what has pushed us in the incorrect direction, we'll avoid repetition of our mistakes. Anger, hatred and accusations never help us. They return us back. People cannot successfully move forward with the eyes looking backwards."

Sasha smiled. He imagined walking forward with his eyes looking back.

"Remember, Sasha, if you want to be happy, you should not allow your mind to circle around the same disturbing thought that somebody did wrong to you, and you did not take revenge or made somebody pay for it. Analyze, why it happened to you, learn the lesson, and let it go. Leave everything in God's hands."

Sasha was surprised to hear mother's position regarding the tragedy in the family. He could not understand, why his father was killed, and why they planned to get rid of the whole family. Now, it was clarified. Obviously, their father mentioned the injustice of the situation and blamed them for everything that had happened to the family since 1946.

"Mama, do you think that people should not try to correct the mistakes?" Sasha asked with hesitation in his voice.

"Sasha, was it only my or your father's mistake that we got in such a tragedy from the very beginning? The terrible war was over, and we believed in peace and friendship between countries. It was the dark history of this country, which we did not know at all. We did not know anything about the existence of another social structure, like socialism or communism that could easily grind innocent people, as the fascism used to do."

"Your father was an honorable man, devoted to his family. Nevertheless, his decisions were not always right. Since 1946, he allowed the seeds of anger, hatred and accusations brewed in his mind. Whatever he did in March of this year did not help him to correct the situation. It took his life and left three of us in the claws of the demons. Only merciful intervention of the Lord saved our lives and gave us the possibility for leaving the Magadan zone."

Then the boy changed the painful topic about mistakes in family life history,

"Mama, what else you remember about Lviv?"

"In 1771, following the First Partition of Poland, the city Lviv became the capital of Austro-Hungarian Kingdom of Galicia and was re-named in Lemburg. During the Austro-Hungarian Empire, the city became one of the most beautiful cities of Eastern Europe with its outstanding example of fusion of the architectural and artistic traditions of Eastern Europe, Italy and Germany. Before the WWII, many magnificent buildings in Renaissance, Baroque, and other classic styles were built. I wish I can show you, Sasha, the buildings with stone sculptures and carvings, particularly on large entrance doors, that were made hundreds of years ago."

"That means that being under the Austro-Hungary did not disrupt further development of the city, am I right?"

"Yes, you are. I remember some facts I learned at school about the changes in cultural life of Lviv under Austro-Hungarian ruling. Austria contributed parks, cobble stone streets and our famous Opera house. At that time many publishing houses, newspapers and magazines were established in Lviv. The literature written and published in Lviv played an important role to Austrian, Ukrainian, Polish, Jewish and Hungarian cultures. The translation work took place between those literatures, creating a truly unique European development that transcended national borders."

Sasha saw that his mother was proud for the history of her land.

"By the way, Sasha, the Russian typographer Ivan Fedorov found his new home in Lviv. He saw the rapid development of the culture in the city and moved his printing business here."

The train was coming closer to Lviv and Maria became more excited. She wanted to bring more interesting facts about her favorite city,

"Historically, Lviv was admitted as one of the most culturally developed cities in Europe. In 1842 the Schaerbeek-Theater was opened, and it was the 3rd largest theater in Central Europe. In 1857 the Baworowski Library was founded. In the very beginning of the 20-th century, the magnificent Opera House or City-Theater was opened, as a copy of Vienna State Opera House. From the very beginning, the Opera House offered different repertoires. They played classical dramas in German and Polish, opera, operetta, comedy, music concerts, performances and shows. I loved the architecture of the theaters and their acoustics."

"Mama, did they build the Universities in Lviv?"

"Oh, yes, they did. I forgot to mention that Lviv University was one of the oldest in Central Europe. Initially it was founded, as a Jesuit school."

"When was it founded?" asked Sasha.

"I do not remember the exact year, but what I know, they founded it at the very beginning of the 17th century. Its prestige was elevated with the incredibly interesting works of one of the world-known philosophers Kazimir Twardowski. He was the founder of Lwow-Warsaw school of logic."

"When did he live?"

"In the 19th century," Maria answered.

Maria was silent for a while, and Sasha saw that she was recollecting something. Then she said,

"I feel really sorry, but I forgot the names of two other mathematicians who worked with Stefan Banach. Three of them turned Lviv in 1930s into the world center of "Functional Analyses."

"Mama, why did you decide to go to Ostrig? I asked you once, but you did not give me a clear answer," inquired Sasha.

"I did not want anybody in Magadan to know where exactly Sister Olga resided after the discharge from the camp. Two days before she left, she talked to me and invited us to come to her place after our discharge. She mentioned that she would always be happy to help us. She kept in secret the place where she was planning to reside, so I learned her address by heart. For administration of the camp, Sister Olga named Korets convent, as a place of her residency in the Ukraine."

"Are we going to Korets convent?" Sasha asked.

"No, Sasha. I hope the address she has left for me is the one, where we can find Sister Olga. It's the address of her parents' house."

Sasha got nervous,

"Mama, but her parents could pass away, when she was in the camp."

"We'll find her, son. Do not hesitate. We'll find her. You will have a chance to see Ostrig, another historical town in Western Ukraine. The Old Russian Chronicle mentioned Ostrig for the first time in 1100. Ostrig was built as a fortified settlement of powerful Ostrogski princely family. From the 14th to 16th centuries Ostrig was the main residence of the powerful Lithuanian-Polish magnets, the Ostrogski princes, in the Volynian principality of the Great Duchy of Lithuania. Upon the extinction Ostrogski princely family, Ostrig was passed to the princes Lubomirski."

"What made Ostrig so famous that it was designated as a historical town?" Sasha asked.

Maria thought for a short while and answered,

"Several historical facts, Sasha, made this small town a well-known historical place. Ostrig was one of the main strongholds against the Tatars' raids in Volynia. In 15th century Jews settled in Ostrig. Jewish community in this town became one of the main Jewish centers in Volynia. They developed one of the most important centers of Talmudic learning in Poland-Lithuania. In 16-th century the Ostrig Academy was founded, as the first high educational institution in the Ukraine."

Maria thought for a while, recollecting the other important facts in Ostrig history and then continued,

"By the way, in 1580 the first typographer Fedorov opened the first printing shop in Ostrig with the First edition of the New Testament and the book of Psalms in Slavonic alphabet. Next year he printed the famous Ostrig Bible, a complete edition of the Bible in Slavonic text version. These events increased the importance of the town, making it a great center of commerce, religion and learning."

"Mama, I like how you tell me about the history of your land. You know it so well. What happened to this interesting town later?"

"Sasha, the history of my land is very interesting. At the end of the 17th century, in the Second Partition of Poland, Ostrig was annexed by the Russian Empire. Then it belonged to the Ukrainian Republic for several years after the revolution of 1917. Then it was again an administrative center of Poland until the annexation in 1939 by the USSR."

Sasha looked at Maria with admiration. He realized for the first time that his mother was an extraordinary person. She was knowledgeable not only in medicine, but she learned and remembered a lot of historical facts. It was so interesting to listen to her. He compared her with his teacher at school whose presentation of the material was emotionless and boring. Maybe, he was not sure that the material he explained to the school children was real, rightful and accurate? He tried to avoid answering the kids' questions, repeating the same phrase every time, "You'll find the answer for your question in the book, if you read it attentively." But the book did not reveal the answers to all the questions.

Sasha sat next to Maria, took her hand and kissed it, as Alexander used to do it. Then he said with excitement and pride,

"Mama, you are great! I would like to learn the history that you learned at school. It's so interesting. One very important fact I have understood today – we cannot change the history just because it happened in our past. Do we need to concentrate our attention on the future?"

"On the future?" Maria repeated and asked, "Why future?"

Then she continued,

"I don't think so, Sasha. If we focus our attention and thoughts only on future, we can lose ourselves in the present moment. If we are lost today, we cannot reach the future. Then all our plans, dreams and desires are worthless. Sasha, live today, and every morning, ask God to bless you just for today. May the Lord make you healthy, successful and happy today."

Maria hugged her son. She liked the way he absorbed everything she introduced him to.

"What do you think about dreams, Mama? Do you think that our teacher was right saying that dreams were good only for aristocracy? He underlined, 'They had nothing to do but sit by the windows and dream.'"

Maria smiled,

"I disagree with his statement. First of all, most of the noble men worked hard, as your grandfather and great-grandfather. They were physicians. Many other nobles were architects, engineers, politicians, diplomates and military leaders in the service of the kings, tsars or government. They did not waste their time just for sitting and dreaming."

"What else you did not like in his statement?" asked Sasha.

Maria replied,

"The second point of my disagreement is in my sincere belief that every person has right to dream, wish and desire. The dream of a person to achieve outstanding results in art, sport, music, in academic or professional fields can be more desirable than to grow only in physical parameters. I could not understand the soviet *law of equality.* It's falsehood and duplicity. All people are different. God created us that way. Different people dream about different things, and different things make us happy."

Maria has stopped in hesitation, whether she should say it to her son now or wait until he was older. Then she shook her head and said in a quiet manner, in order nobody could hear them,

"Every person is created by God and comes into this world with the definite mission to fulfill. The tasks are defined by Divinity. We are not made as Pinocchio or other dolls. Our souls know what we must do, what we need to accomplish, and what we need to achieve during one life. We must be the best in any field of our activity and do everything to the best of our abilities. Our Lord gives us time and opportunities to realize the purpose of our life. Glory to Almighty God for His benevolent patience!"

"Mama, how can I find out, what I must do in my life?"

"God will show you, Sasha. For now, your task is to be patient, organized and achieve the best results in anything you do. School period is given to everyone to collect the general knowledge of the previous generations. Later, you will use this knowledge, as a firm foundation to create something special that you are assigned for. The Lord makes people talented in different fields. One day, you'll discover exactly, what He has created you for."

"Did you discover it, Mama? Do you know undoubtedly that whatever you do is the right thing, and the Lord admits it, as the right choice?" Sasha asked.

"Yes, indeed. I mentioned that we can succeed in different fields. Studying and work are definitely very important. However, there is another important task for people."

"What is it?" Sasha asked.

"It's a family life. It is a very essential part of civilized human existence. To my mind, it is the most problematic part in Russia. In this country, it's much easier to become a good and dedicated doctor, engineer, worker or peasant than to be a loving, caring, reliable, supportive, loyal and responsible spouse and parent."

Sasha was intrigued with mother's explanation and asked right away,

"Mama, what is more important in family life? Where can we learn it?"

"This is not taught at school, son. People must learn how to become a thoughtful, patient, and caring parent and a grateful, supportive and considerate child."

Sasha was surprised,

"Is this all?"

Maria smiled and put her hand on son's shoulders,

"This is one of the most difficult assignments for every human being."

Sasha admitted,

"Mama, I did not even think about it. Who taught you to understand all these things? You did not have your mother."

Maria answered with a smile,

"Sasha, I had a wonderful father. My father was like yours. The dedication to the family and responsibility for well-being, education and happiness of his children meant a lot for him."

Sasha concluded,

"Mama, I was lucky to have you and Dad. I miss my father."

Maria sighed. Small Ivanko turned his sleepy face toward his brother. He stretched his arms and legs after long sleep. Maria sat on his berth and the child smiled.

"Good morning, Ivanko. Let's get up. In an hour, we'll be in Lviv. I'll wash my sleepy boy, change the pajama for something nice, feed you and, with God's blessing, we'll be ready to finish our journey."

The boy smiled again, as if he understood everything that his mother suggested. He was happy to see his mother and ready to go with her anywhere she wanted. Maria kissed him and went along the carriage to the restroom to wash him. She praised the Lord for the strength He returned to her. Maria could easily carry her baby son in her arms.

Glory to Thee, O Lord! Glory to Thee!

Chapter 24

The train "Moscow-Lvov" arrived at its final stop. Maria could not wait to get off the train. They had only one suitcase with them and nearly empty Alexander's bag with some dry bread in it. When they were on the platform, Maria stopped to observe the renovated building of the Lviv railway station. She closed her eyes and recollected her arrival from France in 1940, when her father met her near the train. Then she saw her second arrival with Alexander in 1946. The memories moved in her head like chronicles, quickly changing one after the other. Ivanko touched Maria's face. He wanted his Mama to open her eyes. Maria smiled, saying,

"Sasha, look at this beauty! We are standing near the famous Lviv Railway Station that was built at the beginning of the 20th century by Wladyslaw Sadlowski. It is constructed in an Art Nouvelau style. But the first train arrived to Lviv earlier, in 1861. When the present building of Lviv railway station was built, it was considered one of the best in Europe from the architectural and technical aspects. It was the main gateway from the Ukraine to Europe. What a magnificence! Right, Alexander?"

Sasha smiled, watching his mother. She looked different now. Sasha understood that his mother was happy to be home again. He answered with his father's intonation,

"It's gorgeous, magnificent, and marvelous, Maman."

They laughed, as there was no more tragedy, danger or fear. Small Ivanko watched them with a smile and then made a funny face that Maria and Sasha laughed again.

Maria looked at the huge wall clock. It was 11:47 a.m. She decided to go directly to Sister Olga. Being in the camp, Maria memorized Sister Olga's address and kept it in her memory together with the last words of a wise nun,

"Marie, in case you need, find me and I'll do my best to help you and Sasha with everything I can." Maria prayed every day for her wonderful mother in Christ, asking Lord to bless the spiritual nun with all the best.

Sister Olga was released right after Natasha's execution. They allowed Sister Olga to return to a small town Ostrig in Western Ukraine. She was born in the village, not far from that town. The tragedy with her husband and son took place in Ostrig, as well. Maria remembered their last evening together when Sister Olga mentioned with bitterness in her voice, "Marie, they are so "kind". They killed my beloved in Ostrig, arrested me there, and now, they decided to return me back to my place. I believe that the Lord watches all of us…"

So, Sister Olga did not know anything about Maria's staying in the punishment cell, having only a slice of bread per day and two cups of water. She did know anything of a special order from Moscow to discharge the Kurbatovs from the camps and not to liberate them completely. She did know about Tikhon's birth and Alexander's death. Maria was looking forward to seeing a person who could understand her better than anybody else.

On that morning, everything was so strange. Maria went to the station to find out, how they could get to Ostrig. The answer was short,

"You should go to the bus station and take a bus to town."

The bus station was in another part of Lviv. Maria did not mind taking a ride across the city in order to look at it and show Sasha, at least, something from her previous life.

Maria and children got into a city bus that went to the central bus station. On their way there, she saw a lot of changes in Lviv. Maria paid Sasha's attention to several monuments, buildings and squares that she recognized while they were passing by. It was her dream from student years to take a tour around Lviv with Alexander and show her fiancé the beauty of the city with great architecture and historical background.

Alexander's tragic death blew up all Maria's dreams and hopes. Maria felt lonely, but she admitted for herself that their long trip from Magadan helped Sasha and her to improve their physical conditions. She did not know, how long it would take to gain back completely her strength and usual optimistic spirit. Nevertheless, she was grateful to God for the noticeable positive changes.

The bus to Ostrig was scheduled in half an hour. The trip there required three hours with two stops. Maria was in a hurry to buy some food for kids. Thank God, everything was at hand and, in five minutes to departure, she was already in the bus with her children.

When Maria got into the bus, she noticed that Sasha looked pale. He whispered,

"Mama, I was nervous. I couldn't help waiting for you. It's for the first time in my life when I have clearly realized that Ivanko and I do not have anybody else in the whole world, except you."

Maria cuddled him gently, whispering, "Don't panic, please." Then she smiled and announced with enthusiasm in her voice,

"Look, boys, I found some foods for several days. Let us eat now. I know that all of us are hungry."

"Do we have enough to share with sister Olga?" Sasha asked.

"Yes, we do. I bought enough for four of us. Thank God, they arranged a small farmers market near the bus station. It is very convenient for the passengers. I must say that the prices are half lower than in Moscow."

Maria prayed quietly before and after meal, trying not to attract anybody's attention. After eating tasty foods, the children relaxed and fell asleep. Maria had time to think about everything that she would like to do in the nearest time. "God knows, I am not going to sit a day on Sister Olga's pension, especially with two boys. I must find any job in order to earn something for my kids and Sister Olga. I am forty in July, but she is much older than me plus nine years of unmerciful imprisonment, that distorted her a lot. She is lonely and without any assistancc. It will bc nicc to livc togcthcr. I hope she can stay with Ivanko, when I am at work."

Maria caught herself on the thought that the name Ivanko was tightly attached to her baby. She looked at him and smiled, "He is our patient traveler. He crossed the huge country. I must say that the baby did not give me hard time. Thank God, Ivanko tolerated the long journey quite well. The boy was patient to everything, but hunger. Maria recollected Zina's words: "Your boy is "a true man" and cannot stand hunger at all."

Maria looked at her elder son. She noticed that after Alex's death, Sasha gained non-childish look. She thought, "The tragedy and hardships changed not only the face of my son but his way of thinking and self-expression." She was pleased to conclude, "Sasha is stronger than I expected. I am grateful to You, my Lord, for changing a child into my best assistant."

The feeling of loss occupied Maria's chest with heaviness. She tried to be strong and not to demonstrate her grief in front of kids. However, Maria always remembered that it was she, who brought her Alex to her homeland for tortures, suffering and death. "Oh Lord, forgive me my sins. I did not protect my husband. I did not save my family from the disaster. Have mercy on us, oh Lord!"

The tears rolled out, falling on her black shawl and on Ivanko's coat. The women, sitting on the opposite side of the isle, noticed Maria's crying. One of them reached her with the hand and asked in Ukrainian,

"Who died?"

"My husband," Maria answered also in Ukrainian.

She was surprised that after so many years in France, Germany and Russia, she answered so easily in her native language.

"Oh, poor you," the woman replied. Maria heard how the news was delivered to another trip companion, and for some time, they discussed it between two of them. Then the woman turned again towards Maria and asked,

"Where do you go?"

"To Ostrig," Maria answered.

"You have your family there, haven't you?"

"No, I don't. I have my God-mother there," Maria answered and thought, "Why don't I go to my true God-mother?" Then she answered in her mind, "It is better not to start visiting the places and people where I can be recognized right away. Who knows, what is their attitude toward me after so many years in Germany and Siberia? I am sure that Sister Olga understands me better than others."

"Who is your God-mother?" asked the woman.

"Sister Olga," Maria replied.

"Oh Lord, was she the nun who was taken to Siberia? Were her husband and son killed about fifteen years ago and she became a nun?" The first woman asked.

"Yes, that's right. So, you know her well, don't you? How is she?"

"Poor you! She died two months ago," the second woman said.

"What? What did you say? Sister Olga passed away?"

Maria was panicky. She exclaimed from the bottom of the heart:

"Oh, my Lord! What should we do? I do not have anybody in the whole world. Are you sure about her death?"

"I was sick and did not go for her funeral, but my sister was there."

The other woman confirmed the terrible news, saying,

"Everyone knew Sister Olga. She lived alone. We met her on Sundays in the church. One Sunday she did not come to the service, and our priest sent women to visit her. They found her on the floor in the corridor. The door to the house was unlocked. Sister Olga was dead. People said that she, probably, opened the door to a stranger, and he killed her."

The first woman added,

"It is odd, but the killer did not touch anything in the house. Sister Olga had received her pension a couple of days before. The money was on the table, but the killer didn't steal her money."

Maria understood what happened to Sister Olga and burst into sobbing. Both kids awoke and Sasha asked,

"What's wrong, Mama? Tell me, what's wrong?"

The women looked at Maria with sympathy, but they did not know how to help her. They realized how close the widow was to her Godmother. Maria felt bad, she was about to collapse. Sasha asked the driver to stop the bus and open the doors in order the fresh spring air could draft inside. The passengers of the bus were helping Maria to combat a new shock.

Sasha asked fearfully,

"Mama, what's wrong? Please, don't faint! Not again, Mama! Don't die, please!"

Ivanko was sliding from her knees and screamed nervously. Maria caught the child and whispered in Sasha's ear,

"Alexander, they did with Sister Olga what they did with your Dad. We have to return to Lviv, but we do not have money to go back."

The passengers could not understand the situation. The driver came up closer and asked,

"Do you want to get out? Where do you need to go, Pani?"

She was pleasantly surprised with his old-fashioned "Pani", and Maria thought with hope, "Maybe, in the Ukraine not all of the people are "comrades" and "citizens", as it is in Russia?"

Maria was not able to answer due to a new wave of dizziness and weakness. In a minute, she could not pick up the voices of the people. Maria heard the mixture of sounds in her head, like an echo. She held Ivanko in her arms, and the baby boy was her only anchor that did not allow Maria to lose the connection with her present life.

A fast vision of her nightmare flew through Maria's mind: all three of them were beggars. The vision was so close with the reality that a poor woman felt it with all her inner sensors. She whispered,

"Sasha, we do not have money to return back, I mean to go to… somewhere else. I spent the last money for food."

Maria looked at the driver and whispered louder,

"I have no money to go back to Lviv."

"Pani, is Lviv your final destination?" asked the driver.

"No, it isn't," Maria answered in a low voice.

"Where do you need to go?" the driver asked, trying to find out how to help the poor woman.

"Blue Creeks," Maria answered. The new shock from her answer detached her a little bit from the previous one.

The bus driver asked the passengers,

"Please, help the widow to buy the tickets to Blue Creeks. She needs two tickets to return to Lviv and two tickets to reach her Blue Creeks."

The man from the back seat asked,

"How much do they cost?"

The driver gave him the exact numbers and handed Maria his own portion of money. She took it and whispered in Ukrainian,

"I appreciate it."

The passengers followed the example of the driver, passing to Maria some money. The driver checked the total amount and called Sasha,

"What is your name?"

"Alexander," the boy answered.

"Very well, Sashko. Take off your cap and go to the back of the bus. People will help you with the rest of money. Your bus will be here in five-seven minutes. I'll stop it, and you'll go back to Lviv and from there-to your Blue Creeks. Have you been there before?"

"No," Sasha answered.

"A nice place, I must say."

He pulled off Sasha's cap and pushed him to ask for money. The passengers were giving some money and Sasha whispered in Russian, "Thank you."

The driver reminded people,

"Do not forget, they need to get not only to Lviv but to Blue Creeks. It is one hour from Lviv and additional tickets are required."

The spasm grabbed Sasha's throat. But when he saw that people gave him some money with a supportive smile, he relaxed a little bit. The driver counted money and asked for two more rubles. Four people from the very back passed them to the driver. He smiles, saying,

"Sashko, you have two rubles extra. It's for candies."

In three minutes, the driver noticed another bus, coming in the opposite direction. He picked up Maria's suitcase and commanded,

"Follow me!" and ran out to stop the bus.

He talked to the driver for a minute and called Maria with children. Maria looked at the passengers and pronounced in beautiful Ukrainian,

"Thank you for your help. Be always blessed and happy."

Then she looked at the driver and said,

"I know that you are an angel. God bless you, angel, for good deeds and happiness."

The driver burst into laughing,

"I don't think that I am an angel, Pani".

Maria looked up and said,

"He knows better..."

Maria and children took the bus for their ride into opposite direction. Sasha went to the driver to buy the tickets to Lviv. The driver looked at him and said,

"We'll be there in 50 minutes. The driver from the previous bus asked me not to take money from you. Pay just for your mother's ticket."

"Thank you," Sasha said in Russian and then repeated the same in Ukrainian.

"Sounds better," the driver commented with a smile.

Glory to Thee, O Lord! Glory to Thee!

Chapter 25

Maria left the boys on the bench near the bus station and rushed into station, trying to find a bus to Blue Creeks. She could not find the name of her destination in the Schedule. The disturbed woman ran to the Information Office to get the information about her itinerary. In 40s, there was no bus connection with her Creeks. People used phaetons or cabs with 4 or 6 harnessed horses.

There was a line to the Information Office. When Maria's turn came, she asked the woman in Russian,

"How can I get to Blue Creeks?"

The woman did not look up at Maria and continued recording something in the Journal. Maria asked the same question in Ukrainian. The woman looked at her with a smile and named the bus number that stopped there. Then she looked at the clock and said,

"You should run there in order to catch your bus. It leaves in five minutes."

"I do not know where to run, and my children wait for me near the entrance to the Bus station," Maria answered.

"Today, we do not have another bus in that direction. Run, if you do not want to stay here until tomorrow."

Then the woman looked out of the window, checked that nobody else was inquiring about the buses that departed in the nearest time. She closed the window and rushed to the door of her office with one thought,

"I have met this woman in a black shawl before. I am sure that I have met her before. Where have I met her? Was it here at the bus station? I doubt."

Maria was surprised that the window was shut in front of her face. She needed further explanations. At that very moment, she felt that somebody touched her shoulder. Maria turned around. The woman from the Information Office stood behind her.

"Let us run," she suggested. "Otherwise, you will wait until tomorrow."

On their way to the bus, the woman asked,

"Have we met before?"

"I don't think so. I haven't been here since 1946," Maria answered.

The woman could not understand where it came from, but she felt that she got acquainted with the pale and skinny woman long time ago. She remembered the voice of the woman and the manner she talked.

"Do you live in Blue Creeks?" the woman continued asking.

"No, we don't," Maria replied.

Maria saw that the woman could not find where they met earlier. She picked up Ivanko and a strong woman grabbed the suitcase. She was running to the very end of the bus line, waving with her hand to the driver, asking to wait for them.

When they were moving in the line to take the bus, the young woman from the Information recollected where they met earlier. In 1940, Ganja brought her niece, a nine-year-old girl, for Christmas to the Kotyk's mansion. The child was impressed with tall Christmas tree that was beautifully decorated. Most of all, she was impressed by a young Pannochka that looked so elegant. The girl could not forget Pannochka Kotyk and after so many years, she recognized Maria. The woman put the suitcase on the ground and exclaimed,

"You are Pannochka. You are Pannochka Maria, a young doctor from …"

Maria interrupted her with a smile,

"And you are Oryssia, aren't you? Your aunt Ganja brought you to our mansion for Christmas?"

"Yes, I am."

The woman looked around. She did not want to attract anybody's attention to Pannochka's arrival.

Maria realized that Oryssia learned Kurbatovs' tragic story from nanny Ganja.

"Is Ganja alive?" Maria asked with the tension in her voice. She was not ready to hear that she had lost another devoted person.

Oryssia whispered,

"Yes, she is. She waits for you. For all these years, aunt Ganja was praying and waiting for you and your husband. She'll be happy to see you. I wish I can go there with you! Where is your husband?

"I lost him in March."

"I am sorry to hear that, Pani Maria. Where do you live now? Are you still in Russia?"

Maria sensed how a huge wave of pain arose inside of her. She replied with firmness in her voice,

"No, not at all. I returned home. At first, I go to nanny Ganja, and then I'll find what to do and where to reside."

It was Maria's turn to get into the bus. Oryssia stepped into it in front of Maria and talked to the driver for a couple of minutes. He pulled Maria's suitcase in and handed his hand to Maria, who carried Ivanko. Ivanko hugged his mother's neck tightly, showing that he did not want to be passed to a stranger.

Maria could not get in and called Sasha to help her. She was completely out of strength. At last, they took their seats and Maria heard how the driver promised to Oryssia to stop near Ganja's house in order Maria did not walk with two kids from the stop on the main road to the village.

Sasha put his head on Maria's shoulder and asked,

"Mama, how could you remember the Ukrainian language so well? I have not even known how nice it sounds when you speak Ukrainian."

Maria smiled.

"It's my native language, Sasha. All the rest languages were learned after this one. It was the rule of our house that at home we spoke Ukrainian. Then I learned Polish, French and German."

"Where did you learn Russian?" Sasha asked.

"It was in France, Sasha. I learned it with your father and his mother. They followed the same rule at home – Russian was for their home conversations."

The boy was concerned about learning a new language.

"Mama, what should I do with my Ukrainian?" Sasha asked.

Maria tried to release his apprehension,

"You'll learn it fast, Sasha. It's your mother's language. I'll help you, son."

Sasha looked at his mother with respect.

"I wish I know so many languages, as you do. Five languages! And you are fluent in them. I love you, Mama."

Maria embraced Sasha and answered, "I love you too, son."

It was dusk when the driver stopped the bus in front of Ganja's house. He helped Maria to get off with her heavy suitcase and sleeping Ivanko. Maria wanted to pay him some money for his extra stop, but the man refused to take it. Maria came to the gate and pulled it. It was not locked, but the dog was there, running around the yard and barking loudly. Maria was afraid to get in.

"Sasha, we have to wait until Ganja comes here."

In a couple of minutes, they heard the sound of the house door opened and somebody's steps on the porch. The unfamiliar voice asked,

"Who is there?"

Maria wanted to answer, but the spasm in the throat did not allow her to say anything aloud. The voice on the porch asked again,

"Who is there?"

Sasha saw that his mother was unable to answer and asked in Russian,

"Please, open the gate."

The voice on the porch answered,

"Come tomorrow. I do not expect anybody tonight."

Maria heard that the person opened the door to get into the house and called,

"Ganja, are you there? Pannochka Maria is here."

It was quiet for a minute, and then they heard the steps rushing to the gate. The voice behind the gate asked again,

"Who's there?"

Sasha answered,

"Please, open the gate. My Mama, Maria Kotyk is here. I am her son, Alexander."

Ganja opened the gate and could not move. Maria talked to her,

"Ganja, my dearest Ganja. I am back."

They embraced each other and burst into sobbing, as if they tried to cry out all the bitterness of the long years of separation. Maria was lamenting, when Ganja pulled her inside.

"Ganja, I lost my Alexander. I lost my beloved husband. He could not stand his life, Ganja, and I lost him. I brought him to this country that I considered my homeland, and they murdered him. They brutally murdered my love. How could I live without him? I have no right to live. It's all my fault. I am guilty. It's my sin in front of God. I don't know how to live with two boys without my Alexander. I don't want to live!"

The old woman could not move, she was shocked.

"You brought him again back to the Ukraine?" Ganja asked. "Do you mean that you brought Pan Alexander for a second time to the Ukraine and they murdered him? When had it happened?"

"No, Ganja. No. They murdered Alexander in Russia in March."

Mother's lamenting and disappearance behind somebody's gate, woke up and scared Ivanko. Baby boy began to cry.

"Who is there, Maria?" Ganja rushed to the gate again and noticed Sasha holding Ivanko in his arms. The old woman hastened her guests, taking them closer to the light. Ganja praised the Lord,

"Dear Lord! All my prayers have been answered, and I see Pannochka Maria again. Glory to Thee, my Lord! I prayed to Thee every day and asked for your miraculous protection and support of Your innocent servant Maria. My Lord, You were merciful and saved my Pannochka and her boy. I prayed for the opportunity seeing them before I close my eyes forever, and You had heard my prayers. Glory to Thy mercy, Oh Lord! Glory to Thee!"

The children and Maria entered Ganja's house. Maria blessed herself, looking at the big icons that Ganja brought from the left wing of the Kotyk's mansion after the fire. The fire did not touch the western wing and preserved the holy place where the family prayed daily.

Maria looked at Sasha and asked,

"Do you know, why the government of the Western Ukraine did not waste enormous assets for the construction of the prisons before WWII?"

Sasha shrugged his shoulders,

"Why?" He asked with curiosity, because in his understanding, people could not live safely without prisons. It was Magadan region with excessive number of force labor camps and prisons that presented the boy their incorrect '*protective*' conception.

Maria was proud to answer,

"We did not have so many criminals. Sasha, our people were born in faith. What were we mostly afraid of? The Ukrainians were afraid of trespassing the laws in the eyes of God. Everyone preserved faith in God to the end of the life. The true faith was inherited from parents to their children, as the most valuable gift."

Ganja was bustling near the stove, preparing supper and listening to the conversation of her guests. She decided to interfere,

"Everything had been changed, Pannochka Maria. The soviets ruined not only our life, but people's faith, as well. You do not find icons in most of the houses. It's forbidden to keep them at home. It's forbidden to pray and to attend churches. It's forbidden to teach children the laws of God. Usually, on Christmas and Easter holidays, the soviets arrange Sunday works for kids and workers in order nobody celebrate the Holy days. They send adults and children to clean the streets and collect recycle paper and metal."

Sasha inquired with surprise,

"Why don't you hide the icons?"

Ganja smiled,

"I am too old to be persecuted. Sorry to say, but the younger people were forced to get rid not only of icons, but of following the God's commandments. Pannochka, the crime and alcoholism arose everywhere. The modern people are not afraid of God's punishment."

"I see. They made the second Russia here. Ganja, I feel sorry about this."

Ganja put all the foods she had in her house on the table. The menu did not contain wide variety, but the food was natural, fresh and tasty, especially for hungry travelers. Ganja sliced some freshly baked bread and put it in the basket in front of the guests. Then she brought two crocks: one crock with curd and another one with fresh goat milk. She put a bowl with hot boiled potatoes and another bowl with cottage cheese. Ganja did not forget to slice an onion and sour pickles marinated with dill and garlic. The smell of foods made her guests feel starving.

Ganja checked the foods on the table and invited her guests for supper. The old nanny took a seat across the table in order she could see all of them. She noticed that Sasha enjoyed cottage cheese and curd milk. Maria was feeding Ivanko with some potatoes and cottage cheese. It was joy for Ganja to see how the baby boy tried her foods. Every time he picked up unfamiliar tastes and made different facial expressions while eating.

Ganja poured a big mug of milk for Maria and covered the cup with a slice of bread. She passed it with the words,

"Drink some milk, Pannochka Maria. You look so pale and exhausted. Goat milk and bread will restore your strength."

Ganja went to arrange the beds for her guests. She suggested Sasha to climb the stove and to sleep there. It was difficult for Sasha to understand the Ukrainian language. He tried to comprehend what Ganja meant about his place of sleeping. He walked around the huge stove, observing it with interest from all the sides and thought, "Who could sleep on the stove? Ganja must be joking."

Maria noticed Sasha's confusion and explained,

"There is a special place there on the big stove, where people enjoy sleeping. It is warm and nice there. When children or adults got cold in winter, they healed themselves with sleeping on the stove and drinking the special herbal teas or hot milk with honey and butter. Usually, the process of natural healing went much faster than with taking medications."

"It's interesting. Mama, I agree to try," Sasha replied.

When children fell asleep, Ganja sat down near Maria and cuddled her. Both women were speechless for some time. Then Maria put her head on Ganja's bony shoulder and asked,

"How have you been since they took us away?"

"There is nothing to talk about my life, Pannochka. I was praying and waiting for you."

Maria asked a question that concerned her to a great extent for all the years during and after the war, as well as for long years of force labor camp and after her discharge,

"Ganja, have you heard anything about my family?"

The nanny answered,

"Thank to the Lord, they all alive."

"Alleluia! Glory to Thee, o Lord! You mean that my grandpa is also alive?" Maria exclaimed.

"With God's will," replied Ganja. "We'll visit them one day. It's not fair that they haven't seen you for such a long time. You brought two wonderful boys, Pannochka. They will be happy to see the grandchildren. I told your family about the tragedy that happened to you and your husband Count Alexander Kurbatov. I was not sure that your child would survive after all the torchers and imprisonment. God is merciful. Only God could preserve the boy. Your son is a God's miracle."

"You are right, Ganja. Sasha is a miracle. He is my and Ivanko's support in our uneasy life, especially after Alexander's death. He looks like Alexander Kurbatov, doesn't he?"

Ganja saw Alexander for twenty minutes in the Kotyk's mansion prier the monsters bit him up and prier the mutilation. She remembered that Maria's husband was a very handsome man. The memory of the old woman kept all the details of their appearances so clearly, as if the meeting with the couple was the event of the previous week. Maria and Alexander were dressed in fine cashmere mackintoshes and stylish hats. Ganja thought, "Maria is blessed to see the live portrait of her husband in her son's appearance. Sasha is Alexander's younger copy."

Ganja poured some curd, took a slice of bread for herself and sat down on the bench across the table in order to watch Maria. She forgot about curd and bread, while she was observing her Pannochka.

Maria interrupted the silence,

"Ganja, where is my family? I cannot wait to hear about them. How are my siblings? Did the KGB allow them to return home? Did my grandpa leave the hunting lodge and move back to his house?"

Ganja answered,

"You, probably, heard in Russia that the Ukrainian army continued its fight against soviets in 1950s. Nobody wanted in the Western Ukraine their communist regime that took away God and so many lives from our people. The soviet secret service and NKVD troops eventually liquidated Ukrainian army, as a resistance forth, when they killed Roman Shukhlevych, the last UPA commander-in-chief. Moscow issued the law that they would not persecute people any longer who were in the woods. But who can trust them?"

Maria inquired,

"Who issued the law, Ganja?"

"Nikita Khrushchev did, he is the leader of the soviet government. Our people hate him. At first, they brutally killed so many innocent people, including women and children. Every night they arranged the arrests and deportations of the Ukrainian fighters' families to Siberian camps. What the family members were accused of? After all these inhuman persecutions nobody trusted moskals."

Maria asked with interest,

"Who are moskals?"

Ganja answered with a smile, "People from Russia or Moskovia, as they called."

Maria said,

"I feel sorry for those who are still in the woods."

Ganja continued,

"Last year, right after the announcement of a new law, some men returned from the woods. It is difficult to say, what happened to all of them. I knew one family in our Creeks. All men from that family were in woods in UPA from 1942. The oldest son took a risk and returned home. People said that KGB did not look for him or persecuted him. Since March, he began to work, as a driver in the local collective farm. I want to believe that they will not continue the repressions against those who are still in woods. I wish, your father and old Count Kotyk return to the normal life."

"Ganja, how old is my Grandpa?" Maria asked.

"He was in early 80s when you graduated from school in France. Since then so many years passed. With God's blessing, he is 102-103. He said that he cannot die, Pannochka Maria."

"What did he mean, Ganja?" Maria asked with her beautiful smile.

"He waits for you. He wants to see you and your children, Pannochka. He said that one day, when you come, you'd prove that he was right. Neither your father nor I had understood what the old count meant regarding the proof."

Maria certainly knew what her grandpa meant. It was his prediction. She sensed the chest pain again when Ganja mentioned her grandfather. Maria complained,

"I miss them so much. In the camp, I recollected daily my Papa and Grandpa. It was my dream to come here after the discharge from the camp and meet my family. Alexander was not sure that I could find anybody alive, but to my mind, he did not want to take a risk one more time. Ganja, did you hear anything about my sister Jenny and both brothers?"

Ganja felt sorry about Maria and narrated about them in the softest way.

"Yes, Pannochka Maria. I saw Jenny two times and learned from her about your brothers. Thank God, they are alive and healthy, but…"

Maria became excited,

"What do you know about them? Where do they live? What do they do? Did you tell them that I arrived here and was looking for them in 1946? Did you tell Jenny the ferocious story about Alexander and me?"

For a while, Ganja did not answer. She was silently looking with pity at Maria.

Maria was impatient,

"Ganja, tell me about them, please. I miss them so much."

“I haven’t seen your brothers, Pannochka Maria. I learned from Jenny that they are somewhere in the far north of Russia, working in the mines. From time to time, she received letters from them. She said that they earned good money there. When she was in technical school, they supported her financially.”

“Is my sister married?” Maria asked.

“Yes, she is. Her husband is an orphan, or one of those who was also taken from the decent family, like your sister Jenny. By the way, she considered herself an orphan, though I mentioned to her that your father survived. Do you know, what Jenny answered?”

“What? What did my sister say? Did she want to see her father and grandfather?”

Ganja sighed bitterly,

“She said that she preferred to be an orphan and never hear anything about “people’s enemies” like you, Dr. Kotyk and old Count.”

“Why did she believe in that nonsense?” Maria exclaimed. “How is it possible for my sister to believe in demonic lie? What did they do with my poor Jenny? They completely destroyed her psyche and her normal human perception with brainwashing.”

“As she said, they told her that your husband and you were “spies and terrorists”. Both of you were sent here for terroristic mission. As for your father and grandfather, she considered them “the bandits in the woods” or the active supporters of the bandits. I tried to explain the truth, but everything was in vain.”

"Where does she live? Maybe, I need to visit her one day and open the truth. She needs the truth, Ganja. She needs to hear it from me. Where I can find Jenny?"

Ganja answered with uncertainty in her voice:

"After technical school, they were sent to work at the construction of new collective farms near Odessa. She did not want to leave the exact address for me. In the orphanage, the soviets did everything in order our Jenny forgot her real family, native language and became a cold person with hatred in her heart."

"What does she do for living? Why did she choose the construction work?" asked Maria.

"As far as I understood that in accordance with their technical training at the orphanage school, her husband and she became painters and stucco-workers. They were sent for the constructions of the houses for collective farmers in Odessa region."

"They were small kids, when they were taken from the families to the soviet orphanages. The demons broke their spirits," Maria concluded.

"By the way, Pannochka, both of them are communists and do not believe in God."

The last sentence poor Ganja pronounced in a low voice, like something secret or dangerous. The eyes of a kind nanny were filled with tears.

Lord, have mercy!

Chapter 26

Maria remembered from 1946, how Ganja revealed Alex and Maria the sorrowful story about her fight for a little Jenny. She tried to hide Jenny and protect her from being taken away by special soviet services. The demons broke the arm of the caring nanny but did not leave Jenny with her. Maria was deeply upset with the story about her "baby sister". She admitted with bitterness in her voice,

"The demons won in my sister's case, as they usually won in the cases with younger children. I doubt, Ganja that they were so successful with my brothers. My brothers were older. However, it is difficult to assume. We did not see them for so many years," Maria said.

"You are right, Pannochka," Ganja agreed.

Ganja was observing Maria with attentiveness. She noticed that strenuous, dangerous and challenging life left deep and sore imprints on Maria. "Pannochka has no strength any more to jump in whirlpool of somebody's life in order to save her sister and brothers. She is tired with fights. It is too much for her, and she is right."

Maria verbalized out loud the statement that proved Ganja's observation,

"Ganja, presently my siblings are adults, and they chose their life sets in accordance with their understanding of righteousness. The life proved many times that my arrival here in 1946 was the worst mistake in my life. The demons did not kill my Alexander in 1946, they did it in March of 1958. What can I do for my siblings now? I'll pray for God's intervention. Only our Almighty God will help them to get rid of demonic possession of the *red octopus*."

"I'll pray with you. Every day, we'll pray the "Agreement Prayer" together, and our Lord will save their souls from darkness," Ganja promised.

"Sasha will be the third. He always prays this prayer with me," Maria replied.

She added with hope in her voice:

"One day, they'll come with love in their hearts to visit us and Papa."

"Pannochka Maria, what had happened to Count Alexander in March? If you have strength to talk, share with me your heartbreaking story. Tomorrow, it will be easier for you to wake up with partially unloaded pain. I can feel how your inner suffering rends your heart. It does not allow you to breathe and gain the strength to live."

Ganja stopped for a moment and continued with sincere request:

"Please, do not repeat again in front of God the words that you told me tonight. You must live for you and your sons. Otherwise, where else they will find true care, faith, understanding and mother's love? You do not want the orphanage for them and the replication of your sister's story."

"Ganja, I lost my husband. I lost my dearest Alexander. They murdered him brutally. In March, he visited Magadan KGB office and insisted in repatriation of our family to France. The demons killed him on the train on his way back home. Ganja, they killed him cruelly with an axe and left the axe near Alexander's bag with foods that he purchased for us in Magadan."

Maria became inconsolable. She tried not to awake her sons, but she had a strong desire to howl with all the strength. It seemed to her that she could ruin this old small house with the sound of howl that she suppressed inside.

Maria rushed to the corner with the icons and kneeled.

"Lord, have mercy! Forgive me, my Lord, but I do not know, how to live without my Alexander. The kids and I need the defense and care of a loving father and husband. We need the providing and encouragement of a strong man. We miss him so much. I have no strength to live. Do I need to live longer? Do I need to suffer of my guilt? I wish I have been with my husband on the train! I wish I die together with my Alexander!"

Somebody touched Maria's shoulder. The grip was rather strong, and Maria looked around. It was not Ganja. Ganja was still crying at the table. Maria understood-it was her Angel. He stopped her. He did not want her to sin and to ravage her soul. He did not want her to pay later for her weakness.

Maria closed her eyes and listened to his quiet voice,

"Stop howling, Maria. Do not disturb your late husband with tears and complaints. You survived all the hardships due to your patience. Do not change your essence. Do not make evil happy with your raving lament."

The weakness forced Maria to sit down on the floor. She silently asked the only question,

"What should I do now?"

"Live and prove to other people the presence of God in everyday life. It's your assignment to the end of your human existence."

Maria heard distinctly every word of her Angel. She whispered,

"Please, forgive me."

Ganja came up and helped Maria to get up from the floor. The old woman noticed that something had happened to Pannochka, but she could not understand what exactly.

"Are you all right? You do not feel well, Pannochka, do you?" Ganja asked.

Maria kissed Ganja's hands and answered with her childish smile,

"Thank you, Ganja. I am much better now," Maria replied.

"Pannochka Maria, what do you mean, saying that you are much better now? What do you thank me for?"

Maria explained,

"Ganja, you are absolutely right. I need to move on in my thorny life. I need to become patient again and prove to others the presence of Divinity in human lives."

"Pannochka Maria, it is nice, but not easy," Ganja said.

Then she added,

"I'll help you with everything I can. I have my dream: I want to see you happy again."

The women hugged each other and silently thanked the Lord. Then Ganja shook her head and went back to the table. They sat down at the table, talked and drank herbal tea with honey. It was well-known Ganja's tea. Maria remembered its taste from childhood.

Ganja knew better than anybody else, how much Maria suffered for the last thirty years of her life. The elderly nanny recollected for herself: "Poor Pannochka Maria could hardly survive her mother's departure, when she was ten. Then the war and concentration camp… Then 1946 home-coming with torchers in her own manor… Imprisonment and child delivery in the force labor camp… The draining mine work for ten and a half years in freezing zone… Loss of Count Alexander… They loved each other, they lived one for another…"

Ganja viewed how weak and pale Maria was and thought, "I hope that poor Pannochka Maria did not lose all her strength in the recent fights with demons. I feel sorry to admit, but all the hardships wiped up her beauty."

The tears rolled out of Ganja's eyes on her wrinkled face.

With all Ganja's understanding, the compassionate nanny could not imagine what her Pannochka went through during March and April. Maria tried to narrate in the least emotional way the recent events. She didn't want her nanny to suffer, but whatever she described, made Ganja's flesh creep. Now she knew, how the demons from the Magadan KGB crewed over innocent couple and destroyed the family.

"Beautiful, loving and happy family," Ganja emphasized for herself with disappointment. "They were not happy with their life in Magadan region, but they were happy with each other and kids. Count Alexander wanted better life for his beloved."

Ganja thought,

"Dear Lord! They wanted everyone in Kurbatov's family to be killed. The demons completely forgot one thing-they fought God's children."

Then Ganja looked at Maria and continued out loud,

"They decided to get rid of you and children, when Dr. Alexander refused to comply with their callous lot. The Lord miraculously saved you, Pannochka. He defended your pure soul, and look, you are here. Thank You, Lord!"

Maria was physically tired, and at the same time, she experienced alleviation inside. She thought, "Ganja was right, when mentioned that after my "confession", it would be easier to breathe." It was far after midnight when the women went to bed. When Maria was falling asleep, she recollected again the words of her Angel,

"Live and prove the presence of God in everyday life."

"I will…" Maria promised and fell asleep.

"Glory to You, oh Lord. Glory to You!"

Chapter 27

It was the second day of Maria's stay in Blue Creeks. She decided to walk around and to look at the changes that took place for seventeen years since the beginning of WWII. In 1946, she was not given a chance to show Blue Creeks to her Alexander.

Maria walked along the street in the direction of her mansion. It seemed like an invisible force pushed her there. In a distance, she saw one wing of the main house and thought, "They did not restore the building for twelve years." Maria did not feel bad or distressed, watching her family house in ruins. She felt like she was a complete stranger in Blue Creeks, and everything or everyone she saw on her way were unfamiliar to her.

"Who needed the mansion to be rebuilt? They did not need it. I am more that sure that they successfully have moved the NKVD to another building where they continue their satanic rituals."

Maria met several people in the street and realized that she had never met them before. The whole village looked different. On the fields of their former estate, they built a school and many new houses. The place looked different, but Maria did not feel anything against the changes. She decided to stop at school and ask for any job position. They build the elementary and middle school adjacent to each other, and according to the school schedule, they had children from the first to the eighth grade. Across the street, Maria noticed a kindergarten with spacious playground.

Maria thought, "Maybe, they will hire me, as a teacher of Domestic science. I can teach different classes: cooking, knitting, crocheting, sewing and embroidering. At least, I can ask for this type of job." Maria stopped on the porch of the school and prayed quietly, *"Help me, save me, have mercy on me and keep me, oh Lord by Your grace."*

Maria stepped inside and knocked on the door of the principle. The calm male voice answered,

"Come in, please."

For a moment, Maria felt herself as if she was the first grader, who was scared of opening the door to the office of the school principle. She blessed herself and entered.

The principle was a man in his fifties with multiple medals on his jacket that demonstrated his participation in the WWII. He looked at unfamiliar woman in a black shawl and got up with a hand ready for handshake. His beautiful Ukrainian language had the accent that varied slightly from the local dialect.

"Nesterenko Mykola Petrovych, a principle of the Blue Creeks school."

"Maria Lukjanivna Gnatiuk," Maria introduced herself.

"Please, take a seat," the principle Nesterenko suggested.

He was watching Maria for a minute and asked,

"What brought you here? Do you have your children at our school?"

"Not yet. I'll bring my son tomorrow. I wanted to meet you first and to ask two questions," Maria answered.

The principle smiled,

"What questions do you want me to answer?"

"My son does not know a word in Ukrainian. The area where we lived did not require the Ukrainian language."

"Was it in Russia?" the principle Nesterenko asked.

"Yes, it was," Maria answered, waiting for the next question. But he did not ask right away about the Articles of the imprisonment, and rehabilitation.

"I can see that the mother of our future student knows Ukrainian perfectly well. You will help him at home, and I will ask the teachers to help your son at school. I do not think that it will take long time for him to learn the native language. Usually, the children are good with the languages. I hope that he was a good student in his school in Russia, was he?"

Maria smiled. She was always proud of her boy.

"He was always one of the best in studying and in extra-curriculum activities. It is not only my opinion. The teachers loved Sasha very much, because he was always good help for them with other students."

"Very well. I think the first question was clarified. What is your second question?"

"I am looking for a job position," Maria answered.

"What are you, Maria Lukjanivna?" the principle asked.

"I can teach Domestic science. I was always good in cooking, baking, knitting, sewing and embroidery," Maria explained.

"It's wonderful, Maria Lukjanivna," the principle exclaimed enthusiastically and continued,

"Our teacher of Domestic science left last month on her maternity leave. They found us a substitute from Sambir. She can be here one day in two weeks. In accordance with the subject requirements, it's not enough. It's wonderful that you arrive."

Maria was not so enthusiastic about it. She expected the next question.

"What did you do in Russia? Did you work at school there?"

Maria thought, "Here we are."

She answered out loud,

"Not really, I worked for the local hospital there."

"Now, I believe that you must be a great cook," the principle mentioned.

Maria did not answer. She just smiled, thinking, "He thought I worked there as a cook. It was his personal conclusion. I did not say so."

"Do you have your papers with you?" the principle asked.

"Yes, I do," Maria answered and handed him her new passport and Work registry book given to her in KGB office.

He checked both documents and was surprised that the Work registry book just stated the dates when she was admitted to the hospital and discharged without mentioning her work position. The KGB did not include a statement about her position that she occupied there. Maria could understand the shortage of information. Nevertheless, all the required seals and signatures were on the document.

"How could they write the correct information for Maria Gnatiuk?" She thought. "Such a person had never existed at the hospital."

The principle looked at the clock and suggested Maria to fill out the Employment application. She filled it fast and handed to Nesterenko. He ran through it and gave Maria another sheet of paper for Autobiography.

"You can bring the Autobiography tomorrow. Come at 8 a.m., and I'll introduce you to your colleagues. Then I'll prepare for you the schedule of your lessons. So, tomorrow, you'll start your first working day, as a teacher of Domestic science."

The principle checked the schedule for the next day and said,

"Tomorrow, you have three lessons in the fifth, sixth and seventh grades. You know that every class is subdivided into two groups for Domestic science. Only the girls stay with you. The boys are with a teacher of woodcraft."

"Thank you, Mykola Petrovych."

"Excuse me, please. I have one more question for you. You are in a black shawl. May I ask you, what happened in your family?"

"I lost my husband," Maria answered.

"May I ask, when it happened?" Nesterenko asked with a sign of sympathy in his voice.

"In March. He was sick and died." Maria answered, as she was taught in Magadan KGB. Her heart was pounding, and she wanted to scream out loud, "They murdered my husband. They murdered him brutally, and they wanted to do the same with my kids and me. God's miracle saved us."

Maria did not shout out her pain. She did quite the opposite, she smiled politely when the principle said,

"I am sorry to hear that, Maria Lukjanivna. Do you have strength to work after this recent tragedy? You still look pale and …" Nesterenko did not find the right word for skinny teacher.

Maria picked up the sincere sympathy in the voice of Nesterenko.

"I have to work, Mykola Petrovych. I need to feed my children. May I go?"

"Yes, of course. Don't forget to bring the autobiography for tomorrow. We'll send your papers to Sambir District Department of Education."

"Thank you, Mykola Petrovych. Do I need to fill out the application for my son Alexander to start his school tomorrow?"

"Ask the secretary. All the necessary registration forms for students are in her office."

"Thank you. I'll do it right now."

Maria wanted to add "Stay blessed", as the traditional Ukrainian 'farewell', but stopped herself at the very last second. She thought, "He is definitely an atheist and communist. Blessing from Above has nothing to do with him."

The principle was looking at her, as if he wanted to read her thoughts.

"Good-bye. I'll see you tomorrow," Maria said.

"Good-bye, Maria Lukjanivna," Nesterenko replied.

Maria went to the secretary desk and asked for student's applications. She decided not to take them home, but to complete the applications at school. The secretary noticed that Maria was looking for a place to sit and fill them out and invited her to sit at the opposite side of her table. Maria had finished quickly with the paperwork and ran home. She wanted to share the news with her family. "Why didn't I ask about the salary?" Maria thought. In a minute, she answered herself, "Does it make any difference? They pay some definite salary in accordance with their staff table, as we had it in the hospital. I need to start working, as soon as possible, because we are out of money. Thank You, Lord for Your miraculous support. I found my job!"

Glory to Thee, O Lord! Glory to Thee!

Chapter 28

Maria liked her job at school. She was working a lot at home, preparing different samples for her lessons. She cooked and baked tasty and beautifully decorated dishes at least of expense. Nobody in the village could afford expensive foods. Her students cook Maria's dishes at home, improving the poor variety of farmers' meals. The teachers liked their new colleague, and the friendly atmosphere at school helped Maria to undergo the transitional time. She could not get used to her new last name Gnatiuk and was surprised that Sasha accepted it so quickly.

The principle of the school asked Maria to organize during the lessons of Domestic science thorough cleaning of the school building with the girls of the seventh and eighth grades. The description of the Cleaning project required a lot. They needed to wash all the windows, walls, doors and floors and take care of the plants inside and outside of the school.

The principle explained: "Everything has to be prepared to the Last Bell – the end of the school year and graduation of the eighth graders."

Nesterenko continued,

"I know, Maria Lukjanivna, that the school building needs a lot of cleaning work after the school year. Please, focus the schoolgirls on cleaning the classrooms, offices, windows, corridors, doors and front and back porches, as well as planting the plants inside and outside the school, especially around the school entrance."

During the last two weeks, Maria and schoolgirls spent all the lessons of domestic science with cleaning. While cleaning the principle office, Maria noticed that there were no curtains on the windows there. The room looked uncomfortable.

"It looks like a cold waiting room of the railway station," Maria thought. "The room is long and empty. How could he work here?"

The books were piled just on the floors in each corner of the room.

Maria decided: "I need to ask the teacher of woodcraft, to make the book-shelves with the boys for Nesterenko's office."

She looked at two wide windows. "Something has to be done with the windows. Nesterenko spends all evenings in his office, and everyone can watch him through the windows in his half-finished room. It's not right due to two reasons. First, the office of the principle Nesterenko looked absolutely un-professional and impersonal."

Maria thought for a while and defined another reason of the opened windows, "There is still some danger for a person from the eastern Ukraine. He was sent here for a position of a school principle after being seriously wounded at the end of the war. Without curtains on the windows, everyone could see him, sitting at his desk with his back towards the window."

It took two weeks for Maria to sew with the fifth graders the beautiful curtains for the principal's office. She decided to hang them right after cleaning of the office. Maria was about to finish her job, when Nesterenko opened the door and stopped in the doorway.

"It looks beautiful," he said with his velvety baritone.

Maria liked his voice and the manner he spoke with people. He spoke with teachers and children in the same polite intonation. The man obtained the most difficult goals with the help of his special inner power and persistence. It looked like he could achieve anything without forceful pressure. He asked once and people, even schoolchildren, could not resist following his instructions or requests.

Maria was staying barefoot on his desk, hanging the curtains. She did not know what to answer. She had learned already that the soviet authorities never complemented the personnel for well-performed job. The next phrase made her embarrassed,

"Tell me, if you need any help. You are so tiny, Maria Lukjanivna. You can barely rich the curtain rods."

Maria smiled and did not answer anything. She had finished with hanging the curtains and fixed them evenly. Nesterenko offered her his hand to come down to the floor. Then she stepped back, looked at her work professionally and concluded,

"It's much better now. The office looks better."

"I agree. It's your gift to our school for the Graduation, isn't it?" Nesterenko asked.

Maria made a correction,

"It's a gift, if you want, but not from me, from the fifth graders."

Maria noticed that he felt awkward after her correction.

"Thank you, anyway. I noticed that all the windows in school are cleaned after winter. You did wonderful job, Comrade Gnatiuk. What do you plan to do now?"

"During this week, we'll plant lilac bushes, flowers and plants," Maria answered.

Nesterenko asked,

"Where do you want to plant them?"

"Many of them we'd planted already in colorful pots and put them on the window-sills in the classrooms."

The principle looked at Maria with surprise,

"Do you mind bringing one of the plants to my office?"

"We'll do it after they adjust the book-shelves on the walls. Then we can see how to make the flower arrangement in your office. Tomorrow, the seven graders will take care of your bookshelves, and the six graders will plant the bushes on the territory of the school."

"What kind of bushes would you like to plant?" Nesterenko did not expect that this small woman could be such a hard worker.

"Three lilac bushes of different colors and two jasmine. Now it's a little bit late for planting the trees and bushes, but we'll do our best. We'll bring them with the soil they grow in," Maria explained.

"Where can you get them?" Nesterenko was curious.

He observed Maria with unhidden interest. The way Maria smiled showed him that she had already found the decision.

"There is a burnt mansion at the end of the Blue Creeks. Nobody lives there. One day, we explored the territory with students and found out the wild condition of the bushes there. Nobody trimmed them for years. I'll show the boys how we can get part of the bushes. I promise, we will not damage the whole bush," Maria added.

"You mean Doctor's estate? It's a good idea. I was thinking about that place many times. The war destroyed it completely. After the death of my wife, I was walking there daily. It was August and the apples in that garden were delicious. Nobody collects them. To my mind, people are afraid to be there. It would be nice for our school to take a patronage of that forgotten place. Have you been there before?"

"With seven graders," Maria answered. Her heart was pounding, and she was afraid that the principal could hear its loud sound. Maria's first thought was, "He must know who I am. He must get the information from KGB with the instruction to watch me."

Maria thought: "Recently, just two days ago, Sasha and I went for a walk there. He must know about it."

Nesterenko looked at Maria attentively and suggested,

"You turned pale, please sit down." He poured her a glass of water.

“Thank you,” Maria said and drank all the water to the very drop.

Then she asked,

“In fifteen minutes, the lessons are over. I’ll ask boys to help me, and we’ll go and bring some bushes from the mansion.”

“How do you feel now? I’ll ask Comrade Nitishin and the schoolboys to go with you. The bookshelves can wait. You are still pale,” the principle said with concern in his voice.

“Thank you, Mykola Petrovych. I am quite well,” Maria replied.

Then she asked,

“Do you mind, if we’ll plant some bushes under your windows?”

Nesterenko smiled. He shook hands with Maria, saying,

“Now, I can see that we have a very good teacher of Domestic science. Thank you, Comrade Gnatiuk. Thank you, Maria Lukjanivna.”

Maria rushed to the classroom. She did not understand what made the principal so touched. “Was it our work with curtains and school cleaning? Maybe, he liked my idea of planting bushes under his windows? The front and backyards are completely empty.”

“He liked the apples from our garden,” Maria remembered. She was pleased.

“His hand is so hot,” Maria recalled. “To my mind, he liked the curtains in his office. He did not say anything about them. He just mentioned in general that it looks beautiful."

The school bell rang. Maria entered the classroom, lined up the girls, and they went to Doctor's mansion to get some lilac and jasmine bushes. The Woodcraft teacher followed Maria and the girls with the group of boys.

"The people named our place as the Doctor's mansion. We lived there and did not know that it had that name," Maria thought.

Maria experienced different feelings: in general, she liked her meeting with the principle. To be more precise, she liked his true appreciation of her work. Another feeling was connected with Nesterenko's visiting of her mansion after his wife's death. "He was hiding from the world, from people, from work in our mansion. I can understand him so well. We want to run away from the reality of loss… That place is good for it. Nobody comes there. As Ganja said, people are afraid to be there."

At the moment, Maria went there with unusual purpose to take the parts of the bushes for landscaping of the school. Giving the wild growing bushes to the school does not bother her. She always liked to share with everything and everyone. The feeling that still disturbed her was seeing again the ruins of her home. Maria tried to push away all the unpleasant thoughts and memories by focusing on her new life at the present time. "I must be tired and hungry by this time of the day. These two reasons made me *sentimental*," Maria found the explanation to all her disturbing thoughts.

Maria's day normally started at six in the morning. Sometimes she woke up earlier and could not fall asleep. The worrying thoughts were climbing in her mind. She walked around Ganja's house, as if she was looking for something that she lost long time ago. Several times, she took Sasha to the ruins of her mansion. They wandered there and Maria was crying most of the time. The last time Sasha concluded,

"Mama, I don't want us to come here."

"Why, Sasha?" Maria inquired. "You do not like this place, do you?"

"I do not like you coming here to cry," Sasha replied and continued, "I cannot change anything in your life. I cannot help you. I hadn't helped my father in March. I miss him so much, Mama. Sometimes I want to run away, to disappear, to find another place to live..."

Maria looked at him with sympathy, thinking, "He grew fast after Alexander's death and became depressed. It is not good at all." She came up to Sasha and asked,

"Where can we go, son? Who waits for us? I do not want to be here either. I am sure, that one day, somebody will recognize me, or they will receive the information about me, and it would be the end of our quiet life."

Sasha felt sorry for his mother. Maria continued,

"I promise you not to cry here again. The memory of what had happened here to your father and me struck me with a new strength, when we arrived at Blue Creeks. I could not imagine how painful it could be to return to the place, where normal life had been destroyed forever.

The painful memory interrupted my connection with Universe. Sasha, I am praying but do not feel that I am connected, as I used to be in Russia."

They walked for a while in silence. Then Maria continued,

"The feeling of danger arose again. What kills me most of all is inability to change anything, to become myself and to live my life, as Maria Kotyk-Kurbatov. I did not find anybody of my family. I hoped that we would find my siblings here, and for some time after our arrival, we would live together, as a family."

"It did not happen," Sasha concluded.

When they returned home, Ganja played with Tisha. She had a special talent to be a nanny. The boy liked to be with her from the very first week when they arrived. He sensed the same warmth from her, as he sensed from Zina.

Ganja met them with a smile,

"Look, Ivanko, our scholars are home. We need to feed them. It was nice that you slept well and gave me the opportunity to cook dinner for them."

Ganja served dinner and mentioned the fact that in a week or two after the Kurbatovs' deportation to Siberia, the local NKVD moved from the burnt house. Her goddaughter, who was a janitor at the local committee, helped with packing the documents that survived the fire. They packed eight boxes with half burned documents, and she mentioned that Maria's and Alexander's passports, visas and tickets were not damaged at all.

"Where did they send our documents?" Maria asked.

"I do not know for sure, but to my mind, to Lviv," Ganja answered.

"I do not think that you will start looking for them, right, Mom?" Sasha asked with fear in his voice.

Maria did not like the fearful and depressive thoughts of her older son. Yes, for the present day, she was afraid to interrupt their quiet existence. Still, Sasha's fear disturbed her. Maria needed some time to restore her strength in order to continue fighting. Thereafter, she wanted to restore at least the name of her family-Kotyk, to find her relatives, to live without fear, expecting that earlier or later somebody could recognize her and punish again for using the fake personal data.

"Mama, how is it possible that the local people and the teachers at our school do not recognize you?" Sasha asked.

"Sasha, the local people hadn't seen me since 1941. The seventeen years of hardships changed my appearance very much. The colleagues at school are not from our village. All of them, including the principle of the school were sent from different regions of Ukraine and two teachers were sent from Russia," Maria explained.

Then she looked in a small mirror and added,

"When I look at me in the mirror, I can hardly find anything that reminds the appearance of Pannochka Maria Kotyk."

Maria tried to joke, but Sasha sensed deep feminine pain behind that conclusion.

Maria looked around and asked Ganja,

"Ganja, please do not call me Pannochka. I do not want people to hear this."

"As you wish, Pannochka. But how can I name you then?" Ganja asked with sincere concern.

"Maria. I want you to call me Maria. I am your tenant Maria Gnatiuk. Will you remember this, please?"

Maria came up and embraced the confused woman.

"Yes, I will remember this, Pannochka Maria." All laughed.

Ganja was angry with herself,

"I am old and stupid. I will learn it. If you do not want me to call you Pannochka, then I'll call you Pani Maria. It is natural and nobody will pay attention at this..." Ganja suggested.

"No, Ganja. They know that I arrived from Russia. In Russia they do not use anything except 'Comrade' or 'Citizen'. So, please don't use anything, just Maria," Maria insisted.

"Pani Ganja, Mama does not want to attract somebody's attention," Sasha explained.

Ganja replied with disappointment,

"I understood, Sashko. Years ago, everything was so clear. We did not hide who was who. We had respect toward the educated and noble people. Your grandfather was a very kind man, and he helped everyone who needed health care. Now, everything had been twisted or turned upside down. I am glad that I am old and should not work for them. Sashko, they brought poverty, godlessness and disappointment to our people."

Maria was feeding Tisha and thinking about Ganja's answer. She knew that this uneducated but naturally smart woman was right. Her Blue Creeks looked so ugly in 1958, as if the war was over only a week ago. The local authorities did not care of the village roads, destroyed houses, fences, and trees. For the district and regional rulers, this place had 'small economic and agricultural significance'. It was not her family estate any longer, when her family would do everything to restore its beauty.

Lord, have mercy!

Chapter 29

That morning at the end of June was pleasantly warm and sunny. The school year was over, and Maria worked with other teachers at fixing and painting of the classrooms and corridors, where it was required. The teachers had to finish with repair work before their vocation. At the end of each school year, the principles of the schools were issued the same 12-year old regulation that was defined by the soviet government in 1946, in the first post-war year: "Due to absence of assets for renovation of the schools, all the teachers, students and parents must voluntarily participate in preparation of the school buildings to the next school year".

Maria used to come to school early in the morning. She was given a special assignment – to paint all the window frames inside and outside of the building. It required a lot of time and physical strength. Before the school building was opened, she used to weed and water the flowers and plants around the school building. Many of the plants that Maria seeded and bedded with school children were blooming, making the school yard bright and colorful.

Maria was watering the lilac bushes when she heard somebody's steps behind. It was the school principle who also used to come earlier than other teachers.

"Good morning, Comrade Gnatiuk," he greeted in a distance.

"Good morning, Mykola Petrovych," Maria replied.

The principle opened the entrance door of the school and stopped in the doorway, watching Maria. Maria looked up at him and asked,

"Do you want me to do anything particular today?"

"No, I don't. I was thinking who will help you today with the window painting."

Maria was surprised that he decided to look for a helper.

"You do not like how I do my work, do you?" Maria asked.

He pronounced out loud the thought that bothered him from the very first day of Maria's work on the windows,

"The work is too difficult for you, Maria Lukjanivna. You are such a tiny woman. I don't know where you find the strength to work so hard."

Maria wanted to say that God always supported her, but she knew that he was an atheist and just smiled instead of any answer.

"What did you do in Russia?" the principle asked.

"Different work," Maria answered without naming her mining for more than ten years and the doctor's practice at the hospital after the discharge. She received her new documents that stated that she was a hospital employee. Maria did not see any reason to release any other information for the principle.

“I was a working mother for my children,” Maria joked.

“You are a very intelligent person, Maria Lukjanivna. I believe that you have received good education,” Nesterenko concluded, looking at Maria with interest.

“Oh, really? Do you think that every woman needs good education to teach children how to cook simple dishes, knit the socks and embroider the Ukrainian shirts?” Maria replied with bitterness in her voice.

“You don’t like your job, do you?” Nesterenko was surprised. He did not expect to receive such an embittered answer from a teacher who perfectly complied with all the requirements of her position.

“Comrade Nesterenko, any job is good for me. Presently, I do not even think about preferences, priorities or choices. I have learned to work well, and that is all about job and me.”

Maria was honest, however, in a minute she felt sorry that she made the principle confused and disappointed with her attitude toward her position at school. She looked up at him and thought, “Why did I say this? Am I looking for complications in future? He would never forget my answer.”

Nesterenko came up to her and declared,

“Maria Lukjanivna, you must be hurt a lot in your life, but I am not the one who has attempted to hurt you. I did not mean to do it. If I have asked the wrong question, forgive me, please.”

He turned around and went to school.

Maria finished with weeding and watering the plants and went to paint the windows. Sasha came to help his mother. All the teachers left at 4:00 p.m., but Maria and Sasha continued working. Maria wanted to finish with her pre-vocational assignment sooner and to get principle's permission for summer rest.

She agreed to keep her additional assignment-to water the plants every second day until the teacher of woodcraft arrived from vocation. She was sure that Sasha would accompany her, bringing water from the well to four huge barrels. In the Ukraine, nobody used cold well water for watering. People kept the water in the barrels for several days, warmed it in the sun before they utilized it for gardening.

Every day, Ivanko waited for his mother and Sasha to stay with him, to take him for long walks and to play in the soft green grass. Old nanny did not have strength to play with the boy or catch him when he was running. She was good with cooking and feeding Maria and children. When Maria was earlier from work, they had family dinner outside at the table under the old cherry tree. Maria watched nanny Ganja and made the conclusion: "Ganja needs help with Ivanko. He is heavy for her to carry, and he is too fast with his moving around, pulling and destroying everything that he can reach."

Nesterenko worked in his office with the door opened. For the whole day, Maria felt guilty for her unusual behavior in the morning. She could not forgive herself her explosion and constantly returned to it in her thoughts during the day. Sasha noticed that his mother was sad and did not want to talk much, as she used to do teaching and practicing his Ukrainian language. He tried to find out what was there in her mind but did not receive clear answer. The boy concluded, "Mama is tired."

It was about five o'clock, when hungry Sasha left home. Maria stayed longer to clean and wash several windows, preparing them for painting on the next day. The window frames should be washed, and dried, in order the paint could coat it smoothly. Every day Maria prepared several windows from inside and outside before she left home. It was not easy after the day of painting. Maria saw the principle Nesterenko working at his desk. He wrote something down in a thick notebook, then counted and entered the numbers.

At last, Maria had finished her daily job. She washed the hands and stopped at the Principle office to say "Good-bye". She experienced light dizziness. Nesterenko looked at her and smiled. In a second, Maria noticed that she was losing the ground under her feet and grabbed the door frame with both hands, trying to catch the balance. Nesterenko stood up and rushed towards her. He caught Maria when she collapsed. He did not feel the weight of her body, as he was carrying her to a large leather sofa that was in his office. Then he brought some water and sprinkled at her face. Maria tried to open her eyes but was not successful with it.

"I am sorry," she whispered in a weak voice. "Please, forgive me."

Nesterenko felt scared and confused. He did not know how to help Maria. There was nobody else at school. He looked out of the window and could not see the children that used to come and play on the sport ground. Nesterenko rushed back to Maria and whispered,

"Please, don't die. Maria Lukjanivna, I beg you, don't die. I cannot lose everyone I like. You are a very nice person. Please, stay here. Stay with me."

He touched her face and stroked her hair. Then he sprinkled some more water on her, and Maria opened her large hazel eyes. She saw that the principle kneeled near the sofa, holding her tiny hand in his big hands. The shock from the situation gave Maria strength to sit down and speak,

"I am sorry, Mykola Petrovych. I did not eat today. Now I know, I cannot work for the whole day without food. I planned to come earlier and to leave earlier. O my God! Forgive me please, Mykola Petrovych. I did not mean to disturb you for the second time. What a day!"

He stood up and watched with admiration this tiny bird on his huge sofa. He sat down near her and interrupted her apology with a discomforted sentence,

"Don't apologize, please. I don't need it, Maria Lukjanivna."

Maria imagined, how angry he was with her, if he did not want to accept her apology. She tried to stand up and leave, but the dizziness was so bad that it sat her back on the sofa. Maria became nauseous. She prayed in her mind, “My Lord, help me, please. I am in a very awkward situation.”

Nesterenko jumped up when he realized that Maria mentioned that she did not eat anything. “Today, she did not eat. I must feed her. What do I have with me? I always keep a pack of crackers in my desk.”

The principle rushed to his desk and opened the lower drawer from the right side. He recollected his mother’s visit at 2 p.m. and announced with joy,

“Maria Lukjanivna, you are saved. My mother brought me a sandwich for lunch. It was nice that I did not touch my sandwich.”

He unwrapped it and handed to Maria,

“Take it, please. Eat it.”

Maria took the sandwich with apology,

“Thank you, Mykola Petrovych. I am sorry, I caused too much trouble for you today, and now, I took away your sandwich.”

She looked at the size of the sandwich and said with her smile,

“It’s too big for me. It’s far too big. We’ll share it. Don’t worry, I washed my hands.”

Nesterenko could not stop her. Maria separated the upper and lower slices of the bread, subdivided the ingredients and put them on both bread slices. The bigger half she passed to him. They were eating in silence, thinking about a strange situation they were in. Nesterenko turned to the windows and closed the curtains. He did not want anybody to see him, sitting and eating together with the teacher of Domestic science in his office late in the evening.

Maria felt thirsty and asked for water. He poured it, and she drank fast. When they finished with their sandwichcs, Maria said,

"I am sorry for this morning. It was not me. I like my school job. To my mind, my students liked our lessons, as well. It is much better than mining."

Maria noticed Nesterenko's smile when she pronounced the last phrase. He thought that Maria made a joke about mining. The principle asked,

"Who can mine with the hands like yours?"

Maria was angry with herself for saying too much in the morning and a minute ago.

Nesterenko handed her a candy with the words,

"Your desert."

Maria smiled and sensed that it was time to leave.

"Thank you for feeding me, Mykola Petrovych. I owe you something tasty."

She got up slowly. The weakness and dizziness did not disappear completely. Nesterenko watched her with wariness. Seeing Maria's paleness and feebleness, he got up and suggested,

"We'll go together with you. I think, I worked enough for today."

"No, we should not walk together along the street of our village. You know that we live in a very small place, and we don't need people's gossips about you and me. Thank you for everything. I'll see you tomorrow," Maria said, and her mind ended, "with God's will."

Maria walked slowly along the street to Ganja's house. Her children played outside, waiting for her. Maria opened the gate and sat down on the bench. Sasha was the first near his mother.

"Mama, what's wrong? You do not feel well, do you? You must be very tired, Mama. Please, go inside. I'll help you."

Ivanko also wanted to help his mother but fell on the first step when he lost the canvas of Maria's dress. Sasha picked him up, and they entered the nanny's house. Ganja was busy with cooking supper. She turned to the door and exclaimed,

"What's wrong, Pannochka Maria? You are so pale. The people in coffin look better." Old nanny was honest in her description. Everyone smiled.

"Ganja, I left early today after drinking a cup of curd milk. I did not take any food for my lunch, and at the end of my work, I fainted. I felt bad because nobody was at school, except the principle. I stopped to say "Good-bye" and fainted in his office. I feel awkward for my weakness."

Ganja asked, "Why did you stay so long at work?"

Maria drank some water and came up to the nanny with explanation:

"I worked longer in order to finish my window assignment faster. During my vocation, I'll take care of Ivanko. You need some rest from the boy."

"What did the principle say when you fainted?" Sasha and Ganja asked simultaneously.

"He helped me a lot with sprinkling the water on my face and feeding me with his sandwich. Yes, he shared his sandwich with me. I don't know what to expect tomorrow, but today he was sympathetic to me. I am sorry, but I still feel dizzy. Feed me, please."

Ganja rushed to the kitchen and brought a cup of vegetable soup that she saved from the lunch. Hot soup slightly balanced Maria, however the woman still felt hungry.

Maria said,

"I feel bad about fainting at school. To my mind, Nesterenko was so scared that he wanted to accompany me to our house. I refused, of course. I walked slowly, and now, I am here but still weak and still hungry. Ganja, please feed me, with something else. Your soup flew away so fast."

Ganja put the bowls with freshly made foods on the table. The smell of baked potato made Maria dizzy again. She took one and Tisha immediately climbed and sat down on Mama's lap. He always sat at the table with his mother when the food was there. Ganja wanted to take the boy and let Maria eat, but he missed his mother for a long day and did not want to leave her. Maria fed her chick with love and pleasure. He turned one year and reminded a baby bear when he walked across the room.

Maria noticed that her Ivanko stopped looking and calling for his Dad. In Blue Creeks only once at night he cried and called,

"Daddy, Daddy."

Maria watched her sons and thought, "It must be for better that Ivanko stopped calling Alex. Sasha misses his father a lot, and the loss became irreparable for him."

Maria recalled again the scared and pitiful face of Nesterenko and smiled,

"I frightened the man. He did not expect this from me, 'a hard-working woman'. He must be really scared when he decided to share his only sandwich with me. O yes! I owe him lunch. Tomorrow, I'll prepare something for him."

Maria imagined her coming to school with lunch for a principle. "How will it look? I can imagine the speed of the gossips! If I bring lunch for the principle of our school, who is a widower, our teachers will think God knows what! It's better to prepare for everyone, as I did during the school time, but …"

Ivanko turned and looked at his mother. He had finished with his supper and waited for Maria to wash and take him to bed. Ganja insisted in Maria's eating. Maria fed Ivanko, but she could hardly eat anything except a cup of soup.

"Eat, Maria. Please, eat," nanny insisted.

She was watching Maria for a while and then said,

"You are so exhausted, my dear, that you do not pay any attention to what I have said. Forgive me, please."

Sasha was the first who caught the sense of Ganja's words.

"Mama," he exclaimed. Nanny Ganja did not say 'Pannochka'!" All laughed.

Ganja and Sasha prepared everything for baby's bath while he had supper with his mother. Ganja took the baby, undressed him and sat in the tab with warm water.

Ivanko liked the evening procedure and, in several minutes, the floor around became wet and the house was filled with baby's exclamations. The boy stopped shouting only for a couple of minutes when Ganja washed his short hair and face with soup. The boy turned one in May, and in accordance with Ukrainian tradition, Maria cut his hair very short. Now, it was much easier to wash it, but Ivanko still groaned, quacked and screamed loudly when Sasha poured some water on him, helping Ganja to speed up the washing process. Maria enjoyed watching Ivanko's bath.

From time to time her thoughts returned her to the same subject, "What can I cook for tomorrow? She looked at Ganja and asked,

"Ganja, do you have pumpkins from the last year?"

"I don't know how good they are, but there are two or three left in basement. Why did you ask about pumpkins?"

Maria interrupted her meal, took a candle and rushed down to the basement. In a couple of minutes, she appeared in the room with a big pumpkin in her hands.

"Ganja, look what I found there! What a beauty! I need it for tomorrow."

Ivanko pointed at the pumpkin with his tiny index finger and pronounced,

"A ball."

"No, baby, not at all. It's not a ball, it's a pumpkin. It is a beautiful colorful pumpkin. I'll make pumpkin millet for tomorrow lunch and bake pumpkin sticks with honey," Maria announced joyfully, as if she had found a real treasure in the basement.

"I can make it for lunch," Ganja suggested. "We do not need the whole pumpkin for it. It's too big, Maria."

"No, it is not. Tomorrow morning, I'll make the lunch for us and our teachers."

Then she thought for a while and suggested,

"Ganja, I can prepare everything and put into the stove, but let Sasha bring it to us around twelve o'clock. Everyone at school will enjoy fresh, hot and sweet pumpkin millet. What do you think?"

"It sounds good for us, right Sasha?" Ganja answered merrily. "We'll also enjoy hot pumpkin millet for lunch with goat milk. Am I right, children?"

Sasha made his suggestion,

"Mama, in the morning, I'll go with you to school. We'll paint together, and later I'll run home and bring hot millet to you."

Maria hugged her son. He reminded Maria of her helpful Alexander. He sounded, as if he was much older than he was in reality.

"Thank you, sonny. You are my true help," Maria said.

Sasha answered firmly: "I don't want you to work alone. You are too tired."

"I agree, Alexander. You are my boy."

"And father's," Sasha added.

Maria kissed him on both cheeks and went to her younger one, who waited for his mother to come, sing him a lullaby song, pray and stay near him at least at night before she disappeared to work for a long day.

Glory to Thee, Oh Lord! Glory to Thee!

Chapter 30

Next morning, Maria got up at five o'clock in order to prepare pumpkin for cooking the pumpkin millet and baking the honey pumpkin sticks. She was pleasantly surprised to feel that the exhaustion of the previous day evaporated with the night sleep, and her motions were strong and brisk again. Maria had always prayed in the kitchen before she started her cooking,

"Dear God, please bless with Your Holy Spirit my little kitchen and foods that I cook today. Please, bless me, Your servant Maria, for making the foods tasty and nourishing for everyone who will consume them. May all the meals that I prepare be seasoned with Thy ever-lasting love and grace. Amen."

Maria's memory returned her to the incident that happened at school. "Poor Nesterenko, he was frightened to see me passing out in his office." Maria smiled, "Honestly, I liked his reaction and the kind words that he didn't like when some dreadful things happened to those who he cared about… Yes, he said something like this. To my mind, he mentioned those who he liked…"

"Today, I need to make a new entry in my journal and write a letter to Larissa," Maria thought while cutting and peeling the huge pumpkin.

Larissa was one of the inmates who served her sentence together with Maria in Magadan camp. She was imprisoned in December of 1941 and released in 1955. In August of 1941, the communist committee of her town decided to leave her, a twenty-nine-year-old beautiful teacher of the German language in town for the period of Nazi occupation. They wanted her to work in the restaurant, as a waitress, and collect the information for the soviet intelligence service.

The German occupants moved fast, and NKVD with the local leaders of the communist party were in a hurry with creating the network for gathering data about the military marches of the invaders and the relocation of the German troops and their military supply. Larissa agreed to stay in town and to fulfil their order with one condition: she demanded the committee to assist her three small children and parents with evacuation to war-free zone, as they did to their own families. Her request was denied.

One night, Larissa secretly took her two older children to her cousin who lived in a village close to Odessa. The husbands of both women were taken to the soviet army in July of 1941. In two days, the NKVD officer brought the appalling news to Larissa – *'somebody'* burned the house of her cousin with five children and her cousin in it.

Larissa did not have a single doubt: it was the unmerciful signature of NKVD. The poor mother blamed them and underwent all the consequences for her accusations. She was deported to the Magadan camp with several broken ribs and a double fracture of the left arm. Being physically and spiritually strong, Larissa survived long journey to Magadan zone and fourteen years of mining.

In the camp, they kept Larissa in another barrack, but Maria met her daily in the mine. Sister Olga suggested the young women to pray together for the souls of Larissa's burned son and daughter, as well as for her cousin with her three kids. The mutual worships made the women close friends. Being released a year earlier, Larissa wrote letters to Dr. Leskov, and he took a risk delivering them to Maria. He used to joke,

"Maria, if they dismiss me from my *'valuable'* position of a camp doctor, I know what to do. I'll become a mailman with my long experience of delivering letters to you from Larissa and Alexander."

When Maria settled with her family after the discharge from the prison, she was in correspondence with Larissa. At that time, Larissa was granted her complete rehabilitation status and returned to teaching. In two years, she became a principle of the local high school. Thank God, the demons from NKVD did not take away her baby girl from Larissa's parents. For fourteen years, the child was waiting for her mother's home-coming.

When Maria returned to Blue Creeks, she sent a letter to Larissa in which she described everything that had happened to her family after Alexander's visit to Magadan KGB. She explained where a new last name came from. She also wrote about a tragedy that happened to Sister Olga. Larissa did not like the idea of Maria's staying in Blue Creeks. She wrote, "Maria, I warn you that sooner or later somebody recognizes you, and it can have dangerous consequences. Please, take your boys and come to us. I promise to help you with work and living. In a year or two, you'll decide what to do with your life."

Maria thought, "I need to assure Larissa that everything is not bad. What else can I wish for now? I found my Ganja, her hospitable small house to stay in, my rather interesting work, and one day, I'll meet again my Papa and grandpa."

Maria had finished with the most difficult part of pumpkin preparation – peeling and slicing.

She smiled to her thought and asked herself,

"Should I write Larissa about the school principle who saved me yesterday by sharing his sandwich with me? Or maybe, I should write about bringing my delicious pumpkin millet to him in return? I know that it's nonsense, but it's heart-warming nonsense..."

Maria remembered that she needed to have something for her breakfast, in order to avoid the declining of her strength. She smiled, thinking, "If it happens again, I am not so sure that Nesterenko will save me. He panics so much. I can kill poor principle with my fainting."

Maria heard how Ganja entered the house from the back yard, and the young woman looked out of the kitchen to greet her. Ganja brought a crock with fresh gout milk and a basket with the eggs. The old nanny poured some milk into two mugs and sliced the bread. Then she came to the kitchen and asked,

"Maria, are you ready to eat? I made boiled eggs for everyone. I crashed some of the eggs for our small chicks. They were happy to have nice breakfast."

"Yes, Ganja, I am ready for breakfast. It's perfect timing. I have just finished with all the pumpkin preparations. Please, put it in the stove later, when the stove is ready. I didn't forget about pumpkin sticks with honey. Check on them frequently, when they are in the stove. Don't burn them, please."

"Don't worry, Pannochka."

"Ganja, please don't mention this word again!"

Ganja knocked her forehead with a deformed arthritic index finger and complained,

"It's the age, Maria. Excuse me, please."

She sounded like a small child that complained to adults about a broken toy. Maria felt sorry for Ganja. She hugged the nanny and kissed her on her cheeks. Ganja was pleased, but did not want to manifest her true feelings, and said grumpy,

"No kisses, Maria. I am too old, and my face is ugly. Look at my wrinkled face, dear. Tisha kisses me too, but he is a silly baby."

Maria observed how her arrival with kids made Ganja stronger. The voice and movements of the old nanny became robust. She walked fast again, like a young woman. Maria could hardly catch Ganja's pace, when they walked to the forest to gather the berries.

Maria thought, "Ganja's prayers were answered. She mentioned on the very first day of our arrival, how she prayed daily for three of us to survive and return alive. So, three of us came here. Only my dearest Alex was destined to stay there forever."

Maria finished with her breakfast, hugged Ganja, checked on her sleeping boys and ran out of the house. Even with the preparation of the pumpkin for lunch dishes, Maria came to school half an hour earlier than her co-workers. There was only one difference on that morning-the front and back doors of the school building were widely opened, evaporating all the odors of the school renovation. Maria started with weeding and watering the flowerbeds around the school. She worked near the windows of the Principle office, when Nesterenko opened the window and greeted her,

"Good morning, Maria Lukjanivna. How are you this morning?"

"Thank you for asking. Today, I am very well. And thank you for yesterday."

Maria sensed that the conversation was not over. Nesterenko hesitated with asking or saying something. Maria continued with weeding. In a while, he came up to the window again and asked,

"Did you have your breakfast this morning?"

He pronounced this phrase, as if he asked a lazy student, "Did you prepare your homework?"

Maria looked up at the principle, and both of them burst into laughing.

Nesterenko continued,

"This time, I prepared two sandwiches. Come in, please."

Maria was pleased and answered politely,

"Thank you, Mykola Petrovych, but I avoided my mistake from yesterday, and this morning, I had a good breakfast. Enjoy both of your sandwiches."

Maria picked up the bucket and rushed to bring the water from the barrel. She could not understand why, but she had pleasant feeling inside, thinking about the principle, "Nesterenko is a nice man. I feel sorry for him, because I know what it means to lose the beloved person."

Sasha came right on time when Maria had finished with her weeding and watering the flowers. The boy ran around the school building, counted the windows that they had to paint and suggested,

"Mama, let us complete your assignment by the end of the day."

The boy watched his mother every day and knew that she was completely drained, but never talked about it to anybody. He thought, "Mama definitely needs summer rest in order to gain new strength for another school year."

Sasha was exited,

"Don't worry, Mama. Every day, we used to paint more windows that you planned. Let us finish today, and since tomorrow, you'll be free for nearly two months." He thought for a minute and added, "Except watering the plants every other day. I'll do it for you."

"Thank you, sonny. I appreciate your help. I would never do it by myself."

They were painting the second window when Maria asked,

"Sasha, what should we do with our lunch at twelve?"

"We'll do it a little bit later, when we finish with our painting job. By that time, every teacher will be hungry and enjoy the sweet pumpkin millet with vanilla sugar and honey sticks."

At two o'clock, Sasha brought freshly made food to school. He ran through all the classrooms and invited teachers and principle Nesterenko to mother's classroom for Domestic science. Sasha told the teachers that his mother has finished with her window assignment and celebrates the beginning of her summer vocation.

Maria covered the table with beautifully embroidered tablecloth that she made as an example for students of the sixth grade. She set up the table with a single peony in a small vase. The sweet smell of a pink peony spread all over the small classroom.

Maria's colleagues enjoyed the delicious pumpkin millet and honey pumpkin sticks. Maria saw that they were sincere with their thankfulness for the unexpected and delicious lunch. Only Nesterenko looked seriously disturbed. He was polite while keeping the conversation with the teachers. However, Maria sensed his unusual tension and changes in the intonations of his naturally pleasant baritone.

Sasha left around four. Maria stayed longer to arrange her working supply in the back room. She was sorting out the fabrics, buttons, threads and needles in the drawers of the closet and did not notice when Nesterenko entered the door of the classroom. He called her out loud,

"Maria Lukjanivna, are you still here?"

Maria shuddered from an unexpected sound. She walked out, looked at Nesterenko and asked,

"I am arranging in the closet all our sawing supply for the next school year. Is anything wrong, Mykola Petrovych?"

Maria smiled, but Nesterenko seemed not to notice her smile and hardly heard, what she was saying.

"What's wrong, Mykola Petrovych?" Maria asked again.

Nesterenko looked outraged with something.

"Today, they called from Lviv Department of Education and wanted me to tell you that you cannot work in the system of education without a diploma."

Maria was shocked. Then she asked,

"What kind of diploma is required for a teacher of Domestic science?"

"That's what I asked them. They said, 'Any diploma in teaching'."

The first Maria's thought was,

"It's the result of my yesterday morning conversation with Nesterenko. It's his idea to get rid of me. What should I do?"

It looked like the school principle read her mind,

"Maria Lukjanivna, please don't think that anything stupid was initiated by me. I was greatly surprised to receive such a call. Somebody is against you to the point that they insisted to discharge you today, before they find anybody else who could substitute you for summer assignments and the next school year. I refuse to understand them. I will never find another specialist, like you. You are talented in everything that you taught the schoolgirls. You are not just trained. Maria Lukjanivna, you are talented. Look, how you changed the school and school yard for less than two months with proper cleaning, planting the flowers, plants and bushes. All the parents praised you. You changed the girls for better. You proved for them that the fabric could be inexpensive, but good style and neat sewing work can make the world of difference. The boys are willing to assist you."

Maria put the pile of Manuals for sawing machines on the very edge of the teacher's desk. None of them noticed that the Manuals can fall. She whispered,

"That's all right, Mykola Petrovych. I have to go. Good-bye."

Maria left the classroom. She needed fresh air. She heard just two phrases, ringing in her mind, "They are against you… decided to discharge, discharge, discharge…" Maria was afraid of a new collapse. She could not walk and sat down on the steps of the school porch.

Nesterenko thought, "Today, it is cloudy and windy outside… Poor woman, she needs fresh air."

Maria was sitting for a while on the steps, in order to become conscious of what had happened to her. Different thoughts were climbing in her mind. Then, she got up from the steps and slowly moved forward without concentrating on the direction, where she walked. The ill-fated woman was so distressed that she was unable to focus her mind on the way home. Nesterenko saw from his office window that at first, Maria walked in the opposite direction. Then she realized that she was going in the direction of her mansion and turned back. On that day, it took much longer for Maria to get home.

Sasha saw through the window how his mother was fighting with a gate spring and ran out to help her. The boy noticed right away that Maria was not well. He helped his mother to get into the house. Maria did not give them a chance to ask her about anything that took place at school. She announced in a low voice,

"They discharged me. I am fired since today. The KGB found me again. They want me out of the school system. What should we do? How shall we live?"

Sasha and Ganja were next to Maria, being afraid that any moment, the stressed woman could collapse. Maria was unable to sit on the bench without somebody's support. Sasha shouted,

"Mama, no! Please, do not pass out!"

Ganja brought some water and asked Maria to drink. Then she asked,

"Sashko, run to the well and bring a bucket of cold water."

Cold water had its refreshing effect. Ganja washed Maria's face and gave her some cold water to drink. Maria started to talk,

"They found me, Ganja. Everything was too good to be true. What should I do with two children and no job? How can we live?"

Ganja answered calmly, like nothing dramatic occurred,

"You'll live with God's help, dear. Pray and the Lord will be with you. Is there anything new, Pannochka Maria? Did you believe that they had completely stopped chasing you?"

Maria listened to the old nanny and was amazed with her cleverness. Ganja did not believe that KGB would leave Maria and children alone. They continued hunting the unprotected woman and her sons.

Ganja declared with firmness in her voice, "Something miraculous must happen, in order they forget about you. Maria, it does not matter, that you became Gnatiuk and moved to another side of the country. For the demonic structure, you are the same God's child, that did not allow monsters to win easily. Being demonic, they would never let you liberally breathe, live and work. If they leave God's people unbending, then there is something wrong with their evil cluster."

"Ganja, they left Larissa in peace and allowed her to be promoted to the principle position," Maria contradicted the old nanny.

"Who left Larissa alone? The demons who burned her children alive and caused her suffering? She lives peacefully just because they do not exist already in this world. God got rid of them during the war. Nobody is alive who can revenge her. Your revenge-seekers are living and continue hunting you."

Maria was terrified again for her sons and herself. She thought, "They always succeed with keeping people in fear. Why do they do it again? Why?"

"Everything is over," Maria said out loud. "I have to take my kids and run away. We definitely need to disappear! Where can we disappear, Ganja? Every night, they can come and kill or deport us back to Magadan. O Lord, do they still plan to take our lives?"

Maria looked at Ganja. The old woman was bustling near the stove with preparation of the supper, and she looked like Maria's news did not surprise her at all. Ganja had her plans and she waited for the first day of Maria's vocation. She wanted to take Pannochka and both kids to the woods to meet Dr. Kotyk and old Count. Ganja visited both gentlemen on Friday and prepared them for meeting with Maria and children. Ganja was genuinely kind, and she decided to avoid any additional stress for the family. "Maybe, Maria and kids will stay there for a week or two?" Ganja thought. "Nobody knows what we can expect after Pannochka was dismissed from the school. The KGB can be here any day and any moment."

Somebody called for Ganja at the gate. It was a mailman. He handed Ganja a letter. Ganja put it in front of Maria. Maria opened the envelope. It was Larissa's letter. She invited Maria and her kids for summer vacations. "After long years in Magadan zone, it would be highly beneficial for you and kids to come and to live here on the Black Sea. Maria, don't worry about anything. At the beginning, I'll arrange housing and meals for you, until you find something better."

Maria raised her eyes from the letter and looked at Ganja. The old nanny smiled, like if she knew what was written there.

"Your friend invites you for summer, giving you lodge and board, doesn't she?" Ganja asked.

Maria exclaimed,

"How do you know, Ganja?"

"I am old, too old, Pannochka," the nanny replied. "Go to your friend and stay there for a month. But before you leave to your friend, we must visit somebody else and introduce the boys to them. This is my opinion, Pannochka. Maybe, I am wrong, but the fact that the old Count is still alive in his 103 proves that he patiently waits for meeting you and his grate-grandsons. He has mentioned several times to me that he cannot leave this world until he sees you again."

Maria was amazed,

"Do you think, Ganja he is really looking forward to seeing me? Maybe, he does not remember me, Ganja. The last time he saw me in 1941."

Maria began to cry, saying bitterly,

"It was he, my Grandpa, who predicted my unhappiness, tortures, suffering, and sorrowfulness. Why did he do that to me?"

Ganja came up and sat down next to Maria. She cuddled distressed woman and asked her,

"Was he wrong with anything that happened in your appalling life?"

"No, he wasn't," Maria whispered and added, "But it could be better, if he was …"

"The Lord blessed your grandfather with a very unusual talent. He did not only let people know what to expect in their lives but taught how to survive in all the life-threatening situations. Did it help you, Maria?"

Maria was silent. She experienced severe chest pain again. Her offence toward Grandpa was still there, and every time the recall of her Grandpa's prediction caused that unbearable chest pain that seemed to be able to break Maria's chest right in the middle.

Ganja noticed, how painful was the memory of the grandfather for the young widow. The old nanny advised,

"Maria, stop brewing the old offence inside of you! It was not your grandfather's fault in everything that happened to you. Nobody has the power to change our destiny. Only Almighty God can do it. If it hasn't been done by God, that means that you are strong enough to deal with your life situations."

Maria felt disturbed,

"I do not care about my life. For a long time, there is no life, like life. But how can I protect my sons?"

Maria sensed that her old chest pain was elevating and made her again lightheaded and shaky. She was spilling the water from the cup on her dress. Ganja came closer to Maria, took the cup from her hands and put it on the table. Then she took Maria's pale face in her hands and, looking in Maria's eyes, asked gently,

"Maria, let your childish offence go away, and you'll feel better. Your grandpa loves you more than anybody else in the whole world. He looks forward to seeing you again. Do you know, Maria, he could not forgive me for a long time that he hadn't met you and Count Alexander in 1946, when demons kept you in the servants' lodge. Breathe out your pain, darling, otherwise the pain can choke you."

Maria followed Ganja's advice and started to breathe. At the beginning, she could not inhale. Every time, when Maria tried to inhale, the terrible cough interrupted her breathing. It felt like something blocked the deep inhalation, preventing the release of the emotional pain.

The old nanny patiently repeated,

"Breathe, Maria. Breathe, darling. Let it go away once and forever. May the Lord help you to get rid of the pain that makes your suffering so bad. It was the only reason of your passing out. The demons knew how to make you weak. They mixed your emotional offence toward the grandfather with unacceptance of Count Alexander's death and fears about your kids and yourself. Their evil potion took away your free and deep breathing."

Maria listened to the miraculous diagnostics of the old nanny with a smile. However, she noticed that with each new breathing attempt, she began to inhale deeper and deeper. She was lightheaded, but the chest pain was evaporating with each breath.

Ganja suggested a brake for a couple of minutes. Maria noticed that the children were watching her, and Ivanko tried to breathe deeply, like his mother. Maria warned Sasha, "Watch the baby, please. He can be lightheaded with overventilation and fall from the bench."

"Mama, breathe. Please, breathe again," Sasha asked.

Maria smiled and continued her breathing procedure. She thought, "Ganja created a miracle. No, no, no!"

Maria shook her head and exclaimed out loud, hugging an old woman with strength that she did not experience for a long time,

"Ganja, you are a miracle worker!"

The old nanny blessed herself and said,

"Thank you, Lord for everything You've done for my dear Pannochka Maria. Alleluia, Alleluia, Alleluia. Glory to Thee, o Lord! Glory to Thee!"

Maria got up from the bench and walked around the room. She was not as dizzy, as she expected to be. She was hungry. She sensed, how her stomach was rumbling.

"Ganja, children, I am hungry!" Maria declared in a loud voice.

Sasha exclaimed, "Hurray, our Mama is hungry!" He hugged his baby brother and repeated with joy, "Hurray!" Sasha hugged Ganja and Maria and announced again, "Thank You, Lord! My Mama is hungry!"

The family was sitting at the table and had their cooled supper. They still enjoyed foods because the spirit of joy was with them. Maria asked the question that intrigued her from the very first day when she learned about her Grandpa's life in the hunting lodge,

"Ganja, how is it possible that the soviets haven't thrown my grandpa out of the hunting lodge?" Maria asked.

Ganja answered with a smile,

"All these years they considered him mentally sick. You understand, Maria, for them he was just a crazy old man. Only some people knew that it was not true. Old Count learned how to pretend that he became crazy after the death of his son Dr. Kotyk. He knew how to operate and heal your father, how to hide him from demons for so many years."

"What Grandpa does now? Can he heal?"

Ganja smiled and replied proudly,

"He still helps people with reading the Holy Bible. Every day, he walks for miles in the woods and collects the herbs, roots, mushrooms and bark of different trees. He remembers the recipes of all his remedies by heart. He prepares them and successfully heals different diseases. Every day, he does all these things plus constantly prays for his Marie and waits for your arrival. Sorry to say, but nobody believed that you could survive, except your grandfather."

Maria put her head on Ganja's shoulder and a new flow of tears poured on her cheeks.

"So, Grandpa believed that I was alive," Maria said quietly.

"Every time, he repeated the same phrase to your father and me: 'The Holy Bible cannot lie.'"

"Ganja, why didn't we visit them right after our arrival?"

"None of you were ready. Do you remember in what condition you have arrived?" Ganja answered.

"How do you know that my grandpa looks forward to seeing me? You've visited them recently, haven't you? Why haven't you taken us with you?"

Ganja cuddled Maria, as a small child, and whispered in Maria's ear,

"It's all right, Pannochka Maria. I'll take you tomorrow. We need to go to bed earlier in order to get up early. It's a long walk there, especially with a baby and baskets for berries and mushrooms."

Then she announced out loud in order Sasha could hear,

"Tomorrow, we'll go to the woods to gather the berries and summer mushrooms. The kids do not know, how tasty the mushroom soup or mushroom stew can be. I do not say anything about raspberries. They are absolutely delicious now. We need to bring a lot and make preserves for wintertime."

Sasha looked at Ganja with suspicion,

"Do you want all of us go to the forest to gather berries and mushrooms? I mean, do you think that Ivanko also will go with us? To my mind, he is too small. Mama, what do you think about walking in the forest with Ivanko?"

Maria answered calmly,

"That's all right, Sasha that Ivanko is small. We'll go all together. He also needs the pure air of the forest to breathe. It's rich in oxygen. If it is not good for your younger brother, next time, we'll leave him at home with Ganja. This time Ganja will show us the right places to pick berries and mushrooms. Right, Ganja?"

"It's true. Tomorrow, I'll take all of you in the right place," Ganja answered shortly and began to clean the table.

Lord, have mercy!

⚜

Chapter 31

Maria did not sleep well that night. She saw nightmares with the huge kites that surrounded her and children on their way to the forest. She tried to protect her kids, but they pulled the baby girl out of her arms and flew away. Maria awoke in tears. It was 3:30 a.m. She got up, kneeled in front of the icons and prayed 12 times "Our Father", trying to rich God's attention to her request to deliver them from the evil forces. She ended with her usual appeal:

"Help us, save us, have mercy on us and keep us, oh Lord by Your grace."

At the end of the meditation, Maria noticed the warmth, spreading all over her body and making her relaxed. She was already in bed near her baby boy, when she saw the light. Maria whispered, "Thank you, Lord for sending the Holy spirit that always calms me down." She fell asleep.

In the morning, Ganja returned to the house after feeding chickens and milking the gouts. All of her *'tenants'* continued sleeping soundly. The old nanny sat down on the bench and watched them. She recollected the years, when she was Jennie's nanny, and every morning, enjoyed sitting and knitting in Jennie's bedroom, while the baby was asleep. Ganja always felt guilty to interrupt child's dreams, when it was time and wake her up.

Maria opened her eyes and looked at the clock. It was 7:20. She jumped out of bed. Yesterday, they planned to leave the house at 7:30.

"Sasha," Maria called her son. "It's time to get up. If we come late to the forest, people will gather all the berries and mushrooms in the nearest areas, and we have to go far with Tisha."

It was strange, they called the boy Ivanko, when they talk directly to the child, but very often they continued to name him Tikhon in their conversations about him.

"Mama, where is nanny Ganja?" Sasha asked.

"I am here, children. I am here," Ganja answered. "You want to have your breakfast, don't you? It's on the table."

Maria looked at Ganja and said,

"Good morning, Ganja. Forgive me, I overslept this morning. By the way, I haven't noticed you, sitting there."

"That's all right, Maria. Well, kids, get ready! Your breakfast is waiting for you. We eat and go. I know for sure that it is going to be a very interesting day."

Tisha did not want to move out of bed, until he heard how Ganja named the foods for breakfast. He turned on his belly and slipped down from the bed. The bed was too high, and the baby boy lost the balance when he landed and sat down on the floor. The child wanted to cry, but seeing that nobody paid attention to him, he got up and moved straight to the table. Maria caught her son in a step to his 'destination' and carried to wash and change the pajama for his daily cloths. She was teaching him, "We cannot invite a gentleman in pajama to the table. Nobody insists in wearing the tie for breakfast, but decent cloths are a must."

Sasha and Ganja laughed.

Maria was nervous about her visit to the hunting lodge. Her nervousness slightly decreased, when they entered the forest and began picking up the ripe and sweet-scented raspberries. Tisha liked raspberries and Sasha was gathering them for his brother. Maria flew away in her memories, when she was a girl of Sasha's age, and they used to go daily with her father to gather the berries. It seemed like it was centuries ago. A strange thought came to Maria's mind, "Am I so old?" She could not choose the right answer between 'yes, no, maybe, not at all'. One thing she discovered about her age, "I do not feel that I am 'ancient', but my life made me very weary."

Collecting berries, they continued walking deeper into the woods. Sasha sat his brother on his shoulders in order they could catch the pace of his mother and Ganja.

Sasha asked,

"Mama, are we in a hurry? I cannot carry Tisha, pick the berries, look for the mushrooms and catch your speed. We passed nice places with lots of berries there."

"Leave the berries and mushrooms, Sasha. Follow us, please. When we meet people in the forest, greet them and pretend that you are gathering berries, or even better, feeding your brother with berries," Maria suggested.

Sasha did not understand his mother's advice and asked himself, "Why should we pretend?"

It took longer than two hours of fast walking in the woods to get to the hunting lodge. Maria confessed,

"Ganja, I would never find them there. I forgot all the paths."

Ganja had an opposite opinion,

"Only at the beginning, the forest looks completely unfamiliar, but I am sure that you can find most of the old paths. We brought you to the forest for the first time when you were about one. Every day of the season, the servants were gathering big baskets of berries for making jams, jellies and preserves. Do you remember, your father exported it to Europe? Your mother carried you in her arms. You were dressed in a long pink dress with the white bows around the hem. Pani Anna walked around, picked the ripest berries and fed you. Both of you liked the sweet taste and smell of raspberries. I saw how she blessed the first berry and put it in your tiny mouth to try. You liked it, like Ivanko."

Sasha interrupted old nanny,

"Where is now my Mom's mother?"

"I don't know, Sasha. Ask your grandfather when you meet him. Maybe, he heard something about her."

Sasha came closer to the old nanny and said,

"Excuse me, nanny Ganja. I interrupted you. I wish I can meet all of them, the whole Kotyk's family."

Ganja smiled and hugged the boys. The moment she touched him, Tisha stretched his arms to her. Ganja pulled the boy and carried him, giving Sasha the opportunity to have some rest and to increase the speed. Sasha noticed the hunting lodge in a distance and exclaimed,

"Look, there is a huge house in the middle of the woods. Who lives there?"

Ganja looked at Maria, expecting her to explain something to her son. Maria did not listen to them. She was in a hurry to meet her family. She could not stand walking and ran. Sasha asked,

"Where does our Mama run?"

Ganja answered,

"Let her run, Sasha. Your mother waited for this moment since 1941."

"Ganja, who are those two men on the porch? Why does our Mama run to them?"

Sasha was completely confused, when he saw how his mother flew upstairs and hugged a smaller man there.

"He is your grandfather, Dr. Lukian Kotyk," Ganja answered.

Sasha saw how the older man embraced both of them-Maria and Dr. Kotyk.

"My grandfather? And the taller man must be our grate-grandfather, the old Count Kotyk. Am I right, Ganja?"

"Yes, you are, Sasha. You are absolutely right."

Ganja and Sasha slowed down, in order not to interrupt the re-union of the closest people. All three of them cried on the porch of the hunting lodge. They could not stop hugging and kissing Maria. Father noticed the tattoo number on the wrist of his daughter. Her number from the German concentration camp. He kissed her hands. None of the men noticed Ganja and children until Maria said.

"Look, Papa, here are my sons."

Dr. Kotyk came downstairs to meet them. Sasha moved forward. He introduced himself,

"Alexander Kurbatov."

Then he looked at his mother in bewilderment. He pronounced the real name. She smiled, and it gave Sasha strength and confidence for some correction,

"Count Alexander Kurbatov."

"Count Lukian Kotyk. It's a pleasure to meet you, Your Grace."

Both of them made one more step forward and embraced each other tightly, like if they had known each other forever. The old Count called on them,

"Gentlemen, I am really sorry, but there are two other representatives of the family waiting to be introduced."

Everyone looked at old Count. Sasha ran upstairs and introduced himself to his grate-grandfather. Then Sasha asked him,

"Who else waits for being introduced?"

At that moment, Tisha reminded everyone with loud scream, "Mama. Mama, come."

The old Count pointed at the baby boy and said,

"He and I want to be hugged and kissed, as well."

Dr. Kotyk took his small grandson in his arms and asked,

"What is your name, Your Grace?"

There was silence for a while. Maria was overwhelmed with her feelings and could not present the story connected with the name of the boy. She required some time to tell it. The old Count invited the guests inside of the house. The table was set for seven people. Maria noticed one extra chair at the table. Children were hungry after the light breakfast and the walk in the forest. They enjoyed the lunch at the grandfather's place. Maria could not eat. She experienced the mixture of bitterness and joy at the same time. She wanted to be with her father and grandfather daily, taking care of them and making them happy. She wanted to give them the opportunity to watch her children grow. However, in her unpredictable life, it was not possible to arrange everything this way.

Maria took her father's hand with her small one and pulled him outside. They stood in silence on the back porch of the hunting lodge. Count Lukian touched the black shawl and asked,

"How did it happen, Marie?"

It looked like she was waiting for this question. Father's question released the suppressed force of the willpower, and poor woman burst into loud lamenting. Eco repeated her lament in the deep woods.

Maria shouted out,

"Papa, I lost my husband. I lost my beloved Alexander. It was me, who brought him here. It was me, who sanctified my husband for mutilation and suffering in 1946, and for over than 10 years of inhuman imprisonment. It was me, who did not protect him, and they murdered him brutally on the train after his visit to Magadan KGB. Look at me, Papa! I am a killer of my husband. Can you understand the horror of my life? Every day and every night, I ask the Lord to forgive my biggest sin – my home-coming and the death of Alexander."

Maria did not have strength to stand. She kneeled, took a breath and continued in French,

"Papa, they arrested us in our manor. They beat Alexander to blood and mutilated him to the point that I would never recognize my husband. They raped me, ignoring the six months of my pregnancy. I found my husband in the entrance hall on the floor. He was unconscious. They fractured his ribs, right wrist, and nose. With God's help, he survived. They imprisoned an innocent honorable man for ten and a half years in Siberia."

Maria became dizzy and nauseous. Dr. Kotyk noticed that his daughter is unwell and asked,

"Marie, please stop crying."

Maria did not hear her father's request. She asked him,

"Papa, do you know where Alexander found strength to live?"

Count Lukian answered without hesitation, "He loved you, Marie. Love gives us strength and determination."

"You are right, Papa. He loved me, Papa. He always mentioned that he was ready to suffer and die for kids' and my sake."

Maria continued crying bitterly,

"I cannot live without him. I am lost, totally lost. Yesterday, I was fired. They took away my job. I was a teacher of Domestic science in Blue Creeks school. They continue pursuing me and children. The school principle received a call from Lviv and, as he explained to me, they considered I had no right to teach at school. Why? What did I do to them?"

Maria looked up at her father and saw him crying. She had never seen her father's tears. Maria blamed herself for bringing her unbearable pain to Papa. Maria wanted to get up, and Dr. Kotyk helped his daughter. He said with deep sympathy in his voice,

"Marie, my dearest Marie, nobody can help you. We are outcasts for the communist demonic force. They hate us for being born in noble families, for our faith, for our education, for our understanding that their utopic ideas could not exist long. They stopped hunting me just because they know-I am not in this world. They executed me in order to prove that their satanic power is stronger that the power of our Almighty God."

"Papa, please live long. Now, I know that I am not alone in this world. I will come to you and bring my boys. Since now on, two of us will pray and ask God to forgive my sinful fault in the death of my husband and misery of my kids."

"I'll do my best, my child. I'll do anything you want me to do."

Maria hugged her father and none of them interrupted silence for a rather long time. Then Dr. Kotyk asked Maria,

"What are your plans for this summer?"

"My friend from the force labor camp invited us to Odessa region. She lives on the Black Sea. She promised to help me with everything. I need to go there, Papa. It's good for my boys. They were born and lived in Magadan zone. None of them had ever been at the warm sea. Maybe, I can find my job there. What do you think?"

"Go, Marie, go. You know, girl, that with God all things are possible. I wanted to ask you about so many things. When you come back from Odessa, we'll see each other and talk for several days. Now, you need to go and get home before the sunset."

"Papa, how is Grandpa?"

"With God's blessing, he is 103. Nowadays, he is weaker, but thank God, the Creator blessed him with good health and mind. He always believed that you were alive. He promised me daily, "One day, our Marie will come to see us."

"What do you think, Papa, do they have a suspicion that you have survived?"

“I don’t think so, Marie. You know them better than anybody else. They would never give me a chance to live, if they knew the truth,” Dr. Kotyk explained.

“Papa, do you think that they continue hunting my kids and me in order to finish their ‘dirty assignment’? Poor chicks! How can I defend my sons from the monsters?!”

“Calm down, Marie. Calm down, my girl. God is merciful.”

Dr. Kotyk cuddled his daughter with all his parental love. He reminded her,

“Remember, Marie, there is no any force stronger than God. In your case, you cannot do anything by yourself. Give your fears and concerns to the Lord. Stay under His protection. Keep your kids under the miraculous protection of His Holy Mother.”

Maria did not answer. Dr. Kotyk asked,

“Marie, how can I help you, other than to pay for your train tickets to Odessa? Leave Alexander here, if you want. It would be easier for you to visit your friend with Tisha only.”

“No, Papa. We have learned to travel together. Sasha needs more than Tisha to go to the Black Sea. He is a camp child. He lived ten years on camp putrid wish-wash, made of half-rotten vegetables. Papa, it was awful that I came here before our child was born. Until now, my poor boy hadn’t seen normal life and freedom. I wanted to help you, Papa. I wanted to liberate all of you out of the cage of evil *red octopus*, but instead, my family was trapped and locked in it.”

"Marie, be careful now, when you know that you are still not free."

"I know, Papa, but at least there is no fence with electric wires around, and Sasha attends the school, where nobody names him "camp boy", asking him about the treason or harm his parents committed to this 'most democratic country'."

"Wait, Marie. As long, as they found you again, be prepared: they could fabricate a letter to the local committee with the description of the crime that you and your husband had never performed. People will believe them. Marie, for us, the war is not over. Not yet."

"Papa, I am so glad to see you again, talk to you and get your wise advice. Thank you, Papa. We need to go home."

"I wish I can help you, children," Dr. Kotyk pronounced with deep disappointment.

Maria leaned toward her father and put her head on his chest. She felt happiness inside, or at least something that reminded her forgotten feeling of child's happiness.

"What a miracle, Papa! We are again together."

Sasha opened the door and called them inside,

"Mama, Grandpa, get in, please. We miss you."

Maria took her father's hand and kissed it,

"I love you, Papa."

"I love you too, Marie. You are the only child, who still belongs to our family. They took all my children away from me and twisted their minds and believes."

Maria saw, how painful it was to her father to lose his children. She recollected the similar case with Dr. Leskov's daughters and briefly told him their story.

The old Count stepped out to the porch. He asked the straight question,

"Well, Marie, tell me the truth. Do you still blame me for everything I predicted?"

Maria was grateful to Ganja for releasing her deep pain, and answered honestly,

"No, grandpa. Not anymore."

Everyone noticed that the old Count was happy to hear Maria's answer. He hugged his granddaughter and advised,

"You need to eat more, Marie. There is nothing left of you. You are like a feather. If the wind blows stronger, you can fly far away from us, my darling. My child, we don't want to lose you again. I cannot live forever, waiting for your next visit. I wish, I can see all my grandchildren and grate-grandchildren together before I go home to our Lord.

Dr. Kotyk added,

"I wish all my children find truth of life. Marie, it's not for my sake or grandpa's, not at all. It's for them."

They returned home at dusk. At night, Maria was praying with a smile. She expressed her sincere gratitude to the Divinity for a wonderful day that she spent with her father and grandpa. They helped Marie with the money for the tickets to Odessa. She planned to leave the next day and not to come back in a month. Maria meditated,

"Make haste, O God, to deliver me! Make haste to help me, O Lord! Let them be ashamed and confounded who seek my life and misfortune of my sons; let them be turned back because of their shame. But I am poor and needy; make haste to help me, O God! You are my help and my deliverer; O Lord, do not delay. Amen."

Glory to Thee, O Lord! Glory to Thee!

Chapter 32

Next morning, Maria opened her eyes around 5:30 a.m. It was still dark in the house, but she could not fall asleep again. Maria lit the candle on the table and quietly pulled her suitcase to the bench. She began to pack to Odessa. Suddenly, she experienced an unexplainable wave of icy cold fear that covered her with goose bumps from head to toes. She sensed the presence of a stranger close to their house, if not even in the house. Maria quickly finished with packing and went to wake up Ganja and Sasha. Ganja's bed was empty. Maria's first thought was that something happened to the old nanny. "Maybe, she went outside to the lavatory or the goat house and tripped there in darkness. Maria rushed to look for Ganja outside, and to check the chicken and goat houses.

Maria woke up Alexander and whispered in his ear,

"Sasha, Ganja disappeared. I'll go and check outside. Don't follow me. Stay with Tisha."

Maria rushed to the front door and was ready to open it, when somebody stopped her. She looked back and did not find anybody there. Maria understood-it was her Guardian angel. The frightened woman went to the kitchen window and looked out to the backyard and goat house. She saw that the doors to the goats were opened and not fixed, as Ganja usually did it when she milked the goats. Then she noticed that one of the goats was walking around the dog-house. Maria thought, "Usually, they avoid coming up to the dog. It's strange that the dog allowed the goat to walk there and does not bark at it."

The wind freely moved both doors of the goat house. Maria did not know what to do. She waited for a minute and decided to open the back door. Sasha saw, how his mother prepared a thick stick that Ganja hid under the bench near the entrance door. Maria pulled slightly the handle and the door was opened. She went outside. She did not notice anything strange near the door and on the back porch. Maria ran to the barn and stopped near the opened doors. The wave of fear again covered Maria. She called, staying in the doorway,

"Ganja! Ganja, are you there?"

Both goats answered Maria. Maria did not find courage to enter the barn. She noticed Ganja's neighbor outside. He drove out his cow to pasture. Maria called him,

"Peter, please come here. I cannot find Ganja, and I am afraid to enter the barn."

He jumped over the fence and went inside of the barn. In the doorway he smiled and asked,

"What are you afraid, Maria? Are you still afraid of the goats? They kicked you badly in childhood, didn't they?"

In a minute he went out. The expression of his face talked for him. He showed with his hand inside of the barn and whispered,

"She is gone. Somebody killed her. They strangle Ganja."

Peter blessed himself with a cross and rushed home. In a minute, his wife and another neighbor came to Ganja's backyard. Maria entered the barn. Strangled Ganja laid on the ground with a thin rope around her neck. Maria experienced lack of air. She moved slowly out of the barn and fainted near the entrance.

When she opened her eyes, there was an unfamiliar doctor near her. He listened to her pulse. Maria wanted to get up, but the doctor stopped her. She looked around and saw Sasha who stood on the porch, carrying Tisha in his arms. The militia men worked in the barn near Ganja's body. Maria closed her eyes. Her thoughts were climbing again one on the top of the other,

"This is the end. They killed Ganja. They killed our angel… Yesterday, it was my mistake that I did not leave Sasha with his grandfather… They will arrest me... Sasha will also be sent to the prison "for young criminals", as they call it. Poor Tisha has to grow in orphanage, where demons will twist his mind. He would not remember me, as he forgot his father."

The tears rolled out of Maria's eyes. She was surprised to hear the voice of Nesterenko among all the rest voices. He asked somebody about the tragedy and came up to the doctor.

"Doctor, how is Comrade Gnatiuk?"

"Not stable."

"Why don't you take her right away to the district hospital, if you found that her condition is not stable."

The doctor picked up the anger in Nesterenko's voice and answered,

"I wanted to hospitalize the patient immediately, but Major from militia stopped me. He wants to talk to her. I have no idea, how they plan to interrogatc hcr with hcr blood pressure 57/32."

Nesterenko went to the barn. He came up to the Major and explained the situation. Maria heard their loud voices, but she was not able to comprehend what they talked about. Two of them came up to Maria. The Major wanted to ask something and realized that the principle of the local school was probably right, insisting on taking Gnatiuk to the hospital. Major Kalush looked at Maria and detected that the idea of the KGB officer that citizen Gnatiuk could be the main person under suspicion was a hundred percent gibberish.

"Doctor, take her to the district hospital," Major Kalush ordered.

"Wait a minute," Nesterenko asked. "There are two kids over there. They have to know where their mother is taken."

Maria heard again that he was talking to Sasha for a minute, and they came up to her.

"Mama, please wake up," Sasha asked with a trembling voice.

Maria tried to open her eyes but could not do it. She whispered,

"Sasha, take care of Tisha. It would be better not to stay here, son. They can be back."

"Who could be back, Maria Lukjanivna?" Nesterenko asked.

"Those people who killed Ganja," Maria whispered.

She heard how the doctor asked the people to step aside, in order the ambulance team could take Maria on the stretcher to the ambulance.

"Please, take care of my children, Mykola Petrovych," Maria whispered. "Otherwise, they will kill them. They found us. They will not let us live."

"Who are 'they', Maria Lukjanivna?"

The principle tried to understand. He bended over Maria in order he could hear her better.

Maria whispered,

"People from KGB. They killed my husband in March. This morning, they killed Ganja. I don't know how to protect my sons. Help me, please."

Maria was again in delirious condition, when the doctor took her to the ambulance. Tisha began to cry, and the loud cry of the child awoke Nesterenko. He said to Sasha,

"Don't worry, Sashko, I'll send somebody to stay with you."

The principle left for work. When he was in half a way to school, he noticed a military jeep riding in the opposite direction. He saw that jeep for the third time. At night, Nesterenko could not sleep and was sitting and smocking on the porch of his house. He was surprised to see that jeep around 2 a.m. The day before yesterday, he saw them around eleven in the evening. "Maybe, she was right. The KGB murdered her husband, and now, they scared nearly to death the poor widow and children. How was it possible to kill an old woman in order just to scare Maria and kids? It's unjust and immoral. It's evil. It's criminal." Nesterenko stopped for a couple of seconds and ran back. He was right in time there, when the people from the jeep interrogated Sasha. Nesterenko saw in a distance that the child did not know what to answer. The principle came up and introduced himself,

"Nesterenko. I am the principle of the local school."

The officers looked at him and did not introduce themselves. Nesterenko continued,

"I am here to pick up the children. They cannot stay alone after the tragic event."

Nesterenko saw that he mixed up the plans of the visitors. He explained with a smile,

"You know better than me that the kids' testimonies mean nothing. I feel sorry, it's just wasting of your time, officers."

Nesterenko took Tisha in his arms and said,

"The militia checked the house. So, we can lock the doors and go."

One of the visitors asked,

"Are you relatives?"

"No, we are not. Maria Lukjanivna is our teacher of Domestic science, and Sashko is the student of our school," Nesterenko answered calmly.

"I've heard that she was discharged after a phone call from region Department of education," the second visitor said.

Nesterenko thought, “Maria was right. These visitors know everything. They are after her.”

The principle promised out loud,

“The moment they find the teacher who arrives to substitute comrade Gnatiuk, comrade Gnatiuk is discharged. Good-bye.”

Sasha locked the front and the back doors, and they went to school. Nesterenko suggested to Sasha,

“Now, we’ll leave Ivanko with my mother and go to the district hospital to visit your mother. Do you agree?”

“Yes, I do,” the boy answered without hesitations. “I need to be there with Mama. I did not protect my father in March. Now, I must protect my mother.”

In half an hour, Nesterenko and Sasha were on the road and stopped the truck to hitch a ride. They were close to the town, when the military jeep passed the truck. Nesterenko asked the driver to go faster. He was thinking about a very strange situation, he found himself in. For the first time in his life, he was afraid to be late to see a woman, who was school employee for several months, a stranger to him.

The driver stopped near the gate to the district hospital. They were still in the truck, when they saw, how the officers in the military jeep were driving out of the hospital gate. Nesterenko did not want to frighten Sasha, but his heart was pounding. They rushed to the hospital. The clerk in the Inquiry Box did not want to give them any information or permission to visit a patient. Nesterenko insisted in seeing a doctor-in-charge. The doctor made an exception for “the husband

and son". Maria was in the room with three other women. She was conscious and could talk in a very low voice.

"Where is Ivanko?" Maria asked, when she saw only two visitors coming to her bed.

"Don't worry, Maria Lukianivna. We left the boy with my mother," Nesterenko answered. "He'll be fine there. My mother and sister are retired teachers and know how to deal with children."

"Mama, how are you?" Sasha asked. The boy tried to pronounce the words firmly, but his voice trembled.

"Sasha, I am much better now than I was in the morning. They arrived to interrogate me, but the doctor did not allow them," Maria whispered.

"We saw them," Nesterenko said and noticed that Maria was surprised that he knew who she was talking about.

"Mykola Petrovych, I was thinking. My children and I are in life-threatening situation. I don't want you to get in the same trouble. It's dangerous, trust me," Maria warned.

"What is dangerous for me, Maria Lukjanivna? I am not a coward. I am not afraid to protect a widow and her children," Nesterenko answered.

"Ganja was not afraid, as well, and we lost her," Maria began to cry.

Sasha saw how the principle turned pale. Nesterenko asked Maria,

"Please, don't cry, Maria Lukjanivna. I beg you not to cry. To my mind, it's the only thing that I cannot stand at all."

The nurse entered the room with a syringe filled with medication and ready for injection. She was surprised to see the visitors near Maria. The nurse stopped for a second, then turned around and left.

"She is strange. She is really strange," Nesterenko commented.

He got up and left after the nurse. It took fifteen minutes, until he returned to the room. He tried to find the nurse that 'evaporated' so fast. He was looking for the nurse everywhere and asked the personnel for the nurse with a small syringe in her hand. Nobody saw her, and nobody sent her to patient Gnatiuk. The nurse at the nursing station checked Maria's chart and confirmed that nothing was ordered for Maria in a syringe.

Nesterenko stated with his usual firmness, "Maria Lukianivna, I've decided – Alexander and I will stay with you this night and the whole day tomorrow. If everything is well with you, we'll take you home. One thing I know for sure that you cannot stay alone in the hospital without our protection. Am I right, Sashko?"

Sasha was happy and kissed his mother's hand. Maria wanted to argue and send the principle back to Blue Creeks, "Please, Mykola Petrovych, go and work. Sasha will stay with me."

Nesterenko presented everything, as a joke,

"Maria Lukjanivna, don't push me away from the hospital. At last, I found the way to escape from my office and have some rest. For so many months, I did not have a tiny opportunity for a day off. Today, I arranged my mini vocation for two days."

They smiled. However, Maria saw that Nesterenko was truly concerned. The exhausted woman did not have strength for further arguing. She knew that they would never forgive Nesterenko his attempt to save Maria. "He can ruin his career, because of me," Maria thought. It was her last thought. Her physical weakness and emotional exhaustion put her to sleep.

Lord, Have Mercy!

Chapter 33

In the evening, one of the patients was transferred to another department, and Sasha was lucky to have a bed to sleep. Nesterenko sat down on the chair closer to Maria, blocking the way to her bed from the door. He surveyed the unusual for him circumstances. The man tried to find the reason for his actions. "Why am I involved in the situation with Maria Gnatiuk and her children? Why am I here in the hospital, sitting at Maria's side, as a guard dog? Why do I feel that I must be here?"

He looked at sleeping Maria and continued analyzing the situation, "There is no way that I fell in love with this tiny bird." Nesterenko tried to look in the depth of his heart. "I am too old for love. I am fifty in a month. Then why was my heart pounding since I have learned about the tragedy in Maria's house? I ran there at once, then I returned for the second time and picked up the children.

Nesterenko recollected the situation with the children. He saw that the KGB officers did not expect from the principle of the local school such an action. He smiled, refreshing in his memory the facial expressions of his mother and sister when he brought Ivanko home!

"I am not in love with Maria," Nesterenko tried to prove to himself. The inner voice asked him, "Then why did I take her baby boy and left him with my mother and sister? Why don't I sleep in my own bed this night?"

Nesterenko believed that something wrong was going on around that tiny woman, who was a stranger for him. He admitted that he actually cared about that *stranger.* Then he evoked a single thought that he kept in his mind on his way to Ganja's house, "Please, God do not take Maria away." He repeated that unusual request numerous times. He restored in his memory the picture in Ganja's backyard, when Maria was laying on the ground, and Sasha stood near his mother, holding the younger brother in his arms.

The inner voice prompted, "You are in trouble, Nesterenko. KGB will not forgive you your excessively active intrusion in this case. Your actions will have consequences. Are you ready for them? Do you need it?" He was surprised how fast he answered, "Yes." Then Nesterenko asked the question that was the most reasonable in this situation, "Why do I need to be involved in this unclear situation?" He sensed the disturbance, as if he was a school boy who did something wrong and could not find the reason for it. "We'll see. Time will clarify everything. I mean, the whole situation will be apparent in some time. I am certain in one thing – Maria suffers for nothing. I should stop it." He dozed after the last thought.

Somebody opened the door and quietly sneaked into the room. Everyone in the room was asleep, including Nesterenko. The nurse moved cautiously to Maria's bed.

She did not open the blanket and stuck the syringe through it. Maria moaned and Nesterenko woke up. He registered the syringe with some liquid in it and caught the nurse's arm.

"How can you do it through the blanket …?" Even in twilight, Nesterenko recognized the nurse that "evaporated" yesterday. Maria watched them with widely opened eyes. The nurse could not release her hand. Nesterenko pulled out the syringe and inquired,

"Why did you come here again? Who sent you here? Do you want me to inject the liquid in your arm?"

He looked serious in his intention to do it. The woman was frightened. She whispered,

"You cannot do it. I have two kids at home. They are going to kill them, if …"

"If you do not murder my wife?" Nesterenko asked loudly.

He pulled the nurse's arm and asked,

"Who are *they*, who follows my wife and children? Tell me quickly, or this liquid is in your arm."

"Don't you know? They are people from KGB. But now, it doesn't matter. They will kill me any way."

Nesterenko stepped in the situation that did not show any safe exit for the assassin. Maria watched him. He did not want to return the syringe to the 'nurse' and said,

"Go away."

Then he suggested to the unwilling assassin, "Maybe, you can go to Lviv KGB and describe the situation you are in. Somebody has to cancel the outrageous and illegal order and let your family and my family live without any intrusions."

Maria saw that the woman was crying quietly. Then she answered, "They sent me here, and I failed. It's my loss."

"You did not kill the woman who also has two kids, like you. What makes you so upset?" Nesterenko asked.

"My children and I lost the right to live," the 'nurse' whispered.

"It's serious," Nesterenko concluded. "I can hardly believe that they have power to murder people for nothing…"

Maria registered in her mind, "Poor Nesterenko doubts about me, her and thousands of non-guilty people that KGB executed for nothing."

The woman stretched her hand and asked,

"May I have it? I promise not to disturb you and your wife."

Nesterenko handed her the syringe, and she slowly went out of the room. In a minute, they heard the loud voices in the corridor. Nesterenko looked out of the room: the "nurse" was in convulsions on the floor by the next room. The empty syringe was near her right hand.

"Everything is over there, isn't it?" Maria asked quietly. Nesterenko nodded.

Maria prayed, *"Dear Lord, forgive this woman all her sins, voluntary and involuntary. For her intolerable sufferings, please allow her soul to get into*

Your Kingdom, where she can find peace, comfort and everlasting Light. Amen."

Nesterenko was confused and asked,

"How can you pray for the killer?"

Maria explained,

"Mykola Petrovych, I don't blame that woman. I feel sorry for her. She was a good mother and tried to do everything in her power in order to save the lives of her children."

Maria prayed again for the departed soul of the misfortunate woman. The Divinity stopped that woman, when she was ready to perform the worst sin – to take away life of an innocent person. She did not murder Maria, and the demonic force did not let the woman go alive. It forced her to commit suicide, another transgression in the eyes of the Lord.

"We need to do something, Maria Lukjanivna. We have to find what to do, as soon as possible. What do you think, what should we do to stop them? Who can stop them?" Nesterenko asked anxiously.

Maria did not hear the usual strength in his voice. She recognized the same perplexity, that she observed with Dr. Belikov. For the first time in Nesterenko's life, he was condescended by the force that he was not familiar with. As everything compelling, unknown, humiliating and dangerous, that force affected his mind and will power. Nesterenko found himself in the circumstances, when he was unable to control the situation. His frightened mind drew a dark picture without any light.

He repeated several times out loud the disturbing thoughts, paying no attention that he lost 'Lukianivna', when he addressed them to Maria.

"Maria, if not tonight then another time, they can murder anybody they want."

"Maria, tell me who can stop them?"

Maria felt sorry for Nesterenko, an intelligent, handsome and physically strong man. He was completely lost and terrified. She knew from her life experience that physical strength did not mean a lot when people deal with the demonic force. Nesterenko could not stand the pressure of the unknown and dangerous circumstances. Earlier, he had never been in the situation like the one with Maria and children. In his life, he used to be courageous and straight forward. He could not even imagine that the demonic force made so many cambers and traps on the life paths of other people.

"Mykola Petrovych, go home. You need rest. I appreciate everything you did for me and my children. You asked who can stop them. I believe that only God can stop. It's only in His power to find the resolution of my situation."

"No, Maria Lukjanivna. You know the Russian proverb: "You can keep hope in God but do everything by yourself." We'll go home together. How are you now?"

Maria sat down in bed and felt some light dizziness, nothing in comparison with previous morning. She rang the call-bell. When the nurse came in, Maria asked her to check the blood pressure. It was far from being normal, but functional. Then Maria asked the doctor to come. He flew into the room and asked,

"You want to go home, don't you?"

"Yes, I do," Maria answered with a smile. "I feel better, doctor. Thank you. My one-year-old son is waiting for his Mama to come."

The doctor counted Maria's pulse and decided to listen to her heart and lungs. He opened her gown on the chest so fast that Nesterenko did not have chance to turn away. The traumatized man turned red, as a schoolboy. He stood up quickly and went to the window. Staying there, he tried to wipe off from his mind the picture, he saw seconds ago. He admitted from the very first day that Maria has a delicate complexion, like a figurine from the XVIII century. Her black shawl and long dresses or skirts did not hide the attractiveness of the woman, but he could not imagine that after having two boys, her breasts had beautiful shape and their firmness.

"All right, if you want to go home, I'll prepare all the papers for your discharge from the hospital. The nurse will bring you my prescription. The medication will calm you down after the stress. Do you have lazarette in your Blue Creeks?" Doctor asked.

"No, we don't." Maria and Nesterenko answered simultaneously.

"I would like you to check the blood pressure every day for a week or so," doctor explained. "I want to be sure that it does not drop as low, as it happened on the day of the tragedy."

He came up to Nesterenko and recommended,

"Please, feed your wife and let her rest. Her blood test shows anemia and malnourishment. Take good care of her, please."

"I will," Nesterenko promised without hesitation. The men shook hands, and the doctor ran out of the room with the words, "Comrade Gnatiuk, stay well".

Maria smiled, watching the awkwardness of the situation. She asked Nesterenko to awake Sasha and to hasten the nurse with the prescription and cloths. Nesterenko looked at the watch and said,

"Now, it is 6:20 a.m. Let Sasha sleep for another half an hour. I don't think that they will submit the discharge papers faster. It's the best time to sleep for all the kids."

Maria thought,

"How can I stay here? In blue Creeks, Tisha is waiting for me and ..."

Her tears poured out of her eyes, when she recollected again Ganja's horrible death. "I lost my Ganja, the most devoted person I knew from childhood."

"Tomorrow is Ganja's funeral," Maria said out loud. "You don't know what Ganja meant for me and my boys. She was waiting and praying for me the whole her post-war life. I arrived and brought her death."

Nesterenko did not understand what Maria said about waiting for her. He took Maria's hand in his hands and said,

"Please, don't cry. Maria Lukjanivna, I'll do anything for you that is in my power. Please,

stop crying," Nesterenko begged Maria.

He looked at Maria for a minute and then suggested,

"If you do not mind, since today, we'll do everything together. I propose you my friendship and help."

Maria stopped crying and watched him with interest. She thought, "He is a wonderful person with a big heart. To my mind, I am pleased to see him … here." Maria changed in the very last second, the phrase that was already formulated in her mind, "I am pleased to see him with me." She did not say anything out loud.

"Lord, have mercy!"

⚜

Chapter 34

Ganja's funeral was crowded. Oryssia, Ganja's niece, arrived with her family from Lviv. Maria and Oryssia cried bitterly. Oryssia told Maria her story, how Ganja helped her from childhood. The girl lost her parents when she was six, and Ganja was the only person, who supported her and her older brother, supplying them with vegetables, fruits, berries and mushrooms during summer, unbelievably tasty preserves and sour cabbage, tomatoes and pickles for winter. She sewed all Oryssia's cloths. When the older brother was taken to the military service, Oryssia stayed with Ganja. Poor niece could not imagine who could come in the morning and murder her wonderful aunt.

"Auntie Ganja was always kind to everyone. She loved people and was ready to help or to share the last slice of bread with them. It must be a criminal or a prisoner who escaped from the prison."

Staying near the grave, Maria looked around and noticed several people, who she had not met in Blue Creeks before. Two men in their early forties moved from one group of people to another and listened to the conversations. When they returned from the cemetery, Maria saw them in Ganja's yard and thought, "The killer is always attracted to the place of his crime. They came here again, seeking for new victims." Maria shuddered from the thought about new victims and looked at Nesterenko. During the memorial dinner, he took a seat on the opposite side of the table. Maria motioned with her eyes at one of the unknown guests, and Nesterenko put two fingers on the table, showing Maria that there were two of them.

The neighbors left one by one. Maria and Oryssia cleaned the table and laid it for tea and kuliches that two of the neighbors baked in memory of Ganja. The non-invited guests from KGB left. Only10 people continued sitting around the table-the closest neighbors, Nesterenko, local militia man, Oryssia with her husband and Maria. Sasha and Oryssia's children played outside.

Oryssia asked with real concern in her voice,

"Maria, you must be afraid to stay here after everything that happened to aunt Ganja, aren't you?"

"A little bit," Maria answered and added, "I am afraid for my kids."

Nesterenko touched the shoulder of the militia man and asked,

"Our militia always defends us, right? Will you, Stephan defend Maria Lukjanivna and her children?"

The militia man replied, "Of course, Comrade Nesterenko. Who doubts that we will protect the woman and her kids?"

He looked at the faces of the guests and Maria concluded, "This theatrical phrase was pronounced for everyone to know that they would protect my children and me."

Nesterenko and militia man were the last who left Ganja's house. Oryssia and her family stayed with Maria, so on that night nobody could disturb them. The men paid their attention at the door locks. They found them strong enough. Only Maria knew that the locks could not help in the fight with demons.

She prayed, *"The Lord is my firm foundation, my strength, my refuge and my deliverer. Help us, save us, have mercy on us, and keep us, o God, by Thy grace."*

Two weeks passed since the tragedy with Ganja. Maria sensed the emptiness in the house. The house became unexplainably cold and dark. Maria and children missed Ganja very much. It seemed like the warmness and hospitable spirit of Ganja's place vanished together with Ganja. Sasha and Maria tried not to think about the danger of their stay in the house, but the feeling of the threat did not go away. Maria made her decision not to stay in the unsafe place but to leave for Odessa region to visit her friend Larissa. She could not sleep at night and packed the suitcase. At 4 a.m., Maria took her boys and left for Lviv on the earliest bus.

The train Lviv-Odessa started its journey from Lviv, and Maria did not worry about the tickets. Lviv railway station improved Maria's mood. They arrived early to the station and, after booking the train tickets, they had four hours of free time. In accordance with the schedule, their train departed at 1:45 p.m. Maria did not have strength to take a ride around Lviv, as Sasha suggested. She took the children for breakfast to the café. Then they went to the squire near the railway station. Maria sat down on the bench near the fountain and enjoyed watching her kids playing in the square.

Maria did not notice when somebody came up to her, until he touched her shoulder. The woman turned around and smiled. Nesterenko arrived to talk to Maria. He sat down on the bench and whispered the latest news,

"Maria, they looked for you in the morning. As they said, the KGB started the investigation of Ganja's case. They arrived and did not find you at home. They came to school and talked to me. I said that nearly every morning, you went to the forest and gathered mushrooms and berries for now and for winter. They promised to wait for you in Creeks. Don't come back, until I let you know that there is no more danger for you and children."

Maria's eyes were filled with tears. She complained,

"I am so grateful to God for sending you in my life, Mykola Petrovych. I tried to escape, but every time they found me. After Ganja's murder, I felt that I did not have strength to go anywhere. However, I go. I want them to forget about us. I keep praying about being forgotten."

Nesterenko asked Maria,

"Why do they follow you? Who are you, Maria Lukjanivna?"

Maria looked at Nesterenko and answered,

"I am Countess Marie Kotyk, later after my marriage, I became Countess Marie Kurbatov. Noble people have no right to live in accordance with the soviet laws, rules and regulations. They shot my father Dr. Kotyk on the porch of our estate house. They occupied our manor and used it for the torments and humiliation, until the Lord burned them there. I watched it with my eyes. After all their cruelties and our sufferings, they sentenced my husband and me for 12 years of imprisonment for nothing, just for home-coming with our legal visas and French passports."

Maria stopped for a second, took a deep breath and continued,

"They didn't expect us to survive in the camps. With God's mercy, we made it. My late husband insisted in repatriating us to France. He was brutally murdered on a train after his visit to KGB. As for them, we had no right to live, love, give birth to our sons. They want us to vanish in nowhere."

Nesterenko pronounced with sympathy,

"They murdered your husband in March, didn't they?"

Maria nodded and whispered,

"Now you know, how they killed Count Alexander Kurbatov, a citizen of France. Even after the discharge from the camps, we lived like slaves-without passports, and our children did not have their birth certificates with the identification of the citizenship. We were nobody and nothing in this country. It was God's miracle that the boys and I survived after Alexander's death. The question is: for how long will they keep us alive? They changed our personal data and allowed to leave the Magadan zone."

Maria paused and took a breath again. She decided to tell her life story to the man who was not just curious but deeply involved in everything that had happened to Ganja and herself since she was dismissed from school. Nesterenko listened attentively to Maria's heartbreaking chronicle. He did not interrupt her with multiple questions that arose in his mind. The man was shocked with the data that Maria shared with him. He thought, "Poor woman. How did she stand all the fears, dangers and hardships? How can she live and protect her children? Something has to be done… Somebody must stop the hunting of this intelligent and talented person."

Maria continued,

"From Magadan zone, we arrived to Ostrig to sister Olga who was released from the camp one year earlier than Alexander and I. She invited us to come and stay with her in the house of her parents, until we can find another place to stay. On our way to Ostrig, I found out that poor nun was killed. We took a risk that somebody could recognize Pannochka Maria Kotyk and came to Ganja, a person I trusted from childhood. She worked for our family, as a nanny of my younger sister. Ganja saved Alexander's life after the tortures in 1946. It's a horrible story, Mykola Petrovych. That was our past and now, I don't want to tell you anything about the past. I describe the recent events. They killed my Ganja. An angelic person was murdered because she loved me. She prayed daily for my survival and coming back to Blue Creeks together with my family."

"Maria Lukjanivna, dear Maria Lukjanivna, I knew that there was something hidden behind Ganja's murder. To tell you the truth, I did not expect to find such a heartbreaking story. It's a tragedy. It's hunting of the innocent people."

Maria saw that her life story impressed Nesterenko. He suggested,

"I need to go to Moscow, to … I have to decide, who I need to visit in order to stop the persecution of your family and murder of guiltless people."

Maria sensed like a long, thin needle stuck in her heart. She put her small hand on the top of his hand, looked in his eyes and requested,

"Mykola Petrovych, promise me that you will never ever go to Moscow with such an appeal."

He was surprised,

"Why? Why cannot I protect you and your children? I am a communist for thirty years, I was awarded with orders and medals during the WWII, I was a good teacher, and I hope I am not bad, as a school principle. They should take into consideration my opinion, Marie. I cannot sit and wait until a new tragedy occurs."

"You don't need it. Please, live your life. I'll go to my friend and stay there as long, as I can. Sooner or later somebody will recognize me in Blue Creeks," Maria insisted.

Nesterenko asked,

"What's wrong with recognizing you? You are a wonderful person, Marie. You are a good mother. You are a good teacher …"

Maria interrupted Nesterenko,

"I was also a good physician in Magadan. Everything is good, except my nobility. Please, Mykola Petrovych, stay away from me. Live your life."

Nesterenko looked at Maria and answered,

"I cannot. I don't know what it is, but I cannot separate my life from yours."

Maria did not hide her surprise,

"You do not know me, Mykola Petrovych. You saw me only at school. We did not have a single chance to talk, to spend time together, to bring up our opinions, thoughts and understandings."

"We'll do it in a week. Give me the address in Odessa region, where you go with kids. My vocation starts in a week. I'll be there, if you do not mind."

He looked straight at Maria and saw her hesitation.

"I can give you the address, but I do not feel that whatever you plan to do is the right thing for both of us. At least, for now. I'll be back by the end of summer. Time and distance will arrange everything in the right way."

Nesterenko did not want to accept her idea about later time and distance. He wanted to be with that woman. He thought a lot and had made his conclusions – there was nothing more important for him than to protect Maria and her children. He touched her hand and said,

"It's better and easier to stay together and fight together. Two of us can stop the persecution, Marie. Two adults have more chances to protect the kids," Nesterenko sounded firmly.

Maria opened her purse, took the envelope with Larissa's letter and showed it to him. He read the address twice and handed it back to Maria.

"I will not go to the train with you, Maria Lukjanivna. In case they are here, they should not see us together," Nesterenko concluded.

Maria replied with a smile,

"Oh, really? After sitting together for an hour on the bench in the central square, you decided to hide. Mykola Petrovych, they, probably, made so many interesting photos of two of us. Follow my advice and stay away from me. Only without my children and myself, you can live happily."

Maria looked back to check time on a huge wall clock and noticed, how two men separated and moved in different directions. She concluded out loud,

"They are here, as I said. We need to go. Don't try to cover me and kids when they ask you where I depart with children. Tell them the truth, Mykola Petrovych. It will be better for both of us."

Maria called,

"Sasha, it's time to go. Please, bring the baby."

Nesterenko picked easily the suitcase, and they moved together to the station. The train was already on the platform. They found the number of the carriage and compartment. Nesterenko put the suitcase in the box under Maria's berth. He quickly pulled something from his pocket and put it on the top of Maria's suitcase. Sasha noticed his motion and asked,

"What is there, Mykola Petrovych?"

Nesterenko made a sign to be quiet and whispered in Sasha's ear,

"It's for you and Ivanko. I'll see you soon, boys. Sashko, please take care of your mother and brother."

Maria was busy with Tisha, arranging the seat for him in the corner of the berth. Nesterenko hugged the boys, kissed them in crowns of their heads and moved out of the compartment. Maria stood in the doorway of the compartment and said,

"Mykola Petrovych, I appreciate everything you've done for us. Please, be wise and avoid all the troubles connected with us."

He waved to kids with his hand and answered to Maria,

"We'll fight together."

He took her hand and kissed, as Alexander used to do. Then looked in her eyes and went to the exit door.

Maria saw Nesterenko outside, walking slowly along the carriage. She stepped closer to the window in the carriage corridor and smiled to him. He smiled too. The train shook and moved slowly along the platform. In a moment, Maria did not see Nesterenko. She turned to the compartment and saw her boys watching her. Sasha asked,

"What Comrade Nesterenko left there?"

Maria did not understand,

"Where and what did he leave?"

Sasha opened the box under his mother's berth and took out a thick envelope. Maria closed the door of the compartment in order nobody could see it and opened the envelope.

"It's money, Sasha. Mykola Petrovych gave us money."

Then she noticed a note there and read out loud,

"Enjoy your summer. M.P."

Sasha smiled and proposed,

"He fell in love with you, Madam Kurbatov."

Maria turned red, as a student girl and asked,

"What are you talking about, Sasha? He is the principle of the school, where your mother worked. He can like me, as a teacher, but not more."

Sasha smiled when answered,

"Then why did he look at you all the time while you were talking? Why did he give us money for summer vocation? Does he do it to all the teachers? Do you remember, how actively he helped us with Ganja's funeral? Why did he stay with you in the hospital? Why did he keep Tisha with his mother and sister for three days? O, Mama, don't you see that he is in love with you?"

Sasha's explanation of all Nesterenko's deeds, due to his falling in love with her, made Maria disturbed,

"It's absolutely unacceptable, Sasha. I don't want to see Nesterenko again or continue my friendship with him. And the money … We should send it back. Yes, we must return them tomorrow, I mean on the day of our arrival."

Sasha watched his mother with love. Then he said,

"Mama, he is good. Not so many people helped us here. We were strangers for them. For most of the people, our problems were our problems. Mykola Petrovych was the only one who helped us to deal with difficulties."

Maria did not answer. She thought about Nesterenko, and unexplainable feeling of fear arose inside. She wanted to see him again or at least, hear his voice, in order to be certain that everything was all right with him after her departure.

"Mama, please call him from your friend and say that we appreciate his gift. Do not send anything back. It will hurt him. Nesterenko does not have his family. His wife died and their son was killed at war."

Maria agreed with Sasha but did not say anything out loud. She was looking out of the window. It was a nice summer day, and the train was passing endless fields. The green wheat moved there, as the waves of the green sea. The canvas of the field looked picturesque with red poppies, white daisies and blue corn-flowers. Maria smiled and began to pray, praising the Divinity for introducing her to a wonderful friend Nesterenko, who sincerely supported her in a new, but still unsafe life.

Glory to Thee, o Lord! Glory to Thee!

Chapter 35

Two weeks on the Black sea made Maria, Sasha and Tisha sun tanned and stronger. Maybe, it was for the first time from 1940 that Maria enjoyed life, the sun and the sea. She felt like there was no more danger, death and misfortune in this world.

Larissa and her parents met Maria and children, as if they were the closest relatives. Maria did not know, what Larissa told her parents, but they were sincerely happy to see their guests from Blue Creeks. The house was built on the seashore, and early in the morning, when both boys slept soundly, Maria ran to the beach and swam in the waves of the warm sea. She did not swim in the sea for a long time. The last time her father took all his children to their summer house in Greece in 1937. The threatening events in Europe interrupted their vocations in Mediterranean area. The soviet Russia intervened in Spain and interceded with the change of Spanish government. Then the militarist Germany became a huge menace of war.

Maria remembered the words of her grandfather when they were in Greece, “If you, children, get up early in the morning, before sunrise, the Lord forgives you one sin.” Every morning Maria prayed, asking God to forgive her home-coming, Alexander’s suffering, Alex’s and Ganja’s deaths. Every day, Maria asked the

Lord for one more thing that was important for her – for Lord's protection of Mykola Nesterenko. She did not want to cause misfortune for a man with a big heart.

One morning, Maria was laying on the beach after her long swim in the sea. She was in her dreams and did not hear the steps. Somebody stopped near her, and soft baritone pronounced in Ukrainian,

"Good morning."

Maria s shuddered and sat down. Nesterenko looked at her, smiling,

"Sorry, I did not mean to frighten you, Maria Lukjanivna."

Maria was happy to see him saved and unharmed. The only thing that made awkwardness of the moment was in her wearing the bathing suit in front of the school principle. He tried not to look at her, and Maria wrapped a towel around her slim body. Nesterenko commented,

"You are so … gentle. You need to eat more."

Maria got up and invited him to go to Larissa's place. He said with a smile,

"I've been there and saw that all of them were asleep. It's only six twenty."

Maria inquired,

"Why did you arrive here, Mykola Petrovych?"

They stopped and looked at each other. Nesterenko asked first,

"Do you really want to know why I am here?"

Nesterenko took her cold hands in his and continued without waiting for Maria's answer,

"Maria, you are straight with your question, and I'll give you my straight answer. I am here because I cannot stand my life without you. I cannot live, breathe and work without you. Maybe, it's a little bit late to meet you in my fifty, but now, I know that there is no power in the whole world that can separate us."

"Mykola Petrovych, there is such a power. You met her representatives. They separated my husband from me, and they parted Ganja from us. I do not want to live in fear for your life. We cannot be together."

"Why, Marie? Why can't we be together? Why can't I become your assistance, support and defense? Why should the children have lives without a man in the family? Ivanko is small. Tell me, why you don't want to marry me and to bring father to your kids."

"Just because you are not their father, Mykola Petrovych. If Ivanko is small and does not remember his father, Sasha remembers and misses him a lot."

"Maria, what do you think about you? I love you," Nesterenko exhaled.

Maria explained,

"You are a good man, but I do not love you, as I loved my Alexander. I betrayed him once when accepted changes in our personal data and wiped off his last name. I don't want to betray him twice, having an affair in four months after he was murdered."

Nesterenko looked upset,

"Marie, I did not suggest you an affair. I proposed to marry me. I can wait as long, as you want me to wait."

He made a step forward, put his hot hands on her shoulders, looked in her eyes and asked,

"Will you marry me, Marie?"

He sounded like her Alexander, even the intonation was the same. Maria tried to make a step backward and felt that she was losing her balance. Nesterenko lifted her up and carried to the sea. The cool water returned Maria's strength. She turned to Nesterenko and asked with her weak voice,

"Why did you appear in my life? I don't want any marriage. I am afraid to make your and my life more complicated."

"Marie, come closer, please. I want to see your eyes," Nesterenko asked.

She moved closer and then turned around and swam away. He followed her. They swam fast for five minutes until they reached a tiny island with pure white sand and several huge stones there. Maria was exhausted when she stepped on the land and laid down on the sand. She closed her eyes and listened to Nesterenko's breath. He sat down on a big stone and watched her for a while. Then he asked with noticeable concern in his voice,

"Marie, how do you feel yourself after our swimming race?"

She did not answer. She was analyzing something that she could not apprehend, "Why did I bring him here? It was my hiding place for two weeks. Why am I here with him? Am I in love with this man?"

Maria could not find the answer "yes" or "no". She did not hear the Angel's prompt. She continued thinking about her feelings, "Do I care about him?" She answered without hesitation, "Yes, I do. I care about him." Nesterenko did not interrupt the silence. He sensed the importance of it. He had told her everything, he wanted her to know. "Darling, now, it is your time to decide," he thought. "I am ready for your *'verdict'*." Nesterenko smiled to his thought about verdict.

Maria asked herself, "Why do I care about this man?" She received several answers: "He is a smart man with a big heart. He has wonderful personality. He is full of live, if he has fallen in love in his fifty. He is brave, defending me and my children. He could be a good father for my children, if something happens to me…"

Then a wave of disappointment arose inside, "How can I think about bringing a stranger into kids' and my lives? I want him to stay away from us. And this is not only about me. I don't want to bring any trouble into his life, as well."

Nesterenko did not interrupt Maria's assessment of her mixed feelings. He took off his wet linen trousers and a shirt and put them on the stones to dry. Then he laid down near Maria. He wanted to be with that woman. He had never had such a strong desire to love. Mykola Nesterenko and his wife were students of the teaching college, when they got married. In a year, their son was born. It was difficult time. At night, Mykola was working with loading and unloading the cargo on the platforms of the trains and during daytime, he studied and studied well. After the graduation, they were teaching in the village school not far from Poltava. They lived dissent life and, if not the WWII, they could consider themselves, as a happy couple. The war took away their son in 1942 with the massive night bombing of the village, and Nesterenko's wife was unable to live with that loss.

Maria sat down, looked at him and asked,

"When we are married, where will we live?"

Nesterenko was shocked to hear Maria's question and answered,

"Where do you want us to live? Marie …" he wanted to add something and the spasm in his throat did not allow him to say anything else.

He moved closer and embraced her,

"Is this "yes", Marie? Tell me, dear, does it mean that you agree to be my wife?"

"Only later, Mykola. A little bit later. I want Sasha to agree with our decision, as well."

Nesterenko started to cover Maria's feet, legs, body and face with kisses. She picked up the trembling of his big and strong body. She did not have strength or wish to stop him. Both of them had hunger for true love.

When they swam home, Maria thought, "It was my late Alexander, who sent me Mykola. He did not want me to be alone. He found a nice person for me. Thank you, Alex. Maybe, this man will bring me back to life."

Mykola Nesterenko left in ten days. Everything was discussed with Sasha and Larissa's family, and all of them came to a mutual agreement that marriage will significantly ease Maria's and children's life. Larissa wanted Maria to start working at her school, as a music teacher. Maria filled out and sent the applications to district department of education. The negative answer was received on August 31, one day prier the beginning of the school year.

Maria tried to calm Larissa down, but the school principle made her own decision and wrote an inquiry to the department with the request to explain why Maria Lukjanivna Gnatiuk was rejected, as a specialist needed at school. Days, weeks passed, and nobody sent an answer with any explanations.

In October 1959, Maria understood that they will not allow her to work at school and decided to go back to Blue Creeks. She made the reservation of the train tickets for November 6, when the first quarter at school was over and Sasha could be transferred back to his school in Blue Creeks. Maria felt sleepy and nauseous every day. She walked at the seashore, and it seemed to her that every time the fresh breeze and waves made her hungry and sleepy.

Nesterenko wrote two letters weekly. He could not wait until Maria and children come home. Maria gave him the exact date and time of their arrival, and he promised to meet them at Lviv railway station. Maria experienced two different feelings. First, it was guilt, that she accepted Mykola's proposal. Second, she was happy that he experienced real love for her and children. Even Sasha spent a lot of time with Mykola Petrovych and found him interesting, smart, kind and knowledgeable. He compared Nesterenko with his father and was pleased that his future stepfather was very much alike with Alexander Kurbatov Sr.

By the end of October, Maria understood the reason of her sleepiness and dizziness. Larissa suggested Maria to stay at her place longer and not to return to Creeks until the marriage was registered and the child born. Maria wanted to be with Mykola while she was pregnant. She wrote a letter to him and asked for his opinion. He advised to stay with Larissa, because "some interesting events took place in Blue Creeks. I'll come for holidays and see all of you there. I miss you so much, Marie, and now, I want you to know that our third child is very welcomed."

Nesterenko did not mention the exact day when to expect him. The celebration of the most important political holiday of the communist country-the 42-nd anniversary of October socialist revolution took place on November 7-8, 1959. Nesterenko did not arrive earlier, and Maria understood that the school principle had to take active part in the preparation of the school for the celebrations. He did not arrive after holidays, as well. Maria got nervous. Larissa tried to call to school every day, and every time, another man's voice answered the phone without giving any information about Nesterenko. On November 12, Maria took Tisha and they went to Blue Creeks. She did not listen to Larissa's warnings. Her explanation was understandable, "I need to be with the father of my child that we are expecting."

Lord, have mercy!

Chapter 36

Maria and Tisha arrived to Blue Creeks on November 15th around seven o'clock in the evening. They went directly to Ganja's house. The door of the house was opened, and the broken lock was on the porch near the door. Maria was afraid to step into the house, but she did not know where else to go. She began to pray,

"Help us, save us, have mercy on us and keep us, O Lord by Your grace."

Maria entered the house and switched on the light. There was something on the table. She moved closer and saw a glass of vodka covered with a slice of bread, as it was usually left for dead or departed. Near the glass there was a photo. Maria took it in her hands to see who was there and trembled. It was a photograph of her and Nesterenko on the Black sea. They walked along the sea, and he held her hand in his hand.

"O my Lord," Maria exclaimed. "They killed him."

Maria picked up Tisha and ran out of the house. She was on her way to Nesterenko's house when she met her neighbor Peter, who found Ganja dead. He was drunk, but recognized Maria in a distance.

"A, bitch, you arrived. Do you know that they arrested our Nesterenko and yesterday, we buried him due to massive heart attack? They showed us the photos. It was your fault that he got in trouble. It was your fault that Ganja was strangled. Listen, you bitch, maybe it was you who strangle Ganja and later pretended that you passed out?"

Maria could not pronounce a word. She felt that she was losing Tisha from her arms. The child was sliding down, and she was close to collapse. Tisha screamed.

"Hold the child, you bitch!" her neighbor shouted. He caught Tisha, and Maria fell unconscious.

"What do you think you do?" the drunk neighbor screamed. What should I do now with him and you, bitch?"

Two women from the houses across the street ran up to them. One was a school teacher. She took the crying child from the nasty, shouting man and sent the man home. Another woman brought water from her house and sprinkled in Maria's face. The women helped her to get up and took her to Ganja's house, holding under the arms from both sides.

"What has happened here?" Maria asked. She did not want to keep secrets. "I am pregnant with a child of Mykola Nesterenko. Please, tell me what has happened to him? When he was with us, he was full of energy. He was strong and helpful, when I saw him in August. He was happy. He knew about the child. I do not believe that our love caused his heart attack."

Maria's colleague did not want to say anything. The second woman was more sympathetic and answered,

"We do not know the details. In the morning, they arrived and took him. It was not later than eight. They kept him in Lviv for two days, as people said. Then they let him go home. Next day, there was a district meeting of political bureau and Nesterenko was expelled from the members of the communist party and removed from the position of the school principle. People said that he complained at his chest pain during the meeting, but they wanted to complete the meeting. They considered that he was guilty due to his immoral relationship with a former political prisoner."

"He died at night after the meeting. Yesterday, they organized his funeral. The whole village was there," Maria's colleague added.

"Please leave, it is dangerous for anybody to be with me," Maria suggested. "I became 'leprotic' for people around. If they do not kill my child and me tonight, I'll leave."

Maria's colleague asked,

"Is it true that you are Pannochka Kotyk?"

"Who told you this?" Maria asked. She was not ready to open her identity.

"A man from KGB," the younger woman answered. "They asked several times about you at Comrade Nesterenko's funeral, and then again at the memorial dinner. One of them used this name."

"What else they wanted to know about me?" Maria asked.

"Not much. They were surprised that you were not there," the younger woman replied.

Maria noticed, how Tisha pulled a slice of bread from the glass. He was hungry. Maria stopped the child. Nobody could eat that bread.

"You are waiting for Comrade Nesterenko's child to come, go to his mother. She does not blame you. She said that she trusted the choice of her son. "The choice of his heart was the right one," she said at the cemetery.

The younger woman added,

"That's right. Do not stay here. Save your children. We'll take you there."

Maria got up, took the picture from the table and left the house together with both women. She was under the influence of her new misfortune and did not pay attention at Tisha's loud request for food.

The moment they entered the gate, somebody got up from the chair on the porch. It was Nesterenko's mother. She did not see the faces of the visitors in darkness and invited,

"Come in, please."

The women pushed Maria ahead, and she entered the house. Mykola's mother recognized Tisha, and the boy recalled her right away. He stayed happily with that woman after Ganja's murder. The boy stretched his small hand and asked for food. Maria registered in her mind, "Here we are. We are beggars."

Mykola's sister entered the room and looked at Maria with surprise. She asked,

"Where are you from? Are you from the resort on the Black sea? I mean from the place where you seduced my brother and let him die for your sake."

Nesterenko's mother interrupted her daughter, "Stop it, please." She explained in a low voice,

"We suffer because we lost our Mykola. Don't take personally the words of my daughter."

Maria replied,

"You lost your son. I feel sorry for you. I lost the father of my future child. What else can I say? The only thing I blame myself for is that I have allowed him to return to Blue Creeks after summer vocation. They killed our Ganja, but she was not a communist, she did not take part in the war, she was just a very nice person. Why did they decide to kill Mykola? Was our love so dangerous for KGB? What do you think?"

Nesterenko's sister said with hatred,

"I don't want to blame only you. He was old enough not to ruin his life and reputation."

Maria's eyes were filled with tears. Mykola's mother came up to Maria and suggested,

"Stay with us. You do not have any other place to go. It's too dangerous to be alone in Ganja's house."

Maria burst into sobbing. She took Mykola's portrait in her hands and whispered,

"You were right, Mykola. Your mother is the best mother in the whole world."

Two women hugged each other and cried. They lost a very important person – a son and a husband. They lost the loving and loved man. Both women knew, they lost him forever, and the consciousness of their loss tightened them together.

Maria lived for the third month in Mykola's house. She tried to find any job in order to make some money and return to Larissa's town. Nobody wanted her at school, local store and collective farm. People avoid talking to her and hiring of the person that could cause negative consequences. When the pregnancy became obvious, it made Maria's life more complicated.

One morning, Maria heard rather loud conversation from the adjacent room. Mykola's sister Nina argued with her mother,

"Who is she? Why should you keep her here on our tiny pensions? She is nobody. She caught a respectful but lonely man, seduced him and destroyed his life."

Mykola's mother disagreed,

"It was not Maria who destroyed my son's life. She made him happy. We saw it. My son became alive. He did not live happily with his depressed wife. It was them, the terrible authorities, who did not have mercy for Mykola. Now, you know that they can easily destroy any life. The woman that carries your brother's child is in danger. That's why I keep her here."

Mykola's sister screamed out loud:

"I want her to leave today. She is nobody to us. They did not register their marriage in township. If it was not registered, you should not keep her here with her children on our money."

Mykola's mother tried to bring reasons to her daughter,

"Nina, where will she go? Who will support them? Who will give them a warm place to stay and food to eat? Don't forget, Maria is expecting your brother's child. I would never ask her to leave. It's sinful to push away my grandchild. Will you be happy to see her suffering? I will not take money from you for food. You'll buy your food separately from us."

Nina proceeded with further accusations,

"If you are so humanistic, I myself can tell her to leave. I will not pay attention that it's winter. I am sick and tired to see her here. I want her to go away. Let her try anywhere else but not in our house. The further from us, the better."

Mykola's mother insisted in interruption of their conversation. Maria understood that Nina would never forgive her the death of her brother, so staying in the same house became impossible. She dressed Tisha, and they quietly left the house. Maria went again to Ganja's house. The front and back yard of the house were covered with thick layer of snow. Maria saw that the door into the house was not tightly closed. It was impossible to open the door in order to get inside. She had to shuffle snow and crack the ice around the door. Thank God, there was a shuffle on the porch.

At last, Maria and Tisha entered the house. The temperature inside of the house was nearly the same as it was outside. Nobody warmed it up since their departure to Larissa in summer. Maria worried about Tisha and suggested the boy to go together with her to the shed to get the woods.

"As long as your brother Sasha is not here, you will help your Mama and bring the woods to the stove," Maria said. "Keep moving, Ivanko, keep moving. Don't stay still! It's too cold to stay still."

It took another twenty minutes to clean the deep snow from the path to the shed with the woods. Maria opened it and found out that somebody stole the woods that Ganja and she brought from the forest for winter. "I have woods for two weeks, not longer," Maria concluded. She was too tired to worry. She was happy that at least something the thieves left for them. "Thank you, Lord," Maria whispered.

It took the whole day to warm the frozen house, and only in the evening, Tisha and Maria took off their coats. While warming the house, Maria cleaned the path to the well, and brought home two buckets of cold well water. It was nice that the well was deep enough, and the springs were not frozen in it. She felt happy when she found some pickled, salted and sour produce in the basement. She went up to the attic and brought some dried mushrooms, plums, apples and pears. They were from the previous summer but well preserved in the gauze bags. After Ganja's murder last summer, nobody collected anything in the forest and preserve it for winter. Maria was scared to go to the forest with or without kids.

"Look, Ivanko." Maria showed her findings to the boy. "God provided. We'll have feast tonight. Thank you, Lord!"

Maria cooked mushroom soup and compote. Tisha was tired. When the food was ready, the boy did not want to eat. The child asked for a piece of bread, but there was none of it in the house. He liked fruits from the compote. With each piece of the fruit, Maria pronounced the name of it, and Tisha repeated it several times. When the smiling mother put her child in a warm bed, Tisha fell asleep without Mama's lullaby.

Maria kneeled in the corner under the icons and began to pray. She asked for forgiveness for Mykola's sister. Maria remembered the apostolic words of St. Mark, *"...when you stand praying, if you hold anything against anyone, forgive him or her, so that your Father in heaven may forgive you your sins."*

Maria prayed for the departed souls of her beloved people, who preferred to die, but not to betray her and children. "Dear Lord, forgive me my weakness. I did not push Mykola away. Both of us were burned with hardships in our lives. Our souls matched, seeking for a family, as a restoring harbor. We hoped that the warm and loving atmosphere of our future family would help us to rejuvenate and see again the beauty of life."

Maria talked to the Lord trying to understand the reason, why He allowed a new misfortune to happen. Maria's tears were pouring. "Dear Lord, what was wrong in our intentions? Mykola's loneliness noticed my solitude. He fell in love with me and his sincere love brought me back to life. Why was our relationship cruelly terminated? What was wrong with my acceptance of Mykola's proposal to marry him and to be with him in happy and rainy days? Was it sinful for a widow and widower to love again, enjoy being together and experience happiness? I hoped that the Divinity blessed us with a child for our contentment."

Maria washed her face from tears and returned to meditating. "This morning, I realized that darkness won again. It was not Thee, my Lord, who terminated our relationship with Mykola, his mother and sister. What about the fruit of our unanimity? Soon, the child will come into this world. The child is on the way, and the father is already gone… *Please, do not cast me and my coming child out of Thy grace. Remit, pardon, forgive, O God, my offences, both voluntary and involuntary, in word and deed, in knowledge and ignorance, by day and by night, in heart and thought. Forgive us all sins, for Thou art good and the Lover of mankind. Amen.*"

Maria took Mykola's photo out of her pocket and said, as if he was near her in the real world, "I am sorry, Mykola for shocking events that killed you. It was life-threatening idea to stay with me, and I warned you from the very beginning. To tell you the truth, I could not imagine to the full extend that a death punishment was prepared for you, particularly you. You had proved your devotion to the country and communist party during the WWII and after. I supposed that the demons would 'forewarn' you and 'advise' not to stay with me. However, I had never anticipated them to destroy you completely for your 'apolitical' relationship."

Maria took a deep breath and continued her one-way conversation.

"The worst that I expected them to do was to dismiss you from the position of the school principle. You tried to fight them, proving the righteousness of your choice. You tried to defend me from the kites, but the strength was not equal. You made the same mistake, as my late Alexander. Your decency made me a widow for the second time."

Maria looked again at the picture, made by KGB agent. Mykola and she walked hand in hand on the beach at the time of their happiness. Tears dropped on the smiling faces of two people in the picture. Maria quickly removed her tears from the photograph and put the picture on the table. Staying beside the bed, Maria blessed her child and prayed,

"Dear Lord, preserve us from every evil. Amen."

Lord have Mercy!

Chapter 37

Next morning began in unusual way. Maria got up at six and tried to start the fire in the stove. She could not do it, because the smoke got into the house instead of moving outside through the chimney. Maria ran outdoors, walked around the house in order to look at the chimney. It was impossible to see what was wrong there, looking from the ground. She crossed the street and asked the neighbors' son to check on her chimney. The young man took the ladder, climbed up to the roof and pulled a glass from the chimney. He asked Maria,

"What an idiot covered the chimney with this glass?"

Maria knew well who did it. The smart woman kept her mouth shut. She thanked the neighbor and rushed to the house to start the fire in the stove in order to make the house warm. She needed to cook something for her child. After small breakfast, Maria took Tisha and went to the office of the collective farm. She applied for any job there. The secretary asked her to come on the next day.

When Maria showed up in the office again, the head of the collective farm was there and sat in his armchair, holding her application in his hands. He did not ask her to take a seat.

"So, citizen Gnatiuk, you decide to become a collective farmer. What do you know about the collective farm?"

"The collective farm grows grains, vegetables and kccps cattlc."

The head looked at Maria for the first time and concluded,

"Let me write it down that you know nothing about our collective farm."

"What did I miss? Maria asked.

"A lot. You did not mention our pig and poultry farms. You did not say a word about our orchard garden."

Maria thought, "About our, Kotyks' garden."

"Maybe, I can learn more, when I work here," Maria pronounced with some hope in her voice.

"You must be joking, citizen Gnatiuk. Who will hire you, if you have no idea about our collective farming?"

Maria asked,

"I can do paper-work. I promise to work thoroughly, but please admit me. I need to make something in order to feed my sons and purchase the woods."

"Maybe earlier, I could hire you, but the people with your reputation would dishonor our collective farm. Hey, woman, take you application and go to hell."

"What?" Maria asked.

The head of the collective farm saw her turning pale. He sincerely enjoyed the situation.

"I am not the school principle and will not ask you to sleep with me. You are not of my taste. I hate skinny women. Only that fool Nesterenko could fall in love with a skeletal teacher. We threw him out of our communist organization."

He stood up, came up closer to Maria and Tikhon, saying everything awful about Maria's complexion and cursing her with the worst profanities in every sentence. Maria did not have air to breathe and felt dizzy. Poor woman picked up her son and walked away. She heard the voice of the nasty man, while she was passing two other rooms of the office. The men and women who worked there laughed at her.

The chairman of the collective farm shouted theatrically, in order everyone in his office could prove his detestation towards the immoral members of the soviet society, "I do not collect the prostitutes in my collective farm. Go and die from hunger together with your kids."

Maria was crying all the way home, thinking about her visit to the collective farm. She whispered, "Why are they so nasty? All the authorities are new inhabitants of Blue Creeks, sent here by the communist party and soviet government from different regions of Russia. They rule the life of a big Ukrainian nation. They do not even bother to learn the Ukrainian language or our native history. Thank God, they do not know, who I am in reality. Otherwise, they will tear Countess Kotyk in pieces, as the former landowner of Blue Creeks."

Maria was exhausted and put Tisha on the ground to walk. She was in her thoughts: "All of them lost humanness or probably, they had never gained it. And certainly, they had never learned how to talk politely and behave like civilized people. They are barbarians. I can imagine what Mykola went through. His heart could not stand rudeness and unfair accusations. Poor Mykola! My warning was correct. I had extensive experience in dealing with this type of heartless barbarians."

Tisha was pitiful about his crying mother. From time to time, the boy tried to catch and hug her leg, but Maria was deeply in her thoughts, and it looked like she did not notice his hugs. She was desperately crying. The dirty and obnoxious man took advantage of her woman's loneness. She did not have anybody who would defend her. "My Lord, they did not give me any job in their collective farm. These monsters want us to die from hunger and frost. Please, forbit them watching with their demonic pleasure how my kids and I are suffering."

Maria looked at Tisha and noticed that he was about to cry. She picked up the boy.

"No, baby, don't cry. You should not cry. We'll pray together,

"*Dear Lord, look down at my appeal and soothe the cruel things rising against us. For having you alone, as a firm and famed confirmation, we have acquired your mediation... Transform all our sorrows into joy, all our losses into victory because You are the Protector, Provider and Salvation of our suffering souls. Amen.*"

Maria pushed the gate to Ganja's house and sensed the warmth inside of her weak body. She thought, "God has his plans for me and my children. I have to live one day at a time and ask the Lord daily to bless my kids and myself for the next one."

Lord, have mercy!

Chapter 38

During the first month after Maria's return to Blue Creeks from Larissa, she took a risk and went every day to the forest with Tisha to gather woods and late mushrooms. She dried and salted the mushrooms. Some dried mushrooms she brought to the teachers of the local school and exchanged them for eggs and chickens. A new principle forbite Maria to show up at school.

Three of her former colleagues secretly continued supporting pregnant Maria and Tisha. Every early morning, one of the teachers, who lived across the street, was bringing some fresh milk and woods for the stove. Another teacher baked breads once a week and supplied Maria with her fresh breads. The third used to bring for Maria and Tisha some potatoes, squashes, beets, parsnips, onions and carrots. She delivered the produce to Ganja's gate late Thursday nights, when her husband had his night shift at the dairy plant. She hid the sack with vegetables behind the bushes near the gate, and Maria picked it up.

Nobody should see them helping Maria. Everyone was afraid of tragic consequences. Mykola's mother visited Maria three times without hiding. She always brought some foods. Every time, the considerate woman asked Maria for forgiveness. Maria understood well the situation with Mykola's mother-she could not constantly fight her daughter. The old woman was unable to change her daughter's opinion.

Last time, Mykola's mother brought some fabric and threads, in order Maria could make a quilt, sheets and pillowcases for her baby. She promised to buy more fabric next month upon receiving her pension. "Maria, you'll make the first cloths for my grandchild." Maria was grateful for those gifts. It was very difficult to live, depending on kindness of the people, but Maria did not have other options. She prayed daily for well-being of those caring people who did not let Maria and Tisha die from cold and hunger.

Once a week, Sasha sent a letter to his mother. He wrote a report about his studies. Maria was glad to know that her son is the best in school in mathematics and physics. Sasha always mentioned that Larissa and her parents took good care of him. Larissa promised to take Sasha to Odessa special school during the New year school brake of 1960. The school was named after Admiral Nakhimov. Larissa personally knew the principle of that school. The Nakhimov school prepared the boys for their future service in Navy. Larissa's and Sasha's letters kept up Maria's strength and mood. Maria was grateful to God for her supporters, who took a risk but did not cast her children and her out of their lives.

Every evening when Tisha turned to sleep, Maria was reading Psalms. Some of them impressed her greatly, like that one *"The fool has said in his heart, 'There is no God'. The Lord looks down from the heaven upon the children of a man, to see if there is any who understands, who seeks God. They have all turned aside, they have become corrupted together; there is none who does good, no, not one."*

"It is awful!" Maria thought. "That transformation had happened to our people. They do not seek God," Maria admitted with deep regret. "They have lost their faith and the vitally important connection in their lives – the connection with the Creator and Savior." Maria worried about human civilization, "The Lord is merciful and patient. To what extend can He tolerate human sins?"

Maria tried not to concentrate her thoughts on evil crimes that KGB instigated to her, Alexander, Sister Olga, Ganja, Mykola and so many other innocent people. She carried her child under her heart. The baby should not absorb mother's bitterness and pain that was caused by evil heartlessness, unfaithfulness, hostility and callousness that Satan planted in humans. She did not want to poison the heart of her new child with all the negative experiences and feelings. She loved her child and wanted a new baby to be born healthy, strong and loving.

Wintertime brought more physical difficulties for Maria. Nearly every day, it was snowing, and she had to shuffle the snow daily from the porch to the well, to the woodshed and to the gate. One day while shuffling the snow, she noticed somebody standing not far from the gate and thought, "We need a dog. They killed Ganja's dog in the dog's house. It was dark, and poor Ganja did not notice it, when she went to the goat house. The poor nanny went straight to the barn to milk the goats. The assassin was waiting for poor woman." That *somebody at the gate* walked away, when Maria came closer with cleaning of the path. "We'll keep the dog inside of the house." Maria thought. "The dog will let me know with barking that we have *visitors*."

Maria had just returned into the warm house, when somebody knocked on the gate. She covered herself with a shawl and went there. She opened the gate and stood frozen for a minute. She could not believe her eyes. The woman whispered in French,

"Good afternoon, Marie. May I come in?"

"Come in, Maman."

It was too cold to stay outside, and Maria invited,

"Let's go inside."

They entered the house, and Tisha rushed to his mother, then stopped for a minute, observing the older woman and asked with uncertainty,

"Baba Ganja?"

The elderly woman corrected,

"Grandma Anna."

The child repeated in his way,

"Baba Anya".

The women watched him and smiled. Maria's mother picked the grandson up and covered his cheeks with kisses. She wanted to ask Maria about something or just say something, but Maria turned away, pulled her coat from the hanger and left. For some time, she walked outside back and forth trying to quiet down her feelings and thoughts.

"Why is she here? Why did she arrive to Blue Creeks? In my childhood, I dreamed about my mother's coming back. Today, she has appeared from her voyage. However, thirty years later, I do not feel that I want to see the voyager. It took many years to forgive Maman. Everything was forgiven to adventurer and forgotten – my love, expectations, offense and sufferings, deep pain for Papa's distress and my siblings' hurting. Certainly, I have zero desire to have the incursion of our selfish and treacherous mother in my present life."

Maria walked back and forth near the house, trying to exhale all the negative emotions that could easily poison her baby. She whispered to God,

"Thank you, my Lord that You was merciful and found how to substitute her for me with loving and loyal strangers, like Ganja, Sister Olga, and Zina. I was blessed to have them in my life. Do I hate her? No, I don't. I just don't want this woman to stay with us, playing part of a mother and a grandmother. Dear God, please free my life from the acting of this woman."

Maria took a shuffle and began cleaning the snow, making the path to the shed. There she still stored some woods that she collected in the forest and that her neighbors across the street shared with her. She took some woods and brought them home.

Countess Anna came up to Maria, holding Tisha in her arms and said in French,

"Marie, the woods are heavy for a pregnant woman. How can you manage alone with snow, buckets of water and woods?"

Maria did not know what to say. She kept silence while working near the stove.

"We need to talk, Marie. We have so much to share."

Maria looked at her mother, who tried to build a connection with her daughter and answered,

"Not now, Maman. To tell you the truth, I don't have a desire to recollect and discuss anything with you. My life is not that easy, and I don't have so many pleasant memories, as probably you do. So, I do not want to share with you and, particularly, you anything that made me happy or distressed in my life. You would never understand me, as well as I am unable to understand you."

Maria's denial of having the mother-daughter talk irritated Countess Kotyk. "Thank you, Marie. You are so categorical with your mother. Should I leave now?"

Maria looked at her mother and thought, "Maybe she does not have a place to go. Do I want my mother to become homeless?"

After keeping a silence for a while, Maria asked,

"Where do you stay now?"

"With your Papa, Marie. He is still generous, granting me lodge and board. We don't have our former relationship, but sometimes we talk. It was he, who sent me here. He worries about you all the time."

Maria was surprised to hear the news. Then she recalled the picture of the table, laid for seven people and asked,

"Have you been there in the hunting lodge, when Ganja brought my children and me to meet Papa and Grandpa?"

Countess Anna replied with a big smile,

"Certainly, I have been with Papa for rather long time. Marie, it was too much for me to see you in such a destress. I wanted you to quiet down with your Papa. He always succeeded better with pacifying of our children."

"Nice. You just wanted me to calm down with my Papa," Maria repeated.

Countess Anna continued,

"You have changed so much, my girl. You became a... strong woman. I understand, it's due to your longsuffering life. Marie, you must be tired of adversity. Did they find who killed that servant woman... Jannie's nanny?" Countess Anna could not recollect the name of the late nanny.

"Ganja?" Maria prompted.

Maria thought, "This woman does not have heart. How could she stay hidden in the house, when her daughter came with the grandchildren, who she had not seen ever? She speaks about Ganja's death, as if it has happened not to our family member, but to a complete stranger, who she had not ever met in her life. She left her baby daughter in the arms of *that servant*. That servant was fighting for Jannie, as for her own child."

Maria did not want to continue the conversation. She simply said,

"Leave, Maman. Say to Papa that his Marie is quite all right."

Pani Anna looked around and asked in French,

"How can you consider that you are quite all right sitting in this dark hole without any help? Can you explain it to me, please?"

Maria did not want to explain anything and said firmly:

"First of all, I am not obliged to explain anything to you. I don't need anybody to stay with me and pacify me or my children. I can handle everything by myself. Please, leave. Second, don't forget to tell Papa that I am quite all right with my children. No help needed for now."

Maria saw that her mother was surprised with her daughter's decisiveness. She did not argue and left. Poor Maria burst into tears and ran out of the house in order not to disturb Tisha with her crying. All her emotional pain that was accumulated for 30 years since her mother's departure burst out. She was not able to stand and kneeled near the corner of the shed.

"Lord, forgive me. She is my mother, but I cannot stand her residing with me, touching my child, complaining at her indistinct relationship with Papa. I don't want my new child to know her, as a grandmother. I don't believe that she really can be a grandmother. She didn't even ask about Sasha. Forgive me, my Lord, please forgive me, but do not make my life more complicated with return of this inconsiderate woman into my life. I know that You are kind and do not want me to suffer more than I can stand. Forgive me, Lord but keep this woman away."

Maria heard how Tisha was crying and rushed back to the house. The boy was staying at the door, calling for his Mama. Maria kneeled near him and gave him her hugs and kisses. Tisha stopped crying and wiped the tears from his mother's cheeks with his finger. Then he touched Maria's face with both hands and said,

"I love mommy."

Maria's eyes were filled with tears again. Maria hugged her boy, trying to hide the tears from Tisha. She thought, "What can be more important for a mother than the love of her children? My mother missed something essential in her life. Lord, forgive her."

Lord, have mercy!

Chapter 39

The winter days moved slowly. Maria was tired of snow and cold. She could hardly wait until the winter was over. The letters from Odessa were her only joy. Maria received two letters a month from Larissa and was happy for Sasha. Larissa kept her word and took him to the Admiral Nakhimov Navy School. Nobody from KGB disturbed Maria with their visits for the last three months, and she praised the Lord daily for peace in her house and support from helpful people.

Any day, Maria expected the baby to come, and she did not know what to do with Tisha, if she had to go to the hospital for the delivery of the baby.

The spring sun and warmth had changed Maria's mood. Maria began working in the garden. She planned to grow different vegetables there, in order to stop waiting for her neighbor's supply. She was with Tisha in the garden, when the delivery of the baby started. She knew that she had probably a few minutes to ask her neighbor to keep Tisha with her kids at their place and come and help Maria. A week ago, Maria informed her about the due date.

Maria did not waste minutes and rushed to the house across the street, calling from the gate, "Anna, Anna!"

Anna was a mother of four small children who were successfully born at home, and she realized right away what she needed to do with Maria. She asked her mother-in-law to take care of the children and rushed to Ganja's house. Maria prepared everything for delivery. It did not take longer than an hour, and a beautiful girl was born. Anna showed her to Maria and exclaimed,

"She looks exactly like her father! She is a true copy of Mykola Petrovych! Poor Mykola Petrovych, he did not survive to this day. I need to run and bring the joyful news to his mother."

Maria said quietly,

"Thank you, Anna. She'll be happy to know that Mykola's daughter is born."

The woman wrapped the baby and gave her to Maria with the words,

"She is big and maybe hungry."

Both women laughed when they saw how the baby was turning her head, looking for her food. Maria was nursing and watching her new baby with a smile. Then her eyes were filled with tears that began dripping on baby's quilt. Anna noticed it and adviced,

"You'd better be calm, Maria. The baby can pick up your sorrow through the milk and get sick. I know that your life was not easy, but maybe, she was born for changing it. I'll keep Ivanko with me for a day and bring him to sleep at night. Stay with your new one. Try to sleep."

"Thank you, Anna. You are so kind to me."

At the door, Anna suggested,

"Maria, stay in bed at least for a couple of hours, in order to avoid any complications. Please, drink milk and tea. I left it on the table. Since now, you are a breast-feeding mother of a big and beautiful girl."

Maria smiled, listening to Anna. The woman could not even imagine that she was giving the post-delivery instructions and advices to an experienced physician.

"I am completely lost for these people, as a person and specialist," Maria thought. "They have dragged me in the mire and do not allow raise my head. They have watched me all the time, but, at the same time, they do not notice me. They ignored me. How can I live with three children, being ignored and odious? I did not cause any harm to anybody and suffered all the time. O Lord, please change everything in my life with the birth of my Vira (Ukr.faith). I gave her this name in order to prove my faith in You."

Maria was surprised, how fast she recovered after her third baby. In two weeks, she continued her work in the garden. She knew that there was nobody, who would come and help her there. Everything was all right during summer and fall. They had enough food and Maria's colleagues continued supporting her.

Maria decided to take another attempt at finding job. In order to start working, she needed to take both children to the kindergarten. The director of the kindergarten refused to admit Maria's children, giving her the oddest explanation,

"We can admit the children only of the working mothers."

"How can I start working, if my children are not in the kindergarten?" Maria asked.

The young director refused to take Maria's applications. She suggested,

"To begin with, you should find the working position, Comrade Gnatiuk. Only then, you can come again with your applications. If we have any openings, we'll take your kids."

Maria asked,

"Do you have any vacancy that I can be hired?"

The director widely opened her eyes and asked,

"What can you do at the kindergarten?"

Maria answered,

"I can do anything you need, starting from taking care of children, teaching music, cooking and, at last, cleaning the kindergarten."

The director was confused. Then she waved with both hands and said with anger in her voice,

"No, I will never hire you to be with children. Everyone knows that you dishonored the principle of our school, and he died due to dishonor. Then people talked that you probably killed Pani Ganja, an old and kind person in order to seize her house. I could not understand, why they did not investigate the case to the very end in order to find and punish the guilty person. Nevertheless, all the inhabitants of our village believed that you have appeared at Blue Creeks from nowhere, because you were hiding here from your criminal past."

Maria was shocked after everything she had heard from the director of the kindergarten and asked in a low voice,

"Is that all that you know about me?"

The director of the kindergarten moved forward and opened the door of her office. She was ready to push Maria and her children out,

"What else do you want me to know about you? What? I've heard that you were a good teacher of Domestic science. You wanted people in school to like you, particularly poor Comrade Nesterenko. Now you decided to come to our kindergarten, as a cook, a music teacher, or a genitor. What an obnoxious person you are!"

"I am desperately looking for any job. What's wrong with it? I have my children who need to eat at least two times daily. You do not know me at all, and you have blamed me in so many sins that I could not even imagine, nor commit. What did I do to you, personally you? Why do you allow yourself to blame or judge me? You are an educated woman and collect gossips. Shame upon you."

Maria noticed, how the teachers of the kindergarten gathered in the corridor, listening to the conversation in the director's office. Maria was not able to stand the accusations of the kindergarten director and decided to put everything on its places. "What will I lose if I say the truth about me? Nothing."

Maria made a step closer to the door in order all the teachers could hear her well and said,

"You mentioned that I arrived from nowhere to this village. You are wrong, Comrade director. Have you heard about the first inhabitants of Blue Creeks? Did you hear anything about the founding family of this beautiful place?"

"Who were they?" the director asked.

"Count Lukian Kotyk and his family," Maria replied.

"What does it have in common with you?"

"I am Maria Kotyk, a daughter of Count Kotyk. In Blue Creeks I am at home. I know the spreader of all the gossips about me. I had never ever done anything criminal, and my personal life was so transparent that they decided to reload their evil crimes on my shoulders. I believe in God's punishment. I know that they will pay for the death of Mykola Petrovych. He knew the truth about me and my family. He tried to fight for us. He was a wonderful person. Being a communist did not make him evil. Presently, his daughter was rejected in attending the kindergarten. Do you consider that it's fair?"

Maria saw that the director was shocked and did not know what to answer. She was staying for a moment, catching the air with the opened mouth. Then she asked in a low voice,

"You are Pannochka Maria Kotyk? You studied in France and became a doctor, as your father. I am Natalia, Ivanko's youngest daughter. Do you remember your father's coachman? And you are Pannochka. Why did you come here?"

"Where else should I go? I arrived home. Since now on, I am not going to hide myself and listen to people's unfair accusations. I know that they can kill me any day, as they strangled my poor Ganja. But I do not want to live, as a mole, avoiding the day light and meeting the people. My three beloved people paid with their lives for my free appearance in this place. I am educated enough to advocate my children and myself, and to occupy my place in human society."

The director was completely confused. Maria saw that her weakness did not allow her to make any decision. Maria helped her,

"Do you want me to go to Lviv to the regional department of education and ask for the permission to work in this kindergarten?"

It looked like Maria pronounced something genius. The woman smiled. She still could not talk and nodded with her head. Then she whispered,

"I am sorry, I cannot admit you, because we were instructed not to hire you on any job position in our village. Pannochka Maria, I don't know, how you survived the winter, being pregnant. I felt sorry for you. At the same time, I cannot help you with anything."

Maria was not surprised to hear that and asked,

"Who told you not to hire me?"

"The people from the internal service, from Lviv KGB, when they worked with Nesterenko's case," Natalia answered. "Don't be surprised that the chairman of the collective farm did not hire you, as well. They called the communists for party meeting and gave us all the instructions regarding you."

"Did they mention, who I am and my real name?" Maria inquired.

Natalia answered in a very low voice, in order the curious teachers could not hear,

"No, they didn't. On the contrary, they called you a foreigner and a stranger in our village with still unknown and probably dangerous past. They promised to keep you under surveillance, and they ordered us to keep a close watch on you and report to them about anything suspicious from your life in Blue Creeks."

Maria preferred to interrupt the conversation in order to avoid any sad consequences to Natalia for presenting a lot of information. She thanked Natalia and left. She understood, "Something imperative has to be done that would completely change the situation and my status in the existing society."

On her way home, the disturbed woman was analyzing the conversation in the kindergarten. "Was it right to take a risk and open the secret in front of strangers about my identity?" The answer came immediately- "It will be opened, sooner or later. The escalated situation, as it is now, cannot last forever."

Maria stopped at the gate to Ganja's house and pulled the envelope that the mailwoman stuck in the gate. It was a letter from Larissa. Maria registered in her mind, "Larissa is a very significant person in my complicated life. It's wonderful to have her. Her recommendations are practical, and her help with Sasha is priceless."

Maria opened the door of the house, with pleasant thoughts, "I was happy to meet my Papa again. He used to be my devoted parent, best friend and wise advisor. However, since I found out that he settled Maman there,

I lost him again… And still, I have two wonderful people – Papa and Larissa, who understand me and my life, as is."

Maria's arms felt fatigued to hold Vira the whole morning. She put the girl in bed. The baby was asleep. Maria's thoughts went back to her father. "I miss my Papa and Grandpa. Maybe, I should visit them one day. We'll do it, when Sasha comes for summer vacations. Larissa promised to send me money to come to her place for summer, but I am not sure that it would be appropriate to stay there with three kids without money. It's better, when she purchases just one ticket for Sasha to come home. When Sasha stays with us for summer, we'll make money, gathering, preparing and selling the berries and mushrooms on highway at the bus stops. Thank God, I know how to make them tasty."

Maria rushed to start the stove when somebody opened the door. It was her neighbor with a milk jar in her hands, full of fresh milk. Maria thanked her and handed the empty jar for exchange. The neighbor saved them: a slice of bread and a cup of milk were Tisha's and Maria's snacks, and those snacks were ready in a minute.

Maria was grateful to women who supported her and children's life. She called them "Our angels". They continued sharing some foods with Maria, and all of them were surprised to see the small portions Maria used to eat. Maria only smiled when they asked her, "How is it possible to live, be pregnant, take care of children, do chores around the house and work in the garden on your tiny portions of food?" "God keeps me well," Maria answered with her smile.

Soups were Maria's major food. She missed her tasty soups for more than ten years of her imprisonment. When they threw Maria to the icy cold dungeon cell, as a punishment for writing her journal, they kept her on a slice of bread and a cup of water per day. Maria saw in her short night dreams, how she was cooking borsch, her favorite Ukrainian cabbage soup with a lot of beets, carrots, tomatoes, garlic, sweet and hot peppers. She always added beans to it. People were right, saying that Maria knew how to make soups delicious that everyone enjoyed them. During summer, Maria worked a lot in her vegetable garden in order to have everything at hand for cooking her favorite soups and other nourishing dishes that Tisha enjoyed together with his mother. Vira could not complain that her Mama did not have enough milk. The girl grew fast, gaining nearly a kilogram of weight monthly.

Mykola's mother visited Maria and children every other day. She saw in Vira the live portrait of her son. All the time, she felt sorry that they could not live together. She loved both children and had a special respect for Maria.

Glory to Thee, o Lord! Glory to Thee!

Chapter 40

When Vira was four months old, Maria decided to go to Lviv department of education and get the permission to work in the kindergarten. They talked to Maria politely, let her fill out several applications and sent her home with the promise to clarify the situation during a week. Everything was *clarified* faster than Maria could imagine.

The bus driver made a slight right turn from the highway in four kilometers from Blue Creeks and let Maria and children get out. Maria walked slowly in the direction to her village, carrying two children. Vira was in her arms, and Tisha sat quietly on mother's back in a sack that Maria made for him with her shawl. The boy was hugging the backpack with some food and Vira's swathes. Maria was exhausted when she covered halfway to her village and sat down under a huge oak tree for some rest. She fed Tisha with a sandwich that she purchased at Lviv bus station and nursed Vira. Maria saw, how several fire trucks passed them in the direction of Blue Creeks. Approximately in an hour, Maria saw the same fire trucks going in the opposite direction to the highway.

Suddenly, the wave of cold fear hit Maria. She started to pray. She went faster, feeling that something terrible had happened to her again. Her prayer was interrupted all the time by the cry of the baby. When they entered the village, Maria saw in a distance that in the middle of the street there was a crowd of people. She could not hear distinctly their voices because they were standing rather far from her, somewhere near the former Kotyk's mansion.

Maria felt out of strength and was not able to move forward toward the crowd. In order not to drop her children, she sat down on the bench near the gate of somebody's house. Tisha sled down from her back and showed with his small hand the direction to their home. Maria got up and moved in that direction, sensing something that was against their home-coming. The crowd of loud talking people in the middle of the street frightened Maria. Usually, at dusk the farmers from the collective farm were at home. Maria thought, "Something extraordinary must have happened that all of them are outside after a long work day."

She stopped again and sat down on the bench near the gate of another house. The dogs started barking, feeling a stranger at the gate. Maria heard that somebody opened the door of the house and shouted at the dogs. They stopped barking. Then she heard the steps towards the gate. Maria embraced Tisha, waiting for somebody to open the gate. It was an old man who greeted Maria in an old manner,

"Glory to Jesus, Pannochka Maria."

Maria answered,

"Glory forever."

"I know you, Pannochka. I am Ivanko, your coachman. Please, don't go there. They are waiting for you… to kill. There was a fire in Ganja's house and the next one got burned, as well. I went there to look. Everything was burned: Ganja's house, barn, shed, your neighbors' house and their barn and shed. It started around noon. Your neighbors across the street knew that you left early in the morning for Lviv. It took two hours for the fire trucks to arrive here. Everything was destroyed by that time. They said that you kept a lot of kerosene canisters in the barn."

Maria interrupted the old man with a question,

"What did I have there in the barn?"

"They found six or seven canisters with kerosene in your barn," the old man said.

Maria could not understand and asked again,

"Where did the canisters appear from? I hadn't seen them ever. We do not have kerogas in order to use kerosene. It's strange."

"It's strange," the old man repeated. Then he suggested, "But it's better for you not to go there, Pannochka. Your next-door neighbor waits to kill you. Peter and his family became homeless. When he is drunk, he can kill."

Maria asked,

"Where should we go?"

She comprehended the danger of her return, knowing that KGB started the fire.

The old man suggested,

"Pannochka, come into my house, and when they go to their homes, I'll yoke the horse and take you in my peasant dray to your grandpa in the hunting lodge."

Maria picked up the children and followed the coachman Ivanko. She said with concern in her voice,

"Pan Ivanko, it's risky for you. You are so kind. They can come and find my children and myself here in your house."

"No, they will not look for you in my house. They would never imagine that I know you and hide you here."

"Can they try to find me at my Grandpa's lodge?" Maria asked.

"I doubt. Everyone knows that the young Count Lukian Kotyk was shot, and the old Count is crazy, and it's better to stay away from the lodge. It was me, who heard your father's moaning and dug him out from the ditch behind the garden. Then at night, Ganja and I brought your wounded father to the lodge. Your Grandpa saved his life.

Maria hugged the old man, saying,

"Thank you so much, Pan Ivanko. Thank you for my Papa and for us."

Pan Ivanko waved with his hands, "Thank the Lord, Pannochka, not me. I did, whatever the Lord wanted me to do."

"Still, thank you for taking risk with Papa and now, with us."

Pan Ivanko revealed,

"Ganja told me, what they did to you and your husband in 1946. I remember her waiting for your return. Every day, she prayed for you to survive and come back and asked me to pray. I did it, Pannochka Maria. God was merciful."

Maria said,

"Thank you, Pan Ivanko. Yours and Ganja's prayers were answered. I returned. I returned to be killed."

Maria burst into tears,

"Pan Ivanko, they killed my husband and Ganja. They killed Mykola Nesterenko. Why did they murder the innocent people? Now, they burned the houses. They are looking for my death. This time they want to achieve their goal, using an innocent man, like my neighbor Peter. Why do they do it to us?"

The old man had no answers for Maria's questions. He poured some milk in a big mug for Tisha and Maria. Then he unwrapped a loaf of bread from the linen towel and sliced off a big slice. Maria put Vera on the bench and took bread in her hands. She prayed "Our Father" in Ukrainian and asked the Lord to bless their food, they were about to have. Then she cut off two slices of bread from her big peace and put one in front of Tisha. The boy was hungry but remembered to bless himself before eating.

Pan Ivanko revealed with sadness in his intonation,

"My grandchildren would never believe in God."

"It's sad," Maria answered.

Tisha asked his mother to eat too. Maria moved closer to her son and helped him with milk from a big mug. She could not stop thinking about a new terrible situation the KGB put her in.

The thought that came to her mind in Ivanko's house was strange at the beginning, "I definitely need to go to Moscow." Maria asked herself, "Why Moscow?" The answer was absolutely clear: "The local authorities follow somebody's order – to kill me and, probably, my children. It's quite possible that they received the *request* from Magadan colleagues. Who knows, what the inspector wrote about the obscure activity of the Magadan KGB? Now, they take the revenge."

Maria was hungry but her thoughts did not allow her to notice the taste of bread and milk. She was deeply in her plans. "I must endeavor the visit to the head of the country, otherwise the local internal service will win again. The problem should be resolved on the upper level. I am sick and tired to be an émigré. I don't want my children to become exiles from being born. Now, I need to find out with Papa the possibility, how I can *invisibly* leave for Moscow with two children. I do not want to be thrown out of the train on my way there. I must disappear from their watch, otherwise my journey would never be a success."

Being in her thoughts, Maria did not notice when Pan Ivanko left the house. She shuddered, when he opened the door, coming in.

"We can go, Pannochka."

He turned to the icons and prayed, "*Dear Father, bless us for our ride and protect us on the roads from the evil. Amen.*"

Maria drank the rest of the milk from the cup, bit some more bread and took the rest of her slice with her. Tisha was tired and was falling asleep. She handed her bread to the boy to carry, gently picked up her sleeping Vira from the bench, and they went outside. Mother Maria laid down her children and herself on the fresh, sweet-scented hay in the peasant dray, and the old man covered them with a navy quilt in order nobody could notice his *passengers* in darkness. When they were passing Ganja's house, Maria saw her neighbors wandering on the ruins, looking for something in full darkness. Maria felt sorry for them. Their lives and happiness meant nothing for the demonic structure. They and their two children became homeless due to arson. Satanists were sent to burn not only Ganja's house. With burning the neighbors' home, they found the person, whose infuriation, hatred and anger grew to the level that he was ready to kill the innocent woman with children.

Vira started to move, and Maria began nursing her. She knew that the baby's swaths needed changing, but everything clean that she took this morning was used up for a long day. When they reached the hunting lodge, both children were asleep. Pan Ivanko left Maria and children in the dray and went to the house. He knocked on the window with a special rhythm. Somebody lit the lamp inside of the house and moved to the door. In a minute, Maria saw the Grandpa in the door frame. Pan Ivanko said something to old Count, and two men came down to help Maria and children to get inside.

They moved in quietly, but Vira opened her blue eyes and began to cry. Her unusually loud cry awoke the grandparents, and it was strange for Maria to see, how they rushed together to the baby to calm her down. The grandparents saw Vira for the first time. "What a beautiful girl!" Count Lukian exclaimed. "Marie, she does not look like you, darling. She must be a copy of her handsome father." Vira smiled to her grandparents, as if she understood the complement of her Grandpa.

"She needs a bath, Papa," Maria said instead of greeting. Countess Anna stretched her arms in order to take the baby. Maria said to her,

"Please, don't touch Vira, she is soaking wet. It was a long day that we spent not at home, and we used up all her swathes. Do you have an old sheet that I can cut and use, as swathes for tonight?"

"We'll find, Marie," Anna answered and rushed to her room. In a couple of minutes, she came with some sheets and seizers. Maria put her baby on the sofa and opened her swathes.

The baby stopped crying and looked around. Grandfather Lukian brought a basin and poured warm water that was on the big stove. Maria took raspberry soup and put the girl in the water. The baby was smiling to all the people who watched her taking a bath. The warm bath made Vira hungry. Maria enjoyed nursing her clean and pleasantly smelling baby girl.

Maria tried to be serene, but the events of the day were so dramatic for her that she began to cry. Her father came up to his daughter and said,

"Marie, you cannot cry, when you are nursing the baby. All your emotional bitterness will poison the milk, and this angelic creation will absorb it. This poisonous bitterness can make Vira sick."

Vira stopped sucking not because the baby understood the danger of being poisoned. She just fell asleep.

The father's gentle warning caused the opposite reaction on his daughter. Maria removed the baby from her breast and cried loudly, as a five-year-old girl. The parents were near her. Countess Anna took the baby, and Dr. Kotyk tried to quieten Maria. His daughter was hysterical, as she had ever been in her forty years. She could not stand her life.

"Papa, what is it for? Why me? What did I do that I suffer since ten? I am tired of apprehension and exhausted of suffering. I know that it's not right, but I hate my life."

The old Count entered the room, when he heard Maria's flustered cry.

"Don't say this," old Count said strictly. Then he softened his voice and repeated the same request:

"Never say this, Marie. Tell us, what had happened that you appeared here with two kids late at night?"

Maria could not explain anything. She was bitterly crying on the shoulder of her father, feeling his sincere compassion. Dr. Kotyk was ready to cry with his overwhelmed daughter. He loved his child so much and, being unable to save her, he was ready to scream, as Maria did. His status of a noble man and father did not allow to do it. Dr. Kotyk begged Maria, "Please, calm down, my child. Please, calm down."

The old Count turned to Pan Ivanko and asked,

"What had happened there that Marie needed to run to the woods at night?"

The old coachman briefly reported to the family about the two burned houses, while Maria and her children were in Lviv. He also explained the danger of Maria's return to Blue Creeks. He assured them,

"I have heard with my own ears, how Peter swore in front of people to kill Pannochka Maria. When he is drunk, he does not control himself."

Then the old Count whispered something in Pan Ivanko's ear, and the man left in a hurry.

"Nobody should see him coming from the woods at night", old Count explained.

The baby girl was crying loudly, and Anna could not make her quiet. Maria took the baby in her arms, and the girl stopped crying immediately.

"Look, Lukian, she knows her Maman," Anna noticed.

"I also knew my mother, but my mother forgot me fast," Maria replied angrily and continued,

"I hate to say this, Maman, but it's true. All my misfortunes began with your departure. Let the Lord forget me, if I forget my children in exchange for my happiness."

Countess Anna felt embarrassed and turned away from Maria.

Maria announced,

"I made my decision: I leave for Moscow. I need to meet Brezhnev, the new leader of this country and stop the hunting and killings of innocent people."

"Marie, I doubt that they'll give you the opportunity to meet him," Dr. Kotyk said.

"You'll be surprised, Papa. Your Marie promised to God to protect not only my children and myself, but you and thousands of other innocent people. How did our Lord say? If somebody saves one of His man, that 'somebody' saves the world. I want to serve my Lord and save His people. He helped me today to stay alive and combat my fear. I am ready to fight."

"Marie, maybe, it's better to wait for some time, to gain some strength and let your baby grow?" Countess Anna suggested with uncertainty in her voice.

"Vira is my only concern," Maria agreed. "On the other hand, it is going to be very cold in Moscow, if we arrive there close to the winter. There is another factor, Papa. They will look for me, and one day, they will visit Grandpa's lodge. Those monsters know how to search."

"We'll hide you, Marie," Dr. Kotyk promised. "Nobody will find you here."

Maria looked at her father and asked the question that he asked himself many times,

"You'll hide me from the world, from my children, from love, from my job that I enjoyed so much. Actually, you can hide me from life. Is it worthy to exist without life?"

Dr. Kotyk did not have an answer. Maria continued,

"No, Papa. You cannot hide me. The most important thing is – I don't want to be hidden. I need to go to Moscow, to find the possibility to get to the Kremlin and to visit the General Secretary of the communist party."

"Marie, it's dangerous," Anna said.

"If you do not hear anything about me and children for two months, pray for my soul, Maman."

"No, Marie, no!" Anna exclaimed loudly.

Vira startled in her sleep.

"Quiet, Maman," Maria asked. "Let my baby sleep."

Anna wanted to help Maria and stretched her arms to take the sleeping baby. Maria moved back and said,

"Let her sleep. And you too, go and sleep, Maman. I need to talk to Papa."

Anna felt offended: Maria refused to talk to her father in her presence.

"Marie, please do not keep me in the list of your enemies," Anna asked. "I wish you only the best."

Maria replied with bitterness in her voice,

"Who told you that you are my enemy? You are the traitor and nobody else."

Anna looked agitated and pronounced with real disturbance,

"Excuse me, please. I would prefer not to hear from you such an accusation."

Maria noticed, how her Grandpa smiled and turned to the wall with the icons, saying out loud,

"Glory to Thee, o Lord! Glory forever!"

Then he turned to Maria and asked,

"When do you plan to depart?"

"The day after tomorrow. I need to prepare everything for Vira and Tisha."

Anna stepped forward again and asked,

"Here is the last question, Marie, and I will leave you and your Papa alone. Do you leave both children here?"

"No. What else, Maman?"

"Why can't you leave Tisha with us? He is a good boy, and three of us can take care of him," Anna inquired.

Maria looked at her son, sleeping on the sofa and said,

"My children, Maman are the most important people for me. How can I leave my life, happiness and joy with anybody else? I would never survive then. Good night, Maman."

Dr. Kotyk kissed Maria in the temple of her head and said,

"My child, it will be difficult for you to be there with two tiny children. You do not know, where you will stay and how fast you'll get to the Kremlin."

Maria put her head on father's shoulder and answered,

"It's all right, Papa. The Lord will find the way, how to get there, and guide me how to act under the circumstances. I am completely in His power."

The old Count came up to Maria and said,

"Dear child, may the Lord bless you for your trip! Marie, this time you'll win."

Maria whispered,

"Thank you, Grandpa. I have the same feeling. With God's help, I'll release the chains from my children, father and me. Please, go to sleep. I need to do laundry. Tomorrow, we'll think about money for train tickets. We definitely need two berths."

"We'll give you some money, Marie. Don't worry about it. It will be enough for the first time. Take your fur coat because the temperate will drop in a month," Dr. Kotyk suggested.

"My fur coat? How could it be preserved since 1939?" Maria asked with laughing.

"Your Grandpa knows the secret, right Papa?" Dr. Kotyk asked.

The old Count replied with noticeable pride in his voice,

"I'll better take it out, and let it stay without lavender sticks for a day or two. Marie, I want you to try your fur coat. My child, please follow me."

Lord, have Mercy!

Chapter 41

Maria and Dr. Kotyk went after the old Count to another part of the house. Maria watched her Grandpa's pace and mentioned to her father with disappointment,

"Look Papa, he walks like an old man."

Dr. Kotyk answered,

"Certainly, he does. Marie, what do you think about 103? Isn't it the way people walk at this age?"

Maria smiled and repeated,

"103. Sounds impressive. I am so happy that my Grandpa is alive."

Dr. Kotyk whispered with a smile,

"I am grateful to God that my father has genuine devotion to the Divinity, clear mind, good appetite and the best attitude. He was the only one who believed in your and Sasha's survival and return. However, he had some doubts in Count Alexander's …"

Maria and Dr. Kotyk stopped and talked. They completely forgot about the fur coat. They did not talk for so many years. They had so much to tell each other and to discuss. Before WWII, they were capable to find the best resolutions for their lives, the lives of the younger children, for patients, servants, their farming land, and for their successfully growing business with export of home-made butter, berries and mushrooms provisions to the different European countries.

Under the normal life circumstances, they knew how to implement the found solutions, avoiding the development of different problems. One thing they did not learn-how to handle the representatives of two demonic structures – fascism and communism. Maria and her Papa were people of Faith who belonged to the Light. They knew their determination – to prove with their lives the presence of Light in every day of human existence.

Dr. Kotyk asked the question that he was a little bit afraid to ask. He worried a lot about his older grandson, when Countess Anna mentioned that she did not see Alexander with Marie. Tonight, he saw again that Maria arrived without Sasha.

"You did not say anything about Sasha. Where is the boy?"

Maria answered proudly,

"He is in Admiral Nakhimov Navy School. He is one of the best there. Papa, nobody can compete with Sasha in mathematics and physics."

Dr. Kotyk was surprised with Maria's answer.

"Really? He studies in Odessa? How could you manage to get him there? As far as I know, it's a school for the boys whose parents or at least, fathers were killed in WWII?"

"Larissa's classmate is the Principle of that school. By the way, Sasha's father was killed, as well. It happened not in WWII, or to be more precise, it happened in the war that subsists forever between light and darkness. I miss Sasha very much. I wish, he can be with us in Moscow..."

Dr. Kotyk was happy for his grandson. He also noticed that the conversation about Sasha made Maria sad. He thought, "What a wonderful mother she is!" He kissed her on her cheeks and then did the same to a baby girl. It was ticklish for a baby, and she smiled in sleep with an angelic baby's smile. The grandfather felt how joy and happiness overwhelmed him. It was forgotten joy and happiness that came again to a benevolent man.

"Papa, it was my dream for nearly twenty years to be with you and to talk, as we used to do before the war."

"Like we do now?" Dr. Kotyk asked.

Maria answered,

"Yes, Papa. Thank you, Lord: my dream came true. Papa, if even something happens to me in Moscow, I want you to know that you are the best father. I am grateful to the Lord for giving me such a father. Papa, there is one more thing I need to thank you for."

Dr. Kotyk asked with a smile,

"What is it, Marie?"

"You have never betrayed me. You have never betrayed my brothers and my Jenny. I believe that you have survived, thinking of us, your kids. You could not allow yourself to die and to leave us without your love."

"Why did you say, Marie that I am a good father. I am just your father who is still here, praying for all my children and expecting the best gift from the

Divinity-gathering again together around this table, as one family. Maybe, one day my dream also will come true."

"Papa, I am forty. My life, as a happy life, was over long time ago. I mean, the twenty years of my human life have been elapsed in humiliation, distress, deprivation and sorrow."

Dr. Kotyk embraced his terrorized, long-suffering daughter and answered,

"You are a strong and brave person, Marie. You go to Moscow to open a new part of your life. You'll see the positive changes in a couple of months."

The old Count interrupted their conversation. He brought Maria's fur coat that was purchased in Paris in 1939. It looked trampled. Maria put Vera in father's arms and tried the coat. It still had some chic. Last time, it was worn in winter of 1941. Maria looked elegant in it.

"Look, what else I found there," the old Count handed Maria her hat that she wore with her fur coat.

Maria took off her black shawl and put on her hat. She looked in the mirror and hardly recognized herself. The coat and hat completely changed her appearance.

The old Count said with satisfaction in his voice,

"In two days, your coat will be like brand new, Marie. It will take a little bit longer for the smell of lavender to evaporate. Every year, I changed the lavender sticks for the fresh ones. My child, if you do not use the perfume, people will think that it's the smell of perfume."

Maria hugged her grandfather, saying,

"You are our miracle, Grandpa. I love you so much. I was angry with you for many years. I could not understand, how you were so nice with Anastasia's prophecies, but in my live, you predicted only tragic events. Now, I went through all of them and realized that the last part of your prophesy is still left. Do you remember it?"

Maria expected the negative answer, but her grandfather said,

"Certainly, I do. Marie don't be afraid. The Divinity will guide and protect you in your last battle, my child. They must recognize your dignity, talents, knowledge and humanity. They have to retreat, giving you and your children the way to live decent lives."

"O, my Lord. You kept in your memory for 23 years everything that the Lord let you see and know about my destiny! Thank you, Grandpa. You have proved that I am right in my desire to go to Moscow and let them know that I am alive no matter of what they have done to me. I'll stipulate the leader of the government and party to issue the full liberation for my children, you, my father, myself, and all the innocent people who are still waiting for valid rehabilitation, not the false one that they have given us at the discharge from the camps."

Dr. Kotyk was listening to his daughter with father's pride and gratitude to the Lord. It was late, but three of them could not find strength to be separated and to go to sleep. Maria was exited. She was alive again. She was with those people who understood her well. It was late evening, but she was ready to wash, to prepare her kids and herself for a long and uneasy journey. It was two in the morning when Maria has finished with washing the cloths and swathes and hanging them on the balcony. She stood there for a while, looking at the Ukrainian night sky, covered with thousands of stars. She whispered in amazement,

"It's really gorgeous! It's true royal blue velvet with bright diamantes on it. What can be more precious than the God's art?"

Maria heard the steps of her father and turned to him, asking,

"Why don't you sleep?"

He looked at the sky and answered with a question,

"Isn't it beautiful, Marie? Do you remember our evenings on the balcony of our mansion in Creeks? I was amazed with your description of the night and day sky."

"I remember it, Papa. My life was thorny, but I tried to preserve my good memories about you and our land. The memories helped me in the most unbearable situations. They made me persistent in my dreams and preserved my hope to see you, the sky, our land and this forest – everything that I loved so much. I believe that the Lord has blessed me with the opportunities to raise my children not in a cold zone but in blossom of our native land."

Dr. Kotyk hugged Maria and suggested,

"Let us go and sleep, Marie. You need good rest before your journey. My darling, promise me that you'll take care of yourself during the trip on the train and in Moscow. Remember, I need you alive and healthy."

"I will do my best, Papa. I promise."

They entered the rooms, and in a minute, Maria stifled the candle. She was on the sofa near her children, when the warmth penetrated her tired body. Maria whispered with a smile,

"Glory to Thee, O Lord! Glory to Thee!"

Chapter 42

The old Count took Maria with children not to the Lviv central railway station but to the next tiny one, where the train Lviv-Moscow arrived at 6:45 a.m. and stopped just for a few minutes. He helped Maria with children to get in and handed her backpack with some foods, water and Vera's swathes. The carriage conductor was an elderly man, and the old Count had a second to say something to him and to give him some money.

When the train moved, the conductor brought two mattresses, two sets of sheets, pillowcases and three towels. He helped the widow to do their beds. Then he delivered three hot teas and three bagels. Maria wanted to pay him, but he said that everything was paid by the grandfather. She smiled, thinking, "My Grandpa is amazing. He found time to pay the carriage conductor for the services. Thank You, Lord for keeping him alive."

Maria enjoyed fresh tea with bagel. It was her breakfast. She fed Tisha with farina at the lodge, but she didn't have time to eat. Maria put Tisha to sleep and began to pray morning prayers. At the end, she meditated in her own words,

"O God, our God, the True and Living Way, who traveled with Your servants Joseph and Maria. Travel together with Your servants Tikhon, Maria and Vira.

Oh Master, deliver us from all agitation and slander raised against us. Bless us for happy return. Amen."

The monotonous sound of train always made Maria relaxed, and she dosed sitting near Vira. In her dream, she saw nuns and heard the beautiful sounds of the bells from the top of a magnificent cathedral. Maria had not met those nuns before, but the convent looked familiar. She saw her lighting the candles there. Then Maria felt that somebody watched her and turned back. She saw the woman who stood behind her and stared at the widow with two children. Maria shuddered and opened her eyes.

The dream was so real that she recognized the place. It was Novo-Devichy monastery in Moscow, where she lit a candle for her husband's soul during their tour around Moscow, when they arrived from Magadan. Maria remembered how tour guide told them that Novo-Devichy convent for women was established in Moscow in 1524 by Grand Prince Vasyli III. In mid XVII century, the nuns from the Ukraine and Belorussia were transferred to Novo-Devichy convent. Maria recollected one more interesting fact about the famous convent. In 1812 Napoleon's army made an attempt to blow up the convent, but the nuns managed to save the convent from destruction. Maria was sorry to hear from the tour guide that the communists closed all the churches and monasteries in Russia in 1920s by the Decree of the evil communist regime. The Novo-Devichy convent was closed in 1922, and in seven years, its majestic cathedral was also closed for big services.

Maria thought, "Thank you, Lord. Now, I know where to go. You showed me the way. I need to go to people of Faith. Only the servants of God can assist me in my new Liberation assignment."

Maria concentrated her thoughts on the woman with heavy look that she saw in the cathedral. "Who was that woman that watched me last time in the cathedral? She looked familiar. Did I meet her earlier? Where could I meet her?" Maria shook her head and concluded for herself, "To my mind, my angel showed to me that I need to be careful with people, like her. Thank you, Lord for guiding me. I'll go and find the sisters in faith, if it is possible. Maybe, they know, how I can get to the Kremlin."

Maria fixed Tisha's quilt. "Definitely, I cannot go to the head of the country through the Secretariat or front door. They would never allow the former political prisoner to receive the audience with the leader of the country. Do I need to find somebody who will help me to get to the Kremlin through the service door?" The answer that Maria sensed was: "Yes." Maria wanted to know what to expect then and there, when she managed to get into the Kremlin.

At that time, being on the train, Maria did not receive the answer about '*then*' and '*what*' was waiting for her in the Kremlin. However, she didn't experience any fear or feeling that anything terrible awaited for her and children. "I regret that Sasha is not with us. He was always my best help." Maria missed her son very much.

The circumstances that took place in Moscow were unpredictable. From the railway station Maria went to Trinity Lavra of St. Sergius. Maria recollected that the monastery was founded in XIV century by one of the most venerated Russian Saints Sergius of Radonezh, who was a spiritual leader and monastic reformer of medieval Russia. He built the wooden church in honor of the Holy Trinity. St. Sergius was famous after his blessing of Prince of Moscow Dmitry Donskoi for Kulikov victories battle with Mongol invaders, that turned the war towards triumphant victory. Maria believed that she needed St. Sergius blessing for her battle that she was about to commence.

It was 9:15 a.m., when Maria and children arrived there. The morning service began. It was not crowded in the cathedral, and Maria had an opportunity to move closer to altar. The women's voices of the choir sang repetitively, *"Lord, have mercy."* Maria kneeled in front of the alter, holding Vira in her arms. Tisha kneeled near his mother.

Maria repented her sins of being close with a man, earlier than a year after Alexander's death and giving birth to his child without proper God blessed marriage. She repented her sin for being afraid of the '*KGB hunters*' to go to Lviv and baptize Vira in the cathedral, where she was baptized. The tears poured on Maria's cheeks, and she pleaded,

"Dear Lord, from the bottom of my heart, I appeal for forgiveness of my sins. Punish me but forgive. I don't want my children to be punished for the sins of their

mother. O God, cleanse me, a sinner, have mercy on me and save me, my Lord by Thy Grace. Amen."

The chore of nuns repetitively sang with their angelic voices, *"Grand it, O Lord."*

Maria continued her praying, *"No one is holy as You, O Lord my God. Amen."*

She looked at Tisha and smiled. Her child kneeled near his mother. Maria prayed to the Most-pure Theotokos, *"Appealing now to you, Mother Maria, for a stream of cleansing tears and washing of my sins. Please, accept the repentance of my heart. In you I have placed my hope, O Good One, that you will deliver me from the torment, for you are the Fountain of Grace and Mother of God. Stretch out your most-pure and honorable arms like the wings of a hallowed dove and cover my children and me under their shelter and protection. Thank you, O Sovereign Lady. Amen."*

The tears continued running, and Maria did not notice, when one of the nuns came up to her. She gently touched Maria's shoulder. Maria turned her head. There was no bright light in the cathedral and Maria did not see the face of the nun.

"Stop crying, Maria, Lord is merciful," the nun whispered and stepped aside in order not to interrupt the prayers of distressed woman.

Maria was surprised that somebody knew her here. She did not recognize the nun, though she had heard her voice before. "O, yes! It was Sister Irena from Lviv prison. They deported us on one train to Magadan, but later, separated to different camps. It's a miracle that she recognized me. In Maria's head the bells sounded, "Miracle, miracle, miracle..." and the floor, seemed began to move. Maria did not feel well. "My Lord, please help me, don't let me faint."

The disturbed woman looked around in order to find Sister Irena, but she went away. Maria took Tisha's hand and moved to the exit door. Only now, she noticed that the child still held in his hand three candles that she wanted to light for the souls of her departed – Alexander, Ganja and Mykola. Maria lit them and prayed, asking the Lord to forgive the sins of her beloved and settle them in His Kingdom, where there was no fear, worries and suffering, where they could see the everlasting light of God's Glory.

Vira began to cry, and Maria walked out of the cathedral. She still felt dizzy, and a cool morning air pleasantly refreshed her. Maria walked around in order to find the place where she could change Vira's swathes and nurse her. Vira cried louder and louder, and the people, who were passing by, paid attention at Maria and children. Maria noticed in a distance that Sister Irena is coming. They embraced each other, and Sister Irena asked.

"What happened, Marie? Why are you in black?" Sister Irena asked it with concern in her voice.

Maria did not know what to start with. Her eyes were filled with tears again.

"I lost my husband." Maria answered.

Sister Irena asked, "How did you lose him? What happened to him?"

"They murdered him. He visited the Magadan KGB and insisted on our repatriation to France. They brutally killed him on the train on his way home. Then they strangle Ganja, the old and kind person who allowed me and my children to stay in her house in the Ukraine. They killed my best friend Mykola Petrovych, who wanted to prove my guiltlessness in all the accusations of KGB. A few days ago, they burned Ganja's house, where we lived. They also burned the neighbor's house and left us and our neighbors homeless."

Sister Irena hugged Maria and said,

"I am sorry to hear, Marie that the persecution is still going on. Why did you come to Moscow? What are you going to do?"

Maria explained,

"I decided to come to Moscow and get to the Kremlin. They did not leave anything for me, except finding the possibility to see the head of the country and prove to him the illegal actions of some KGB officers, who continue hunting and murdering of innocent people."

Sister Irena replied with hesitation,

"It is nearly impossible to reach Brezhnev, Marie."

Maria answered with firmness in her voice,

"I believe in God, and He sees that they did not leave another choice for me. Very soon, they will come closer and kill my children. Sister Irena, I must protect them, otherwise I am not a mother."

"Do you have where to stay?" the nun asked.

"No. I don't have anybody in Moscow," Maria replied.

"I have to think, what to do with you, Marie. It's not easy to find a place for you with children. You don't have money, do you?"

Maria shook her head.

"My father gave me for a week. I wish I had more, or I wish I could go and earn something," Maria said in a low voice.

Sister Irena suggested to Maria,

"Marie, I'll take you with me to sisters. Three of us live together in an old house in suburban area of Moscow. Our house used to belong to one of our sister's late parents. We'll feed your son and you at our place. Then we'll decide what to do with you, and how we can assist you with your Liberation assignment."

Sister Irena picked up Maria's bag, and they went to tram stop in order to get to the suburbs of the city. It took fifty minutes to get to the old area of Moscow with one-storied houses and green gardens surrounding them. When they came to sister Irena's home, she introduced Maria to two elderly nuns, as her old friend from Lviv. Sister Irena mentioned right after the introduction,

"My guests are hungry. We need to feed them."

Maria felt awkward. The distressed woman thought, "My family has always supported the nuns and monks with significant donations and quantities of produce and honey. Here they are old and sister Irena brought me with two kids for lunch. It's not right."

The nuns brought two bowls of oatmeal and two cups of milk to the dining room. Maria turned to the icons praising the Divinity for unexpected joy from her meeting with Sister Irena and having food in a pleasant company.

While Tisha and Maria were eating, all three nuns talked in the kitchen about Maria's and kid's life situation. Maria took the dishes to the kitchen and thanked the nuns for meal. They watched how she washed the bowls and cups and did not say anything to her. They wanted to finish the discussion before they can bring their decision to a widow with two kids.

Maria nursed Vera and changed her swathes, constantly thinking about where to go and what to do. The thoughts climbed one on the top of another, "All the convents are closed. Nobody would allow me to stay at the railway stations with two kids longer than two days, and I do not have money to move from one station to another."

She shook her head and reminded herself,

"The children need to be washed and Tisha needs hot food every day. Even on our long journey from Magadan, I purchased soups for them on the train stops."

Maria looked at the kitchen door and thought, "They are too old to keep us. They do not have much space for three of us. I have to thank them and leave."

She fixed her shawl and decided to go. The angel stopped her with the question, "Where can you go? On the street and become homeless? Nobody can help you there. Be patient, Marie."

At that very moment the nuns appeared into the room and sat down near Maria around the table. Sister Irena began the conversation,

"Marie, we made our decision. You'll stay here with us, until we find people who will help you to get into the Kremlin and meet Brezhnev. Please, Marie, do not speak with anybody. People, even other nuns in the church or who visit us should not know anything about you, your life and the reason of your arrival to Moscow," Sister Irena warned.

Maria raised her eyes at Sister Irena and said,

"I appreciate your hospitality and willingness to assist me in achievement of my goal. I promise to help you with household, cooking, cleaning, sewing and doing whatever you ask me to do."

All three nuns praised the Lord for being able to support the family in need.

Mari turned to sister Irena and asked,

"Do you know what they did to Sister Olga in Ostrig?"

"Yes, Marie. By the way, I am already Mother Irena," the nun announced calmly.

Maria felt uncomfortable,

"Excuse me, please Mother Irena."

"That's all right, Marie. Don't worry about this. We have other things to focus our attention on. Tonight, I'll talk to one person and ask her to help you to get to the Kremlin. She is a nice faithful woman. Her daughter works there in the kitchen. I don't want to promise anything beforehand, but we'll try to help you to get there. All the rest things will be on your own."

"Thank you, Mother Irena."

The owner of the house Sister Kathrine took Maria to the guest room. The room looked spacious because it had just a few pieces of furniture in it: two narrow beds from both sides of the room, one small table near the window, and two chairs from both sides of the table. Sister Kathrine watched Maria, when they entered the room and noticed that poor woman was happy to see tab water in the room, but there was nothing else, besides the tiny sink in the corner.

"You need to wash your kids daily, right?" Sister Kathrine asked.

"Yes, Sister," Maria felt ashamed, that she caused so many inconveniences to the nuns.

Sister Kathrine promised,

"Don't worry, Marie. I'll give you a wash-basin for children."

Maria was happy to hear that. Her children were saved.

"Thank you, Sister Kathrine. I feel uncomfortable that you have extra work with our arrival."

"That's all right, Marie. Our restroom is further in the corridor. We have a tab and shower next to the lavatory," Sister Kathrine added.

Maria hugged an old nun and said in a weak voice,

"You are sent by God. You know that you saved us today. Thank you very much for your hospitality and kindness."

Sister Kathrine looked at Maria and noticed that the widow could hardly talk. She suggested,

"Marie, you need some rest, dear. You can hardly stand."

The nun blessed Maria and kids in their new room, prayed "Our Father" together with Maria, wished then good stay and left. Maria put Vira on the bed. Her arms were fatigued from holding the baby during all morning hours.

The preparations with getting inside to the Kremlin took longer time than Mother Irena expected. The woman, who worked in the kitchen of the Kremlin, left for vocation two days ago. She went to the sanatorium in Odessa due to her trauma of her back. So, the cook needed to stay there for twenty-four-day course of treatment, plus two days trip back to Moscow. Mother Irena mentioned that there was another obstacle-nobody was sure that the cook would be able to help Maria to get into the Kremlin. Maybe, the assistance of somebody from the guard team would be required. It would make the operation more complicated.

Maria prayed days and nights. She prayed while cooking, cleaning, doing laundry, ironing and sawing for nuns and children. The nuns gave Maria the small pieces of cotton and linen fabrics that were left after the sawing of their clothing and bed linens. The offcuts were too small for the purposes of adults. Maria was grateful to God for nuns' gifts. She enjoyed sawing, combining different fabrics and creating amazing dresses, shirts, vests, jackets and pants for her children.

Maria learned to pray at work in German and Magadan camps. She always felt the necessity of worshiping. The belief that God brought her to the nuns in Moscow and supported from the first hours of her stay here, gave her hope in successful resolution of her vitally important Liberation assignment.

The days crawled slowly, as never before. Maria was exhausted not with chores but with waiting. Mother Irena comforted her from time to time. The nuns avoided attracting the neighbors' attention to Maria and her children. However, it was not possible to hide them all the time or to keep them indoors. The children and Maria needed some fresh air. The sisters explained to curious neighbors that Maria came to Mother Irena from the Ukraine to pray with her for the soul of her late husband, who unexpectedly died. Everyone felt sorry for the widow and her children.

One evening, Mother Irena and sister Kathrine came into Maria's room. Maria was washing her children. She washed and put Tisha in bed and prepared everything for Vera's bath. Both nuns decided to help her, but Vera was not happy with seeing strangers around her and began to cry. At the end of the washing procedure, Maria poured some water, rinsing the baby from the head to toes and prayed, *"Glory to Thee, O Lord! Glory to Thee! You are the Holy One always, now and ever and unto ages of ages. Amen."* Maria covered the girl with the towel and put her on the other bed. The baby found the face of her mother and smiled. Maria swaddled her in fresh swaddling-cloths and began to nurse. In five minutes, the girl fell asleep and the women could talk without anybody's interference.

Mother Irena explained the reason of their visit,

"We brought news for you, Marie.

On that day, Mother Irena visited and talked to the Kremlin cook Elena, who arrived from vacation. The young woman asked for two days in order she could check the possibility of realization of Maria's plan with another person. She had only one guard there that she could talk to. The rest of the guards were new, and she would never take a risk of talking to them.

Mother Irena continued,

"You have to be there with Elena at 5:00 a.m. that means thirty minutes earlier than the rest of the cleaning and kitchen personnel arrives. Remember, Marie you have only half an hour to reach the main building and hide somewhere in bushes closer to the building. I don't know how you can manage everything with two small children. Will your kids allow you to stay hidden? Can they be quiet at night?"

"Yes, Mother Irena. It's sad that my son Sasha is not with us. He can be a great help with Tisha, and I'll take care just of my girl. I am sorry, but this is just Mama's dream to have all three kids there with me," Maria said.

"You did not say a word about your eldest son. Where is he?" Mother Irena asked.

"He is in Admiral Nakhimov Navy School in Odessa," Maria answered.

"How did it happen? How could he get there?" Mother Irena was surprised.

Maria explained, "I served with onc woman in the camp. After the rehabilitation, she became a principle of one of the schools in Odessa region. She took Sasha with all his school reports to her classmate in Odessa. He is high ranking officer and helped with Nakhimov school. Larissa told him my story and Sasha was admitted."

Mother Irena asked,

"Where is your friend, Marie?"

Maria checked her purse and handed to the nun Larissa's address and her school phone number.

"Let me think. I do not promise you anything, but you know that *'With God all things are possible,'*" Mother Irena said.

"I live with this belief," Maria answered with her smile.

Mother Irena looked at the watch and whispered,

"We have to leave. It's time for bed. Keep the kids sleeping longer tomorrow. You also will need extra strength in a couple of days. Gain it now."

Mother Irena blessed the sleeping children and Maria with her beautiful pearl cross and wished quietly,

"Good night. God bless you, children with sweet dreams!"

"Thank you for everything. Good night," Maria replied.

When Maria was in bed after washing the kid's cloths, she saw the light in the room and sensed warmth, coming from the light. Maria appreciated everything that Mother Irena and Sisters did for her. The disturbing thoughts, feelings and tiredness mixed together, and she dozed fast near her baby daughter. The night dream was about her visit to the Kremlin. She saw the cortège of beautiful cars and a smiling face of the leader. He was surprised to see her and three children there. Maria saw Sasha with her. She did not remember what she said to Brezhnev, but he let her talk. Then she saw her children and herself in a beautiful and spacious car. They brought her and kids to Blue Creeks. She remembered the thought, "Why do they take me to Blue Creeks? Our family manor was burned and never reconstructed. They burned Ganja's house to ashes. Where do they want us to live?" Maria woke up with a pleasant feeling.

Glory to Thee, O Lord! Glory to Thee!

Chapter 43

Mother Irena visited Maria late in the evening when Maria had finished with the chores of the day. She asked,

"How were you today, Marie? You work hard. You must be tired."

Maria answered, "I am all right, Mother Irena. Did you hear anything from the Kremlin girl?"

The nun looked at Maria with condemnation and advised her,

"Be patient, Maria. Wait until everything is ready. This time, you must win, otherwise you are not the only looser in this matter. Remember, you have three children."

Maria imagined the seriousness of the situation and exclaimed,

"Help us, save us, have mercy on us and keep us, O Lord in Your grace."

Mother Irena replied with a smile,

"This is right. Now you sound much better. I believe that a real God worshiper is in front of me. Do you remember, Marie how the commandant of the camp and all the overseers called you? To my mind, the inmates of all Magadan camps heard the stories about your worships. Those stories worked like nourishing remedy for those who lost their hope to survive the inhuman camp conditions. Poor women considered you, Countess Marie Kurbatov, God's messenger, Divine angel, Saint Martyr."

"Who told you about me?" Maria asked with surprise. "Who was so kind to bring good word about my faith to you?"

Mother Irena warned,

"Marie, never allow pride to talk. I met you personally and knew that you were a woman who preserved faith in the heart. You, Marie were gentle but not weak to be broken. Faith kept you alive though endless sufferings and hardships. I saw you in Lviv prison, as a persecuted, tortured, humiliated and misfortunate pregnant woman. For many years, your faith has been nourishing your hope that one day, the trepidation and terror will be over, and the truth triumph. That's why you are here. I like the way you sound now."

Mother Irena smiled and added,

"Maybe, the inmates were right to some extent. I am again regarding your worship at the camp."

Maria still wanted to find out who told Mother Irena about her praying but did not want to interrupt the nun.

"You are right, Marie that you never fed ego and pride. What you did was correct: you preserved true faith. Any person can be blessed with ascension for our earthly deeds, faithful thoughts and sufferings," Mother Irena concluded.

"Ascension?" Maria interrupted. "It's not about me. I am a sinner, Mother Irena. I am a true sinner. I brought my husband Alexander to this country for torments, sorrows, distresses and death. My nanny Ganja was strangled because of my stay with her, and last month they burned her house. The intelligent and honorable man Mykola Petrovych, who was my close friend and fiancé was killed because he was defending my children and me. He wanted to prove that I am innocent. Now, I have to raise my children without fathers' care, protection and love. I am a sinner, Mother. I am a sinner."

Mother Irena did not agree with Maria. She said with the firmness in her voice,

"It was not only your fault, Marie. It does not put you down in the eyes of the Lord. Now, you arrived to stop illegal persecution not only of you, but also your children, beloved and other victims. God bless you, Marie! I believe that Holy Mother of God, as a woman and our Mother, will patronage and protect you in your mission, as well."

Maria hugged her sister in Christ. She was grateful to Mother Irena for her kind words. Maria did not know earlier, how her God's worship affected the lives of other inmates in her and other camps. She considered that she lived and worked with prayers just because she did not know how to live without the connection with Divinity and the assistance from Above. Who else was able to help, protect and preserve the human life in GULAG, the hell on Earth? Maria prayed and her prayers were answered. Another thing was how people responded to the God's miracles. If her sincere worship saved the life of at least, one inmate, she did it right.

Mother Irena watched Maria thinking about something important for her and said,

"Everything is going to be all right, Marie. You know that our Lord is merciful. Wait until tomorrow. Pray and wait. Be always patient. Good night."

The nun blessed the sleeping children. She looked again at Maria and thought,

"It's true that Marie looks like a real martyr in her black shawl. Poor woman, she suffered so much. Her loses were very precious for her."

Then she smiled and wished again,

"Stay always blessed by God, Marie. Have a good night."

"Good night," Maria answered quietly. She meditated her evening prayers and at the end, the disturbed woman asked, "Dear Lord, forgive me, your servant Maria, for my impatience. If I need to wait, I'll wait with Your help and Your blessing."

Lord, Have Mercy!

⚜

Chapter 44

It took two more days before Mother Irena said,

"Everything is going to be arranged the day after tomorrow."

Maria was nervous, and she knew that the only medicine for her nervousness was her sincere prayer during the day work and reading of the Psalms every evening. She prayed to the Lord, requesting for the deliverance from affliction, wrath, danger, every snare of seen and unseen enemies. She asked the Lord to deliver her and kids from the temptations and attacks of the adversary. Maria supplicated the Divinity to destruct every evil counsel directed against her and children during their visit to the Kremlin.

Every morning, Maria took some Holy water and gave it to her children, asking for Lord's cleansing of their souls and bodies and for filling them with His Holy Spirit.

She found time to read out loud daily the Holy Bible,

"Brethren, he who observes the day, observes it to the Lord; and he who does not observe the day, to the Lord he does not observe it. He, who eats, eats to the Lord, for he gives thanks; and he who does not eat, to the Lord he does not eat and does not give God thanks. For none of us lives to himself, and no one dies to himself. For if we live, we live to the Lord; and if we

die, we die to the Lord. Therefore, whether we live or die, we are the Lord's."

Maria believed that the Lord would control the whole situation in the Kremlin. She repeated by heart several times a day, *"The Lord is my Light and my Savior; whom shall I fear?"* or *"The Lord is the Defender of my life, of whom shall I be afraid?"* Many times, during the last two days, Maria asked the Lord, *"My Lord, please do not cast me away from Your presence, and do not take Your Holy spirit from me..."*

It was around 2 p.m. when somebody knocked on the door of Maria's room. Both children were taking a nap. Maria rushed to open the door in order the visitor did not awake the kids with the knocking. What was her surprise! Sasha was standing there. He looked much older in his Navy uniform. Mother Irena watched them with a smile. Maria stepped out, hugged her son and covered his face and head with kisses. She repeated his name, "Sasha, Sasha, Sasha… O my Lord! Today, You have granted me the best gift, sending my son to me. Thank You, Lord! I am so grateful to You and Mother Irena."

Maria was interrupted with Mother Irena's voice, coming from the end of the corridor,

"Marie, it's good enough with thanking me. I had nothing to do with it. I'll see you later. I have to bring something to you for tomorrow."

"Thank you, Mother Irena," Maria answered joyfully.

The nun left with the words, "O Lord, she is a genuine mother. Help her to find justice and protection for her children. *You are a merciful God, who loves mankind, and to You we ascribe the glory: to the Father, to the Son, and to the Holy Spirit, now and ever and unto ages of ages. Amen.*"

Maria let Sasha in. She could not help admiring her son. He looked hansom in the Navy uniform. He looked even more alike with his father. The tears filled Maria's eyes. Sasha could not see his mother crying and begged her with his father's intonation,

"Maman, please don't cry. I'll do anything you want me to do, only stop crying. Show me my sister, please. I feel sorry that I was not able to kiss her five months ago."

They came up to the bed where Vira was asleep. Sasha kneeled near her and said quietly in Russian,

"Hello sister Vera. I am your brother Sasha. I love you, and I hope you'll love me too."

Vira smiled. Sasha got exited,

"Mama, do you remember, every time when I spoke to Tisha in his sleep, he smiled to my words. I mean, when he was a baby and slept in his crib."

Maria answered,

"And now, he is smiling."

Sasha turned to his brother. Tisha was sitting in his bed with a smile on his face. Sasha rushed to him, hugged tightly and said,

"I miss you, Ivanko. My younger brother, I miss you so much. Very often, I looked at small boys like you in the streets of Odessa and wished to be with you."

Tisha did not move, he closed his eyes and smiled. Maria came up to her sons and embraced both boys. It was a moment of their mutual happiness, the most desirable for their mother. All three kids were with her. What else could she wish? Sasha was the first, who interrupted Maria's thoughts with several questions,

"Mama, why did Father Nikolas bring me here? What do you do here? Why is it so that Mykola Petrovych does not accompany you and Vera?"

Maria sat down on Tisha's bed and told Sasha the tragic story about her home-coming after summer vocation. At the end, she concluded,

"They killed Ganja and Mykola; they burned our house together with the house of our neighbors; they refused to hire me on any job, even the one in the collective farm, where they always experienced the shortage of farmers."

Sasha asked,

"So, you are hiding here, aren't you?"

Maria continued,

"Why should I live with my children in hiding places? What crime did I commit?"

Sasha looked at his mother with concern, asking,

"Then what do you do here?"

Maria explained,

"I came to Moscow, because I decided to meet the Head of the country Brezhnev and to ask for his personal intervention. I need to stop persecution."

"Mama, wouldn't it be Dad's appalling finale?" Sasha asked in a trembling voice.

Maria sensed in Sasha's question that he would never take a risk after his father's murder. She felt sharp pain in her heart, when she understood, "My Lord, they did terrible thing to my son – they frightened him."

"Sasha, I was scared for a long time and avoided fights. However, following their orders, hiding without taking any actions and growing inner fear did not help me to resolve the problems. It made the demons think that they are allowed to execute anything dismaying to me and my beloved, and they would never be punished for it. I must stop them."

Maria came up to Sasha and said firmly,

"Now, I feel different. Thank God, I am inspired for fighting. I know exactly what my requests are. I understand that it's dangerous. Sasha, you should not go with us, if you have hesitations. Thank God for giving me the opportunity to see you before my visit to the Kremlin. You know, Sasha how I love you."

Sasha got up and walked out of the room. Maria followed him to the door, but something stopped her right in the doorway. She thought, "I should let Sasha make his own conclusions and decide what is right and wrong for him. It's his time to make a choice." Maria came up to the window and watched how Sasha walked slowly along the street. In five minutes, Maria saw her son coming back. When he looked at her window, she waved to him. He smiled.

Maria opened the door in the vestibule, and Sasha entered the house with the words,

"Mama, tomorrow, maybe it will be the last day of our lives. Nevertheless, if I do not go together with you, Tisha and Vera, I would never forgive myself. I won't be able to live peacefully. We must be together. Up till now, I blame myself for not being with my father on that terrible day, when he visited Magadan KGB."

"Thank you, Sasha," Maria said quietly.

"What is it for?" Sasha asked.

"For being our son." She accented the word "our." Sasha smiled.

Maria explained,

"I know, my boy, it was not easy for you to make this decision. I myself checked many times: it's not my ego, pride or self-respect that pushed me there. It's the understanding of human dignity. Your father died for it. I was a sinner, because I considered his death, as a manifestation of his pride or impatience. No, children, he was completely right. A man cannot live hidden from the light, as a worm. It's the most important philosophy of a human being-the Creator made a man, as His own replica with His belief that a man would never become a slimy worm."

Maria felt exhausted and changed the subject, "Tell me, how is everything in your school? How do you explain to classmates, why you are there?"

"All the students lost their fathers due to their military missions in Spain, Africa, Japan, China or WWII. Nobody asked anything about my father's mission, and I did not volunteer to say anything. They know that I have my mother. I think that Larissa knew how to correctly introduce my case to our principle."

"How are Larissa and her parents?"

"I think that everything is all right with them. She works a lot. Every time, when she arrives to Odessa, she visits me and brings something tasty. She used to bring candies, cookies, fruits and pastries. I always share with my friends, as I did it in the labor camp. So, they also like my *aunt's* visits."

Maria joked,

"You were lucky to find a good aunt, Sasha."

The small children interrupted the conversation. They woke up nearly simultaneously, and Tisha called loudly,

"Sasha, come here."

In a blink of an eye, Sasha was near his brother. He hugged him again and "smell" him, as he did it, when Tisha was a baby. Then he seriously concluded,

"The boy smells good, let me eat him for dinner."

Sasha made a face of a monster, who was ready to eat a child. Tisha enjoyed, how Sasha pretended that he was biting his younger brother. Tisha and Maria burst into laughing. Vera started to cry. She did not want to be alone, but she was too small to take part in her brothers' game.

Maria held Vera in her arms and watched her sons with joy that she did not experience for a long time. The boys were playing and laughing. They missed each other and were happy to be together again. Maria thought, "They looked different, but both are the Kurbatovs'. Sasha is a copy of his father, and Tikhon copied his grandmother from France." Maria smiled bitterly to her thought, "My children are not destined to live with their fathers, as well as they are not destined to live with their grandmother."

Maria shook her head to the next thought, "I decided to take a huge risk, and they can lose me, as well..." Then she said out loud, *"Help us, save us, have mercy on us, and keep us, O Lord by Thy grace."*

It was 7:15 p.m. when Mother Irena came to Maria's room. The nun brought a big pack with something and left it on the bed. Maria turned to Mother Irena and asked,

"What is there in the pack?"

"Open it fast, Marie. It's your cloths. Everything was cleaned and ironed. Don't even think that you can go to the Kremlin in the way you are dressed now. They'll immediately throw you away," Mother Irena explained.

Maria took out a brown cashmere dress with a color made of off-white lace, a pair of dark brown shoes, silk stockings, gloves, light brown coat and a beautiful hat. Everything looked elegant. Maria smiled, recollecting, how the grandfather suggested her to wear the fur coat in order she could look presentably. She recollected how the old fur coat had immediately changed her appearance. It looked that she became again Countess Marie Kotyk in her fur coat and matching hat.

"Try them on, Marie," Mother Irena suggested. "The woman who donated you these cloths is your size, but it is better to try beforehand. If something needs the alteration, you'll do it now."

Maria took a dress and shoes. She stood behind the headboard of the bed. Sasha thought,

"Our Mama is so short. We can hardly see the crown of her head behind the headboard. How was it possible that I hadn't paid attention to that before? She is so petite. My God, only now, I have realized how difficult it must be for her to live alone with two small children without work and anybody's help. I must be with her not only tomorrow, but always. My Dad would never be happy with me, knowing what hardships our mother is overcoming alone."

Sasha's thoughts were interrupted when Maria stepped out of her hiding place. There was a silence in the room for a minute. Even Vira stopped sounding.

Mother Irena was the first who started to talk,

"It looks all right, Marie. Put on a coat and a hat, please."

Maria put them on and looked around for a mirror to see, how she looked in somebody's rather expensive clothing.

"There is no mirror in the room, Marie. Take everything off and hang it until 2:30 a.m. All of you must be ready by three. They'll pick you up. Please, don't waste your time in the evening. Feed the kids, wash them and go to bed. Sleep for a couple of hours and get ready. With God's blessing, tomorrow is the day of your liberation…"

Mother Irena did not finish the last sentence. She suggested,

"Let us pray to the Lord and ask Him to bless you for a desired outcome."

They prayed "The Agreement Prayer". Maria was happy to see that her Sasha remembered it very well, though they did not pray it together for a year. Mother Irena blessed Maria and children for good night and left. Maria did everything, as Sister Irena advised. Tisha was happy to sleep with his brother. It, probably, reminded him how they travelled for nearly a month together on one berth from Magadan to Moscow.

Maria did her evening laundry fast, praying all the time to the Holy Spirit *"Heavenly King, the Comforter, the Spirit of Truth, who arts everywhere and fills all things. Treasury of Blessings and Giver of life: come and dwell in us, and cleanse us from every impurity, and save our souls, O Good One. Amen."*

The moment she stopped praying, a strange thought sneaked in Maria's mind,

"Why do I do now my chores and laundry? Will it be tomorrow for my children and myself? What should I expect from tomorrow? Will they allow us to come back here after our visit to the Kremlin? Will they allow us to leave the Kremlin on our own or they will arrest me and send the children to different orphanages? Am I right to put my children in unsafe situation?"

The fearful thoughts and hesitations conquered Maria for a moment. She kneeled and pleaded,

"O Lord Almighty, the God of our fathers, I pray to Thee, have mercy on us according to Thy great mercy. Protect us with Thy eternal power and save us by Thy grace. Amen."

Maria felt that hesitation and fear retrieved, and she continued,

"My Lord, I ask this with my pure heart and with my honest mind: deliver my children and me from all afflictions, wrath, danger, and necessity this night and tomorrow. Amen."

Maria looked at the clock. It was 10:10 p.m. She took her towel and went to take shower. When she came back to the room, it was a quarter to 11 p.m. The children slept soundly. Vera smiled in her sleep. Maria thought, "She is a good girl. She knows that her Mama has to prepare herself for tomorrow." Maria combed her long hair and thought, "Maybe, I need to cut my hair? The long braids always require additional time and strength."

She recollected, how late Alexander loved her long hair. The length of the braids has already reached her knees. He asked her to keep her braids unplaited at night and enjoyed hiding his face in her long hair. Maria thought, "Nobody needs it now. Nobody enjoys my braids. I should cut my hair short and forget about my femininity. Should I?"

Maria heard her Angel's answer, "No, Marie. Don't do it. Never destroy your natural beauty. Look always decent in the eyes of the Lord. He blessed you with wonderful hair. If nobody else, then you should enjoy your prettiness, as God's creation."

Maria finished with braiding and checked again on her sons. She put two towels on her pillow in order not to make it wet and laid down near her baby daughter. She did not turn off the table lamp, thinking that she could stay in bed only for one hour. "I will not fall asleep, just let my legs have some rest," Maria thought, and in a minute, she dozed.

Lord, have mercy!

Chapter 45

Maria jumped up from the bed, when somebody knocked on the door. She rushed to the door with a single thought, "My God, I overslept". She opened it and did not find anybody there. "It's strange." Maria locked the door and checked the clock. It was 1:55 a.m. Five minutes earlier than she planned to get up. She smiled, "Thank you, my Angel."

Maria was dressed up in her new cloths, when she awaked both boys. It took only ten minutes for Alexander to get ready.

"Now, I can see, Sasha that you are a student of the Navy school," Maria commented with her smile.

Sasha was happy to see his mother smiling. He believed that the coming day was not expected to be easy, and mother's beautiful smile cheered him up.

Then she noticed with theatrical intonation,

"Look, Sasha but we have Tisha, who is still not trained, as a military man."

Maria tried to wake Tisha up with kisses, repeating, "Wake up, my dear. Get up."

Sasha helped his mother to dress a sleeping Tikhon, who could not open his eyes. The boy looked unrecognizable in his new shirt, pants, vest and jacket. Then Maria nursed her baby girl, changed her swaddling clothes and was ready to wrap her in a warm quilt, when somebody knocked on their door. Sasha opened it. Mother Irena came with a woman who arrived to take Maria and children to the Kremlin. The woman introduced herself,

"I am Elena. Let us go."

Mother Irena blessed everyone and prayed out loud, *"Dear Lord, bless Maria and children with reinstatement of justice. Almighty Father, save Maria and children with your miraculous intervention. Holy Spirit of Truth, make their liberation from evil pursuers peaceful and successful. Amen."*

Maria picked up her daughter from the bed, and Sasha carried his sleeping brother. They followed Elena and took the rear seats in a van.

"When we stop at the gate, keep your heads down. Hide yourself," the driver instructed. The driver started the engine, and the car moved right away. Maria noticed Mother Irena, standing on the porch of the house. Maria was ready to cry, thinking, "Why do I have to go there? Why do I need to put in jeopardy my children and myself?" Then she started to pray and calmed down to the point that fell asleep. Her sleep surprised Sasha. He could not imagine to be so serene in the situation, like theirs.

The driver stopped at the rare gate, prepared the documents and handed them to the guard. Elena found the way to attract the guard's attention with her morning greetings. Everything went smoothly at the gate and nobody checked the rear seat. The car moved slowly to the garage area. The driver ordered briefly,

"Get out fast!"

Sasha and Tisha were out in a couple of seconds, and it took nearly a minute for Maria and Vera to be out of the car.

"Where should we go now?" Maria asked.

Elena showed the direction to the road where usually the cortege of the leader's cars was proceeding. She also warned,

"Don't come up to the front car, please. It's his security team in it. He is in the second car. Try to stop his car, and then you may have a chance. Should I mention that you have not ever seen me and the driver? God bless, Marie!"

Maria just shook her head and moved forward. Then she looked back and pronounced with a low voice,

"Thank you so much, Elena. Don't worry, we haven't met both of you before."

Maria looked at her watch. It was difficult to read time. It looked like it was 5:05 a.m. All-embracing darkness covered Maria and children. They moved in the direction, pointed by Elena. It was a chilly autumn morning with the wind, bringing cold from the north. Maria covered Vera's head and face with the quilt.

Maria whispered the instructions,

"Sasha, in darkness, we need to come up closer to the main building and hide there in the trees. They said that Brezhnev comes around 8 or 8:15 a.m. When his cortege comes, please don't be afraid and follow me. Stay next to me, please."

"All right, Mama. I'll be with Tisha next to you," Sasha promised.

They walked for thirty-forty steps forward and had to hide deeper in the bushes. A big truck with soldiers moved in the direction of the main building.

"Change of the guards," Maria whispered. Then she suggested,

"Let's walk deeper in the trees. It will be less dangerous then to walk along the road. When we walk close to the road, the headlights can trace us."

It was difficult to move forward in darkness, carrying children in the arms and stumbling all the time over the roots of the trees.

"Sasha, while it's dark, we have to get as close to the building, as we can," Maria suggested.

"So, we have probably half an hour to get there, Mama. The park is big," Sasha replied. Maria whispered,

"With God's help, if nobody stops us, we'll get to our destination point on time."

Then she continued,

"Do you remember our trip around Moscow? You wanted to be in the Kremlin, so here you are." Maria smiled.

Sasha was amazed, thinking, "How can Mama joke now? She is brave."

When they were ready to cross one of the alleys, Maria noticed a figure of a man on the alley, coming in their direction. Sasha did not notice the man. Tisha's head blocked his vision. Sasha made a step forward, and Maria pulled him back. The man noticed some motions in the bushes and stopped near them, trying to see what animal could be there. The grass was wet. For a while, the man stood in hesitation, choosing between checking the bushes and walking straight to his work.

Maria noticed that Vera did not sleep, and she could start crying any moment. The man continued staying from the other side of the bushes. Vera made a face that was usually followed with loud cry. Maria covered the face of the baby with her face. The baby smelled her mother and began to gasp, looking for her breakfast. The man moved forward and stopped again. Maria unbuttoned her coat and dress and began nursing. The man walked away. When Maria finished feeding Vera, the day was breaking.

"Mama, how are you there?" Sasha asked.

Maria was speechless. She fixed her dress and coat and walked further. They crossed two more alleys. In both cases they did it cautiously. It became more difficult to sneak up to the main building. The people started to walk back and forth along the alleys, and Maria had to wait for five or more minutes in order to catch the moment and cross the alley with children. At 7 a.m., the yard cleaners began to clean the territory. Their work made Maria's trekking more dangerous.

By 7:40 a.m., Maria and children reached their destination point, where they needed to stay about thirty minutes in order to meet the cortege. There was one big complication there – the place around the main building was too opened, and there was no possibility to stay unseen. Maria decided to sit down on one of the benches in the square and wait for the arrival of the head of the soviet government.

"Sasha, if somebody comes and asks you why we are sitting here, say that your mother was given an early appointment to see somebody in the main building. Our documents were taken at the entrance."

"I wish nobody will ask us for anything," Sasha answered.

Maria watched how two male yard cleaners looked from time to time at Maria and children. They moved toward them from two opposite directions, and Maria prayed the Lord to send Brezhnev, as fast as possible. Sasha noticed,

"Mama, do you see how muscular the yard cleaners are?"

Maria answered with big smile that both cleaners could see her smiling face in a distance,

"They will definitely try to control the situation and not allow us to reach his car. I beg you, Sasha, stay next to me all the time. Don't focus your attention at them. Brezhnev is our target. We must be next to his car in several seconds. All the rest things will be arranged by the Lord."

Then she estimated the distance from the bench to the road and asked,

"What do you think, Sasha, how long will it take for us to reach the cortege cars from this bench?"

"As for me, it's probably 30 seconds from this spot. With Tisha in my arms, it will take a little bit more."

Maria saw that both yard cleaners were in less than fifty steps from her children and her. She smiled, talking to her children. Then she changed the position of Vera in her arms and looked at her watch.

"Sasha, it's already 7:58 a.m. Where is the cortege? The cleaners will be here earlier than Brezhnev," Maria said. *"Lord, have mercy. I ask for Your mercy not only for me, but for my innocent children and thousands of other non-guilty people."*

Maria tried to pull herself together because she was ready to cry. When the distance between Maria and the yard cleaners was not longer than ten steps, the cortege appeared on the road behind the trees. Maria looked at Sasha and suggested with a big smile,

"Sasha, sit quiet, until I say to you, 'Go'. We move straight through the bushes to meet them there on the road."

The noise of the cars was close enough, when Maria commanded,

"Go."

In a second, Maria and children were running between bushes and fur-trees. She heard the steps of yard-cleaners behind them.

"Sasha, don't look back. Run to the second car and stop it."

They appeared on the road when the first car was passing by. Maria jumped out in front of the second car. The driver stopped immediately. She moved to the right rear door. She did not know that Brezhnev was there, and she did not know, why the right rear door was chosen. She tried to see him through the tented window.

The yard-cleaners were near and pulled Sasha and Tisha from the car. The guards from the first car were already out and circled Maria. Maria called,

"Comrade Brezhnev, please open the window."

The guard pulled her, but she did not let them to separate her hand from the handle of the rear door. The tears were running on her cheeks. She repeated persistently,

"Comrade Brezhnev, please open the window."

Two huge guards jumped on her from both sides, and a miracle happened: the door was opened, and Brezhnev stepped out.

"What is going on here?" He asked and looked at Maria with surprise. Then he ordered to the guards, "Let her come."

"I am Countess Maria Kotyk-Kurbatov. Please, find a couple of minutes of your time and listen to my story. Then you can do whatever you decide is right. I agree with any of your personal decisions."

Brezhnev smiled and noticed out loud,

"Good start."

One of the guards came up to Brezhnev and said with a smirk,

"Look at this countess. She 'arose' on the territory of the Kremlin with all her children and demonstrated her impudence in her obnoxious desire to talk to you Two prisons, Lubyanka and Crosses, are waiting for her I prefer Crosses."

That was a moment, when God demonstrated Maria that the country had a new leader, but the KGB acted by old laws regarding its people. It looked like the invisible spiral moved inside of Maria's tiny body, and she began to scream, naming everything what was done to innocent people, like her, her father, husbands, children, Sister Olga and Ganja. After each accusation, Maria asked Brezhnev and people who surrounded her and her children,

"What was it for? Why do you allow the KGB to murder innocent people? Why does the KGB have all the rights to persecute my beloved, my friends, my children and myself? Why is the KGB allowed to hunt and slaughter the elderly women? Why was the KGB allowed to burn our houses and the house of my neighbors, making the families with children homeless? How can I, a highly educated woman with medical degree from Sorbonne University, survive with three children without any job just because the representatives of KGB gave the orders to the local authorities to keep me unemployed, and to kill my children with cold and hunger? Where is justice, humanity, democracy and freedom?"

Maria turned towards the guard, who suggested to arrest and depart her to Crosses prison and asked,

"When will you stop hunting the innocent people? My husband and I had never been the citizens of your country. You threw us to the camps for 12 years, illegally making us "people's enemies, spies, terrorists and ideological saboteurs." Maria pulled Sasha forward and asked again,

"Why should he be born in GULAG? Why should he spend ten years of his childhood there? What was it for? I came with my husband with all the legal documents in 1946. I arrived home to visit my family after the war. They arrested us, tortured, mutilated my husband, humiliated me as a woman. I was six months pregnant, when I arrived. What was it for? They killed my dear friend, a father of my daughter, who tried to prove my innocence. Why should the veteran of the war and the principle of the school pay with his life and dishonor for honorable actions? They murdered two old women for nothing. Why? What was it for? They occupied our manor and shot my father, when he tried to take his personal things and the instruments for his medical practice. Why did they shoot him? He did not mind moving out of the house and his private clinic. He asked for permission to take his personal things and his medical supply. Do you personally see any crime in it?"

Brezhnev listened attentively to Maria and realized that that woman underwent a lot, and he was her last hope. He asked,

"How do you want me to name you?"

Maria answered,

"During forty years of my life, I was named Her Grace Mademoiselle Kotyk, Madam Kurbatov, by my prison number and citizen Gnatiuk after the discharge from GULAG. Which one is good for you?"

Brezhnev made a step towards Maria and offered his hand, introducing himself,

"Leonid Ilych."

Maria answered,

"Maria Lukianovna."

Chapter 46

Brezhnev ordered somebody to take Vera, and they walked toward the main building, talking quietly, as if they knew each other for a long time.

"Maria Lukianovna, I can see that an extraordinary reason brought you here. You are fearless. When do people usually lose fear? It happens when their suffering and pain have escalated to the highest level. You have no more strength to tolerate your suffering and pain. So, you decided to arrive here in order to stop it. Am I right?"

Maria could hardly believe in what she heard. Her mind reminded, "Be careful, Marie. Now, you've stepped into the building, and they can arrest you and children. He was smart not to do it outside, because too many witnesses were there."

Brezhnev tried to calm Maria down, saying,

"I know that you do not trust me. Who can blame you? You went through terrible illicit accusations, humiliation, unlawful sentence and long-term imprisonment. Sorry to say, but those facts took place before and after the war. We cannot be kept responsible for Stalin's orders. We need to check and correct all the facts that take place today. I need to find out who continues tracking and destroying you and your family. If there is no reason for persecution, people must be punished for misusing of their power. Otherwise, we would never stop uncontrolled actions."

Maria did not believe his words, though he pronounced them naturally and without presence of theatrical intonations.

"May I ask you, Leonid Ilych about one thing?"

"Yes, Maria Lukianovna. What is it?"

"I would like to see my children all the time. Is it possible?" Maria asked.

"You are a good mother. They will be in the secretary room, so that you can hear them, but they will not interfere with our conversation and my calls to some administrative institutions in Lvov region."

Brezhnev turned around in front of the doors that were opened for him and ordered to the person who followed them along the corridor,

"Take good care of the children, Major. They did not have breakfast, and the youngest one probably will need her mother from time to time."

He turned back to Maria and asked with a natural smile,

"Your youngest child is breast fed, isn't she?"

Maria smiled for the first time and answered,

"Yes, she is."

The office of the party and country leader was spacious. He did not go and sat down in his arm-chair at the end of a long table. There was a small table with two cozy armchairs in the corner of the office. Maria registered for herself, "It's probably a place for 'non-official' conversations." The secretary took Maria's coat and left. Brezhnev invited Maria to take a seat at the small table.

The moment he took a seat, the secretary brought a tray with the breakfast. When she was leaving, Brezhnev requested in a polite manner,

"Please, do not allow anybody to disturb us for an hour."

"Certainly, Comrade Brezhnev," the secretary replied and left.

Brezhnev looked at Maria and announced,

"Breakfast first. We need to bring fuel to our body and brain in order to function well and resolve successfully different tasks and situations."

Maria did not believe in everything that was going on. She thought, "O my Lord, I have my breakfast with the leader of the country. Does he plan to put me in prison right after the breakfast?"

Brezhnev invited,

"Maria Lukianovna, please try our sandwiches. Look, they brought mineral water, coffee and tea. So, we have choices here what to drink."

Maria did not move. The initial part of their meeting was extremely intensive and burned all Maria's energy. She was moving her eyes from Brezhnev to delicious food and felt that she was unable to stretch her arm and take anything from the tray. Brezhnev, on the contrary, put several sandwiched on his plate and enjoyed the smell of his fresh coffee.

"Due to absence of free time, we'll eat and work on your case at the same time, but please, eat first. Will you allow me?"

Brezhnev took Maria's plate and put several sandwiches on it. Maria replied with a smile,

"Thank you."

Poor woman was completely confused, "Dear Lord, what is going on? Why do they need to pretend that they trust me?"

"What will you drink?" Brezhnev asked.

"Coffee, please," Maria answered.

For some minutes, there was silence in the room. They were chewing. Then they looked at each other and smiled.

"How do you find the taste of this coffee, Maria Lukianovna?" Brezhnev asked.

"It's wonderful. To tell you the truth, I forgot already the taste of good coffee," Maria replied.

"At least, you know the difference between good and bad," Brezhnev noticed with a friendly smile.

Maria had her own opinion about such knowledge,

"Sometimes, it's better not to know, Leonid Ilych. I am honest with you. I don't know what to expect in a minute, but I hope that you will not feed me here with this tasty breakfast before sending to the Crosses prison."

Brezhnev covered Maria's tiny hand with his and promised,

"I do not keep it in my plans, Maria Lukianovna. Continue eating your breakfast, please."

He called somebody, and the person that followed them to the office with Vera in his arms appeared instantly.

"Write down the dates of the most important episodes in the life of Maria Lukianovna. They were tragic, but we must restore the panorama of those events, then names of the people that took '*active*' parts in the events."

Brezhnev turned to Maria and continued, "Maria Lukianovna, when we collect the facts, dates and names, I will ask those people your questions: '*Why*? and *What it for?*' If they were wrong, we'll find how to correct everything that is still possible to correct. Nobody is able to bring back to life the diseased people, who were precious to you. We'll force the authorities to change their approach toward you and living members of your family."

Maria brought all the information written on one page of the school notebook and submitted it at once. Brezhnev read very attentively the both sides of the page. She saw that every tragedy of her life reached the mind of the leader. The heartbreaking chronology was registered with the names of the organizers and executors. Brezhnev handed the information to the KGB officer with the order: "You check all the facts." When the officer was at the door, Brezhnev stopped him with one more order: "First of all, make a call to the Lvov KGB office and order them to find the Kurbatovs' original passports and entry documents. Give them 5 minutes to report."

"Maria Lukianovna, we did not finish our breakfast. Please, continue eating," Brezhnev invited in a casual manner.

He called the secretary, and when she appeared in the doorway, asked her politely,

"May we have some fresh tea, please? We still need to wait for some information."

Maria knew that at that very moment her future and the future of her children depended on how fast the original documents would be found. The minutes lasted forever. She could not take any food from the plate. The tea was miraculous. She smelled it in a distance, and actually enjoyed it with the chocolate candy that the secretary put on her saucer.

The door was opened, and Maria heard the voice of the security man who wanted to arrest her from the very first moment and put in Crosses. He was talking loud enough that Maria could hear every word. "So, you found them. We'll send the inspectors to your office not later than today." The phone conversation was over, and the younger officer entered the room with the request,

"Comrade Brezhnev, may I report?"

"Proceed," Brezhnev replied.

"The Kurbatovs' original documents were found in their files. They arrested the Kurbatovs on the day of their arrival. No factional evidences of espionage or terroristic acts on the territory of the Ukraine were found. Colonel Petrov decided to send the inspecting group to the Lvov KGB in order to inspect this particular case and two others that require additional investigation."

"Good news, Maria Lukianovna," Brezhnev said.

Maria was afraid to move. She felt dizzy again.

In five minutes, there was another report regarding Magadan KGB persecution of the Kurbatovs and their illegal action with changing of the names and personal data.

"I believe that the rest of the information you submitted is based on true facts," Brezhnev concluded without any hesitation.

Then something happened that Maria could hardly hope or dream about. Brezhnev ordered to connect him with the Chairman of Samburovsky district soviet government administration. The assistant began the conversation with local Samburovsky authorities with the phrase,

"Good Morning. Be prepared. In a minute, you'll be connected to the General secretary of the communist party and the leader of the soviet government-Comrade Brezhnev."

Maria could imagine the shock of the person on the other end of the phone connection, when he received a call from the head of the country. Brezhnev asked the Chairman to introduce himself and ordered him to write down all the instructions. The orders to the region administration were brief but clear:

"We give you two weeks to build two houses that were burned in Blue Creeks. You personally, as the Chairman of the regional government, are assigned to be responsible for the terms and quality of the construction. Your work will be inspected."

Maria realized that the Chairman asked about the size of the house and Brezhnev replied:

"Comrade Gnatiuk's family requires five house-bedroom house. She has three children and brings her father and grandfather to live in Blue Creeks. That's why you must build the house with spacious kitchen and well build attic garret and basement cellar with shelves where they will keep the dry, preserved, salted and marinated mushrooms, fruits and vegetables for autumn, winter and spring for their large family."

Maria could not hear the other person and his questions. She apprehended them from the Brezhnev's answers:

"Of course, they need a barn. Do not forget to build it. Order the Chairman of the Blue Creeks collective farm to deliver the best milking cow and two milking goats. Again, do not forget about the feed for the animals for the winter and spring time. Make a chicken house in addition to the barn."

Brezhnev looked at Maria and probably noticed for the first time that she is tiny. She looked like a person after the concentration camp. He made his next order:

"The winter is coming. Supply Comrade Gnatiuk's big family with different grains, sugar, salt, oils, rye and wheat flour for breads and Ukrainian perogies. Do not forget about the vegetables for winter and spring. Everything must be prepared for Maria Lukianovna's family in two days before her arrival. Everything must be fresh and the best quality. We'll inspect the delivery."

Brezhnev looked at Maria and smiled. He covered the phone with his hand and whispered,

"I like Ukrainian perogies. One day, I'll stop at Blue Creeks. Do you mind?"

"You are always welcomed," Maria answered.

He made notes of all his orders. Then he continued:

"Prepare enough woods and coal for a Russian type stove. Ask the women of the village to prepare the cooking ware for the Kotyks family. Don't forget about plates and cups, knives, spoons and forks. There are six people in the family and one day, I'll be their guest."

The last Brezhnev's order surprised Maria even more than all the previous:

"You personally meet Maria Lukianovna and her children at the Lvov railway station and deliver them to Blue Creeks, in order they do not have any complications there. My secretary will let you know the exact day of their arrival. Is everything understood?"

Maria did not hear the next question of the regional Chairman. Brezhnev's answer was well-defined:

"Our party is strong enough to admit the unlegislated prosecutions of the NKVD/ KGB in the particular case with Maria Lukianovna Kotyk-Gnatiuk and her family. The widow, her children, her parents and grandfather are found innocent, and I personally, recommend you, as the head of the reginal communist committee, to demonstrate your humanity and political literacy in comprehensive support of the victims that I named earlier. Arrange the descent introduction of the founding family to the residence of Blue Creeks. We wish you success in your social and political activity. Is it clear?" Then Brezhnev ended:

"I believe, you'll do everything in the right way. Good-bye."

At that moment, Maria realized one thing-God's miracle happened.

Glory to Thee, Oh Lord! Glory to Thee!

Chapter 47

Maria's eyes were filled with tears, and she could not distinctly see the face of Brezhnev and the security officer that came into the room. The security officer put a document on the table of the General secretary. Brezhnev looked through the paper and came up to Maria with the words,

"Maria Lukianovna, everything is exactly, as I have heard from you. Now, the inspectors will personally ask your questions "Why?" and "What is it for?" In a week, we'll receive the written reports of the inspectors with the answers from the Lvov and Magadan KGB."

Maria stood up and said in a weak voice:

"I don't have the right words to thank you, Comrade Brezhnev."

Brezhnev shook his head and asked, "How could it be, Maria Lukianovna that you did not mention that Blue Creeks was founded by Count Kotyk family? In the document, they mentioned three generations of physicians. I understand that you are the third doctor Kotyk after your grandfather and father."

Maria answered,

"Yes, I am. You were given the true facts. The lands were purchased, and the Blue Creeks estate was founded by the Kotyks in Poland. That's why I mentioned that we did not have citizenship of the Ukraine or the Soviet

Union when we arrived after WWII. My late husband was Russian who was born in France. With marriage, I became the citizen of France."

Brezhnev continued,

"They found the facts in your father's file that the doctors Kotyk, a father and a son, were loyal to the soviet power. Your father and grandfather continued their medical practice for all the people of the area, until they were evicted from their houses and medical offices, as well as restricted to reside in Blue Creeks. Sorry to mention the fact that your father was shot."

Maria's eyes were filled with tears again. She added a new fact,

"God was merciful to him. My grandfather provided multiple surgeries and brought his son back to life."

Brezhnev continued,

"Now, it's time to correct the impacts from abuse of power. I admit, the soviet power was presented in Blue Creeks in an ugly way. Maria Lukianovna, you are also Kurbatov and the citizen of France, and now I know that you are also a good physician, aren't you?

"I hope, I am," Maria answered.

Brezhnev continued,

"This country and your native land are in need of knowledgeable and experienced doctors. I would request that you stay in your Blue Creeks and provide the medical services to the local population. We'll provide you a medical facility."

"Don't be afraid to become yourself. Sometimes, the political and government authorities need to be stopped to recognize the apolitical mistakes and activities of their representatives in order to correct them right away on the local level. Then I and other members of the Central committee should not spend our time for such corrections."

"I am so grateful for your time and understanding. When I took a risk to come here, I believed in God's providence that a new Head of the country will see me to liberate my family and me from wrong accusations and persecutions," Maria said.

"Where do you stay?" Brezhnev asked unexpectedly.

"With the local nuns," Maria replied.

The assistant of Brezhnev asked,

"You do not have money for a stay in another place, right?"

"No, I don't," Maria sensed awkwardness of the situation and explained,

"They gave the order to the local school, kindergarten and farm not to hire me for any position," Maria could not control the tears and they dropped on the dress.

Brezhnev noticed,

"They did everything to destroy you. You are like the bird phoenix. They burned you, and you raised up from the ashes and landed in the Kremlin".

Brezhnev gave the instructions to his assistant and the assistant asked,

"Now, we'll give you the tickets to return to Blue Creeks. However, you have to wait for two weeks until everything will be prepared for your arrival."

"Sasha needs to attend school. He is a student of Admiral Nakhimov Academy. Tomorrow, I must send him to Odessa."

Brezhnev laughed,

"The nobility, like your husband's Kurbatov family, has always been on tsar's navy and diplomatic services. They represented their land with honor. So, Maria Lukianovna, your son inherited to be a defender of the seas."

Brezhnev turned to the assistant,

"Get the ticket for the future navy officer for tomorrow on the direct train "Moscow-Odessa".

Maria and Brezhnev shook hands and the grateful woman added,

"I believe in God, Leonid Ilych. Today, God's miracle happened, and you took the important part in this miracle. May I pray for you and your success in my daily prayers?"

Both men looked at Maria with surprise. Brezhnev smiled to his thought, "She is a believer. Let this woman think this way."

He said out loud,

"You are free to do whatever you think is right."

When the assistant opened the door for Maria, Brezhnev stopped her with the question, which she expected from the very beginning of their conversation,

"Maria Lukianovna, may I ask you, how did you get here? I mean to the Kremlin."

Maria turned to Brezhnev and answered with her charming smile,

"From above, as a burned phoenix. There was no other way to come here."

All three of them laughed. Maria saw the faces of the people in the secretary office, watching her with surprise. She thought, "They are ready to arrest me any second in order to check, whether I can miraculously disappear from here, as I have appeared in this place."

Then she noticed her children and a woman in an adjacent room. Sasha got up from the chair when his mother entered the room. Maria sensed his tension and said,

"Alexander, everything is all right. Thank God, we are completely liberated, and since now on, nobody will persecute you, my children, your grandfather and me."

Maria thanked the woman who took care of her children for an hour. A new miracle was created by God. The assistant helped Maria to put on her coat, while the secretary prepared an envelope with some papers in it. Maria asked,

"May I ask, what is there in the envelope?"

Maria was still afraid that at the end of a nice visit, they would convert everything into a terrible ending. The woman with the envelope in her hand noticed Maria's hesitation. She opened it and named everything that was there,

"Don't worry, Comrade Gnatiuk. Here is the reservation for your tickets in thirteen days from today; the copy of instructions to regional authorities regarding your delivery to Blue Creeks and a new introduction. You keep them, in case they 'misplace' or 'lose' the phone instructions." The woman smiled to her own remark.

"Here, you'll also find some instructions to your local Blue Creeks authorities. You'll hand it to them, when you meet them in person. The rest of the documents will be delivered to Lvov KGB directly by the inspectors of the case. You may also find some money for your stay here in Moscow and for your re-integration in Blue Creeks. Maria Lukianovna, we wish you all the best! Good luck, children. By the way, you have a wonderful baby daughter. She forced us to change her swaddling-cloths twice for one hour."

Maria felt awkward,

"Excuse me, please. Usually, I stay with Vera all the time."

The elderly secretary smiled, watching Maria's embarrassment.

"I joked about your baby. We did whatever we needed to do. It was nice to meet you. Have a safe trip."

Maria and children followed Brezhnev's assistant along the endless corridor. In the morning, they came in from the other side of the building. Only now Maria noticed the guards along the corridor. She thought, "How was it possible that I did not see them in the morning? I was really in the condition that people used to describe, as being 'out of mind'."

Maria could not walk fast with Vera in her arms, and Sasha observed the magnificence of the building. Maria smiled to the thought that explained her morning poor focusing on the same building and the same guards, "My Lord did not want me to notice anything or anybody that could distract my attention from the conversation or even worth-frighten me."

Sasha came closer to Maria and whispered,

"Mama, I wish we know where this man takes us. I don't trust him."

Maria answered in a calm manner,

"Don't worry, Alexander. We go home."

The exit doors were opened by two guards after Brezhnev's assistant handed them a pass.

Near the exit, there was a car, waiting for them.

"You'll be delivered home, and when you are ready to go back to Lvov, give us a call. You'll be taken to the railway station and assisted with taking the train."

Maria thought for a second and asked, "Is this an obligation that I have to follow? I do not want to disturb your office again."

"No, it's not a disturbance. Comrade Brezhnev considers that you have undergone too many life complications due to unfair actions of different authorities, and now, it's your time to receive the assistance and their time to learn justice."

"I appreciate the understanding of Comrade Brezhnev and his personal concern. Thank you, people for everything."

The children have been already on the rear seats of the car, patiently waiting for their mother.

Brezhnev assistant asked before the opening the front passenger door for Maria,

"Did anybody tell you, Maria Lukianovna, that you have an irresistible smile?"

Maria smiled and answered,

"Thank you for the complement, but only you noticed it."

The assistant opened the door and ordered to the driver,

"Go."

Maria blessed the road and the driver smiled.

Glory to Thee, o Lord. Glory to Thee!

Chapter 48

The car moved fast along the roads to deliver Maria's family to the nuns' home. Vera began to cry. The baby missed her mother and '*insisted*' in compensation for the time that her mother spent in the office of the leader of the USSR. Sasha carefully passed his sister to Maria, and baby smiled, seeing her mother again.

"How was Vera in the Kremlin?" Maria asked.

"She was very well. She slept most of the time, and between her naps, she enjoyed the washing and changing of her swaddle-cloths."

"Who did it?"

"There was a woman with us all the time. Did you notice the one, who stood near us? She was tall and strong. She washed Vera twice and, to my mind, they threw away her used swaddles and changed them for new. We have several new sets with us in Vera's bag."

Maria covered her shoulder and Vera from the driver's side with a light shul in order not to be exposed while nursing. She nursed Vera and smiled. The girl stopped sucking and smiled to her mother. The driver stopped at the red traffic light and watched a strange company in his car. Maria knew that he would like to talk to them, but it was not allowed. Not every visitor to the Kremlin was delivered by government car to their residence. There were so many questions in his mind to ask, but his job description prohibited any questions and conversations.

The car stopped near the nuns' house. The driver looked at Maria and Maria said,

"Thank you very much. You drove so smoothly that my younger kids dozed."

Then she asked Sasha to help her out with Vera. Maria felt inner shaking and dizziness again. She commanded to herself, "No, Maria. Not now. Be strong."

The driver noticed that Maria turned pale and asked,

"Are you all right? Do you have anybody here, who can help you to get in?"

Maria tried to pull herself together,

"I think, I'll make it."

She made one step and exclaimed,

"Vera ..."

In a second, the driver was near Maria and caught the falling baby. He asked Sasha to run to the house and ask somebody to come out and help his mother. The front passenger door of the car was opened, and the driver managed to sit Maria on her seat.

Sasha brought three nuns, and they took Maria out of the car. She was not able to stand or walk by herself. The driver suggested,

"Call the ambulance. Do you want me to call the ambulance?"

The nuns did not answer him, and the driver called to his office with the report about the unexpected situation. He had not driven away until the ambulance came. The doctors rushed to the room where the sisters put Maria on the couch. She was unconscious.

Sasha made his report regarding Maria's previous manifestations of critically low blood pressure after stressful situations. The boy mentioned,

"Dr. Leskov knew better than anybody else how to stabilize Mama's blood pressure."

One of the doctors asked,

"Dr. Leskov? In what clinic does he run his practice?"

Sasha answered,

"He is in Eultin, Magadan region."

The doctor concluded,

"At the moment, he cannot be a big help. How long did your mother stay unconscious?"

"She was unconscious for five days after the murder of our father. They could not help my mother in the hospital and called Dr. Leskov."

The team prepared Maria for hospitalization.
The doctor continued questioning,

"When did the previous cases take place?"

Sasha answered,

"It happened in the labor camp, after giving me a birth. And the second episode occurred last year in March."

The doctor was confused and asked,

"She got pregnant at the camp, did she?"

"No, she did not. She was six months pregnant when my parents arrived to the Ukraine in 1946 and were taken to the labor camps."

The second doctor had finished with paperwork and was listening to the conversation.

"Who was your father, boy?"

"Count Alexander Kurbatov. He was Russian who was born in France."

The first doctor concluded,

"Everything is clear. We'll take your mother to the hospital. I'll leave you the address and the phone there."

"No hospital, please," Maria whispered. "I don't want to go to any hospital. I refuse going to the hospital. In an hour, I will be all right. We need to go home."

At that very moment Mother Irena entered the room. She removed the team from Maria and asked,

"How are you, Marie? Tell me the truth, please. If you need to go to the hospital, we'll go."

"I don't need to go to the hospital, Mother. Please, let me stay for a day with you. Let Sasha help me to get to my room, and he'll take care of children. Tomorrow, I'll be all right," Maria whispered.

Mother Irena turned to the ambulance team and announced her decision with the intonation that was beyond any hesitation or discussion,

"Marie needs some rest. Where can she find better rest from life vanity, if not in our surrounding? We should not keep you longer. Go, please. Go. She'll stay with us. If tomorrow she is as weak, as today, I personally will call the ambulance, and you'll hospitalize her. Good-bye, doctors. Have a blessed day."

Maria smiled. She knew the kindness of Mother Irena, but listening to the intonation of her deep voice, the team realized that they dealt with a nun, made of iron. The supervisor of the team left the phone number of their medical institution. The team belonged to the Kremlin hospital.

Mother Irena burst into short laugh. She tried to cheer up Maria and asked her with her usual gentle voice,

"Well, how good was I, Marie? What do they think about me now? They hate all of us just because they are atheists and consider that the clergy people are fools with our tales about God. I feel sorry for them. Do you remember, Marie what had happened to those misfortunate women who did not carry faith in their hearts?"

"You are great, Mother Irena," Maria said in a low voice.

"Now, our sisters will bring food and some milk for you," the nun said.

Maria looked around and did not find her children in the room.

"Where are the kids, Mother?"

"They all have their lunch in the dining room, Marie."

Maria smiled and asked,

"All three have lunch there, especially Vera?"

Mother Irena stroked Maria's hair and asked her question quietly,

"Did you see him? Did you have a chance to talk to him?"

Maria turned to Mother Irena, hugged her and answered,

"With God's help. We talked longer than an hour. Five minutes outside, when we stopped the cortege. Right there, I described the major tragic events of my life, expressing all my thoughts and feelings regarding the prejudiced, unlegislated persecution toward my family. I brought his attention to the recent tragic incidents that forced me to arrive to Moscow. I think my fearless narration impressed him, and he continued the conversation with verifying the facts when we came to his office. By the way, he invited me for breakfast with him."

"Glory to Lord! What did Brezhnev suggest you for breakfast? It was not our cream of wheat or oatmeal with a cup of tea, right?"

"No, Mother Irena. They made different tasty French type sandwiches and brought delicious tea and coffee. I mentioned to him that I forgot the taste of good coffee."

"He is a new person. How did he sound, Marie?"

"I don't know, how he plans to rule the life of the country, what laws and regulations he prefers to follow in future, but presently, he is a person with a good heart," Maria concluded.

Mother Irena blessed herself and said out loud,

"Glory to Thee, O Lord! Glory to Thee!"

Maria sat down on the sofa and smiled, looking at Mother Irena.

"Why do you smile, Marie? Do you feel better?" The nun inquired.

"I've told Brezhnev that I believe in God and that our meeting today with positive results I've seen, as God's miracle. I've mentioned to him that he has played an important part in the miracle after the Divinity."

Mother Irena smiled. She wanted to comment Maria's last sentence, but two other nuns appeared at the door and announced,

"Mother Irena, your soup waits for you. It's on the table and getting cold."

"All right, all right. We are coming. Can you walk, Marie? I wish, we can have our soup together."

Maria stood up and, in a second, she sat down. She joked,

"I did my best with standing up. However, the floor tries to run away from me. I can walk only with somebody's help."

Both nuns simultaneously suggested their arms to support Maria,

"Here we are," Mother Irena said.

At the lunch, Mother Irena and Maria discussed the details of Maria's visit to the Head of a huge country. Both women were sure that another God's miracle happened.

"You suffered a lot, my child," Mother Irena said. "You needed real help. Our Lord changed the Head of the government for the person with good heart."

"I have to send Sasha back to school," Maria said. "Brezhnev ordered a ticket for Sasha. So tomorrow, my boy leaves for Odessa."

"Marie, we talked to the principle of his school, when we decided to bring Sasha here. He allowed the boy to stay in Moscow, including tomorrow. Everything goes right with God's blessing."

"Thank you, Mother. However, I need to stay at your place for extra thirteen days. Do you know why?" Maria asked with her smile.

"Why, Marie? Why?" Mother Irena liked Maria's mood.

"Brezhnev ordered the district Chairman to build our and the neighbors' houses for two weeks."

"Really? What else he wanted them to do?" Mother Irena asked with satisfaction in her voice.

"To build a barn, to bring a milking caw and two milking goats. He ordered to supply us with firewood, foods, produce, salt and oils for winter. He did not even forget about the feed for animals."

Maria's face expressed sadness, and Mother Irena asked,

"What else makes you sad, Marie?"

"In summer, I grew a lot of vegetables. They were so nice. The fire destroyed my work."

"Next summer, the soil will give you better crop. The soil is fertilized with the burned vegetables."

"It's hard to believe, Mother. We have to wait until they finish with everything that I could hardly dream about."

"The most important, Marie, you'll have your family together. Your children will see the grandpa and grate-grandfather daily. They will learn a lot from them. As for your mother, let your mother visit her younger daughter Jenny. She might like it there," Mother Irena suggested.

After lunch, Mother Irena asked another nun to take Maria to her room.

"Let Marie have some rest. The morning was very intense for her."

Sasha put children to sleep, and Maria had an opportunity to rest. She slept soundly for several hours, and the loud cry of her hungry daughter awoke her. Maria looked at the clock on the opposite wall. It was 5:17 p.m. Maria's weakness did not completely disappear, but she felt better and was ready to go for evening church service with the nuns. Maria wanted to express her gratefulness to the Divinity for everything that took place on that wonderful day. One more God's miracle happened in Maria's life.

Glory to Thee, O Lord! Glory to Thee!

Chapter 49

Maria hesitated regarding the phone call to the Kremlin and reminding their promise to assist her with children to take a train Moscow-Lvov. Mother Irena did it for her. The car was near the nuns' house in an hour to departure. The same driver that brought Maria after her visit to Brezhnev appeared in Maria's room to pick up her belongings.

Thanks to the nuns, the luggage significantly increased in size and Maria purchased a big suitcase. Maria used all the pieces of the fabrics that the nuns gave her for making the kid's cloths. The children were prepared to go to the kindergarten in new and very beautiful cloths. Maria made the shirts, vests and pants for Tisha, as well as two nice jackets with adorable applications. The girl's dresses, skirts and blouses were so amazing that Mother Irena made the *exhibition* of Maria's works in the living room, and the sisters brought more pieces of fabrics with the explanations,

"Marie, the children grow very fast. We give you more fabric and you'll make more cloths for them. You'll make various combinations of the fabrics. The multicolored clothing looks very beautiful on your kids. You are a talented mother.

Mother Irena added,

"Look, Marie. You've also sowed two backpacks for the kindergarten with funny applications and embroidery, in which you'll carry all necessary things for Tisha and Vira."

Maria was grateful to God and nuns for her amazing stay for a month and a half in a hospitable atmosphere and for the opportunity they gave her to dress her children in everything new and beautiful. This time, Maria helped a lot to the wonderful hostesses with house chores and sawing. She had a chance to knit same type of a warm wool vest for Mother Irena, as she made it for Zina. She planned to knit at home two more vests for sisters and send them for Christmas.

Mother Irena and nuns were already waiting near the car. Maria hugged them all, and the tears covered her eyes, when she turned to Mother Irena,

"I will miss you there. I will always miss you, Mother Irena."

"Write me, Marie. I'll keep you and your children in my prayers. May our God bless you with all the best in your new life!"

The train was on the platform, when the driver brought Maria and children to Kiev railway station. Her first pleasant surprise was waiting for her on the train: the whole compartment belonged to Maria and children.

"Nobody will disturb you for two days and nights," the driver promised.

Then he put a rather heavy package on the table "Here is your lunch and dinner for today. Enjoy it. You are a breast nursing mother. You need to eat and gain strength. I reported about your weakness, and Leonid Ilych gave me the permission to prepare you for the surprising events, arranged by important authorities in Lvov. They will meet your train and take you to Blue Creeks. They will do the presentation of the founding family in the right way with granting the citizenship to your father and grandfather, as well as the documents on your house. The keys for your new house have already been presented, but they'll do again."

"What do you mean 'presented'?" Maria asked.

"You are not the first resident there. For two days, your father and grandfather are staying in the house and supervising the last touches of the constructive work. Today, they are receiving the deliveries of food, feed and firewood supplies. During the meeting, the officials will issue them and you the new soviet passports with the right last names."

"Thank you. I appreciate everything that was organized for my family and me," Maria replied with tears in her eyes. She continued,

"I'll do my best to prove that the assistance was provided to the right person, who is valuable to the human society."

"Maria Lukianovna, everything goes in the right direction. You should not worry about anything again. You have no strength for apprehension. Here is the direct phone number to the administration of Comrade Brezhnev. Leonid Illich insisted in giving you this number. Please, call right away, in case some other *corrections* need to be done. Just mention your case number. It is in the right top corner of the card."

Maria expressed her sincere appreciation,

"How nice that you decided to prepare me to all the *surprises*. I can hardly stand even the most positive and happiest overwhelming. I need some time to gain my physical endurance."

Maria thought,

"Poor driver, he saw the sensitivity of my nervous system and reported to Brezhnev about my unpredictive *misbehavior* that he witnessed last time. Any stress can cause the drop of blood pressure and coma."

"Thank you for making me ready for good events," Maria repeated again.

"You are welcome. I am sure that with the strength of your spirit and determination, you'll rebuild your physical power very fast."

The driver hugged the children and rushed to the door. He waited on the platform for the departure of the train. Maria was happy with the first news from Blue Creeks.

"Children, your grandpa and grate-grandpa are waiting for us at home. Isn't it wonderful?"

Tisha asked,

"Where is our home, Mama?"

"In Blue Creeks, my boy. It's in my favorite Blue Creeks. Children, your Mama is happy. Thank God for everything."

The trip home was pleasant. The train arrived to Lviv at 8:45 a.m. Maria noticed that two big men were running to their carriage. In a minute, they were in Maria's compartment, introducing themselves. They picked up children and a suitcase and moved to the exit door. Maria could barely chase them.

They were outside with children, when another person came to the steps of the carriage and stretched his arm to support Maria on the steps. He introduced himself in the Ukrainian language with heavy Russian accent, "I am the Chairman of the district committee. We'll deliver you to your new home in Blue Creeks. Welcome home, Maria Lukianivna."

"Thank you," Maria answered.

They were already in the car, when Maria thought, "I love my Lord and I am grateful to Him. He had heard the voice of my supplication. I kept my faith even when I said: 'I am considerably afflicted!' They take us home, our home. What can be more important for now? I feel sorry for Sasha. My son should see the Lord's victory over the evil forces."

The three vehicles from three different administrative organizations entered Blue Creeks. Maria was in the car with the District Chairman of the communist committee. Another car brought the representatives of the regional administration. The representatives of the Lviv KGB were escorting them in the military Jeep. Maria registered for herself, "Everything is under control."

In a distance, Maria noticed a big crowd of people on the road near the new houses. Maria thought, "May these houses receive the blessings from the House of the Lord, with God's protection and love!"

Two cars stopped in parallel at the same time. Maria recognized the people from KGB, when they came closer to her vehicle. She felt frozen for a second. One of them hold a big envelope. The Chairman of the Blue Creeks local committee opened the door of the car, and invited Maria to step out with deep theatrical bow. The Regional Chairman interrupted his comedy. He briefly whispered something to him, and the local authority retreated quickly away.

When Maria was out of the car, she noticed her father and grandfather in the crowd of the people. The Regional Chairman stood up on the prepared platform and started his welcome speech to the founding family of Blue Creeks. It was not their natural desire to say good words about the Kotyks, however they have brought their apology in public to the family that was mistreated since 1939. Maria heard how the Regional Chairman rephrased the words of Brezhnev,

"The Head of the soviet government comrade Brezhnev accented in our conversation, 'We are strong enough to admit our mistakes and to correct what is possible to be corrected." This innocent woman lost two loyal men who were not guilty, as well. Her children lost fathers who could be good support and example in the kids' lives."

Maria noticed that Mykola's mother and sister moved forward. She saw their crying faces. The Distric Chairman continued,

"A desperate woman and a single mother of three kids found herself in the circumstances, when nobody even tried to bring sufficient changes into her life. She discovered the way to see comrade Brezhnev, the General Secretary of the communist party and the leader of our country."

People interrupted the speech with loud applauses.

The Chairman jumped down from the platform and pulled Maria closer to it. He continued his speech,

"Look at Maria Lukianivna. This tiny woman is a woman of courage and unpredictable strength. Years ago, she could occupy her place in our socialist society. She is a highly educated woman, a physician who successfully worked in the hospital in Magadan region. She continues the family tradition of well-known doctors in Blue Creeks. Since today, she is an honorable member of our society."

The crowd applauded again.

He turned to his assistant and whispered,

"Passports. Give me the passports."

The District Chairman pronounced the next part of his speech with the voice and intonation that usually people pronounce on the cemeteries:

"Today, we correct the most terrible mistake of the soviet bureaucracy and return the citizenship to the Kotyk family with presentation of their passports."

The speech was interrupted again with a round of applause and loud ovation.

Maria marked for herself, "Why '*return*' the citizenship? You had never issued it to my father and grandfather, as well as to my late husband… You had never issued it to Maria Kotyk-Kurbatov, as well."

The Chairman jumped down again from the platform and handed the passport to Maria's grandfather with the comment,

"This man is 103, and he did not allow himself to die without the document that proves his belonging to this land and the soviet country. Congratulations!"

People applauded.

The Chairman continued his speech and handed the passport to Dr. Kotyk, Jr.

"The older population of the area remembered Dr. Kotyk, as a devoted physician, who saved many lives for the years of his medical practice. We believe that your knowledge and experience will be appreciated again in a new clinic of Blue Creeks. We received the order and documentation for the restoration of your family manor that you will use for medical needs of the local population and inhabitants of the surrounding villages."

People applauded loudly. They were happy to receive the important news regarding the medical care in their village.

Maria noticed, how the Chairman glanced at two representatives of KGB. They probably decided that he said too much. However, they knew that the scenario was sent from Moscow. The Chairman pronounced loudly:

"Dear Maria Lukianivna, the leader of our great socialist country Comrade Brezhnev wanted me to ask for forgiveness on behalf of all those who mistreated you. Please, forgive us for terrible mistakes that were done and caused the deaths of your beloved. Forgive us for your sufferings."

There was a complete silence in the crowd. The Chairman looked at the crowd and rushed to the mother and sister of Nesterenko.

"Comrade Nesterenko, I ask you, as a mother of Mykola Petrovych Nesterenko, to forgive us. Your son was right, when he tried to prove to the communist bureau the innocence of Maria Lukianivna. He wanted to go to Moscow in order to protect her and children from the false accusations. His heart was broken. Your daughter-in-law Maria Lukianovna returned his honorable and respectful name, and we return to you his document, his membership of the communist party of the Soviet Union and all his awards from WWII."

The Chairman jumped on the platform again and called the crowd: "Please, honor the memory of Nesterenko Mykola Petrovych with a minute of silence."

Men took off the hats and the crowd stood still for a minute in complete silence.

The Chairman looked at Maria and proceeded with the last part of his performance.

"Now, we are back to alive. Maria Lukianivna, Comrade Brezhnev gave me all the instructions regarding your house. He is an example of lawfulness and generosity for all of us. We invite you into your house, where every resident of Blue Creeks participated in making the Brezhnev's order to be fulfilled in time and with good quality. We wish you and your family success and happiness in your new home."

People applauded loudly. The district Chairman took Vera from Maria's arms and handed her a key to the house. The performance had to be ended in a nice way. Maria opened the door and staying on the porch of her new house, addressed her words to the crowd,

"I am grateful to God and all of you who made my home-coming so warm. I promise to be a decent citizen of our big country and hard-working member of our society."

Maria's strength was over. The exhausted woman needed to get in and sit down. Maria took Vira from the Chairman's arms and entered the door of her new beautiful house. Somebody wanted to follow her, but she heard, how the District Chairman thoughtfully stopped them on the porch. "She needs some rest. It was not easy for her to undergo all her adventures in the Kremlin."

Maria stopped in the middle of the living room and pronounced distinctly with a new strength in her voice the words from Psalm 28:7 that worked for her, as a miraculous key to success:

"The Lord is my strength and my shield; my heart trust in Him, and I am helped."

THE END

Autobiography

I was born in 1952 in the Ukraine, part of the former Soviet Union. My father was a high-ranking military officer in the Soviet army, and my mother was a housewife. Being a single child in the family, I grew in atmosphere of pressure to succeed. My parents did their best to develop my skills and talents. From six years of age, I remember myself in a tight schedule of different activities, such as musical school, the studio of young actors, dancing, as well as seasonal sport activities, including skiing in winter, as one of my favorites. Every Sunday, I had two hours of leisure time, playing chess with my father.

In 1959, I became a student of one of the best schools in our region, where the talented and knowledgeable teachers introduced us to a fascinating world of knowledge. I should be honest saying that from ten years of age my teachers and parents motivated me to write. I was an editor of middle school newspaper and later, high school newsletter. Most of all, I enjoyed writing my personal journal. My daily events were recorded in the form of poems and short stories. On Saturdays, my parents invited their friends and arranged the family candle lit gatherings, where I read out loud my first literary works.

During the school years, I participated and won multiple essay competitions in the Ukrainian and Russian literatures. The teachers of languages encouraged me to undergo the university studies in journalism and creative writing. In 1969, I graduated from high school. Being interested in learning the foreign languages and literatures, I continued my studies of German and English and graduated in 1977 with a diploma and degree, as a specialist in both languages.

From 1977 to 1988, I worked as a teacher of foreign languages in one of the Ukrainian high schools that specialized in teaching the number of subjects in German and English. I would never forget my room of the German and English literatures. The sponsor invited a talented young artist to paint marvelous portraits of world-known authors. I tried to perform each lesson in a way so that my students became the participants of an amazing play. What child could be bad in performing? The world of grammar, words and phrases became as interesting, as the world of the German and English literature. During the years of my professional career, I continued exercising the skills in creative writing. Writing the journals in foreign languages was not only my favorite hobby; it became the preferred hobby of my best students.

In 1988 my family arrived in the United States. We were fighting for life of our daughter Tatania. Eleven surgeries with one clinical death and numerous complications proved the words of my mother-in-law "Ask the Father Almighty, and He will help the girl in

His miraculous way." Due to seriousness of Tatania's condition, I do it daily up till now. I praise the Lord for blessing to be in this world together with a unique child, like her. Living in constant pain, she has a special attitude towards those who are in physical and emotional pain. She helps them to rise above the disturbing pain and hardships in order to successfully fulfill all the assignments of their destiny.

Immigration is never an easy process in people's lives. I had to resolve a very complex situation. We came to the USA with a medical visa issued to a child who had right side paralysis after the polio vaccination that was provided six years ago. Tania suffered from S-shape scoliosis with severe compression of the internal organs. The girl was dying. After three months of evaluation in the US, the orthopedic specialists of five children's hospitals pronounced the verdict:" It is too late to start the surgical treatment. Why didn't you bring her three years ago when the formation of the scoliosis just began?"

People from the civilized world could not understand that I was fighting with soviet officials for my daughter's arrival to the American hospital for long six years. I believed that in the United States, my child could find the necessary help, because American medicine has a vast experience in treating people with polio disease. Every year the Health Ministry of the Soviet Union rejected my daughter's case. We lived in a communist cage. Professor Gusev explained it in a simple way, "You have to understand that she is dying. If she had not died right after the polio vaccination, she'll die in the nearest future. Our country will not pay the capitalists for her treatment abroad."

What could I do after the verdict? I prayed to God, as my mother-in-law taught me, and the miracle happened. Dr. Betz from Philadelphia Temple University hospital called me three days prier the expiration of our visa and suggested to include Tania in his experimental group. He offered one percent of survival out of a hundred during the cycle of spinal surgeries, but it was still better than none. We signed the Agreement that in case of her death, we would not keep liable the surgeon and the hospital. Instead, I praised the Lord for a given chance to save my daughter's life. However, there was ***one impairment*** that arose with signing of the Agreement. The Agreement required Tatania's stay in the United States until 21 years of age.

The ***second*** obstacle was connected to the change of the family status, that could allow us to legally live and work in the country. We arrived here not as the permanent residents of the USA but, as the parents of a nine-year-old girl, who was seriously ill and could not live without us. Legalization process required time and money. The Soviet Union allowed every person to leave the country with a hundred-dollar bill. It was nothing. We learned hard way the process of immigration. Some lawyers were just layers. It took time and assets to find the right Law firm that helped with legalization.

The ***third obstacle*** was very important and required fast actions. Our 16-year-old son Roman was stopped by KGB from coming together with the family to the United States. They assigned him to the military service in the USSR. There was a dilemma. Our daughter was barely alive. Our 16-year-old son was in dangerous situation without parents.

What could I do for free to save both children? I prayed and asked the Almighty God to intervene and help me in resolution of our hardships. As long, as we were not allowed to make any income and rent a room, I found the barter position of a cook, cleaning lady, laundry maid and care giver for a paralyzed elderly woman in exchange for a room in attic without air conditioner and 2 meals daily for three people. I prayed days and nights during my stay near Tania about the lodge and board, and the prayers were answered.

In those multiple job positions, I worked for 15 hours daily for four months without a single day off. As my master clearly explained, the family could not have our 2 meals, if I decide to have a day off. The 4-th of July came. It's one of the best holidays in our family. Our daughter asked us to show her the parade and firework in Philadelphia before the surgeries began. With the permission of the master and his wife, we took our child to parade, and we enjoyed the firework at the Art museum. We "paid" for the celebration of our Independence Day. When we returned, our suitcase was on the porch. We became homeless.

I would never forget the questions of my daughter: "Mama, where should we go? I can sleep in my wheelchair. But where will you sleep?" What could I answer except: "God will take care of us. You'll see." We walked for an hour and stopped in the Rittenhouse Square. There was an empty bench there. We stayed there for three days. Since then, I have my special attitude towards the homeless people. Yes, they are different. However, in our case, the Lord sent us the compassionate "neighbors". Every day, they shared with us pretzels or bagels, a bowl of fruit salad and water. I praised the Lord for introducing us to that experience. I learned that somebody was in much worse situation than us for many years, not for three days. They did not lose the humanity. They felt sorry for our sick child and fed her without asking any questions. As soon as our financial situation has improved, I participate in feeding the homeless people and supplying them with readymade foods.

The ***fourth obstacle*** is also well-known for many new immigrants. My husband could hardly master all the subjects and medical terminology in English, including computer that we did not see in the Soviet Union. All the hardships made him depressed and nostalgic. He did not believe that we would overcome the problems in our American life. Even the work authorization could not give us the job positions in accordance with our diplomas and degrees. We needed to study again and pass the exams in order to prove our education. It is not easy, but right and doable.

Being a mother, I did not allow myself any depressive thoughts and feelings. When we received the work authorization, I was so grateful to the Lord

My husband went to college for studies, and I started my working carrier with cleaning the houses. I am not ashamed of that step. My Bachelor and master's degrees could not bring food on the table and payment for the rent right away. On that moment, we had bigger priority: we needed to bring my son Roman to the United States. He was already 17. In a year, they planned to take him to army service. If he survived two years of military service, he had to stay for additional five years in the native country. My son was my pride. He was a brilliant student. He needed better life. Mother had to clean two houses daily in order to pay the attorneys who agreed to bring my son to the US. Senator Heinz considerably helped me in Roman's case. Up till now, I am grateful to God for sending me the right people who understood me, as a mother.

When Roman arrived, he was seventeen and a half. It was one of the happiest moments in my life. He went to school and graduated with amazing scores. His test results impressed the Harvard university. They invited us to Boston for an interview. We could not travel anywhere: Tania was not stable after the second surgery and required our presence in Philadelphia all the time. The Harvard professors visited us at home. They wanted to meet my genius boy and interviewed him for several hours. I've done whatever a mother could do, in order he lives and succeeds in the country of grate opportunities.

Roman's and my professional studies began at the same time. In a year, I proved my diploma and received a teacher's position in one of the privet schools in Philadelphia, and in two years, at Widener university. As a teacher, I was always happy. God gave me the skills to teach, and it was always interesting for me. Nevertheless, life changes our plans. My ex-husband started his medical practice and insisted in my help. I was taking one college course after another in order to run our new business. He needed the specialist in nutrition, and I graduated from nutrition and fitness. He was interested in Enzyme Replacement therapy, and I became an enzyme replacement therapist. He wanted to add hands on procedures, I learned all the courses of Cranio-Sacral, Manual Lymph Drainage and Maternity massage, etc. and worked successfully.

With time, my dear daughter Tatania became part of the family practice. She graduated in 2% of the best students in the world, and I was not surprised that after the college studies and with years of experience, she became a world-known counselor and crisis management consultant. In 2006, Tatania founded her International Wellness Foundation and brought me in her philanthropical world. With the help of the generous sponsors, we do our best for wellness of people and improvement of their lives.

Now, the name of her International Wellness Foundation is well-known in different countries, such as Columbia, Poland, India, Ukraine, Kenya and Ghana Africa. The project "Wheels of Life" succeeds with the delivery wheelchairs for free to the underprivileged people. The mobility opens new opportunities for those who had lost the hope. At the present time, Tatania and I work on the second major project "Veterans and disabled formula to success". Her fight for life after 11 major surgeries became an example for many people. My life experience with the handicapped daughter gave me the right to participate in her projects and to prove that the most valuable that people received from the Creator is our life. It is our choice to win or lose in this life.

In 2007 I began to write the family saga, a trilogy called "God's Miracles in Lives of Regular People". The trilogy is based on the journals of my mother-in-law Countess Kurbatov. She chose me to be an author of the trilogy, and I appreciate her faith in my skills to transform the 'dry' data into an alternate historical and inspirational novel.

I started my Autobiography in the first book with the words, "I am a happy person in this life and grateful to God for everything that He helped me to overcome and achieve." This is true up till now. My life had never been easy. I learned hardships, bitterness and losses. Not only death separates people. Weakness, cowardice and betrayal still exist in our human world. May our Almighty God strengthen the spirit of people and bless us for true faith, fidelity, love, loyalty, respect and success. It does not matter how distressed our life is. We are born to accomplish our mission and be grateful for every moment of our life.

With deep respect to my readers,

Author Angelic Tarasio

Author Angelic Tarasio

Bibliography

Suicide Fact Sheet N398 "Methods of suicide: international suicide patterns derived from the WHO mortality database" (www.who.int/mediacentre/factssheets/fs398/en)

CBD "Mortality and cases of death": Global, regional, and National life expectancy, all-cause mortality, and cause specific mortality (www.ncbi.nim.nih.gov/pmc/articles/PMC5388903)

"Preventing Suicide: A resource for Media Professionals" (www.who.int/mental_health/privention/suicide/resource_media.pdf)

"Suicide prevention strategies revisited 10-year systemic review" (www.thelancet.com/journals/lanpsy/article/PIIS2215-0366(16)

Suicide in the World" www.ncbi.nim.nih.gov/articles/PMC3367275

The ArtScroll Tehillim by Mesorah Publications, Lid

'Mortality and Causes of Death" "Global, regional, and national age-sex specific all-cause and cause-specific mortality for 240 causes of death. (www.ncbi.nim.nih.gov/pmc/articles/PMC4340604)

"Suicide rates per 100,000 population (www.who.int/gho/mental_health/suicide_rates_crude/en/)

"Suicide and psychiatric diagnosis a worldwide perspective" (www.ncbi.nim.nih.gov/pmc/articles/PMC14898480)

"Reporting Suicide and Self Harm (www.time-to-change.org.uk/node/75408)

"Media Guidelines for reporting Suicide" (www.samaritans.org/sites/default/files/kcfinder/files/press/Samaritans20Me)

"The Power of Words" (https://web.archive.org/web/20130513011216/http://www.suicideprevention.ca/abosuicide/the-power-of-words/)

"Vital Signs: Trends in State Suicide Rates – United States and Circumstances Contributing to Suicides" (www.cdc.gov/mmwr/volumes/67/wr/mm6722a1.htm)

"Contact with mental health and primary care providers before suicide: a review pf the evidence" (www.ncbi.nim.nih.gov/pmc/articles/PMC5072576)

"Suicidality and aggression during antidepressant treatment: systemic review and meta-analyses based on clinical study reports" (www.ncbi.nim.nih.gov/mpc/articles/MPC4729837)

"Adverse Childhood Experiences and Suicide Risk: Toward Comprehensive Prevention" (www.ncbi.nim.nih.gov/pmc/articles/PMC2585177)

"Stereotypes, Prejudice, and Depression: The Integrated Perspective" (http://pps.sagepub.com/content/7/5/427.abstract)

"Suicide" Wikipedia: Definitions, History, Risk Factors, Previous attempts and Self-harm, Substance Misuse, Media, Methods, Pathophysiology, Prevention, Epidemiology, Sex and Gender, Age, Legislation.

"Preventing Suicide after Traumatic Brain Injury" (www.ncbi.nlm.nih.gov/pubmed/17708726)

"Best evidence topic report: Suicide at Christmas" (www.ncbi.nim.nih.gov/pmc/articles/PMC1726490)

"Research on Religion, Spirituality, and Mental health: a review" (www.psychology.hku.hk/fibcstudies/refbase/docs/hill2003/29 Hill+Pargamei)

"Relative Status and Well-Being evidence from U.S. Suicide Death" (www.frbst.org/publications/economics/papers/2012wp12_16bk.pdf)

"Suicide Screening in schools, primary care and emergency departments" (www.ncbi.nim.nih.gov/pmc/articles/PMC2879582)

"Suicide rates Data by country" (http://apps.who.int/gho/data/node.main.MHSUICE?lang=en.)

"Suicide rates rising across the U.S." (www.cdc.gov/media/releases/2018p0607-suicide-prevention.html)

https://en.wikipedia.org/wiki/Sorbonne_University

https://en.wikipedia.org/wiki/Robert_de_Sorbon

https://en.wikipedia.org/wiki/Trinity_Lavra_of_St._Sergius

https://en.m.wikipedia.org/wiki/Sergius of Radonezh

"Suicide and suicide risk in lesbian, gay, bisexual and transgender populations review and recommendations" (www.ncbi.nim.nih.gov/pmc/articles/PMC3662085)

"Religion and the risk of suicide: Longitudinal study of over 1 million people" by Dermot O'Reilly and Michael Rosato

"Suicide is on the rise in the US, and Muslims aren't immune" by Hannah Allaman

"Suicide Prevention program for at-risk groups: Pointers from an epidemiological study" by T. Mariam, Karuth Chinna, C.H. Lim, I. Nurashikin, A.A. Salina, Jeevitha Mariapun

"5 facts about military suicides" by ERLC (www.thegardian.com/world/2013/feb/01/us-military-suicide-epidemic-veteran)

"U.S. military veteran suicides rise, one dies every 65 minutes" (www.reuters.com/article/2013/02/02/us-usa-veterans-suicide-idUBRE9101E320130202)

"Suicide rate among vets and active duty military Jumps – Now 22 A Day" (www.forbes.com/sites/melaniehaiken/2013/02/05/22-the-number-of-veterans-who-now-commit-suicide-every-day/)

"Youth suicide rates rose by nearly 30% in the US in the month after '13 Reasons Why' first aired" by Jill Serjeant, Lisa Richwine, Reuters

"Kids' Suicide Risk Tied Parents' Religious Beliefs" by Steven Renberg

'Religion and Completed Suicide: Meta-Analysis" by School of Medicine, Vanderbilt University USA;

Department of Epidemiology, School of Public Health, China; Center for Suicide Prevention Research, Shandong University, China

"The Road to Recovery Report" (www.saluteheroes.org)

Bridge To The Sky

Table of Contents

Printed in the United States
By Bookmasters

Printed in the United States
By Bookmasters